MANAGEMENT AND PEOPLE
IN BANKING

Management and People in Banking

2nd Edition

Editor: Bryan L. Livy

The Institute
of Bankers

First Published 1980

Reprinted 1981, 1984
Second Edition July 1985

Enquiries should be sent to the publishers at the undermentioned address:

THE INSTITUTE OF BANKERS
10 Lombard Street
London
EC3V 9AS

© The Institute of Bankers 1985

ISBN 0 85297 143 5

British Library Cataloguing in Publication Data
Livy, Bryan L.
    Management and people in banking. — 2nd ed.
    1. Banks and banking — Personnel management
    I. Title   II. Institute of Bankers
    332.1'068'3   HG1615.5

    ISBN 0–85297–143–5

Typeset in 10pt Times by MULTIPLEX techniques Ltd, St Mary Cray, Kent.
Text Printed on 90gm^2 Dundee Offset, Cover on 180gm^2 Chromocard.
Printed and bound by Dramrite Printers Ltd, Southwark, London SE1, England.

CONTENTS

EDITOR'S GENERAL INTRODUCTION

First published in 1980, 'Management and People in Banking' is now produced as a second edition. Revised, re-written, updated, it has also been expanded to probe more deeply the human implications of a fast-changing banking scenario.

The history of the book pre-dated its first edition – at least the ideas behind it go back to the Wilde Committee[1], a working party appointed by the Council of The Institute of Bankers in 1972 'to undertake a comprehensive review of the Institute's future role as a qualifying association', and which first reported in 1973. The Wilde Report heralded an extension of 'professionalism' in banking, and advocated those 'who are likely to reach senior positions in their banks to start studying systematically the ways in which problems of management must be approached and decisions taken.'

A new response in education and training was called for. The dynamism of change in banking was accelerating. Changing attitudes towards employment, changes in the educational system, the need for long-term career development, keen competition in financial markets, disappearing boundaries between financial institutions, a sharper commercial awareness – all pointed the way towards a planned programme of professional education. The impetus has not diminished. Pressures have increased.

The world today has little reward for static or backward-looking attitudes. Banking services and the management of large-scale enterprises are becoming more complex, more difficult, more demanding. These facts of life speak for themselves. The Wilde Report predicted: 'Future managers, even more than today, will need marketing and administrative skills of a very high order'. The outcome was a new structure for the IOB diploma examinations, and the launch of the Finanical Studies Diploma, a degree level qualification. Successful candidates are entitled to the designatory letters Dip FS. Other educational innovations quickly followed, augmenting the scope, encouraging effort.

The FSD has not been designed for those who are unlikely to progress beyond a first managerial appointment; it has been designed for those with ambition and potential. It provides opportunity for the study of banking and management at a high level – including advanced studies in banking practice, human aspects of management, marketing, business planning and control. The objective is to provide expertise specific to banking, plus a broader background of business information, skills and acumen relevant to the formation of organisational policies and their implementation.

The prime purpose of this particular book is to support teaching programmes leading to the examination in *Human Aspects of Management* which forms part of Section 1 of the FSD. The syllabus aims to provide insight into:

(a)   the problems of individuals and groups in a working organisation;
(b)   the process of managing people;
(c)   the personnel function as an aid to management;
(d)   the contribution of behavioural sciences;
(e)   legal and institutional factors affecting employment in a banking environment;

All these issues are encompassed within these pages. The subject matter is broad. Briefly – in a nutshell – we need to examine organisational design, management styles and psychological insights into leadership, motivation and group behaviour. We consider employee relations, attitudes and expectations, and contemporary issues like the management of change, the impact of technology, politics and participation. As a starting point for manpower 'resourcing,' we need to consider forward manpower planning as a derivative of corporate planning; the appropriate gearing of policies for recruitment and selection, including how to interview, and how to make assessments. We look at performance appraisal and how to apply it properly, at methods of staff training, management development and how people learn. We study rewards, pay systems, job evaluation, financial incentives. We review the backcloth of industrial relations, the purposes and methods of collective bargaining, problems of staff representation, the legal and institutional factors affecting employment in a banking organisation. In short, the aim is to educate the student in ways of raising staff performance, to help him or her understand inter-related policies for human resource management and, hopefully, to make a useful contribution.

Most students find it fun. For a start it often comes as a breath of fresh air after studying more conventional banking subjects. Secondly, the emphasis in teaching courses is on the *application* of existing knowledge and theories to particular banking problems; trying to evaluate the merits and demerits of any particular course of action or any set of techniques. To some extent, students are encouraged to look at comparative practices in other industrial or commercial organisations. The syllabus follows on naturally from the broader *Nature of Management* at the Associateship level, and for which this book may also be useful. Courses of instruction leading up to the examinations aim to be both informative and to develop critical judgement.

Success rates in the FSD examination have improved gradually since the inception of the scheme in 1979. Currently, almost half the candidates pass. In the early days, too many candidates thought they could get through simply by quoting their own anecdotal experiences, waffling about generalities without supporting evidence, or uncritically reciting their own bank's policies. This dead-beat approach was squashed right from the start. Such candidates were failed.

In the examination, questions have a practical slant. Examiners are not just looking for book-learning, although this forms the background. They are looking for balanced, analytical, critical and constructive answers. Most importantly, the purpose of the programme is to help banking managers do their job better, through a sharpened awareness of the core issues of human organisation. Candidates should be thinking ahead as managers and seeking ways to improve their own and their bank's management performance.

With the needs of the senior banker in mind, the crux of this book pivots on the corporate problems of man-management. Practical decisions are what matter at the end of the day. However, there are certain theoretical issues which have not been ignored. Hopefully, the book provides the right blend of academic and pragmatic thinking which has been found to be useful, not only in banks, but also in other industries and organisations for those whose task is to watch over how an organisation works and how the people within it may be provided with the best opportunities.

The material in the book has been arranged into three sections:

    I.   Managing People and Communications.
   II. Staff Policy and Administration in Banking.
 III. Employment Conditions and Industrial Relations.

This book is not an end in itself. There is much more, as the reader will be aware, to the human problems of management than a tool-kit of theories, examples or case studies. Management is a very personal thing and requires a personal touch. Armchair reading alone cannot make a good manager. But it can help those who take their job seriously, those who are prepared to think critically about what they are doing, those who are receptive to new ideas, and those who are sufficiently sensitive to the changing world around them. Rarely can the study of management be prescriptive. In no way, therefore, does this book provide all the answers. It was not intended to be a complete and definitive statement of good management practice. It was designed as supplementary reading to the existing literature. Its unique distinction is its focus on banking.

People too numerous to mention individually – bankers, educationists, trade unionists, managers, students – have contributed their ideas and the benefit of their experiences both to the book and the FSD syllabus which it supports. One of the strengths of the book is that it combines the wisdom of many. All the contributors have been involved in banking – either as managers or consultants – and some are still very much in the hot seat. Many too have comparative experience in other industries on which to draw. The 'experiential' input is rich and diverse. Contributors have been free to express their own views. The theme of the book is in its title 'Management and People in Banking'. The aims of the editor have been to integrate the various parts into a coherent exposition of the human problems which can beset managers in a banking organisation and how they might be approached; and to generate informed debate about the issues.

Reference
1.   The Institute of Bankers: Educational Policy Review, 'A Report by the Wilde Committee', Part 1, *The Institute's Future Role as a Qualifying Association*, London: IOB, 1973.

THE CONTRIBUTORS

The Editor

Bryan Livy is Chief Examiner in *Human Aspects of Management*, which is one of the subjects in The Institute of Bankers Financial Studies Diploma. He is a graduate of the Universities of Exeter and London, and began his career with a short-service commission in the Royal Army Educational Corps, serving in Germany. Thereafter, he went into industry with Ford, British Steel and Glaxo.

Since 1971, he has been Lecturer in Personnel Management at The City University Business School. From there he has undertaken a number of research and consultancy assignments – as External Specialist, Petroleum Industry Training Board (1977–83), developing personnel selection criteria in off-shore North Sea oil drilling and gas operations, and assessment centres for rig management; as External Collaborator, International Labour Organisation, Geneva (1980–82), reviewing international practices in job evaluation; and various ad hoc assignments. He has also researched recruitment and retention problems in NHS hospitals, aspects of the 'hidden economy', and for six years participated in management training courses for a major clearing bank.

He is the author of 'Job Evaluation: A Critical Review' (Allen & Unwin, 1975), which is also translated into Spanish, and of 'L'evaluation des Emplois' (ILO, 1984), plus various articles. He is a Fellow of the Institute of Personnel Management.

Malcolm Bennison joined the Institute of Manpower Studies in 1974 from the Organics Division of ICI, where he was responsible for manpower planning and developing personnel information systems. He has worked in the productivity area of both chemicals and steel. He became Deputy Director of the Institute in 1978 and Associate Director in December 1983. He is responsible for leading and co-ordinating IMS services to employing organisations. The services include the advisory service, the education and training programme and the development of methods and techniques to improve the effectiveness of manpower management. Additional IMS responsibilities include personnel policy, publicity and overseas work. At IMS, he has been responsible for many projects in a wide variety of industries and organisations in the UK and overseas. He is joint author, with Roger Morgan, of 'The Management of Career Structures' and with Jonathon Casson of 'The Manpower Planning Handbook' (McGraw-Hill, 1984). Mr Bennison is a graduate of the University of Manchester.

Richard Boot is currently Lecturer in Management Learning at the University of Lancaster. He started his career working for a major UK oil company with which he spent a number of years, initially in marketing and subsequently in personnel development. Since that time he has held a number of academic posts at various institutions including The City University Business School and London Business School. In parallel with these posts, he has acted as consultant in management and organisation development to a wide range of organisations. He has a long-standing interest in small group processes and is a past Chairman of Group Relations Training Association. His two main current research areas are experience-based approaches to management learning, and factors which influence outcomes of educational innovations in management settings. He has published a number of books and articles. He is a graduate of The City University.

Bill Braddick graduated from Exeter University and pursued a further year's study in Education. He worked at Cadbury Brothers, Bournville and subsequently was Assistant Education and Training Officer with West Midlands Gas. He joined Portsmouth Polytechnic in 1962 and introduced a range of residential short courses for practising managers. He has worked closely with a number of companies helping to develop appraisal systems and management development programmes. As a result of a study sponsored by the Chemical Industry Training Board, he published 'Design of Appraisal Systems' with Peter Smith. As a result of a research project carried out in 1980, he has published 'The Challenge of Change' with Denis Boyle. He has acted as an examiner in Management Studies for a number of professional examinations and is currently Chief Examiner in *Nature of Management* for The Institute of Bankers. He joined Ashridge Management College to teach personnel management and industrial relations. He was Director of Studies for several years before becoming Deputy Principal in 1978. On behalf of Ashridge, he has organised and run seminars in many parts of the world. He has been Secretary of the Association of Teachers in Management and is a Fellow of the British Institute of Management.

Rani Chaudhry-Lawton, a graduate of the Universities of Wales and London, is an occupational psychologist who also trained at the National Training Laboratories in the USA. She has worked for the Abbey National Building Society in the field of counselling and management development. She is an associate member of Ashridge Management College, tutoring on a number of organisational behaviour programmes. For the last five years Rani has also been working as a freelance consultant, predominantly in the financial sector, but also in industrial and service sectors. One of her current major interests is to help individuals and organisations plan and implement change effectively.

Nick Cowan has been Director and Secretary of the Federation of London Clearing Bank Employers since May 1980. Previous appointments include Director of Personnel and Industrial Relations of the Perkins Engines Group, Director of Personnel of Phillips Industries, and a Member of the Board of Unigate Ltd. Mr Cowan's other activities include being a member of the Employment Appeals Tribunal, the Central Arbitration Committee, and of the Civil Service Arbitration Tribunal. He is a member of the CBI Pay Policy Committee, the CBI Council, and a member of the education boards of 'Personnel Management,' and 'Industrial Relations Law Reports.' Mr. Cowan is also Chairman of West Lambeth Health Authority, and is very active in National Health Service matters.

Eric Glover graduated from Oxford University with first class Honours in Classical Moderations and a second in 'Greats'. After a short spell in teaching, he had five years with Shell International in Borneo and Uganda, mainly on the personnel and training side. He joined the staff of The Institute of Bankers in 1963, was appointed Under-Secretary (Director of Studies) in 1969, Deputy Secretary in 1977, and in 1982 became the Secretary-General.

Keith Hillyer, JP was, until 1984, Group Training Manager of the National Westminster Bank Group. After a traditional banking career in his early years, he spent nearly all of the last fifteen years in various management posts in training and management development. These included data processing and personnel as well as the more general aspects of technical and management training. His last post included overall control of the Group's training function as well as personal responsibility for the bank's Staff College at Heythrop Park in Oxfordshire. At present he is working at home and abroad on consultancies in the personnel and training fields and is, *inter alia*, Director of the Banking and Financial Studies Department of the Middle East Centre for Management Studies in Nicosia. He is a Fellow of The Institute of Bankers, a Fellow of the Institute of Personnel Management and a member of the Association of Teachers of Management.

Philip Hodgson is Director of the Leadership Design Programme at Ashridge Management College where he lectures and consults in leadership and people skills. His background is in industry and commerce where he worked for many years as a management development adviser. He is currently working on the effects of information technology on management. He is a graduate of Bristol and London Universities.

Tony Jackson joined Westminster Bank Ltd. in 1962 in the Leeds Office. He completed his degree in Business Studies at Bradford in 1973, and his Doctorate in 1982. He joined the full-time staff of Henley – The Management College – in 1976, where he is now Senior Lecturer in Occupational Psychology, and a member of the Directing Staff of the College. He has been concerned with the introduction of appraisal and selection systems in organisations since 1973. Amongst external examinership roles, he is an assistant examiner in *Human Aspects of Management* in The Institute of Bankers Financial Studies Diploma.

Sid Kessler is Professor of Industrial Relations at The City University Business School. He graduated from LSE with first class honours and then took a postgraduate Diploma in Business Administration. There followed three years research at The National Institute of Economic and Social Research and eight years as Head of the Research Department of the National Union of Mineworkers. Professor Kessler has been at City University since 1964. During this time he has acted as part-time industrial relations adviser to the Prices and Incomes Board; was seconded as Director of the Commission on Industrial Relations; was industrial relations adviser to the Royal Commission on the Press and to the Clegg Commission on Pay Comparability. Currently he is a Deputy Chairman of the Central Arbitration Committee and a member of the ACAS independent panel of arbitrators. He is a Fellow of the Institute of Personnel Management.

Richard Lawton is a Client and Programme Director in Organisation Behaviour at Ashridge Management College. He is a graduate of Trinity College, Cambridge and York University. In 1976, he worked for the Greater London Council in the personnel area. On leaving the GLC in 1978 he joined the Abbey National Building Society as a Training Officer, developing interpersonal skills programmes. For a brief period he worked as the Training Officer with the Housing Corporation before returning to take up a senior position in the Abbey National in 1980, running the management training and development function. Since joining Ashridge, Richard has worked with a wide variety of clients ranging from international banking and insurance companies, through to manufacturers of both computer hardware and more traditional products such as steel.

Leif Mills has been General Secretary of the Banking Insurance and Finance Union since 1972, having joined NUBE/National Union of Bank Employees in 1960 as a Research Officer. He was a member of the TUC Non-Manual Committee; the Committee to Review Financial Institutions; and the Civil Service Pay Research Unit Board. He is currently a member of the Armed Forces Pay Review Body, the Monopolies and Mergers Commission, and the TUC General Council; and also Chairman of the TUC Financial Services Committee. He is a graduate of Balliol College, Oxford.

Tim Morris graduated from Jesus College, Cambridge, and the London School of Economics. He worked in banking for three years before undertaking research in that area. His PhD. thesis looked at the development and operation of industrial relations in the London clearing banks, and in due course he will be publishing a book based on his research. His current research interests include employment strategies of firms in the financial sector. He is a lecturer in industrial relations in LSE.

Margery Povall is a Research Fellow in the Centre for Personnel Research and Enterprise Development (C–PRED) at The City University Business School. In her career in personnel management and research she has specialised in organisational opportunity and equal opportunities for women and men. She has worked as both researcher and consultant to banks, drawing on international experience, including organising a seminar for the EEC on 'Equal Opportunities in Banking'. Margery is a graduate of Witwatersrand University and the University of South Africa.

Sheila Rothwell is the Director of the Centre for Employment Policy Studies at Henley – the Management College. She has researched and lectured in industrial relations and personnel management at London School of Economics, was Assistant Secretary (Negotiations) of the National Union of Bank employees, and then Assistant Chief Executive of the Equal Opportunities Commission. Current interests include collective bargaining and worker participation; future trends in employment and unemployment; women's career patterns; technological change, and manpower utilisation. Sheila is a graduate of London University.

Brian Stone, graduated from London School of Economics in philosophy and economics. He worked in various capacities in the advertising industry until 1969; then attended the Manchester Business School to take the Diploma in Business Administration, followed by three years in the same institution as SSRC Senior Research Fellow, engaged in study and teaching in occupational behaviour. He joined Williams & Glyn's Bank Management Training Centre in 1973, with responsibilities for management and business development training. In 1978, he completed The Institute of Bankers examinations and was elected a Fellow in 1984. Mr. Stone is currently Senior Lecturer at Manchester Polytechnic Business Studies Department teaching business skills via supervised consultancy projects conducted by student groups. He is an Assistant Examiner for *Human Aspects of Management* in The Institute of Bankers Financial Studies Diploma, and Moderator for Correspondence Courses in that subject. He has recently contributed to the book of case studies for *Nature of Management* at AIB level.

Deryk Vander Weyer was appointed full-time Executive Deputy Chairman of British Telecommunications plc on 1 October 1983 after being a part-time member of British Telecommunications Corporation since October 1981. He was previously a Group Deputy Chairman of Barclays Bank plc and Chairman of Barclays Bank (UK) Limited.

A Yorkshireman of Flemish ancestry, he joined Barclays in 1941, was Manager at Chester in 1960 and Local Director in Liverpool in 1964. In 1969 he was appointed a General Manager, setting up the first UK Clearing Bank Marketing Department, and was Senior General Manager by 1973. He was Chairman of the Chief Executive Officers' Committee of the Committee of London Clearing Bankers – 1974 to 1976. Between 1977 and 1980 he was Chairman of Barclays Merchant Bank Limited and Group Vice Chairman, Finance and Planning. He remains a Director of Barclays Bank plc.

Between 1979 and 1981 he was President of The Institute of Bankers and at various times has been a Governor of the Museum of London, a member of the Royal Commission on the Distribution of Income and Wealth, and a member of the Board of the English National Opera. Currently he is Chairman of the Board of Companions, British Institute of Management, and serves on the CBI Council.

John Waine is the Assistant Director of the Federation of London Clearing Bank Employers. He was formerly employed by Barclays Bank where he was a Chief Programmer and Senior Systems Analyst before holding managerial appointments in investment and personnel. He is currently a member of the Education and Training Committee of the CBI and of the North East London Area Manpower Board of the Manpower Services Committee. He is a graduate of Durham University, an Associate of The Institute of Bankers, and formerly a research associate of The City University Business School.

Jane Welch is the Senior Research Fellow in Company and Commercial Law at The Institute of Advanced Legal Studies, University of London. She was formerly legal adviser at the Inter-Bank Research Organisation. She is a joint author of a commentary on the Banking Act 1979, and editor of 'The Regulation of Banks in the Member States of the EEC'. Her principal interests are in banking, company and commercial law in the EEC, subjects on which she has published a number of articles. Jane is a graduate of Trinity College, Dublin and of the University of London.

Allan Williams is Reader in Organisational and Occupational Psychology, and Director of the Centre for Personnel Research and Enterprise Development at The City University Business School, London. After graduating in psychology from Manchester and London Universities, he then spent three years in market research with Marplan Ltd., where he headed their Communications Research Division. Since joining City University in 1963, he has acted as a consultant to numerous companies, and as an external examiner to six universities and polytechnics. Dr. Williams has served as Honorary Treasurer of the British Psychological Society and Chairman of its Occupational Section. For 12 years he was a member of the Psychologist Assessors Panel of the Civil Service Selection Board, and has researched and published widely in personnel management and organisational behaviour. Through the consultancy research activities of his centre, C-PRED, he is currently studying conditions leading to the effective use of research in organisational problem-solving.

PART I

MANAGING PEOPLE AND COMMUNICATIONS

Introduction

The opening chapter of this book sets the scene. From the pen of Deryk Vander Weyer, a Past President of the Institute, comes an enthusiastic and thoughtful review of some of the structural and organisational choices which face a large, international bank. His central theme is to ask and answer the question: what is the best way for a bank to organise itself? He discusses the broad problems of planning and strategy, the formal processes of direction, control and decision-making. But he does not ignore the nuances of the informal organisation. The executive must understand where the main springs and rivers run; how things actually get done. The wise senior manager is a politician; he practises the art of the possible. He must learn to 'work' his own organisation. This opening chapter addresses itself broadly to management in a banking environment.

The management of people in a large-scale enterprise is a shared responsibility. Both line managers and staff (or personnel managers) have a part to play. The exact delineation of these responsibilities may sometimes be difficult to define. The problems of line/staff relationships are discussed in the second chapter, together with an appraisal of the role of the personnel function.

The book then moves on to important behavioural issues – organisation theory, motivation, group behaviour and leadership styles. Bill Braddick summarises the main schools of thought relating to 'organisation theory' and the assumptions on which they are based. As he says, there is no shortage of theory. Whilst each theoretical approach has its own short-comings, an analysis in this area is important intellectually and historically. The search is still on for ways to facilitate effective organisational performance and personal satisfaction simultaneously.

From this mould, further avenues can be explored. Of paramount importance to all managers is staff motivation. Richard and Rani Lawton provide a synopsis of the main motivational theories and show how they may be applied in a banking environment. What dominant needs motivate people to work? Is it greed and fear? Is there deeper psychological significance? To what rewards will an individual respond? What are the driving forces? Why are some people high achievers? There is more to motivation than a crack of the whip.

People as individuals also work in groups. Their motives and attitudes are modified by colleagues. Richard Boot looks at some of the 'hidden' processes which go on in groups – at communications, personalities, power politics.

Managers have to deal with people as individuals as well as collectively. Managers cannot avoid exercising their authority – indeed, that is their job. But managers can choose *how* they will exercise it – their *style*. It is their style which can make or mar success. Philip Hodgson tackles the tricky issue of successful leadership – leadership in different situations and the difference between leadership and management. Drawing from a complex network of research evidence, his aim is to show how the performance of managers and subordinates may be raised in mutually satisfying and fulfilling ways. There is more to leadership than a blast on the bugle.

An understanding of motivation and leadership is critical for any manager who hopes to get things done – at any time, and particularly when times are moving fast. Today, technology is the accelerator. Bankers must clearly know the mechanics of the new electronic gadgetry, understand the implications for staffing, the problems and possibilities which ensue. Nick Cowan paints a detailed picture of contemporary developments and employment trends in banking.

Will far-reaching changes be accepted or resisted? The two concluding chapters in this section come to terms with these issues from practical and theoretical positions respectively. Leif Mills faces the big issue of sharing information and of involving people in decisions which affect their working lives. He debates the thorny problem of staff participation, and reviews various approaches. Whatever the outcome regarding possible forms of 'industrial democracy' in the years ahead, and to whatever degree, most people would agree that there is a need for better communications and consultation. At least a participative/consultative structure would go a long way to ensure that changes are widely understood before they become a matter of dispute.

Change creates uncertainty, and possibly anxiety. Innovations resulting from new technology or working practices may therefore be resisted by people whose jobs are affected. Management, therefore, in seeking to advance the well-being of the enterprise may face immediate reactions. The problem is not so much how to overcome resistance, but how to prevent it. Allan

Williams brings behavioural theory to bear. He discusses a process known as 'Organisation development' and shows how strategies for planned changes may be introduced.

The chapters in this section are concerned with organisational, motivational and communications problems. On balance they focus equally on the needs of employers and employees. The various contributions are concerned to show the inter-relationships of working life.

CHAPTER 1

Structural and Organisational Choices in an International Bank

Deryk Vander Weyer FIB

Deputy Chairman of British Telecommunications plc,
Former Chairman of Barclays Bank UK Limited, and
Deputy Chairman of Barclays Bank plc;
Past President of The Institute of Bankers

A. THE APPROACH

In *The Second American Revolution*, John D. Rockefeller 3rd said, 'An organisation is a system with a logic of its own and all the weight of tradition and inertia. The deck is stacked in favour of tried and proven ways of doing things and against the taking of risks and striking out in new directions.'[1]

This paper examines some choices available to those who must continually watch over the way their organisation works, for structure is a vital element in efficiency, and for senior executives, an area prone to much thought, though junior management tends to take structure for granted, ascribing problems to personalities rather than illogical relationships.

As the writer is still a bank Director, too detailed a reference to other banks' organisation systems could be invidious. The approach is to suggest some criteria and point to some choices, illuminating them by reference to international banks. Organisation structure must be fitted precisely to the style and character of the business and simple comparisons can hide deeper and more complex issues.

Structural Criteria

It may be helpful to approach organisation structure in the way an engineer looks at a machine. He builds it, tends its, modifies it and re-designs it, all for the purpose of keeping it running smoothly at the right place in the right direction. Both pace and direction will change continually. Its purpose is to enable management, from the supervisory or 'Group Board' to the most junior decision maker, to marshal most efficiently, three sets of resources – human, financial, and physical.They must meet the aims of the enterprise, be they commercial needs of profitable markets or non-commercial needs based on social or cost-benefit criteria.

Because organisation structure is a set of human relationships, problems and choices are often unquantifiable and non-standard. There is no kit on the shelf. This is why the achievement of the best structure is not subject to the application of desk calculations. Boards and senior executives must personally review their structure.

The ideal solution when found is unlikely to remain so for long, such are changes in markets, resources, skills and attitudes. Because it involves personal status, responsibility and commitment, it is perhaps the most difficult area to attempt change and the executive who adopts the engineer's analytical approach will find that his professionally analysed proposals for innovation may meet with responses more emotional than in any other field. Human structures cannot simply be taken to pieces and rebuilt like a physical machine. Very sensitive problems of morale and motivation are involved. It is noticeable that management consultants often meet hostility from clients in respect of suggestions for changing the corporate structure, whereas in other areas, change is quite acceptable.

Before isolating some major components of the organisation, we may note underlying sources of its complexity. Size is a major determinant particularly in communications and human motivation. Also important are:

- the width and diversity of products and markets;
- the geographical spread of activities;
- the number of required skills;
- the variety of asset and liability requirements;
- the relative degree of interface with the general public, government, unions and other groups;
- the increasing impact, particularly overseas, of corporate and statutory requirements.

Formality of Systems
The more complex the organisation, the more difficult it is for humans to manage it and the greater the tendency to formality. A very large organisation needs substantial motive power and strong steering gear to make it move in the desired direction. A large international banking group, especially one

which has a world wide network of retail outlets and a wide range of corporate activities in various legal forms, has probably as interesting a structural problem as any, whereas a small investment bank may have virtually none.

It is tempting to think that major change, with its disruption of personnel and customer relations, its distortion of the on-going data base for decisions, its learning and settling down period, should only be attempted perhaps once in 5–7 years accompanied by a major communication plan. The intervening years may need to be used for expedient tuning of a structure seen to be no longer functioning effectively. For leaders, judgment about the rate of change an organisation can absorb is crucial.

B. ORGANISATIONAL CONCEPTS

It may be useful to consider three concepts:

- the formal organisation structure;
- the formal process of direction, control and information;
- the informal organisation.

The Formal Organisation Structure

This is often depicted by various levels of interconnecting, continuous or broken lines and boxes. The whole takes the form of a pyramid or set of pyramids one above the other; sometimes the apex is one man, sometimes the pyramid has a flat top. The chairman and board of the parent company or group is at the top, and at the bottom is the lowest level of management depicted by the chart, perhaps 'branches' or the 'Marketing Department'. This structure forms the vertical, lateral and diagonal relationships through which flows the information, direction and control by monitoring.

Most major US banks appear to favour formalised, published organisation charts in the interest of clarity of authority and responsibility.[2] The British tradition of flexible pragmatism may have influenced British banks in being slow to formalise charts and some do not care to publish them too widely or too often.[3] It is desirable to let everyone know by chart what the formal relations are but it may not be wise to enshrine them too deeply in dogma. To do so makes it more difficult to make subtle or frequent changes, or occasionally allow some 'stretch' to accommodate personalities, though a chart which is simply a reflection of personalities is a recipe for organisational chaos.

The Formal Process of Direction, Control and Information

This is the decision making structure by which management information and direction flows upwards, downwards and laterally and diagonally. Information is gathered for a proposal, a proposal becomes a decision, a decision is implemented, controlled and reviewed. Decision points are established by a hierarchy of authority to make them. This is the dynamic process within the static chart of lines and boxes.

The Informal Organisation

Within the formal structure is an informal infra-structure of consultation, motivation and personal commitment. As any general manager who has dealt with a strong minded specialist below him will witness, ostensible authority is not the same as power. It is essential for executives to know where real power lies and to what extent management can exercise authority. Branch managers may be instructed to promote say insurance or in-house trust units; if they lack faith in the market prospects or the product themselves they will not do much about it. It is hard to enforce them.

There emerged in the sixties the doctrine of 'acceptability'. The executive must 'sell' his authority to peers and juniors. To this extent, the skill of senior management was not only in making the right decision, but in persuading the organisation to endorse that decision, by confirmation and implementation. The larger the organisation and the more intelligent and organised the work force, the more important is the informal organisation. Knowledge of who can make a proposal work and the identification of resistance points do not appear in the charts and boxes but they are the reality. Taken too far, the doctrine of 'acceptability' can be dangerous. It can be taken for managerial weakness, but there is no doubt that there are limits beyond which managerial action is not acceptable. It is a matter of judgement where those limits are in relation to the enterprise itself. In recent years a firmer management style has appeared, welcomed by many who found management by consensus a slow process in adapting to change, whatever its social merits.

C. WHAT THE ORGANISATION MUST DO

Through the three components outlined, the organisation, in marshalling resources to meet needs, has certain essential activities:

- it must develop objectives;
- it must form strategies and make plans;

- it must manage 'operations' designed to sell products to 'customers' (the line function) – the word product is used as a shorthand for financial services;
- it must manage functional support activities.

How is it best organised to carry out these tasks and to arrange for the co-ordination of all these activities?

The Development of Objectives

Whilst the objectives of the business are essentially a matter for the board of directors they cannot as a group write objectives unless they are, in reality, working committees. An organisation unit, probably in the planning area, must develop aims for the chief executive who seeks approval from his board. This is the normal process of upward proposal and response. A board may call for reports, ask questions, criticise, comment, but generally it has no base on which to initiate policies or decisions in isolation.

Objectives often start with an ideological statement. Such a declaration might be:

> 'The objective of this bank is to prosper as a leader of private sector banking, optimising the interest of stockholders, consistent with duties to personnel, customers and the public of communities in which we trade.'

Such an objective is virtuous and embraces all. Perhaps it is useful as a motivational device for the less sophisticated but it does not encompass firmly enough the realities of organisational survival! For an international bank. They are likely to be:

- earnings per share, as a trend over three to five years;
- risk control;
- capital maintenance;
- liquidity maintenance;
- the strategic distribution of sources of profit contribution.

Market share, volume, margins, personnel policies, investment criteria are generally best regarded as strategies or constraints since they are not in themselves unqualified objectives. The wider the areas treated as objectives the deeper becomes the philosophical muddle, because objectives will be in conflict.

The planning organisation at group level in an international bank must have a strong financial orientation. The objectives tend to be largely a set of numbers covering the above 'realities' and lead to the numbers which form divisional or subsidiary objectives which must harmonise with them although the measurements may be different; for example, subsidiaries whose capital is arbitrary may find it more meaningful to use return on allocated capital plus return on gross assets rather than return on stockholders' funds. At every level, targets set will derive from the requirements of the ultimate group stockholder, but in reality they must be modified by what the resources within, and the environment outside, permit. The organisation must produce realistic appraisals of competitive strengths and weaknesses and internal constraints. Boards cannot set whatever objectives they like. Therefore, group planners must also be involved in broad strategic concepts which underpin the financial aims.

Strategy Formation

At every level, strategy is the business of the chief executive and his senior colleagues backed by strong analytical support. At the group level in an international business it will cover:

> *manpower* – senior development, succession and cross divisional policies and transfers;
> *the management of financial resources*, particularly capital appraisal, adequacy, raising and spending, liquidity, tax and cash flows, and financial and management accounting changes;
> *liabilities management*;
> *asset risks* on broad bases – currencies
> – countries
> – industries
> – products
> – major single lendings or investments;
> *organisation structure and controls;*
> *volumes and contribution levels* on a broad base;
> *management information and planning;*
> *broad social policy, public relations and publicity;*
> *competition.*

If an international business has a group chief executive, (in some banks it may be a top executive group), these areas are his essential functions rather than the making of operational decisions which can be made at lower levels within the strategic framework.

Duplication between group and division must be avoided. As soon as the group strategist extends his thinking to the marketing of individual products, say, cheque book accounts in UK, or to planning within particular territories (apart from the broad exposure control), he may duplicate the thinking of the responsible operating unit, which incidentally will know more about the theatre of action.

Another problem is the 'profit centre game'. Profit centres are essential to measurement of contribution and helpful to motivation but they may result in the development of local strategies which do not suit the whole organisation. For example, a fee earning service, such as trust or corporate advice, may decide that its profits will look better if it boosts them by some judicious lending; conflict with commercial banking operations will be likely and it may not suit the parent faced with scarce skills and marketing confusion for parallel lending activities to develop. So strategy at divisional level must be subservient to group although at some peril to motivation. A number of major banks are now also making significant investments in the securities industry and this adds an extra element to the strategies available to international banks.

Planning

Planning is the codification and quantification of strategy, and the research and development of specific projects e.g. strategic acquisitions. There should be group planners and there may have to be product, territorial or functional planners. In an international group there will be several levels. The operators themselves are unlikely to plan successfully, particularly if they are traditionally trained bankers who are traders and risk-takers and may be suspicious of planning. Negotiators and controllers of operations find that planning tends to come last, so it may best be a full time function, reporting direct to the chief executive at each level. In an international bank at group level it will be highly sophisticated and backed by automated systems capable of carrying out sensitivity analysis on planning assumptions.

A true plan can, organisationally, neither be completely 'top-down' nor entirely 'bottom-up'. A top-down plan will not be successful unless the top-down planner has total information about practicalities internally and in the market. Without this, his plan may fail through lack of credibility or be incapable of being implemented. Either people will do what he has directed at risk of disaster, or they will fail to accept the reality of his plans and overtly or covertly dodge them or do little. Only the lowest rung, say the branch manager, can have a completely top-down plan. No one knows more than he about what is possible on his 'patch' and unlike higher rungs of his ladder, no one is likely to argue! In some ways, the lowest rung of profit centre manager is the most free.

Yet a bottom-up plan is not a plan at all. In group terms, it is merely the collation of a set of loosely federated profit and cost centre policies. So the two must meet. The aims of the business must survive intact but modified by the realities of 'the grass roots'.

Within the time span, say the planning year, carefully orchestrated systems are needed to keep the group planning machine moving. It will never stop, for as soon as one plan is endorsed by the board and goes into implementation through divisions, the chief executive will be working on the next. Those in charge of operations tend to distrust planning since they lack faith in futurity and their conception of priorities is today's deal. But in a complex organisation, the chief executive should live and breathe with his strategy as embodied in his plan. It is his marker against which to judge policy decisions. Perhaps as important, it is his tool for maintaining control over a chaos of individual operations and decisions.

If it is to become a firm framework, the plan must be seen by modern management as logical and a good way to ensure that, prior to board endorsement, is an exposure of the draft plan to implementing management. If it is a good plan based on logical analysis, it will survive, possibly with some alteration to meet field experience and a few cosmetic changes to soften the ardour of operational activists. A thoughtful professional executive should achieve broadly the strategy he started from, with some change perhaps, in detail.

The Management of Operations
We need next to be clear about the use of the terms 'operational' and 'functional'.

Every business has some structure by which, at various levels, executives do the deals, lend the money, meet the customer and take day-to-day risk and commercial decisions. These are the operators, product or geographical managers, whether they are regional or branch managers, head of credit card operations or corporate finance directors of a merchant bank. There are grey areas between these operators and functional managements, say, the chief internal auditor, the chief personnel manager and other 'functionaries'. For example, the treasurer of an international bank is functional in his management of the bank's liquidity but if he controls the dealing rooms and makes day-to-day decisions on 'spreads', he is operational. A functional manager can be operational within his sphere, but here the term operational is related to the management of products.

A key question is whether to manage by geographical area or by product line, or a mixture of both. Can there be a matrix reporting system (one of the largest US banks has one) by which there are both geographic and product reporting lines?

If so, how can conflict be avoided? The most simple criterion is whether product specialisation, both technical and marketing, is more important to effective operation than geographical knowledge of market environment and personalities. The choice is not always clear cut. Of five of the largest US banks, published reports indicate that one has a matrix system with strong product input, one other is moving that way and others have a complex mixture of both product and geography.

Most merchant banks with little geographical spread of outlets divide their management by products – the corporate advice department, the banking department, the investment department. They may do this partly for security reasons but they choose also to do it because specialisation in product and marketing is essential. To complicate matters they may have a geographical breakdown within functions; for example, the banking department may have a Scandinavian 'desk', but typically, product management is the pattern.

The clearing banks in the United Kingdom and the traditional British owned overseas retail banks tended, until recently, to be managed geographically. Historically, they offered a range of general banking services to a very wide market in which the technology could all be grasped and handled through the same outlets. The management pre-occupations were short-term lending, people, properties, systems, deposits and local politics and economics. So the geographical system seemed right and it proved hard to change. It still has advantages in managing a geographical spread of general commercial banking business, where local conditions are more important than across-the-board product characteristics. But in an age of sophisticated product development and competition, it has come under strain, particularly as such products as medium-term lending to companies, acquisition advice, project finance and leasing, cannot effectively be sold by generalists and need not always use the traditional outlet, the branch bank. Once the clearers dropped the concept of leaving special products to other specialist institutions and tried to do almost everything, they found that the geographical concept produced too little specialist expertise applied to competing in the market against banks which do specialise – and this means nearly all their non-clearing bank competitors.

The US banks, however large, have never had major domestic branch retail networks (with one particular exception) so they have found product management natural and they claim to deliver their chosen product at a particular location with concentration and skill, not diffused by a multi-product, geographical approach.

For the British international banks, wide and dispersed historic retail networks have found it more difficult to change to product specialisation though they realise its importance, particularly in dealing with multi-national corporate customers where a geographical style of management by territories has led to some fragmentation of contact.

They will run the more specialist services (merchant banking, leasing and credit cards) through separate managements, but their dilemma is over what used to be known as general branch banking, namely retail services such as savings and cheque accounts, consumer credit, small business credit and corporate credit for medium and very large business. Running these services through geographical managements does produce considerable conflicts of marketing priority, fragmentation in customer contact, and lack of expertise, inseparable from a situation where one generalist management is offering a range of services against concentrated competition.

So in the retail operations of the British clearers one can see a gradual change to product rather than geographical management, but the change will produce some problems. It is easy to see a move from say, regional management in the UK to the concept of a consumer credit division, a corporate lending division, a retail division, but what new grey areas and cross-conflicts does that change itself produce? How would the branch manager relate to several reporting lines rather then one general regional manager? All sorts of untidiness can be foreseen. For instance, should the credit card be part of the consumer credit division or part of the money transmission service management? If the branch manager reports separately to consumer credit, trust and corporate business divisions who determines the priorities in his branch plan? Who else but a geographical controller – who can say 'Consumer credit division stand back, the priority in this location is corporate lending'?

There is a wider issue. Even though banks move to product management within one country, to what extent should it cross frontiers? Should the corporate advice activity at London head office, control the merchant bank offering the same product in Hong Kong? For product synergy, the answer is probably yes, but what of the group's general banking business in Hong Kong? Does that report to a separate London banking division and what problems does that produce locally, particularly in relation to politics and personalities? Does one need a local, general 'leader'?

A further difficulty is that in some products, particularly consumer related, expertise in one country does not imply expertise in another. Can a UK consumer credit operation effectively control such a business in Australia?

Wherever possible, an arrangement by which two managements are offering the same product in the same territory is to be avoided.

So the final answer may be the following global groupings within the total business:

- commercial banking, including correspondent banking (probably excluding small business);
- dealing, foreign exchange (all currencies including sterling);
- trust and investment, including eurobond issues but possibly not bond trading which might be under 'dealing';
- specialist corporate services – leasing, project finance, export finance, corporate advice, 'marriage broking', equity capital provision (except on a portfolio basis), acquisitions – i.e. the 'merchant banking function';

- retail services – domestic money transmission, savings accounts, small business services, possibly including loans, probably with 'home' and 'abroad' sections;
- consumer credit, probably split at lower levels to 'home' (branch and direct), overseas, and credit card. (Another alternative is to regard consumer credit as essentially part of retail banking.)

There is another finesse on this complex issue. International banking is no longer operated entirely through line manager relationships but through participation in subsidiary or associate companies. Where the subsidiary is wholly owned, management accountability on traditional lines may work, but where there are minority (or majority) partners, the group must work through boards of directors, not single employee managers. Then the head office function becomes closer to that of a holding company and it becomes harder to interfere in marketing or product technology and administration. The parent can only make sure it has the required board and top managers and the adequate control data so that it receives the right contribution and is not led into bad risks. In that situation, local personalities and politics become more important than product and territorial skills.

Where board, rather than individual accountability exists, a 'protocol' is needed as to what data is provided by the board to head office of the group, how many members represent the parent (or minority as appropriate) and what issues will be at the control of the group. Such reportable matters may be:

- liquidity and capital adequacy;
- capital investment;
- risk exposure;
- public relations and advertising affecting group;
- social responsibility;
- personnel policy (in broad terms);
- profit contributions;
- basic managerial control systems – lending authorities etc.

There will be numerical reporting levels where appropriate. The one market, with which it is difficult for banking organisations to deal, is the demand by multi-national companies for across-the-range, global, financial services. Multi-nationals themselves have different ways of handling their banking relationships, so the first task of any bank is to find out how the customer wants to do business and adjust the approach of the bank accordingly. Evidence is that some multi-nationals centralise major banking decisions, perhaps leaving their retail requirements to local management, others require local management to negotiate all requirements. Another customer may want to deal with local bank managers for wages and other retail services and global corporate division of the bank for its major borrowing or treasury function. In the face of this confused pattern of demand, banks should have some organisational back-up which identifies where the negotiation points are, perhaps a multi-national corporate division equipped to marshal the services in the right way. The degree of authority of such a division in relation to other bank operations dealing with the customer varies. It can at one end be R & D support; at the other, it can control the total relationship.

Finalising this broad sketch of the choices and conflicts in operations, let us summarise:

- There is no clear cut advantage in product or geographical management which will apply to every product and every market, but those products which cross geographical lines, such as lending to multinational corporations, probably should lean towards product organisation, as should those where the special technology crosses borders. When the customer is essentially local and where the product is also parochial, the best organisation is geographical.
- Whichever divisional system is used, bridges between geographical and product management are needed to make sure geographical knowledge is available to product divisions and technical skill is available to the geographical manager.
- Dealing with multi-nationals needs special co-ordination.
- The trend is towards product management.
- The golden rule is – identify the needs of the customer in his environment and match them.

The Management of Support Functions

In commercial organisations, the operational units are the spearheads and the functional managers are in support. The latter do however, have some power, which arises more from their special responsibility and knowledge than from their ostensible place in the structure. It is a foolish chief executive who instructs his chief accountant, albeit junior, to ignore the Companies Acts. He may have the authority but should he exercise the power? This creates an interesting organisational balance which the chief executive must get right. Undue authority to operations will mean rapid business development, high short term profits, high risks and some lowering of professional and legal and safety standards – cutting corners; excessive power to accountants, inspectors, auditors and automation technicians will result in the customer and perhaps market share and profit coming last. Functional managers, who tend to be highly trained specialists, can have divided loyalties, between the organisation and their speciality. More practically, they tend to be highly marketable so their career prospects lie more widely than to any slavish loyalty to the ethos of the business. In technical fields, no policy or operations manager dare move without them; yet sometimes he may have to over-ride them in a commercial judgment. A business ruled by the functional manager risks becoming a bureaucracy which may fail in the market place just because many functional managers provide a control mechanism.

Thus the problem of the top policy group is to build up the finest expertise and then temper their power and judgments continually, with the attending morale problems. However, the provision for the specialist of a broad management perspective by training and development will help him to balance his specialism with operational judgment.

International groups are so large that functional departments must be built up locally. Some saving of expensive personnel such as accountants, inspectors, public relations, advertising can be achieved by centering major departments at the group level reporting to a group executive, but this may result in inefficiencies because divisional managements require much more detailed functional support in their areas than does the parent. So there will be a pull between creation of functions at division and sub-division (and even lower down) and functions at group. A typical example is an in-house credit card, say Barclaycard. A keen management needs its own marketing and advertising department yet it carries spin-off for Barclays as a whole. What liason systems are needed between it and the marketing and advertising competence of Barclays' operations in the UK and overseas? Sometimes, these problems can be solved by appointing a group head of marketing or public relations with functional lines of accountability from managers across the group. However, where the group exercises a purely strategic role, he may find that power really rests in divisional managers reporting to him.

The crux then is the reporting line. If there is no group executive then group functional heads lack a source of authority.

Multiple reporting is sometimes possible in functional areas. It is feasible for the head of public relations to report to the group chairman and equally to the chief officers of divisions and others who need him from time to time, provided that all understand the priorities of activity.

Another difficulty in managing functions is that their managers can be perfectionists. They wish to have the best accounting or automation system; they find beauty and safety in quality of systems. This takes time and money and the business is operating against nimble competitors, so there must be a balance. In the more esoteric areas such as computers, it is difficult for a general executive to control the specialist spending budgets because he lacks technical knowledge of the real requirement. He may need outside consultants to check on his inside specialists; this will make him unpopular but can save the business cash. In operations, he normally has clearcut income flows and profit contributions as his guide. In functional departments, the guide is cost benefit analysis which is more difficult and sometimes impossible.

Moreover, functionaries like management systems, and their installation of systems in place of intuition tends to formalise. Formality can destroy flexibility and erode the authority of the individual to make exceptions, use expedience and compromise, all of which is part of the role of the manager.

An example will illustrate. The installation by personnel departments of a complex job-evaluation system for management, based on carefully structured weighting of responsibility factors, may please managers with its benefits of fairness and objectivity. (Incidentally, it can be inflationary of status, job and so salary.) It makes job comparisons more systematic and less arbitrary and it will be accompanied by a panoply of evaluation and appeal committees. So far, so good, but the chief executive now finds he has lost his authority to move people across lines where, as previously, he could finesse the relative seniority, or reward exceptional people's performance or down-grade jobs that needed it. The system now will not permit it; it has taken over from him. Budding executives should beware that the application of management systems does not castrate the managers who build them.

The opposite policy of flexibility may produce such variable standards of performance and inequity as to be unacceptable. So the executive watchword is balance.

D. THE FORMAL PROCESS OF DIRECTION, CONTROL AND INFORMATION – THE DECISION PROCESS

The Roles of Various Groups in Relation to Each Other

THE GROUP BOARD

The co-ordination of planning, operations and functions is the role of boards and general executives. Let us begin with the group board and group executive in relation to executives and subsidiary boards. We must here assume some division between the role of board and management, even though it is blurred, and between group and subsidiary. Chief executives and subsidiary boards may seek autonomy, and they normally do, but they cannot forget that the board of the group or parent is ultimately, in law and spirit, responsible to the stockholder and must retain authority and an information base in major policy areas. In identifying these areas, one is brought back to certain fundamentals which have threaded through earlier parts of this paper, they are:

- the profit contribution;
- dividend policy;
- capital adequacy, raising, spending;
- the divisional plan;
- major diversification;
- senior manpower plans;
- risk management;
- liquidity management;
- major public relations and social or political policy;
- major personnel policies and relations.

Whether the board wishes to give prior approval or post facto report, and which 'floor' limit it requires for reporting, are for arrangement. Efficiency may suffer if the group board strays much beyond these areas into matters such as consumer marketing, or middle management disciplines or the actual approval of loans, unless the area is so exceptionally large as to have real bearing on the group capital and reserves. Normally, such matters are best left to divisions, either at board or management level.

One part of the formal organisation structure containing nuances not describable in formal terms, is the relationship between the chairman of the board and the chief executive. The chairman must do the following:

- maintain satisfactory relations with his stockholders (or parent company);
- plan the mix of age and speciality of his own board;
- ensure that the board gets from management the information it needs and that a proper relationship between board and management is maintained, shielding executives from the board's undue interference in management matters;
- monitor the work and plan succession of chief executive and his most senior colleagues;
- exercise organisational leadership by his operational style;
- keep a sharp watch on the general health of the business and its internal and external relations.

Since the interests of stockholders and management can differ, it is usually unsatisfactory for the chairman to be chief executive unless the company is in a period when swift authority is exceptionally needed to meet a special challenge. It may occasionally work in subsidiary companies but it reduces the status of the board and creates a situation where the chief executive is not clearly accountable. In large organisations (such as major banks) that have to take very substantial risks, it arguably puts too much strain on one man's ability and judgment. Transactions are quick and reasonably individual, but policy is slower and lacks benefits from group thinking, so there should be an interplay of at least two minds on these major matters. A separation of the roles also works against the development of an executive clique or power vacuum around the top man.

THE GROUP EXECUTIVE

How is the group board to ensure that major policy areas are effectively administered and reported at the group level? There must be an executive group above divisional level so that the board can receive recommendations that do not purely represent divisional views and so that group matters can have executive attention.

Since this executive group is primarily policy making, there is no need, necessarily, for one group chief executive. It is possible to work with a small peer group. But, such is the range of external issues, nearly all major banks now have a full time chairman of the board. If he chairs all policy committees both at board and sometimes at group management level, is he the chief executive, even though he disclaims such a role? Thus the phrase chief executive begs some questions.

At group level these executive functions seem clearly indicated:

- group finance;
- group manpower;
- group planning, marketing and development.

Economics and public relations' support will be available to the top group. Generally, the top executive group members should not also act as divisional executives, though the chairman and/or chief executive of major divisions may come into the top executive committee. Arrangements as to the degree of group or individual decision-making are again matters of style and tradition in the company. The group executives may be non-executive directors on operating boards for purposes of communication, but this can create an invidious position as on those boards they will be neither 'insiders' nor 'outsiders'.

If this top group of five or six people were on the group board, US practice (and UK practice in some cases) indicates the rest of the group board should be outside non-executive directors. Stockholders need an independent audit on management and the top management need advice outside their in-house support. Subjects such as their own salaries and succession may need to be dealt with by a committee entirely composed of outside directors. Again, it is a strength, both for the board and for the group finance director in dealing with auditors, if the board has a non-executive manned audit committee. In some countries it is mandatory.

Recent strengthening of the role of non-executive directors is a welcome attempt to bridge a gap that arose when companies ceased to be managed by their owners. The UK stockholder in particular had become somewhat impotent and the non-executive is one good way of strengthening his powers. In an international bank it is helpful if the outside board, which should have an age balance, can encompass some of the following expertise:

- – finance, investment and the stock market, for advice on stockholder relations, capital raising and acquisition policy;
- – personnel;
- – social policy;
- – political conditions;
- – broad geographic areas – North America, Europe, Africa, Middle East, Far East;
- – very broad industrial skills.

This, together with an age balance, is not easy to arrange. Technical banking probably, is not on the priority list for outside directors of banks. Expertise should be supplied by executive directors or possibly, retired executives. The latter however, can find that they feel uncomfortable. Their in-house knowledge quickly gets out of date and they have no independent expertise. Possibly, retired executives are best used for special projects where an elder statesman is required, say, a divisional boundary dispute, rather than as purely non-executive directors.

DIVISIONAL BOARDS AND EXECUTIVES

It is hard to conceive of an international bank having no divisional structure. Large businesses can become inefficient because human communication and commitment are hard to achieve in big units. To run an international multi-product bank with only one board and one executive is probably not feasible, though in a one-office bank with just a few products, say a small British merchant bank, or consumer credit organisation, it may work.

Since divisional boards have no direct stockholder responsibility and are only a legal requirement if the division is incorporated, need they exist at all? This choice turns on whether it is wise for one man or group to have total power and be largely self reporting, or whether every man should have somebody to whom he must be accountable. For major products or geographic areas, say consumer credit in UK clearing banking, a board has uses, but excessive proliferation of small activity boards is a waste of management time, especially if manned by executives who would probably be better employed in their executive tasks than sitting around a board table.

Subsidiary boards can, of course, be used as promotion ladders to the top board for younger, non-executive directors though it is not usually tactful to tell them so.

Centralisation and Decentralisation

This commonly mentioned antithesis is usually oversimplified. One has to ask two questions. First, decentralisation of what – strategy or operations? Secondly, which decisions within the scope of an individual are we talking about?

The overall strategy and its framework in a plan are the functions of the centre, whatever local modifications are permitted around the edges. In an investment trust of banks, one strategy, to maximise stockholders' return, may be enough; in effect, all other decisions are then decentralised. But an international bank must create synergy in business and cannot entirely control banking risk on a mere investment portfolio basis, and it must keep the enterprise on course and the strategic plan is the tool for so doing.

On the other hand, commercial decisions made daily in the field probably are best made as close to the data base as possible. Decisions are then based on knowledge of facts and judgment. To take the decision away from the commercial point of contact is to widen the area of unknowing; hence the value of decentralised operational and functional decisions. Yet excess of decentralisation makes more difficult the task of the centre in monitoring the degree to which policy is followed and the quality of executives; hence the value of a post facto reporting system and some form of management audit as a compromise between total absence of control and prior approval requirements.

The amount of decentralised authority an individual needs and should have, depends on the extent to which the particular decision is crucial to his role performance and central to his skills. To be quick and competitive, a branch manager must have reasonable lending authority. This also, is the area of his personal expertise. He need not be given much authority on premises expenditure which is not crucial to his role and not within his functional expertise.

It is also true that, particularly in the business of banking, (essentially concerned with taking risks), individuals can bear much more delegated authority when removed from the market pressure point than when faced across the desk by a pleading or threatening customer. Commonly, a man who last week had authority to lend £X to each customer as a branch manager, this week has £X × 5 authority as a head office controller. The new role is supported and protected, the old was not.

In large branch banks there are hierarchical tiers of recommendation that permit large individual discretions 'up the line', particularly when the authority covers short-term current asset finance. In non-branch banks, such as merchant banks, the authorities are probably rather smaller, for lenders face customers direct, without a filter or recommending offices. Moreover, in such banks, commitments may be longer term, the transactions more complex, so more investigation is needed, and decisions can be slower.

In summary, decentralisation can bring greater market sensitivity but greater professional variability in performance – more risk and a less rigid adherence to the central plan. Centralisation implies tight adherence to the plan. One disadvantage of centralised organisations is the lack of development of individuals implicit in not allowing their independent responsibilties to expand. Some risks must be taken if people are to grow.

Spans and Levels of Control

The appropriate span of control depends largely on the nature of the work. It is a practical question. For example, in a retail branch network, very few complex types of decision pass between branch and its next upper 'control'. Thus a control team may supervise and motivate up to say 100 branches. However, in a complex operation, say a merchant bank dealing in very technical corporate advice, or in a functional department in which complex legal papers are moving across desks and much discussion is needed, perhaps one to three or four is not too narrow. Certainly, a one-to-one manager relationship is nearly always unsatisfactory, the junior being a bottleneck through which those below cannot easily reach the man above and vice versa. A one-to-one structure tends to lead to by-passing.

One effect of narrowing the span of control is to increase the number of management levels. A narrow span is better for communication between any two levels, but it lengthens the distance from 'top to bottom'. However it is virtually impossible for so complex an organisation as an international bank to work with less than five or six executive levels.

Some Principles of Delegation

In bringing to a close this discussion of the formal organisation, one may mention some principles of delegation without which the machine will not function properly:

- A policy maker should avoid, where possible, interfering in operational decisions within the authority of those charged with operating his policy; nor should a manager make decisions in areas delegated to subordinates, though he must have an effective monitoring system.
- Decisions are normally made on the basis of detailed presentations by subordinates. Thus the decision-making process is normally recommendation and response. A manager should not normally act without the recommendation of those who have worked in the area.

- Managers must 'grit their teeth' when decisions are taken at lower levels which they themselves might not have taken (unless they have such alarming implications as to take the matter out of subordinate discretion).
- Managers should try to act consistently when acting on their own authority and when recommending to higher levels. This may be a counsel of perfection, but no one should allow himself the self indulgence of recommending weaker decisions to head office than he would take himself, hoping to shuffle them through on someone else's responsibility. He should not stand aside from the negotiations between head office and the customer or employee. He represents the company and he must accept that responsibility; this is his professional integrity.

This brings us naturally, to the matter of human character and management style and the informal organisation.

E. THE INFORMAL ORGANISATION

One does not need a machiavellian mind to stress how important is the informal organisation. An organisation is a society – human beings in relationship. The executive must not only understand this but know where the main springs and rivers run; how things actually get done. In all organisations the formal boxes will expand and contract or distort with personality, and the lines between them will sometimes have power flowing through them; sometimes they will appear blocked. The wise senior manager is a politician, he understands what is possible. He must learn to 'work' his own organisation, but honestly, for deviousness will quickly bring its own penalties.

Limitations on Formal Authority

Our forefathers in management would have been horrified at the limitations placed on modern management authority, particularly at the top. A modern executive must live with severe constraints on his power to get things done. In banking, constraints may well be less than in industry as a whole, because of the good industrial relations and the ability of work people to move from the bottom to the top throughout their career. Even in lower ranks, their commercial and personal motivation is high and is generally tuned to the business. The 'we and they' syndrome may be less evident than in other industries.

There have always been problems in the exercise of ostensible authority. Greater energy is required to move something than not to move it, or to stop it from being moved. There are always those who, through inertia or resistance, try to prevent the flow of decision into action. One must learn how to persuade, by-pass or remove structural, human or other obstacles. This can take time and hard work. It is one measure of the strength and subtlety of a senior manager as to how long he takes to achieve clearly correct aims against this sort of resistance, without undue fuss.

In the move from owner-managed businesses to manager-run enterprises, we have swapped one sort of informal power which lay with the family to another – the specialists and the work force. In family businesses, key members of the founding house, though not always ostensibly in executive authority, could wield influence. In modern business, informal power lies with specialists or with personnel and their representatives. Moreover, in the developed, industrial democracies,the modern manager's burden of legislative constraint has been growing rapidly, particularly in non-banking matters, race and sex discrimination, consumer protection and job retention, though in the UK he has been fairly free of regulatory banking law. Changes are occurring. The relationship between the supervisory authorities and the banker is becoming tougher again. On top of this is the activity and power of the unions, particularly in the UK, although this is in retreat.

Managers have one weapon which is their support against all the pressures nowadays placed on them; their skill and professionalism which must be heightened to meet challenges to their authority.

Proposals made and decisions implemented must command respect by the quality of their arguments. The able executive who can analyse, present and handle effectively policies and decisions, will make organisations move, but the process is demanding and requires high intellectual qualities and social skills.

Management Style

Every business has its own style. A critique of the four major London clearers (and subsidiaries within them) or of the five or six largest US banks would reveal quite different styles – even though all of these banks compete effectively in the same market. Whatever the style, it should support individuals in their roles. Such manifestations as cliques, courtiers, 'gentlemen and players' and intrigues are anathema to professional managers and must be discouraged by leaders. The prolonged retention of ineffective executives due to excessive and misplaced 'kindness' is frustrating to those above, below and alongside and unfair to the person concerned. The by-passing of chains of authority, the reversal of decisions and the setting of head office against branches, and the reverse, by senior people are all withering to organisation vitality; generally only directors and senior executives can prevent the onset of some of these malaises. Managers are entitled to have recommendations heard, their specialisations consulted though they are not entitled always to win their point; if they lose it they are entitled to know why. What hurts executives at every level is any suggestion that decisions, which may be accepted even if hard and adverse, are unfairly made or made without unprejudiced professional analysis and discussion.

Of course, the true professional cares much that the eventual decision taken by the organisation is the right one, but he cares almost as much that the decision is made by the best assembly of facts and balanced judgments that can be brought to bear upon it.

Communications

In small organisations, communications are relatively simple and this is one reason why large organisations should try to break down their working centres into small units. Personal and 'industrial' relations have traditionally been good in banks, unionised or not, and this is partly because bank work forces are organised into small groups. Nevertheless, the communications problems for the British clearing bank groups are as difficult as in any bank in the world. The major US banks may have far bigger balance sheets but they have fewer people in a smaller number of offices. The bank that can get the whole of its top and middle management in one room is lucky indeed.

A whole range of communictions systems, expensive and time consuming have been developed, bearing in mind that the written head office letter is only suitable for certain procedural and technical instructions and quite inadequate for motivation.

Explaining why the group takes certain lines of action and persuading people themselves to do things, obtaining a personal commitment, are matters for personal contact where possible. Hierarchies of conferences backed by attractive brochures and visual aids are essential.

Most major banks now have their public relations departments and have been persuaded to engage them fully as professional, external communications technicians, even though the message itself and its presentation must come direct from management, not a PR front man. His role is stage manager, not lead performer. Not all banks have committed themselves to the public relations arm as internal communications technician. It has such a role and need not detract from the leadership and communication job of management itself.

Leadership

This brings us to the intangible factor of leadership. It has changed, but it has not become an anachronism. Leadership is a different function from management, though individuals may combine the two roles. The manager is a problem solver, his or her energies are directed to goals, strategies, decisions and actions. He directs affairs to reduce uncertainty. Leadership however, consists of heightening imagination, considering wider choices, production of ideas and the personification of the most outward looking aspects of the business. It should infuse human warmth, enthusiasm and generosity into the enterprise.

Modern leadership should be professionally inspired. Managers do not expect leaders to have detailed technical knowledge, but they do expect a general professional grasp of the business, intelligent self-criticism and penetrating questions. And an understanding of managers' problems and frustrations can gain respect.

Managers have not become so sophisticated as to divorce policies and principles from personalities; and they are still all too willing to develop leadership cults. Carried to excess, this can cause dangerous instability in the organisation which will become unbalanced by the excessive power and influence of one individual and the consequent vacuum around him. Unfortunately, loyal employees in large businesses do tend to be moulded and conformist, so one often regrets a lack of healthy independence and scepticism. But intelligently used, the force of personality can create a focus of commitment, and the skills of the platform, the radio and television must be cultivated. Without these skills, a modern leader is professionally incomplete. He must be able to write reasonably well in his own field and speak effectively to any size of group on every occasion. He must learn sensitivity to audience groups. This is a product of experience and flair.

Different organisations need different kinds of leadership at various points in time. At one time, a sound, solid administrator may be followed by someone of flair and charisma, outward looking. There should also be a balance between chairman and chief executive and where possible one should complement the other. So boards of directors and chosen leaders must sense the needs of the business at the time, seeking to cement the inevitable cracks. Leadership, even though not itself innovative, should provide a climate where carefully thought out innovation is possible, particularly in the area of structure where human investment in status quo makes change so difficult.

F. SOME CONCLUSIONS

Is it possible in such a short tour d'horizon to isolate from the complexities of organisation structure any general principles? Let us mention some:

- There is a balance continually to be watched between the need for a formal organisation and decision process and the need for speed and flexibility in competitive environments. The balance best rests between a secure central strategic framework and flexible operations within it.
- Within the formal organisation, informal systems operate so that differing characters and styles may develop within a secure policy framework. The organisation must be so structured that individuals feel secure in their role and their authority to carry it out.
- Whatever the formal and informal systems, they must continually be adjusted to meet organisation needs.
- Management must now make acceptable its policies and decisions to secure commitment, because the age of management participation in whatever form is here and is healthy if intelligently organised. This puts much greater pressure on management to perform professionally.
- Some people are favoured by natural aptitudes, but all must train themselves to provide leadership in the way that the organisation needs. In the area of structural change, leadership is required more than in most other areas of the enterprise.

References
1. John D. Rockefeller 3rd, *The Second American Revolution*, New York, Harper & Row, 1973, p. 72, as quoted in 'Managers and Leaders Are They Different', A. Zaleznik, *McKinsey Quarterly*, Spring 1978.
2. Most include some form of organisation chart in their published accounts.
3. Lloyds Bank published a chart in its 1977 Report and Accounts; it has been followed by other banks since.

CHAPTER 2

THE ROLE OF THE PERSONNEL FUNCTION

Bryan Livy

Lecturer in Personnel Management,
The City University Business School, London

We all know about 'people' and those of us who are managers know how to 'manage'. We think we do, anyway. The statement is truthful, but only a partial truth. There is much more to the management of human resources than the lessons of our own personal experience, prejudice, intuition or 'gut feeling' (although these are important).

For some time now – for over seventy years – researchers, consultants and managers themselves have investigated all manner of human problems at work. The core issue is essentially the quality of human organisation in pursuit of common goals.

Whilst our knowledge has increased, we still cannot be prescriptive in novel situations, although we can offer systematic approaches. 'People' problems at work are dynamic. This makes the study of human relations more, not less, imperative.

As members of the human race, we all know that our behaviour is sometimes rational, sometimes emotional, sometimes conscious and deliberate, sometimes unconscious and confusing. We may respond mechanically to the world around us if we find it dull or boring, or if we feel powerless. In such cases, our performance is likely to be limp. At other times, we seek to change things. We are not robots; we are self-willed, thinking, creative, purposeful human beings. We are individuals; but we are also members of working groups. We are affected by what others think. We also have loyalty to a wider organisation – the bank. The bank is provider and custodian of our future. Our individuality is necessarily compromised. We may sometimes feel frustrated.

However, the employing organisation is equally restricted. Designing, producing and marketing a product or service has obvious technical, cost and profit constraints. Pure engineering is not enough. People have got to work the system, and also to make it grow. People must respond positively. There is a world of difference between what people *can* do and what they *will* do. At the heart of management lies a neat balancing trick – reconciling the 'needs' of individuals with the 'needs' of the organisation.

'Banking above all things is about people'.[1] The major clearing banks are large-scale employers. Some of them, with over 50,000 people, rank amongst the giants, both nationally and globally.

High street banks have a long history extending back to the amalgamation movement in joint-stock banking in Britain in the late nineteenth century, and continuing today. They have further grown by the extension of the market and the innovation of new facilities. Now they form highly stable organisations, but in competition with each other and with other financial institutions.

Human enterprise on such a scale creates problems and possibilities. Many of these are related to size itself and are endemic to other giants, oil companies, the motor industry, steel-making; some are special to banking, which is still labour intensive, like the Civil Service, and also fragmented, with a large number of retail outlets. The principal problems engendered by geographical dispersion, by the employment of large numbers, by the exercise of control through various levels of authority in branch, regional and sometimes district units are essentially human ones; coordination, cooperation, communications.

For years banks have been regarded as excellent employers. A career in banking is regarded as a profession. The traditional concern which banks have always shown for their staff is not simply a matter of welfare. Managing people means getting the best out of them, developing their talents, creating opportunities for their growth, promoting their positive contribution to the success of 'the bank'.

However, we should not assume all employees have a unitary, undivided loyalty. Within a bank there are differences in the aims and ambitions between individuals and groups; there is competition between employees for resources, promotions, recognition, rewards and status. A bank, like any other organisation, is better regarded as a 'pluralistic'[2] collection of interests within the common weal. The job of management is to seek reconciliation, harmony, and a stimulated, satisfied workforce.

Noble ideals are not easily translated into practice. Nor does the responsibility for welding the disparate interests and aspirations of the people employed into a cohesive, manageable whole rest solely with any one individual, neither Chairman, nor branch manager. It rests with all who hold managerial or supervisory positions. Concerted effort is required. Responsibility for the management of people is collective.

To help meet this challenge there has grown up over the last half century or so, at first gradually and then at an accelerating pace, a body of knowledge, a discipline, which offers advice and guidance: personnel management. Personnel management is not simply for specialists; it has lessons for all who manage people.

What is Personnel Management?

Personnel Management is part of the process of management in general; a constituent element in the complex business of running an enterprise. At first sight a personnel function can take some of the load from over-burdened line managers and can provide a specialist, advisory service. At second sight it can provide a valuable input into the planning, control and management of an entire organisation.

What does this specialist advice consist of? One leading academic[3] has described personnel management as the 'technology of the behavioural sciences'; in other words the application of behavioural science to the human problems, frustrations and conflicts to be found in any work situation. Behavioural science is really the combined contribution of what is termed occupational psychology (the way in which individuals adjust to job demands, and conversely, how jobs may be adjusted to individuals) and sociology (the ways in which people behave as members of various groups, and respond to their neighbours).

All this is not just 'moo-cow sociology' (contented cows give best milk). Economic rationale motivates good employment policies as well as social justice. But it is broader yet; for the law, questions of engineering and technology, work methods, politics, costs, markets and productivity all impinge on the processes of managing people. The approach is multi-disciplinary.

Personnel management is not philanthropic or paternalistic in style, nor is its place the 'bleeding heart' of the organisation; it is the formation and execution of policies for getting the best from people at work.

The Oxford English Dictionary defines personnel as 'staff or hands of a business as opposed to equipment or plant', and management as 'administration, skilful handling'. Thus Personnel Management has a distinctive focus, which 'justifies the separation of the function in spite of the fact that every other person in the enterprise must also be concerned with personnel'.[4] It is the job of *all* managers to manage and *all* managers have a responsibility for people. There are two sources of responsibility for people at work. Responsibility is shared between line and staff functions.

Line and Staff

The line and staff concept is an old one. It describes an organisational interaction. To define it is simple enough. To make it work has beset organisations for generations. Probably the best definition comes from a contemporary writer. 'Line functions are those which have direct responsibility for achieving the objectives of the company. Staff activities are those which primarily exist to provide advice and service'.[5] Underlying this concept is that of the division of labour. Units of work become specialised and have to become integrated. Further, the system of authority (the line organisation) represents a basic division in work structure and consists of direct vertical links between different levels. Advisory services can make inputs at any of these levels. The concept derives from military organisations and is akin, for example, to the 'teeth' and 'support' arms in the Army, representing line and staff functions respectively.

A word of warning is called for. The word 'staff' is generic. Strictly defined it does not simply mean the 'people' element. Specifically and accurately it includes *all non-line* activities, all supporting management services (such as supplies, properties, financial control systems) as well as the 'personnel' element. Semantic confusion often arises over this definition. In the context of this book we are primarily concerned with 'staff' in the 'people' sense.

Looked at another way, the line has 'executive' authority for getting things done, achieving primary objectives. Staff activities may have varying degrees of functional authority in advising line management. And specialist advice is indispensable in a complex commercial world. The precise degree of authority and responsibility accorded to the staff function is often ambiguous insofar as it may vary from one situation to another.

There is no doubt that line management (e.g. the branch manager) has executive authority over his domain, and therefore, responsibility for it. He is responsible for its success or failure. He must therefore be accorded a degree of judgemental freedom in deciding the best way to do things. He is as directly responsible for his staff and getting the best out of them as he is for the equipment and other resources under his control. But does he know all the answers? Does he not have a responsibility to act in compliance with bank policy as a whole? Do there not need to be uniform policies between branches and between local areas? Is not fairness and consistency achieved by some regulation over such matters as manning levels, contracts of employment, pay, training and promotion, disputes and discipline, redundancy, redeployment, industrial relations and negotiations? If these questions suggest an affirmative answer, then the branch manager cannot act in isolation. The issue neatly resolves itself into a line/staff interactive problem with all the possibilities of cooperation and/or conflict which might ensue at both operational and policy-making levels. In any large-scale organisation, some centralisation of 'personnel' functions is both inevitable and desirable for purposes of coordination and control. But then there comes the threat of remote, bureaucratic inertia. The problem is common.

How much authority should a staff man have? Should there be a 'right given to a staff specialist to command compliance with methods, procedures, policies and timing of one unique function of the organisation . . . requiring specialised knowledge'[6] with the dire possibility that the 'line manager may feel that his customary and well-tried ways of doing things are being threatened by new-fangled specialists, whose advice he may yet be afraid to ignore (and) become unsure of his authority?'[7] Will staff people 'interfere' with the time-hallowed custom of the line to do their own man-management?'[8] Or should staff be meekly advisory, subservient and impotent? Where does the balance of advantage lie, and where should the line be drawn?

The issue is not even as simple as that. A further complication arises from the fact that staff men may themselves be in a direct hierarchical relationship with their bosses in the staff function at the policy-making level – i.e. the personnel director or staff general manager. They therefore themselves have a kind of line responsibility – to get the job done – i.e. the implementation of company policy. As such they may regard themselves, or be titled, as managers, charged with achieving certain organisational goals, and if they 'consider themselves fully responsible for its success or failure . . . their work is therefore not indistinguishable from that of line management.'[9]

The line/staff concept is a pillar of the traditional organisation; it provides for a patterned, structural relationship which in practice can become blurred. Traditionally, the staff function is there to give advice, provide services to the line, develop plans and policies, follow them through, evaluate them (in cost-benefit terms), validate them (to see if they are achieving their purpose), and to initiate change and improvements. Indeed, the relationship is as much influenced by the personalities performing the various roles, if not more so, than would appear to be suggested by inanimate boxes on organisation charts. The sources of influence and power are partly personal, partly political and partly derived from expertise, particularly if that expertise is not a shared resource.

Remedies must therefore be found to deal with any conflict in line/staff situations, to reconcile the aims and objectives of each. Ignorance of each other's purpose and each other's problems is probably a major cause. Training programmes may go some way to alleviate this, but can provide no substitute for grass roots experience. An interchange of personnel between line and staff functions at different points in their careers proffers a better means of gaining understanding. This is practised in banks and certain other large organisations, but in turn creates problems. Not all managers are suitable for a staff appointment; nor do all wish it – they may see it as disruptive to their careers. In addition, the staff specialisms are becoming so much more professional and technical that it is not always possible to cross-fertilise in this way. A mainstream of professional expertise needs always to be on tap. This in turn requires career paths for staff specialists comparable with opportunities in the line.

All specialisms have become more esoteric in recent years; it is certainly true of personnel management. The line manager, of necessity, must rely more and more on the specialist. This must inevitably mean more power for the specialist and probably some erosion of the line manager's prerogative. McGregor[10] has argued that where two people in line and staff roles interact, the effective performance of one will generate a deficiency in the other. Could it lead to duplication? Does the line/staff concept overlook too many human realities? One critic, Argyris[11] argues that formal organisational structures inhibit psychological development. Further, organisations cannot speedily and appropriately react to changing conditions if impeded by traditional organisational structures and the prescription of roles and responsibilities. Research has shown that successful firms in a dynamic environment need flexibility.[12,13] The bureaucratic model which has nice, clear-cut divisions of labour necessarily assumes a mechanistic view of man who will respond to and submit to the parameters placed on his behaviour; who will accept the prescribed restriction of his individuality, without which the system would not work properly. And if the organisaion needs to respond to changing circumstances, the structure will stop it from doing so.

Out of this debate, what lessons can be drawn?

(i)   There is no universal prescription for the role and status of the staff specialist.

(ii)   The staff man, by definition, must be a specialist, and the line manager a generalist.

(iii) There can be no abdication of the line manager's responsibility for managing people simply because a specialist service exists.

(iv)   There is a collective responsibility for managing people. Both line and staff managers have something to offer; both observe organisational problems from different angles.

(v)   The staff officer can never impose his ideas on line management. Respect for his expertise must be *earned*. Line managers will not cooperate unless the advice proffered them is acceptable. Line managers have ways of doing their own thing and they have the right to reject recommendations which do not help them to achieve their objectives.

(vi)   The duality of responsibility implies that by some means or other, a *joint* approach between line and staff managers, both in the formation and execution of policies, is called for.

(vii) In a fast changing world, any strategy must be *flexible*.

Permutations of the various ways in which personnel management may be integrated into general line management all stem, fundamentally, from a common root: role definition (i.e. who does what). Given that some responsibility must be held somewhere for human resource management, the argument for one kind of structure versus another are choices of organisational design; they are administrative matters, not matters pertinent *per se* to the justification of personnel policy; they are peripheral and not central to the *raison d'etre* of personnel management. Perhaps, in some ways, it does not matter too much which choice is adopted. Under different circumstances all could work well or badly, depending on a number of factors – environmental, political, technological – but most of all on the will to succeed.

Responsibility for people must rest somewhere, and it must be clearly delineated. 'Personnel management is the responsibility of *all* (my italics) those who manage poeple as well as being a description of the work of those who are employed as specialists.'[14]

Human Resource Management Planning

Staff management cannot take place in a vacuum. Policies must be planned and specifically tailored. Comprehensive techniques are nowadays directed at large-scale human resource management. Probably the most fundamental of all these is manpower planning, from which all others emanate. Manpower planning is the corporate overview of the manpower stock: the skills, qualifications, knowledge and experience required for different levels of responsibility within the organisation, the age distribution of its members, the rates at which they leave, the prediction of future manpower demands according to the way in which the organisation plans to grow (or contract) and forecasts of recruitment, training and development which will be necessary to meet the corporate objectives. Strategies must be devised for meeting the bank's staffing requirements overall, both now and in the future. This requires that careful consideration be given to such matters as career planning, professional education, training, management development, job evaluation, pay systems, terms and conditions of employment, the kinds of people to be selected to work in the bank, how their performance is to be appraised, on what criteria they are to be promoted.

At root, the demand for manpower is a derived demand – people are taken on or trained to provide a supply of skills according to the bank's operational needs. A collection of interlocking plans must be geared to organisational objectives. These plans are both quantitative and qualitative. Projected changes in the total manpower stock and its 'mix' or composition reflect moves in the state and direction of the organisation. Clearly, predictions of any business plans have wide-ranging staffing implications. A systematic model is depicted in Figure 1. Planning is concerned with securing an optimal adjustment in 'matching' job demands with people's abilities and aspirations. Although the work itself may be the main priority, modifications can be exercised to meet human needs by the design of the job, equipment, methods of work and reward systems. People can be steered towards the desired goals through appropriate selection, training, experience, etc. But we should not forget that the process might be further influenced by broader environmental considerations – such as employment trends, government policies, legal requirements, industrial relations, union agreements, social attitudes, and so on. The disparate elements need to be reconciled, and staff policies hammered out accordingly. Let us crystallise the main aspects:

Resourcing implies generating a manpower input into the organisation via recruitment and selection procedures, gearing the 'flow' of people through organisation levels and occupations over time, and taking tactical steps to meet short-term contingencies.

Training and development activities are aimed at the growth and enhancement in an individual's ability to perform – for current jobs, for promotion, or new assignments. Programmes are concerned with the inculcations of skills, abilities and attitudes, whether at operational, supervisory or managerial levels. And performance needs to be appraised.

Motivation is of concern to all managers. People need to be inspired. Sensitive and sensible leadership is essential. But the motivational pull (or push) is not one-sided. People's natural capacities and aspirations demand outlet and opportunity. Work must be consciously designed to accommodate human potential. Symptoms of dissatisfaction such as absenteeism and labour turnover must be investigated.

Financial Compensation involves the design and administration of payment systems, job evaluation, salary structures, incentive schemes, collective bargaining. People expect to be paid fairly for their work.

Although this classification depicts certain key staff management activities, they are by no means discrete. They are all interwoven and operate, inter alia, within the broader context of industrial relations and employment legislation.

Employment legislation is chiefly concerned with people's rights at work, both individually and collectively. Government enactments affecting employ-ment in recent years, together with Codes of Practice have galvanised the personnel management function into a hub of activity, regarding contracts of employment, employment protection, fair and unfair dismissal, redundancy, sex and race discrimination, equal pay and opportunities, health

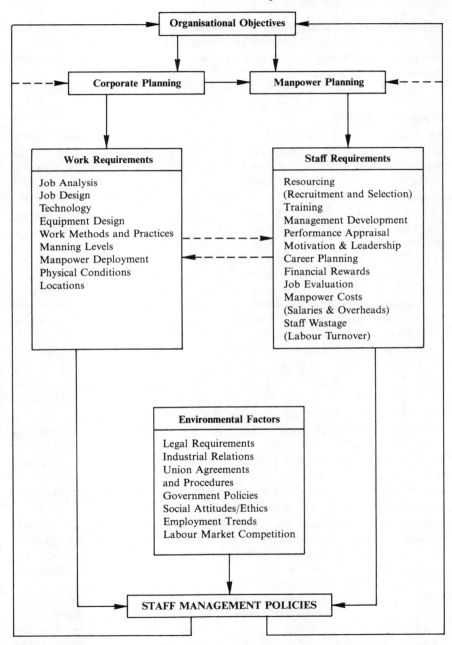

Figure 1 Systematic Model Showing Inter-Relationships in the Information of Staff Management Policies

and safety, industrial relations. Many personnel policies have assumed the force of law. As the wind has veered at Westminster, the volume of legislation has grown rather than diminished. Certain issues have become political footballs.

Industrial Relations

The growth of trade unionism, from about 1871 onwards, when trade unions became legal entities, is probably one of the major factors giving rise to the contemporary personnel function. Through combination, forming a 'collective' body into which individual identity was partially submerged, people at work could press for improvements in terms and conditions. By concerted action more could be achieved. From origins in blue-collar unions, white-collar unionism developed much later, particularly in the post-war period.

Today, industrial relations is concerned with a panoply of roles and collective organisations at work – trade unions, staff associations, employers' associations, procedures, agreements, negotiations, settlements, staff representatives, union officials, duties and obligations, the role of government, the provision of conciliatory and arbitration machinery for the settlement of disputes, the 'web of rules'.

Collective representation developed initially in the High Street banks more by way of House or Staff Associations than through the normal channels of trade unionism. Bank staff come from a fairly homogeneous social background. The development of their collective behaviour parallels that of staff with similar social backgrounds in other industries. Homogeneity of interests and values is often thought to be a causal factor in motivating collectivity. Employees become conscious of group or team affiliations. Relationships tend to be lateral and communal rather than vertical and individual.

In banking, other factors are also present. One of these is 'employment concentration' – the extent to which types of workers are grouped in units (even if these units are scattered). With concentration often comes bureaucracy, because large numbers of people engaged on similar work need systems and policies for control and coordination. Here is fertile soil for trade unionism. From the trade union point of view, large blocks of employees justify the recruitment effort. From the employers' point of view, collective representation has an administrative advantage. No longer, with increasing size, can employers form personal, individual relationships.

Although paternalism may still linger in places, banks as institutions are highly systematised. Communications become more difficult. Links between policy-makers and branch workers become de-personalised – even tenuous. Local management is physically out of contact with the nerve centre of the bank. 'The process by which activity generates profit is diffuse and not immediately obvious, so that the individual's sense of involvement tends to be limited. It is easy to see why a merchant bank with its much smaller proportion and therefore concentration of clerical staff would be less prone to collective white-collar activity. There is less necessity to institutionalise its working processes and any disparity in the treatment of individuals is less likely to create dissensions. Communications are easier, and even relatively humble staff feel they can approach those who control their destinies personally without the need to form some sort of caucus.'[15]

Clients

A pertinent question is: who is the client of the personnel manager? Personnel managers occupy mediative positions in the middle ground of the employer-employee relationship. But personnel managers are part of the management team, paid for as such. Personnel management is a cost centre. The staff manager is a manager first. His clients are other managers and the workforce. For the workforce he has a shared responsibility, but he is not their 'representative' nor is he directly responsible for the management of the organisation. Staff managers act reciprocally as representatives of management and as their advisers.

Any attempt to develop the personnel function interdependent of business considerations is unlikely to succeed. The staff manager, particularly in industrial relations, is something of a diplomat, balancing the interests of the respective parties, seeking common ground, acceptable outcomes. There are two sets of clients: employers and employees.

There is often a dilemma in the diplomatic role.

Economic, Social and Technological Change

World wide recession, reduced economic activity at home, massive debts in the third world have all made banking business harder. Coupled with increasing competition from other financial institutions, building societies and the like, the battle is firmly on for new market, new sources of profit. Attention is focused on the quality of service and the quality of management. As banks fight to become fitter, they become increasingly fluid.

Social change has also had its impact. People today are better educated than their forebears – they have a wider range of skills and talents which they seek to deploy. An aspirant workforce is now the norm. Frustration of opportunities breeds apathy and resentment. Attitudes have changed – to authority, to work, to the purpose of life. Trade unions, temporarily weakened, may well devise more socially significant ways of asserting power than mere monetary demands. Indeed, the clamour is on for participating in all forms of work organisation and re-organisation.

Associated with social change has been the impact of technical change. Old jobs are in demise, new ones in ascendancy. Revolution in information processing opens a new scenario. There is no looking back. Technological advance bodes dislocation, if not upheaval, of established banking careers. Maybe we need to re-appraise the whole career concept. Maybe 'work' itself is in demise.[16] Just as people hope to grow and reap the rewards of success, so do they become jittery about impending change, uncertainty, insecurity. Successful management of change is now critical. Organisational development (OD) techniques aimed at facilitating adjustment, encouraging employee acceptability and responsibility, are in the forefront of novel approaches to human resource management. Characteristically, they seek to secure permanent, long-term benefits for the organisation as a whole, aimed at the resolution of conflict, at smoothing the transition inflicted by technological progess, and improving job satisfaction.

All these trends bring personnel management into a central arena. They open up doors for fresh approaches to consultation, participation and planning. New problems are the hardest to handle.

CONCLUSION

We may all know something about people, but we cannot formulate informed opinions until we are able to analyse problems clearly, understand all the threads in the fabric, the institutions and customs, and draw on relevant knowledge and behavioural research.

People who work are humans. They prefer to be happy not miserable, to grow not to stagnate, to be interested not disinterested, involved not neglected. They hope for ambitions fulfilled, anxieties allayed. This is the 'social responsibility' of the employing organisation be it bank, factory or public service.

Man-management may be regarded as the leader's job. But he cannot do it single-handed. So personnel managment becomes the contribution of specialist expertise on the one hand, and the commitment of line managers on the other. Responsibilities are shared. Personnel management is an interactive and interpersonal process. It must surely mirror the realities and priorities of the moment. Its thrust is both social and commercial.

References
1. Watkinson, Viscount, 'The Social Responsibilities of Big Business – A Personal Note' in *The Banks and Society*. Cambridge Seminar 1974. London: The Institute of Bankers.
2. Fox, A., 'Industrial Relations: a Social Critique of Pluralist Ideology' in Child, J. (ed), *Man and Organisation*, 1973. London: Allen & Unwin.
3. Lupton, T., *Industrial Behaviour and Personnel Management*, 1964. London: Institute of

Personnel Management.

4. Thomason, G., *A Textbook of Personnel Management* (3rd ed.), 1978. London: Institute of Personnel Management.
5. Stewart, R., *The Reality of Management*, 1963. London: Heinemann
6. Megginson, L. C., *Personnel and Human Resources Administration*, (3rd ed.), 1977. Illinois: Irwin.
7. Stewart, R. (Ibid)
8. Heller, F. A., 'An Evaluation of the Personnel Management Function', in McFarland, D. E. (ed), *Personnel Management*, Penguin.
9. Heller (ibid)
10. McGregor, D., *The Human Side of Enterprise*, 1960 New York: McGraw Hill.
11. Argyris, C., *Understanding Organisational Behaviour*, 1960. London: Tavistock.
12. Burns, R. & Stalker, G., *The Management of Innovation*, 1962. London: Tavistock.
13. Lawrence, P. & Lorsch, J., *Organisation and Environment*, 1969. Illinois: Irwin.
14. Niven, M. M., *Personnel Managment 1913-63*, 1967. London: Institute of Personnel Management.
15. Lyons, R. P., 'Industrial Relations in Banking' in Livy (ed), *Management and People in Banking*, 1980. London: Institute of Bankers.
16. Handy, C., *The Future of Work*, 1984. Oxford: Blackwell.

CHAPTER 3

ORGANISATION THEORY

W. Braddick

Deputy Principal, Ashridge Management College

The question of how to link people and tasks in ways which encourage both organisational effectiveness and personal and group satisfaction is one which has long preoccupied researchers, consultants and businessmen. There is certainly no shortage of theory. As the industrial revolution began, the growth of large scale business organisations stimulated new ideas about how organisations function and how they should be managed.

THE CLASSICAL SCHOOL

The early theories are usually classified under the heading of the Classical School of Management. They represent the work of a number of managers, consultants and researchers who, although they approached the study of organisation from differing vantage points, produced a group of concepts and ideas which have much in common.

(a) Scientific management

There are three major streams of thought. The first was concerned with everyday operational efficiency at shop floor level and resulted from the practical experience of F. W. Taylor (1856–1917), usually called the 'father of scientific management.' He started life as an engineer and made important contributions to productivity through the technical innovations and changes he introduced. He soon realised, however, that to get the maximum benefits from his work, he would have to do something about the widespread inefficiency on the factory floor which resulted from a combination of poor management and what he claimed was the natural tendency of work people to protect their own interest by working below their potential.

He set out to build a series of 'laws, rules and principles which would become the basis for economical ways of doing work' and would create a true science of management. He saw the key factors in improved efficiency as:

the separation of *planning* (scheduling and supervision) from *doing*;

tasks should be broken down into their component parts after detailed analysis; methods standardised and carefully timed;

employees should be carefully selected to undertake a specific element of work and they should be thoroughly trained to do it efficiently;

reward should be directly related to the quantity and quality of output.

His work (which was developed by others like the Gilbreths and Bedeaux) produced spectacular increases in productivity.

Taylor rejected the notion that the working man should fear productivity increases. Like many of his contemporaries, he believed that his country, the United States, passing through a period of rapid industrialisation, was the land of opportunity and that employers and employees could only benefit from increased efficiency. The emerging trade unions did not share his views, which were not borne out in reality, as strikes and violence often erupted both in the US and later in the UK, when managers and consultants attempted to introduce his ideas and those of his followers.

His work is usually criticised on the grounds that 'scientific' management is, in fact, a systematised set of values, beliefs and subjective judgments: that the simplification of work results in boredom, monotony and the alienation of the worker from his job; and that his view that money is the only motivator is a gross oversimplification. Nevertheless, Taylor was undoubtedly one of the great pioneers of industrial organisation and social engineering. He invented a new division of labour concept which was widely adopted. This influence is still felt, not only on the shop floor but in the organisation of clerical operations too.

(b)   Administrative management

Whilst scientific management was concerned particularly with organisation at shop floor level, Henri Fayol a French engineer was working in organisation at the managerial level. His book 'Adminstration Industrielle and generalle' 1916 was a landmark in classical management thought.

The principles which he formulated (later expanded and developed by others) resulted from personal experience, thinking and judgment rather than systematic research, and they have had a powerful effect on the thinking of several generations of managers. Briefly the principles may be summarised, as follows:

Effective organisations need:

(a)   clear objectives;
(b)   one focus of loyalty (unity of direction);
(c)   one source of authority (unity of command);
(d)   clear lines of authority;
(e)   equality of responsibility and authority;
(f)   a rational division of work and logical grouping of tasks into sections, departments and higher administrative units;
(g)   a clear definition of accountability for performance and the establishment of formal relationships so that everyone in the organisation knows his role and position in the team;
(h)   an opportunity for subordinates to show initiative.

These principles have been vigorously criticised at several levels. It has been suggested that the principles are more accurately termed 'proverbs' and, for every one enunciated, another of equal and opposite value could be produced. The principles are often vague. A case in point concerns the number of employees a manager can control. The classical theorists attempted to produce numerical rules about the span of control. But the nature of the work, the complexity of decisions, the degree of training given to the subordinate, all affect the span of control so that there is no general rule, only an answer specific to each situation.

Similar ambiguities arise in the realm of coordination. Gullick suggests a sub-division of activities based on purpose, process, clientele and place, but these factors are often in conflict with each other and in any case the key terms are unclear. The same activity might be described as purpose or process according to the view of the person describing the job. A bank clerk completing a ledger entry might fulfill the purpose of his job, but for his manager it will be a means to an end.

This leads to more fundamental criticism. In practice it is very difficult to identify any universal principles of management which give clear guidance in a specific situation where managerial judgment will remain paramount. If the classical view is accepted that it is difficult to supervise more than five people at senior levels in the bank's hierarchy, then one might have to create a multi-level organisation which will be expensive to monitor, might cause delays in decision-making and lead to over-supervision of subordinates: the benefits would have to be weighed against the material and psychological costs. In the end someone will have to decide as a result of judgment, experience or intuition which is the best solution in a given situation. No principle seems to help.

The proponents of the classical school also assume that business organisations have clear overriding and unchanging objectives and all that needs to be done is to divide the work into convenient units to achieve them.

In practice, most businesses pursue a multiplicity of aims, which vary in importance over time as the dynamics of the environment and the organisation change. Procedures will change according to circumstances, and managers will be faced with constantly conflicting choices for which no set of principles is in itself adequate.

Perhaps the most searching criticism of all is concerned with the role of the employees. They are seen as passive agents bound by the rules. It is assumed that people are quite content to be part of a system which they do not want to change. The possibility of growth and evolution is ignored. Structure and anatomy rather than progress and change are seen as the key features in the life of the organisation.

It is, of course, very easy to be critical after the event. Circumstances were very different forty or sixty years ago and it is easy to judge with hindsight. There is no doubt that the work of Fayol, Urwick and others was, and is, extremely influential and the results can be seen in many modern business and governmental organisations.

(c) Bureaucratic theory

The word bureaucracy is now often used as a form of abuse. This was not the intention of Max Weber who, writing of bureaucracy in the 1940s, used the word in its precise meaning – rule by office holders.

Weber identified three forms of organisation. *Charismatic* organisations are led by men who can project a powerful personality and inspire others to work for them without question. Some of the great political and military leaders as well as great business entrepreneurs possess this quality.

Charismatic organisations characteristically are loosely structured and controlled. They operate on a basis of intuition rather than authority. They are stimulating to work in, but also cause anxiety, insecurity and rivalry. The organisation often lacks managerial depth, and the departure of the charismatic leader can cause a severe crisis of succession from which the organisation might never recover.

In *legal-traditional* organisations, leaders occupy their positions as a result of tradition. The most common example in business is where the firm is passed from father to son with no reference to talent or ability. This type of business is less common than formerly, but many examples still exist. Even in public limited companies the inherited power has not completely disappeared.

Bureaucratic organisations derive from *rationality* rather than from charisma or tradition.

Typical features of a bureaucracy are:

(i)   a *well-defined chain* of *command* in which *authority* and *responsibility* are *equal* and in which the network-linking positions are clearly defined and understood;

(ii)   a system of *procedures* and *rules* establishes the working *relationships* between people and tasks. They are designed to ensure consistent behaviour and cater for contingencies. They preclude the use of the organisation for one's own ends;

(iii) the *division of labour* is based upon *specialisation* and *competence*;

(iv)   *selection, placement and promotion* are *based on merit* and not on tradition or whim;

(v)   *impersonality* in *human relations*. People are more concerned with performing their tasks than with involvement in the needs of others. The bureaucracy is about a set of relationships between positions and not between people. Each position or office reacts to the behaviour of other positions or offices and not to the individual occupying these positions.

The complementary and mutually reinforcing nature of these approaches to organisation is clear, and their impact has been enormous as a cursory study of large scale organisation will testify. The influence of classical thinking in the large clearing banks is demonstrated by the hierarchical structures, the chain of command, the characteristic coordinating committees and working parties, the detailed job descriptions and the career structures based on merit and achievement. Banks are sometimes criticised for some of the limitations which are allegedly typical of organisations designed on classical lines:- their slowness to adapt to changed circumstances; their concern with role and ritual; their over-insistence on formal procedures. Yet it is not always easy to justify these criticisms. It can be argued that, in spite of their size and structure, many large banks have shown a remarkable ability to adapt to a turbulent environment and to respond successfully to a variety of new markets. Perhaps bureaucracies are not so slow to respond as their critics suggest. Alternatively perhaps banks are not pure bureaucracies and have adapted themselves to the more recent organisational concepts.

THE HUMAN RELATIONS SCHOOL

Researchers who wanted to find out the effect of the levels of lighting on productivity conducted a simple experiment in the 1920s at the Western Electric Company in Chicago. They put equally sized teams of workers in two similar rooms and both groups did the same type of work. The levels of illumination were increased in one room but not the other. Surprisingly productivity increased in both rooms. To help them understand what had happened, the researchers called in Elton Mayo, an Australian consultant and Professor at the Harvard Business School, to give them advice. In doing so they launched a study which became a milestone in the development of organisational and management theory – the 'Hawthorne' study, named after the site where the works were located.

The first investigation involved the separation of five workers from their fellows doing the same work (relay assembly) and setting them up in a room of their own. The conditions of work, rest pauses, starting and stopping times, and the method of payment were varied systematically whilst productivity rose steadily.

A second experiment was tried with a second relay assembly group. This time the whole group (a group of five) was kept together with the main group in the same shop,but they were given a special financial incentive bonus (like the first group) and this resulted in productivity increases of 12%. A third group in the mica splitting room was set up in the same way and shared a 15% increase in productivity. This suggests that the financial incentive alone could not account for the large differences in productivity which occurred during the first experiment.

A further investigation was carried out in the bank-wiring room where fourteen men worked together in three teams wiring, soldering and inspecting electrical connections. In spite of financial incentives the men restricted their output and worked to their own standards (enforced by the group itself) rather than that of the company. The significance of this study was that it directed attention to the group as a very important factor in influencing organisational behaviour and it created an interest in the study of group behaviour which still continues.

From these beginnings there has sprung a whole body of research and many theories which attempt to explain why and how people behave as they do in organisations and what managers can do about individual and group behaviour, productivity, individual development and job satisfaction. These issues are dealt with at length in Chapter 5. At this stage it is sufficient to concentrate on Mayo's conclusions and their effects. Mayo summed up his views (which went far beyond his research) in a book entitled 'The human problems of an industrial civilisation' in which he argued that the workplace can be the only link between the individual and society at large. This link must be developed to avoid anarchy and chaos. Its development depends critically upon the role of the manager. He must be trained to become an effective leader. The Hawthorne investigation indicated that this would involve the ability to understand the needs of individuals and groups, to listen carefully to problems at both these levels, to be able to interview skilfully to discover the things which bother people, to be able to give sound counsel as a basis for persuading work people to accept change. The influence of these ideas is still apparent today. The management development programmes of many large organisations still reflect the importance which is attached to training managers in interviewing, inter-personal relationships, understanding groups, the relationships between behaviour and performance and other social skills. All these concerns derive more or less directly from the work of Mayo. Behind them lies the idea that it is possible to create an organisation which achieves its aims through the satisfaction of the needs of its members.

Mayo's views have been savagely criticised at many levels. His most severe critics attack his unitary view of society because they claim that a variety of power centres is vital to a free society and a protection against the corporate state. Other critics point out that Mayo examined all behaviour from the managerial point of view. They claim that this concentrates too much on the role of the company in the life of the employees and ignores the wider economic and social factors which have a profound effect on the way in which people behave. Mayo's work has been dismissed as 'moo-cow' psychology – a process in which a worker is manipulated to higher productivity through false expressions of esteem. The proposals and remedies which Mayo proposed – counselling, the fostering of a group spirit and joint approaches to discipline are said to be weak and inadequate responses to deep-seated industrial problems which Mayo barely identified.

Nevertheless, Mayo is a major figure. From his work sprang a whole tradition in social science research and his research methodology was pioneering. Studies in leadership, productivity and work group behaviour have all emerged from these early efforts. Many of the solutions proposed by Mayo have certainly appealed to managers, if not to sociologists. The greater concern for human problems, an increased interest in communication and consultation, a belief in training in social and leadership skills are now part of the accepted practice of management training. They have their origins in the puzzling experiments in a Chicago factory more than half a century ago. Within a very short period Mayo succeeded in translating 'economic/rational' man into 'social man'. Later generations of behavioural scientists translated him into 'self actualising' man.

THE SYSTEMS APPROACH

A major figure in the development of the systems approach to management was Herbert Weiner. In 'Cybernetics', published in 1948, he built on his war-time work which was concerned with the development of weapons systems. His research helped him to identify similar problems of communication and control in animals, human beings and machines. Weiner's ideas were further developed by engineers, biologists and social scientists. It is the inter-disciplinary nature of systems thinking which is attractive to the student of management who must himself draw on ideas from both the natural and social sciences, pure and applied, to make sense of business organisations.

Systems theory deals with the analysis, design and operation of systems; entities which comprise interacting, inter-related and interdependent parts. Clearly a business organisation fulfils these criteria and can be studied using the concepts and tools of systems theory.

A business is a system which converts a series of inputs (raw materials, machines, people) into goods and services. It operates within a larger system – the external political, economic, social and technological environment with which it interacts continuously in complex ways.

It is made up of a series of sub-systems which are also inter-related and interact. A malfunction in one part of the system will cause difficulties in other parts.

An investigation of a bank along systems lines would begin with a specification of objectives as a means of understanding the nature of the decisions which must be taken to achieve them. The external environment would have to be investigated to grasp the ways in which the bank interacts with its wider environment.

The researcher would then turn to the internal environment. He would want to understand the major sub-systems of the business; how they interact and how their operation relates to the system as a whole. He would investigate the ways in which decisions are made, the critical information needed to make them and the communication channels through which the information is conveyed.

Decision-making, the information system and communication channels are particularly important to the systems analyst because these are critical to the achievement of the organisation's goals. In each area the systems approach has produced fruitful new concepts and techniques.

In the field of decision-making, systems thinking has enabled the development of types of decision to be classified. Concepts of certainty, risk and uncertainty have been developed. Logical approaches to the making of complex decisions have been evolved and systems thinking has encouraged the development of techniques (many of them mathematical) which are a great help to managers.

The nature of the information at the disposal of the decision-maker has an important influence on the quality of the decision itself, and it is not surprising that this has been given a great deal of attention. Those who design management information systems try to get the right information to the right person at the right time. To do this they will need to know the decision which will be made when the information is provided, and they will also be concerned about the speed with which this is made available, (if this is an important element of the decision-making). The provision of relevant data which could improve the quality of the decision (and the elimination of unnecessary data which will simply increase the cost) is also an important consideration.

The communication channels in an organisation are important elements in the decision-making process as they convey the information required. Systems analysts have provided many useful insights into organisational communication. They have drawn attention to the need to analyse the types and patterns and networks which are likely to produce effective communication. Considerable advances have been made in understanding and overcoming problems of 'noise' and interference in communications as well as the identification and resolution of problems which arise at the boundary of one system or sub-system with another.

The implications of the systems approach is that managers can more easily relate their particular job to that of the organisation as a whole. It is particularly useful to the general manager because it encourages him to maintain a balance between the needs of particular departments and the goals of the total organisation. It encourages him to think of the flows of information throughout the system. It directs attention to the importance of communication. It helps to identify the reasons for ineffective decision making and it provides the tools and techniques to improve planning and control.

Not only has systems thinking encouraged new thinking about organisation – particularly with its emphasis on the integrated nature of a business and on the crucial importance of information and communication systems, but many useful mathematical tools and techniques have been developed which have greatly helped in managerial decision-making and assisted in the development of more sophisticated planning and control systems.

In spite of all these benefits, systems thinking has yet to fulfil its early promise. The claim that it would allow the application of modern scientific method to management has yet to be established. This is partly due to the complexity of large scale systems. It is not easy to understand the multifarious ways in which the external environment affects the internal organisation. The interaction of the variety of sub-systems within the business is imperfectly understood. Systems boundaries are difficult to define: too wide a definition will result in the accumulation of costly and irrelevant data; too narrow a definition will result in partial solutions to problems. It is not easy to define the issues which a business will face and it is thus difficult to define the information needed in the future with any precision. Even if the best technical and most logical solution is found, it might not be politically feasible. Nevertheless the systems approach offers useful insights into the way an organisation works.

It will become even more important as the information revolution makes it imperative to understand the true nature of the business as a system to obtain the full benefits of expensive technology.

CONTINGENCY THEORIES

Many people have had the experience of trying to solve a problem in one organisation by applying approaches and techniques which worked in similar circumstances in another, only to find that this does not work.

Contingency theory helps us to understand why this happens by clarifying the unique nature of each organisation and providing an analytical framework through which its problems can be diagnosed. The five key elements are the organisation's environment, its task or overall mission, its technology, structure and people.

The Environment

Burns and Stalker[1] made a distinction between *mechanistic* and *organismic* systems of management. Mechanistic systems have the following characteristics:

the specialised differentiation of functional tasks into which the problems and tasks facing the concern as a whole are broken down;

the abstract nature of each individual task, which is pursued with techniques and purposes more or less distinct from those of the concern as a whole;

the reconciliation, for each level in the hierarchy, of these distinct performances by the immediate superiors;

the precise definition of rights and obligations and technical methods attached to each functional role;

the translation of rights and obligations and methods into the responsibilities of a functional position;

hierarchic structure of control, authority and communication;

a reinforcement of the hierarchic structure by the location of knowledge of actualities exclusively at the top of the hierarchy;

a tendency for vertical interaction between members of the concern to be, i.e., between superior and subordinate;

a tendency for operations and working behaviour to be governed by superiors;

insistence on loyalty to the concern and obedience to superiors as a condition of membership;

a greater importance and prestige attaching to internal (local) than to general (cosmopolitan) knowledge, experience and skill.

Organismic structures characteristically show:

the contributive nature of special knowledge and experience to the common task of the concern;

the realistic nature of the individual task, which is seen as set by the total situation of the concern;

the adjustment and continual re-definition of individual tasks through interaction with others;

the shedding of responsibility as a limited field of rights; obligations and methods. (Problems may not be posted upwards, downwards or sideways.);

the spread of commitment to the concern beyond any technical definition;

a network structure of control authority, and communication;

omniscience no longer imputed to the head of the concern; knowledge may be located anywhere in the network, this location becoming the centre of authority;

a lateral rather than a vertical direction of communication through the organisation;

a content of communication which consists of information and advice rather than instructions and decisions;

commitment to the concern's task and to the 'technological ethos' of material progress and expansion is more highly valued than loyalty;

importance and prestige attach to affiliations and expertise valid in the industrial and technical and commercial milieux external to the firm.

(From Burns and Stalker, 'The Management of Innovation', 1966)

In summary they suggest that organisations which operate successfully in a 'turbulent' environment characteristically have a decentralised structure and are governed by few rules, whilst those where decisions are highly centralised and which are governed by a web of rules or regulations will have a much greater struggle to survive. The research of Lawrence and Lorsch[2] in ten firms in the United States supports and extends this view. It suggests that not only do firms in different environments need to evolve differing approaches to organisation if they are to be successful, but that departments within the same firm need to be differentiated in relation to their particular environment. They find that in highly performing organisations departments varied on four dimensions:

the formality of the structure;
time horizons;
orientation to the market;
inter-personal relations.

Successful departments in uncertain environments coped best with an informal structure, a long time orientation, very specific goals and strong emphasis on task. In stable environments, formal structure and short-term orientations were suitable; more generalised goals could be set, but a strong emphasis on task was still necessary.

Subsequent studies have done much to confirm that complex environments need complex organisations to cope with them.

Technology

The importance of technology as a significant variable in organisation design was identified through the work of Joan Woodward[3] who set out to test how far classical principles were applied to 100 small firms in the South East of England. She found that there were important variations in organisation according to whether the firm was involved in unit, mass or process technology. The length of the hierarchy, the span of control of the chief executive, the proportion of managers to men all increased with the shift from unit to process production. The mass production system was the most formalised and mechanistic. The most successful firms were those which were nearest the norm for each category. The conclusion to be drawn from this research is that *as a firm moves from one technology to another it must redesign its organisation.* Careful thought must be given to the organisational implications of this change if the full benefits are to be obtained. The significance of this finding for banks which are going through a profound technological revolution is obvious.

Size

Size has long been recognised as an important variable and the work of researchers in the University of Aston[4] have stressed its importance. With growth in size, there is usually an increase in specialisation; the organisation becomes more complex as jobs and departments become more differentiated. The organisation becomes more formalised to facilitate control and more decentralised to foster effective coordination.

People

People are another important factor which the manager must consider. People with high security needs will find rapidly changing highly flexible organisations threatening, whilst people who value freedom and autonomy will be bored with the monitoring of the routine production of stock products. Low calibre people will require a different management style from those of high calibre and, by the same token, differing managerial styles will attract a differing calibre of staff.

History

The history of the organisation is also important in that style, beliefs and values are very much influenced by the origins of the company and the subsequent experience of its management and staff.

Those who favour contingency theories contend that each organisation must be studied in its own setting, bearing in mind its goals and technology, the expectations of its employees and its size and history. Only when these factors are fully taken into account can the appropriate organisation be designed. Practitioners of this school, therefore, stress the need for managers to become skilled at the analysis and diagnosis of organisational problems and to seek a specific solution rather than to try to work from general principles.

BANKING

An analysis along contingency lines for banking as a whole would take into account:

Environmental factors

the political stability of key markets;
government programmes in relation to industry, commerce and banking;
government economic and fiscal policy;
the economic situation globally;
the world monetary system;
economic opportunities in key markets;
demographic change – implications for marketing;
changing consumer expectations in all markets;
levels of employment;
social consensus/conflict.

Task

The transformation of the financial sector – the development of banks as financial supermarkets.

Technology

    technological change;
    speed of implementation;
    effects on customers;
    effects on staff;
    effects on branch networks.

People

    numbers employed;
    skills and occupational status;
    training and development;
    expectations;
    trade unions and staff associations;
    degree of consensus/conflict;
    key managerial changes;
    managerial style.

Structure

    operating network;
    decision making;
    information flow and feedback;
    communication systems.

This list could be extended considerably but it would only be useful in relation to a specific bank operating in its unique market, taking into account its history, size and the ambitions of those who guide it. If this were done for the bank as a whole so that the key variables affecting organisation development could be identified and their meaning understood and acted upon, then the same process would have to be undertaken for key sub-units and departments so that each of them could adapt itself to operate as effectively as possible in its specific situation.

Contingency theories make a lot of sense to practising managers. They fit in with their experience that what works in one situation does not work in another and that each issue must be studied in its own terms.

But the oversimplified example above indicates some of the problems in analysis and diagnosis of organisational change in a large business. The number of variables is enormous. It is not easy to understand their relative importance, nor how they interact to cause even further complexity. The dynamic nature of the business means that the analyst has to behave like a doctor trying to diagnose a patient on the run. Even if the major variables can be understood, there still remains the problem of understanding how they affect major units and departments and what factors operate at these levels which should be taken into account in deciding how best to organise them effectively to adapt to their particular circumstances. Nevertheless, the use of contingency theories provide many useful insights into the key factors which drive the business and it helps to identify possible courses of action.

There appears to be no universal truth, no blueprint emerging from organisational theory. Protagonists of one school vigorously advance their case whilst passionately demolishing that of another. But organisational theory is useful. It helps managers to check their models of the world against those of others and offers them new frameworks which they can test against the reality of their everyday work.

References
1. Burns, T. and Stalker, G. M., *Management of Innovation*, 1961. London: Tavistock.
2. Lawrence, P. R. and Lorsch, J. W., *Organisation and Environment*, 1969. Harvard University Press.
3. Woodward, J., *Industrial Organization: Theory and Practice*, 1965. Oxford University Press (2 edit. 1980).
4. Pugh, D. S. and Hickson, D. J., *Organisation Structure in its Context* Saxon House, 1976.

CHAPTER 4

Individual Motivation At Work

Richard Lawton,
Client and Programme Director, Ashridge Management College and

Rani Chaudhry-Lawton
Independent Management Consultant

In this chapter, we shall examine two aspects of motivation. Firstly, we shall review all the key theories of motivation, and secondly consider the implications of these theories for a bank manager in trying to understand individual motivation at work.

If managers are to make decisions which improve the performance of individuals and increase their contribution to organisational effectiveness (among other things), then those managers will require an understanding of motivation. The principles behind motivation form the basis of numerous managerial decisions: for example, the design of jobs, the design of wage and salary systems, the style of leadership and management to be adopted and assumptions about subordinates. Motives are the forces underlying human behaviour. The cue for action is the desire to satisfy personal needs or wants. The trigger for action is *Motivation*; the willingness to exert effort and energy in order to achieve a desired outcome or goal which will satisfy the individual's need. Therefore the basic model of motivation looks like this: Need→Action→Goal.

For example: Need (thirst for water)→Action (drinking water)→Goal (quenching of thirst). Action is considered finished if the goal fulfils the need; any gap between the goal and the need will lead to further action.

Differences in performance at work can be attributed to two factors. First, different people have varying abilities according to their education, training and experience. Secondly, differences in performance levels may be due to different levels of individual motivation: individuals vary in their willingness to direct their efforts towards the achievement of personal and organisational goals.

Therefore performance at work can be seen as a combined function of the individual's ability level and his or her motivation. The individual must satisfy his or her own needs through job performance while at the same time meeting organisational criteria for effectiveness. The subject of motivation has attracted considerable research, from which we have inherited many theories. Nevertheless, our understanding of the whole area of individual motivation is still limited. It is not always easy to make predictions about which needs give rise to particular actions, which may in turn be directed to achieving organisational goals. Moreover, needs vary between individuals, and each individual's needs may vary from one day to the next. This all goes to form a very complex set of circumstances, making it a far from simple job for any manager to motivate staff. However, it is worth examining some of the theories of motivation in order to draw some guidelines and indicators in understanding individual motivation.

MOTIVATION THEORIES

Motivation theories can be divided into two main categories:

1. Theories which address the question of *what* motivates people. These attempt to identify the needs which cause individuals to act in certain ways.
2. Theories which address the question of *how* certain actions are determined. These concentrate on the processes which individuals undergo before being motivated to act in a certain way, i.e. how an individual decides on the action which they think will meet the need.

Maslow's Hierarchy of Needs[1]

Maslow, an American psychologist, was one of the first major researchers to differentiate between needs and to draw up a hierarchy of higher and lower orders of needs. Maslow's 'Theory of Motivation' (1954) comprises a hierarchy of five levels of needs which, arranged in ascending order of priority to the individual, are as follows:

1. PHYSIOLOGICAL: The need to survive, as manifested in the desire for food, water, air and warmth. Whatever is necessary to keep the body in a state of equilibrium is important at this level.
2. SAFETY/SECURITY: The desire for protection against danger, and for physical and psychological safety and security. Shelter

and freedom from attack on the body or the personality are the focus at this level.

3. BELONGING AND LOVE: The desire to fulfil the need for belonging, for love, affection and friendship.
4. ESTEEM: The need for recognition, for competence, independence, self-confidence and prestige. This is exhibited in two ways: self esteem and esteem from others.
5. SELF-ACTUALISATION: This is more difficult to define, but it is viewed as the need for self-fulfilment and self-expression. It is seen as striving to realise one's full potential and to become everything that one is capable of becoming.

In Maslow's hierarchy of needs (illustrated in Fig. 1), the Physiological and Safety/Security needs are considered lower order needs, while Esteem and Self-actualisation are considered higher order needs. According to Maslow, individuals can pass to higher order need levels only when the lower order needs are satisfied. For example: a starving man will concentrate on satisfying his hunger, if necessary taking great risks to do so, even if it means ignoring the safety need. Once that is achieved, however, the need to protect himself from danger takes priority. Therefore, the physiological needs must be satisfied to an acceptable level before an individual will pass upwards to attempt to meet safety/security needs and so on up the hierarchy until self-actualisation is reached. Once a need is satisfied, it no longer monopolises an individual's behaviour; behaviour will then be directed towards satisfying the next need level. The conclusion is obvious – *only unsatisfied needs act as motivators*. However, Maslow makes an exception to this rule when considering self-actualisation. At this level, increased satisfaction, instead of decreasing need strength, tends to increase the desire for further self-fulfilment. Complete satisfaction of the self-actualisation need is rarely, if ever, achieved. The individual seems constantly to strive for improvement.

Maslow's theory presents needs conceptually. To define them in operational terms, which can then be empirically tested, is a problem. He did not design the theory specifically for the organisational setting, but rather for application to an individual's whole life. Clearly, needs may be satisfied outside work and questions can be raised as to the applicability of this theory to work situations, although subsequent researchers have applied the self-actualisation level to the work setting.

The principal lesson to be learned from Maslow's work is that all needs must be considered in an attempt to motivate people to work or to work harder. It is especially emphasised that higher needs should not be disregarded, particularly in a society where the physiological and safety/security needs are in most individuals at least reasonably satisfied. Individuals

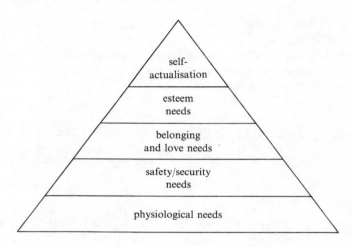

Figure 1 Maslow's Hierarchy Of Needs

may differ with regard to the needs that are dominant; the same incentives cannot be expected to motivate everyone and attempts should be made to recognise the dominant needs and to act accordingly.

Alderfer's Erg Theory[2]

More recently, Alderfer (1972) has suggested a modification of Maslow's Hierarchy of Needs theory. In his modification, he recognises only three categories of need. Identified as the ERG Theory, the three categories are: *Existence* (close to Maslow's lower order needs of a physiological and material nature), *Relatedness* (close to the love and esteem levels in Maslow) and *Growth* (rather like the self-actualisation level in its emphasis on creativity and self-fulfilment). Alderfer sees these as a continuum rather than a hierarchy, thus permitting different personalities to 'fit' themselves at different points along it without presuming that the point of 'fit' must be better or worse than another's because it is 'higher'. His theory also allows that some needs can be treated as persistent over time, while others are more intermittent.

'The difference between Alderfer and Maslow can be described in both content and process terms. They differ in content terms – for Maslow there are five needs, for Alderfer there are three. They also differ in process terms – for Maslow the process is one of fulfilment – progression; for Alderfer, both fulfilment – progression, and frustration – regression, are important dynamic elements.[3]

'In a sense, Alderfer's view of motivation is a more hopeful one for managers. It provides them with the possibility of constructively channelling the energy of their subordinates even when the individual's high level needs are blocked. This energy can be directed towards lower-level needs. The ERG variation is a very new one. A good deal of research will have to be done before it can be accepted as a reasonable view of how and why people expend energy in work settings.'[3]

McClelland's Achievement Motivation[4,5]

Implicit in Maslow's higher order needs is the desire for achievement or accomplishment. Using personality tests, McClelland studied the characteristics of people whom he identified as being achievement oriented. Higher need achievers, he found, were always exhibiting behaviour designed to better themselves, and working harder in order to accomplish their goals. They shared a number of common characteristics:

1. A preference for performing tasks over which they had sole responsibility, to enable them to identify closely with the successful outcomes of their actions.
2. They were moderate risk-takers, and to maximise their chances of success they set themselves moderate goals. This does not mean that they avoided challenging situations, but simply that their goals were within an attainable range.
3. They needed continual feedback, since it is only from the knowledge of success that satisfaction can be derived.

McClelland tried to find why some people were low achievers and concluded that the major reasons lay in parental influences, education, cultural background and the value systems dominant in society. The obvious conclusion is that organisations, therefore, should be concerned with selecting high achievers as managers. Even more significantly, however, McClelland suggested that low achievers can be trained to develop a greater urge to achieve.

Relating McClelland's work to management, various authors have suggested that recognition of motivation patterns should enable managers to distinguish between those who are self-motivated, and those who require external motivation in terms of financial or solid rewards. It should also be possible for an organisation which discovers its personnel to have a low rate of achievement motivation to introduce training to help individuals develop a greater level of motivation in this area.

His ideas have two important implications:

1. The importance of reinforcing achievement motivation through the mechanism of recognition of achievement, such as praise, advancement, monetary reward and recognition.

2.   People with high achievement motivation are capable of being identified during selection processes and people with low achievement motivation can be trained to develop a higher achievement motivation.

McGregor's View of Man[6,7]

McGregor attempted to apply some of Maslow's thinking to the work context. He argued that managers' decisions that were intended to influence the behaviour of their staff were based on their assumptions about human nature. McGregor divided managerial assumptions about human nature into two schools of thought – Theory X and Theory Y.

Theory X consists of a set of 'traditional' assumptions. Man is seen as inherently lazy and unambitious, slow to seek or accept responsibility and prepared to work only when it is unavoidable. Management of people based on this underlying assumption is commonly known as the carrot and the stick approach. According to this theory, direction, motivation and control must come from outside. Thus the employee is viewed as someone who must be driven by greed, fear and coercion if he is to work at all, and who must be under constant surveillance. McGregor regards the theory and these assumptions about man as outdated, rigid and inappropriate. He argues that if management acts on Theory X assumptions, the approach arouses a defensive reaction in employees who, resentful of the fixed norms and rules enforced, try to beat the system whenever possible by acting in ways which do not meet the needs of their managers.

Theory Y is seen as a 'modern' view. This theory holds that work is a natural human activity, capable of providing enjoyment and satisfaction and that external control – the carrot and the stick – is not the only means of getting people to work. People can exercise self-control and self-direction if they are personally committed to the objectives towards which they are working, and individual higher level needs can be satisfied in the pursuit of organisational objectives.

In applying Theory Y successfully, the chief task of management is to bring about those conditions under which work can and does lead to the satisfaction of individual needs and a source of achievement. Their objective is to enlist commitment to organisational goals and to arouse a sense of personal responsibility and self-control in their staff, which necessitates a minimum of supervision and external controls. Frequent and open discussion, leading to better understanding at all levels, and mutual target-setting, are seen as the main mechanisms by which maximum efficiency and productivity may be achieved by applying Theory Y to the work context.

Herzberg's Two Factor Theory[8]

Herzberg's Two Factor Theory was specifically developed to improve our understanding of people at work, in particular the factors which determine job satisfaction or job dissatisfaction.

Herzberg considers that man has two sets of needs – maintenance needs and motivational needs. The first are concerned with avoiding pain and dissatisfaction, the second with actively seeking and achieving satisfaction and fulfilment.

Those factors which have to do with maintenance needs Herzberg calls maintenance or hygiene factors, because attention to them can only prevent or eliminate dissatisfaction, without promoting satisfaction or happiness. In the work situation, maintenance factors are all contained in the total environment in which the employee works, including physical conditions, salary, social factors, interpersonal relations, etc. The manager must attend constantly to these factors if the employee is not to be dissatisfied, but cannot and must not expect this attention to lead to active satisfaction.

The factors which can lead to fulfilment are those concerned with the motivational needs: the need for growth, achievement, responsibility and recognition. These needs can only be met through what is actually done – the job itself, which according to Herzberg, can provide a potentially more powerful motivator than any extrinsic incentives. Herzberg claims that the results of a number of empirical studies he carried out show that at all levels employees can be actively satisfied only when the work done is perceived by the employee to be meaningful and challenging, and thus able to fulfil his or her needs.

If managers *fail to recognise this distinction between maintenance and motivational factors, it can lead to a complete lack of understanding* of the employee's concerns. The employee, perhaps not satisfied by a job which is perceived as meaningless and repetitive, may react to work only with apathy and detachment, even if the work conditions are excellent.

Herzberg recommends as a solution to the problem of meeting motivational needs, job enrichment; one of the methods of job redesign which has been applied in a number of companies. Some methods are:

1.   JOB ROTATION: This involves moving employees between a number of jobs on a regular basis so as to introduce some variety into their activities.

2.   JOB ENLARGEMENT: This means not only vertical job enlargement (promotion) but also horizontal enlargement by changing the content of a specific job without any increase in responsibility levels in order to build in additional tasks.

3.   AUTONOMOUS WORK GROUPS: This method attempts to derive an optimal match between technology, social needs and

economic factors. It involves groups of workers engaged in a complete area of work, such as assembling engines. The group is given considerable autonomy over how it performs that particular work and is made responsible for its own planning, organisation and co-ordination of tasks. 'The Volvo Experiment' is the best publicised example of autonomous work groups (even though more recently, this experiment has attracted some criticism).

Herzberg points out that benefits derived from catering for both motivational and maintenance needs do not benefit the employee alone. The dissatisfaction generated if maintenance needs are not met leads to a restricted productivity or poorer performance. Elimination of this dissatisfaction removes an inhibitor of performance, but does not bring about any real improvement. Only the motivation provided by a challenging and rewarding job brings about a positive pay-off in terms of genuine improvement in standards of performance.

Determinants of job satisfaction	*Determinants of job dissatisfaction*
MOTIVATIONAL FACTORS	**MAINTENANCE FACTORS**

Achievement
Recognition   Higher order
Work itself   needs
Responsibility   Intrinsic
Advancement   factors
	Company policy &
	   administration Lower
	Supervision order
	Salary needs
	Interpersonal Extrinsic
	   relations factors

— Presence of these factors WILL equate to job satisfaction.	— Presence WILL NOT equate to job satisfaction
— Absence WILL NOT lead to job dissatisfaction	— Presence WILL equate to no job dissatisfaction
— Absence will lead to LACK OF job satisfaction	— Absence WILL equate to job dissatisfaction

Figure 2 Herzberg's Two Factory Theory

EXPECTANCY THEORIES

Other theories concentrate not on *what* motivates people at work but *how* they are motivated. This is done by examining the process which individuals go through before behaving in a certain way. Individual differences in this process will occur, because people's expectations vary and so the theories are sometimes referred to as EXPECTANCY THEORIES. An expectancy theory is a cognitive theory of motivation, since it assumes individuals are consciously aware of goals and direct their behaviour rationally towards achieving those goals.

Vroom's Expectancy Theory of Motivation[9,10]

Vroom explains motivation as being a function of two factors:

1. VALENCY (V) This is the preference an individual has for a particular outcome and equates to the individual's perception of the satisfaction he will gain if he achieves the particular outcome.
2. EXPECTANCY (E) This is a subjective assessment of the probability that doing something will actually lead to a particular outcome.
3. FORCE (F) This is another term for motivation, being the result of the interaction of VALENCE for various possible outcomes with the EXPECTANCY that action will lead to those outcomes.

Therefore the relationship looks like this:

MOTIVATION $F = f \Sigma (E \times V)$
E = expectancy that action will be followed by a desired outcome
V = strength of preference for a particular outcome
Σ = summation – because a particular course of action typically has more than one outcome.

The main conclusion of the theory is that individuals are motivated to behave in certain ways by choosing from a range of possible outcomes, the ones which they judge to have the best odds of occurring. For example, if an individual strongly desires promotion as an outcome (valence) he will be motivated to perform well if he thinks that there is a high probability that the organisation will actually reward him with promotion (expectancy). In short, people act in different ways as they seek differing outcomes and in accordance with their perception of the relationship between performance and outcome.

Porter and Lawler: Expectancy – Instrumentality – Valence Theory[11]

The most comprehensive theory of motivated behaviour is that which has been developed from the work of Tolman (1932), Lewin (1938), Vroom (1964) and Lawler (1968), by Porter and Lawler (1968). Their theory is known as 'The Expectancy Theory', and includes a number of refinements of Vroom's (1964) theory.

In its simplest form the theory states that the individual's decision to expend effort will depend on three perceptions about the particular situation:

1. If effort is expended, there are available for successful achievement, rewards which are attractive and have some value for the individual.
2. That the achievement of success as a result of expending effort will in effect bring forth these rewards.
3. The expenditure of effort will result in successful achievement.

The theory also states that achievement will depend not only on the decision to expend effort but also on the skills and traits of the individual, and on the role perceptions of the individual (which here means how well the individual understands his position relative to the situation he finds himself in.) It also states that rewards associated with performance may be either 'intrinsic' or 'extrinsic' and that they must conform to the individual's perception of what is 'fair and equitable' in the way of reward for the performance. Those rewards, when evaluated, are the source of satisfaction to the individual and this satisfaction in turn influences the value which the individual will place on any subsequent reward.

Expectancy theory has been criticised for being far too rational. The question which is often asked is whether people actually go through the process of weighing up expectancies and placing values on the attractiveness of outcomes. This is quite difficult to test empirically.

Motivation in Banking

Having examined the theoretical base of motivation studies as they apply to all sectors of industry, we shall in this next section apply some of these theories to examples drawn from the banking sector. There are three main areas which raise particular problems and opportunities for motivation: the public image of banks and the way this reflects on the internal culture; the changing environment in which banking operates; and the multi-site nature of many banks.

Image and Culture of Banks

Banks rely heavily on the confidence of their investors and depositors. They generate this confidence by projecting an image of security, integrity and attention to accuracy and detail in financial dealings. Clearly, this image cannot be maintained unless it is constantly being demonstrated by the behaviour and attitudes of the employees. The need to maintain their image

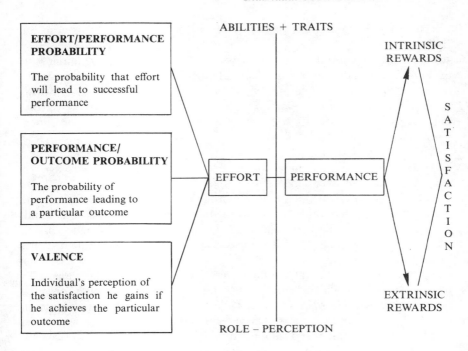

Figure 3 The Porter and Lawler Expectancy Model

in society influences the banks' recruitment practices and the way in which they reward their staff once they have joined. In behavioural terms, 'What you reward is what you get.' This maxim, based on some of the experiments of B. F. Skinner[12] and a host of subsequent research work, applies at an organisational as well as an individual managerial level – many managers have learnt its truth for themselves.

It is no surprise, therefore, that when they are recruiting, the banks often attract people who are seeking security, a degree of status in the community and who are attracted to operating in a methodical, accurate fashion. Banking work is likely to appeal to the convergent thinker, the person who is able to make logical links between items of information in order to narrow their focus to follow a set procedure or to solve a particular problem.

In terms of motivation theory, the typical bank can expect to have a large number of employees who are operating on the Safety/Security and Belonging levels of Maslow's Hierarchy of Needs. Security in this context does not just mean security of employment, but the security that comes from knowing that most situations are guided by procedures and protocols already established by the organisation.

The salary and grading structures in the banks often reflect this need for status and security. Gradings tend to be well defined and visible. The salary structures often guarantee small incremental steps to reflect merit and length of service. In addition to this there will often be an inbuilt protection against some of the impact of inflation by the provision of a cost of living award. It is rare that such a system will provide the glittering prizes in money terms, but neither will it seriously handicap the person who is average or under-performing to a moderate degree.

A number of banks extend the security and protection offered by their reward package by including in it a reduced rate staff mortgage or private health insurance scheme. In terms of Maslow's[13] model, this is the organisation taking care of the lower order needs which form the base of the pyramid, namely health and shelter requirements. These additions to the basic salary are not directly related to the day to day performance of the individual, but may help to buy long-term loyalty and commitment to the organisation.

Rewarding individual performance is a wholly different process from providing rewards which largely meet status and security needs. In fact, there are times when one system can work in almost direct opposition to the other: for example, a system which clearly identifies high performers and gives them significant financial rewards might actually promote insecurity amongst some of the staff. Leon Festinger's[14] work indicates that when trying to gauge how well off they are, people tend to compare themselves with others, rather than with an absolute standard. In a system which pays relatively small merit increases, nobody is likely to suffer too many shocks or agonies of comparison. Conversely, in such a system it is hard to provide the 'positive reinforcement' of the type of behaviour which is associated with high performance standards.

In a recent survey of a number of successful companies, Peters and Waterman[15] look at some common themes which have helped to promote success. Amongst other things, they identify a number of elements which help to guarantee positive reinforcement of productive behaviour. Rewards should be immediate, specific and achievable, although from time to time there should be an unpredictable element in the reinforcement and the sources of reward should be intangible as well as tangible. In practical terms, this means that, if members of staff have performed well on a particular task or duty, they need to know this soon after the event (immediacy) and they should have a clear picture of the exact nature of their achievement (specific details). The aim of positive reinforcement is that the successful behaviour should be repeated again in other circumstances. The organisations which reward only outstanding performance (which is likely to make many staff pessimistic about their ever achieving this goal) are therefore reducing the probable frequency of such performance. Therefore there needs to be a means of supplying some small 'wins' for the staff.

The value of the element of unpredictability in reinforcement is that it overcomes the problem of institutionalised rewards, which in time cease to have a reinforcement effect because they are taken for granted. One of the best examples of unpredictability is what Peters and Waterman refer to as 'management by walking about'. This is the manager who is in contact with the staff often enough and on a sufficiently random basis to be able to identify examples of excellent performance and reward them on the spot. In this instance a more intangible reward, such as praise, might be the most appropriate. McClelland's[16] work suggests that this would be crucially important for the high achiever.

The power of intangible rewards should not be ignored in the context of banking for managers seeking additional sources of motivation. There are many reasons why the tangible reward system (typically the employee's remuneration package) may not produce the motivation required for achieving high standards of performance. Firstly, a system geared primarily towards meeting people's needs for security and status breaks many if not all of the rules of positive reinforcement – the cost of living awards are often larger than increases paid to reward merit. A requirement for business success specified by Peters and Waterman, that there should be an immediate and specific link between performance and the reward, is thereby not met. If a significant part of the remuneration package is fixed, as in the case of a staff mortgage, there is again no link between performance and reward. Some employees refer to the staff mortgage as 'golden handcuffs' – the message here is that they are certainly committed to the company but not necessarily through choice.

Secondly, individual managers in banks find themselves with relatively little control over the tangible reward system that affects their staff. This may be because their recommendations are filtered through several layers of management or central control, or because financial constraints make the merit payments fairly modest. What they often have more influence over, however, are the intangible rewards. These may take the form of praise, recognitioin (through special titles or special duties) and job enrichment in the form of allocating additional duties. In the area of intangible rewards it is often easier to adhere to the principles of positive reinforcement. This fact is highlighted in Blanchard and Johnson's[17] book, 'The One Minute Manager', where the impact of 'One Minute Praisings' is celebrated and the value of low cost, high impact, immediate positive reinforcement is demonstrated. The authors also echo Peters and Waterman's comments about the walkabout manager when they refer to the One Minute Managers trying to 'catch their staff doing something right'.

Despite these strong benefits, though, the intangible reward system should not become a convenient substitute for the tangible reward system. Employees will be very quick to devalue the significance of praise which is arbitrary, excessive or which is not backed up by other forms of recognition and reward. In a witty reply to the One Minute Manager, André and Ward[18] tackle the problem from the point of view of 'The 59 Second Employee' – on the topic of One Minute Praisings they advise, 'Don't settle for them. Turn them into something concrete.'

THE ENVIRONMENT OF BANKING

The fact that banks face a rapidly changing commercial and social environment means that a major problem facing management is that of motivating staff to do things differently. There are many forces of change which require significantly different actions and behaviours from employees: a need to become more customer-conscious and responsive, a need to provide a wider range of services, a need actively to market those various services, and a need to master the impact of new technology. As we have argued earlier in the chapter, the image presented by the banks both externally and internally has been until recently one of conservation and security and we noted that the tangible reward system tends to emphasise these features.

Under conditions of rapid change, managers need to think carefully about whether they are providing the motivation for their staff to make the necessary adjustments. All alterations to routine and established practices initially constitute a threat to the majority of people (even if it is in their long-term interest to adapt), through the destabilising effect of moving from the known to the unknown.

However, some changes lend themselves more readily to providing sources of positive motivation. For example, an increased emphasis on being responsive to, and having closer contact with, the customer can provide a source of motivation to those staff who would enjoy more direct dealings with the public. Instead of investment counselling being seen as an additional burden, some employees may welcome it as a source of increased job satisfaction (this would be an example of a motivator that is intrinsic to the job itself). The type of staff who might be attracted to this sort of work are the ones who are motivated by the belonging and esteem needs in Maslow's model.

Other changes may require more careful handling because they constitute a bigger distribution to the *status quo*. Many banks have diversified the services that they offer in order to remain competitive within the overall financial sector. In 1982, for example the clearing banks made a significant inroad into the house purchase market. Lloyds took a step into the estate agency business with their purchase of the six-office Charles Hawkins group in Norfolk. In our discussions with banking employees, we encountered a range of reactions from eager anticipation through to resistance at having to learn new procedures and attitudes (the ones associated with mortgage lending). Some went as far as to argue that a specialised function such as mortgage lending should be left to the building societies. Against this background there is a clear need for management not only to communicate to such staff what is expected, but also to outline the benefits to them of the new work. Communication in itself is an act of basic recognition of another person and usually has a positive effect in meeting esteem needs, whether or not it is favourable news that is being communicated. Inadequate or infrequent communications is one of the commonly cited reasons for people feeling demotivated or even hostile about a proposed change.

Some bank managers that we have talked to have referred to the need for themselves and their colleagues to become more marketing conscious. They have acknowledged that this may require different behaviour and attitudes on their own part and that it is, in turn, also likely to change some of the criteria by which people are recruited into the bank and then advanced within it. Clearly, this influence is going to have an impact on motivational factors. A marketing orientation is associated with divergent thinking, that is a willingness to think around an issue, to look at a number of different perspectives and possibilities before deciding on the correct approach. We have noted earlier in the chapter that building a reputation of security, orderliness and financial probity tends to emphasise the need for convergent thinkers. At the present time the banks need both convergent and divergent approaches but are usually staffed with a majority of convergent thinkers. If the marketing orientation is to be successful, there is a need for the banks to encourage and motivate their staff in this direction. This suggests an increased emphasis on initiative and creativity as opposed to conformity and the maintenance of established procedures. In terms of McGregor's[19] theory, it means motivation based on Theory Y as opposed to Theory X assumptions.

When a bank is introducing a change that has far reaching consequences it will often have implications for the method of communication, as well as the terms and conditions of employment. Thus, Barclays' reintroduction of Saturday morning opening in 1982 was accompanied by offers to appropriate staff of separate contracts to work agreed numbers of Saturday mornings (in addition to the contract to work their five day, 35-hour week). Those staff who volunteered were given special payments from £24 to £40. At an individual level, there appeared to be very few motivational problems and Mr John Quinton,[20] Senior General Manager, described the staff reaction as 'pretty relaxed'. However at a union level, in this case the Banking, Insurance and Finance Union (BIFU) together with the Barclays Group Staff Union (BGSU), there was concerted opposition. BIFU called for 'blacking' of the move by its members and Mr Eddie Gale[21] (General Secretary BGSU) was quoted as being 'outraged' at the lack of prior consultation. The unions' reaction emphasises the need for an increased effort to communicate the need for and the benefits of change. One of the concerns of the unions was that the move would lead to compulsory Saturday work once the supply of volunteers had been used up.

THE MULTI-SITE NATURE OF BANKING

Many of the operations of the bigger banks are multi-site, which presents its own particular set of opportunities and problems in the area of motivating employees.

Problems can be created if local conditions require patterns of working which are possibly out of step with the rest of the company. Shift working, for example, is a necessary part of working in some of the branches in airports, shopping centres or in-store branches. In such cases, opportunities are presented for the managers to vary their management style and the service that they provide to suit both the demands of the local customers and some of the working traditions of the local labour force. However, too much autonomy at branch level can sometimes be a bad thing – the manager who will only favour for promotion, his or her own staff, because they have these 'local' strengths, can block the possibility of new talent moving in from other branches, and can create resentment amongst employees in neighbouring branches who might see people less able than themselves advancing up the banks' hierarchy.

How To Improve Motivation?

The business of achieving enhanced performance through an appreciation of an application of motivational factors is a difficult one. We have already highlighted the fact that motivators vary from person to person, that they vary over time and that the success of a particular approach to motivation must be judged in relation to the culture of the organisation. In order to be successful, managers need to keep in touch with the shifting needs of their employees and of the organisation. When they are attempting to provide the stimulus to motivation they should communicate clearly and frequently, bearing in mind the principles of positive reinforcement.

At Ashridge Management College we have designed an open programme entitled 'Performance Through People' which recognises the complexity of the motivation problem. Our model encourages participants to look at opportunities for enhancing performance in three main areas: their own style of management; the approach of their management team; and the organisation's systems, such as appraisal and remuneration. Thus some participants might choose to examine how they are operating individually and to modify their approach in favour of increased participation. Other participants will sometimes look at ways in which they can help their team to achieve greater job satisfaction through an approach such as job enrichment. A third category of participants might leave the programme with an action plan for persuading their organisation to provide, say, extra training and development as a means of enhancing performance. Under conditions of rapid and far-reaching change, such as those which face the banking sector, there may be a need for managers to respond to motivational issues at each of the three levels: personal; team, and organisational.

Given the complexity of motivational issues, it is hard to distill basic principles from the range of theory. Some authors have recognised this and have opted for offering practical guidelines instead (Peters and Waterman[22] together with Blanchard and Johnson[23]). But even here there are dangers. Peters and Waterman recently met with criticism[24] when a number of the 'successful' companies on which their study is based started running into difficulties. This does not invalidate their findings, but merely emphasises the need for all guidelines, theoretical and practical, to be amended and interpreted in the light of what is known about a particular company or working team.

One thing is clear – that the most powerful source of motivation is intrinsic, that is, generated by the job itself. This source of motivation does not require that the manager should do all the motivational work, and stresses the worth and responsibility of the person being managed. Once the sources of extrinsic motivation have been taken care of, the manager then has the challenging job of trying to create an environment in which others can motivate themselves.

References
1. Maslow, A. H., *Motivation and Personality*, 1945, Harper, New York.
2. Alderfer, C. P., *Existence, Relatedness and Growth, Human Needs in Organisational Setting*, 1972, Free Press Glencoe.
3. Landy, F. J. and Trumbo, D. A., *Psychology of Work Behaviour*, 1976, Dorsey Press.
4. McClelland, D. C., *The Achievement Motive*, 1955, Appleton-Century, New York.
5. McClelland, D. C., *Achievement Motivation Can be Developed*, Nov–Dec 1965–7, Harvard Business Review.
6. McGregor, D., *The Human Side of Enterprise*, 1960, McGraw-Hill, New York.
7. McGregor, D., *Leadership and Motivation, 1966, MIT Press*.
8. Herzberg, F., *Work and the Nature of Man*, 1966, World Publishing Co, New York.
9. Vroom, V. H., *Work and Motivation*, 1964, Wiley.
10. Vroom, V. H. and Deci, EL., *Management and Motivation*, 1970, Penguin.
11. Porter, L. W. and Lawler, E. E., *Managerial Attitudes and Performance*, 1968, Irwin-Dorsey.
12. Skinner, B. F., *Beyond Freedom and Dignity*, 1971, New York, Knopf.

13. Maslow, A. H., *op. cit.*
14. Festinger, Leon., *A Theory of Social Comparison Processes*, 1954, Human Relations 7.
15. Peters, T. J. and Waterman, R. H., *In Search of Excellence, 1982*. New York: Harper and Row.
16. McClelland, D., *op. cit.*
17. Blanchard, K. and Johnson, S., *The One Minute Manager*, 1982. New York: Morrow.
18. Andre, R. and Ward, P. D., *The 59 Second Employee* 1984. Houghton Mifflin.
19. McGregor, D., *op. cit.*
20. *Financial Times*, 14 May 1982.
21. *Financial Times, op. cit.*
22. Peters and Waterman, *op. cit.*
23. Blanchard and Johnson, *op. cit.*
24. *Business Weekly*, 5 November 1984.

CHAPTER 5

Group Behaviour

Richard Boot

Lecturer in Management Learning,
University of Lancaster

A bank, like any formal organisation, can be conceived of as both a task system and a social system. As the former, it represents the conscious attempt to coordinate the activity and effort of individual members of the organisation in the service of an overall commercial purpose. As the latter, it represents a fairly stable pattern of interactions and relationships between members of the organisation based upon widely accepted, and often taken for granted, rules governing behaviour, resulting in a distinctive way of life or organisational culture. The two systems, however, are only separable in theory. In practice they are inextricably intertwined, each having a significant effect on the other. And in either case the individual is integrated into the system via the various groups of which he or she is a member. As such, a manager can gain greater understanding of the relationship between the two systems by examining the processes within the groups for which he/she is responsible and indeed of which he/she is a member. These processes can have a significant effect both on individual satisfaction and on individual and collective performance.

The Nature and Formation of Groups

But first it will be useful to clarify what we mean by the term 'group'. In this context we are using it to apply to a collection of people who interact with one another, are aware of each other as individuals and, most importantly, regard themselves as being a group, that is as having some common bond that distinguishes members from 'outsiders'. It is likely that the 'average' branch with a staff of between ten and twenty will fit this definition. Clearly the whole organisation does not, but neither would a larger branch in which, although there may be some shared sense of belonging to the same social unit, the individuals probably do not all interact with one another, nor are they all aware of each other. On the other hand, four or five individuals entering a lift together may pass the time of day and discuss the weather or test-match scores, but despite interacting with and being aware of each other, they are unlikely to regard themselves as a group with a shared identity.

It is common for a distinction to be drawn between formal groups and informal groups. This distinction in some way parallels that mentioned earlier between the task system and the social system, and in the same way is clearer in theory than it is in practice. Thus, formal groups are created to carry out some specific task or meet some organisationally required goal. Some aspects of their structure, procedural roles and membership are likely to be explicitly stated. As we have seen, a branch as a whole might fit into this category, and within a branch so might the Securities Section, the Terminal Room or indeed, together, Manager's Assistants, Assistant Manager and Manager may constitute a formal management 'team'. Informal groups on the other hand are not explicitly 'set-up' but emerge spontaneously, possibly on the basis of friendship or some common interest which may or may not be work-related. In a sense it could be said that they function to meet the needs of their members as human beings, rather than to coordinate their activities as organisational units. The formally prescribed groupings, however, may significantly influence the emergence of informal relationships and groupings. The more individuals are formally required to deal with each other and the more they formally have in common, such as nature of work, physical location and grading, the more they are likely to develop a common identity. So, taking our earlier example, it is not surprising that informal groups emerge in the Terminal Room. It is clear then that an individual can be a member of a number of different groups within the organisation at the same time.

Individual Benefits from Group Membership

It is also clear that group membership means more to an individual than simply asistance in getting a job done. In fact in some cases we shall see that perhaps individuals would be more productive working alone. But there are needs other than task ones which group membership can satisfy, and in so doing have a significant effect on behaviour. In the previous chapter you will have seen that people have varying degrees of need for friendship and affiliation. Almost by definition, association with others in a group activity, be it formal or informal, is capable of satisfying such needs.

The opportunities provided by group membership for social comparison are also important. It seems that we all have a need to compare our opinions, beliefs and activities with others. This is particularly so in social situations which, by their nature, tend to involve a fair degree of ambiguity. By comparing our beliefs with those of others in the same situation, the discomfort associated with this ambiguity can be reduced. In other words we can gain a clearer definition of social 'reality'. So for example, a school-leaver entering employment in a bank for the first time will have to discover what life is like in the branch, what is expected of him or her, what are regarded as 'acceptable' attitudes and behaviour. No doubt he/she will have some prior expectations and (mis)conceptions and is also likely to have gone through a formal induction process. On arriving in the branch it is likely that there will be some general introductions and some specific instructions in his/her new role and duties and the technical aspects of the job. All of this inevitably leaves a large amount of detail still to be filled in, particularly in connection with ways of reacting to colleagues and informal norms and standards of behaviour. The groups of which the new entrant becomes a member are important in filling in that detail. As such, they play a major part in the early process of socialising the individual into the bank. Problems obviously arise when the informal definitions of reality do not coincide with the formal ones. We shall return to these processes later. We shall also see that group processes are significant in establishing informal roles for individuals. Through these emergent roles, group membership provides opportunity for those individuals to develop or test their sense of self-identity at work. Finally, group membership can provide a sense of relative security and greater control over the environment, particularly the social environment. This derives from the belief that a number of people of like interest will be better able to achieve their own ends if they band together than if they continue to operate separately.

Groups, then, would appear to be as important to individuals in meeting their needs for affiliation, social comparison, self-identity, security and influence as they are for getting a job done. But what does this imply for performance effectiveness? Is it enhanced or inhibited? What follows is an examination of behavioural scientists' attempt to shed light on such questions.

The Dynamics of Group Effectiveness

One of the first things of interest we find is that there is evidence to suggest that the mere presence of other people has a significant effect on individual performance, but whether this effect is positive or negative will depend on the nature of the task. The presence of other people tends to increase an individual's general level of arousal. This can have a positive effect on simple tasks which involve little in the way of new behaviour. On more complex tasks, however, in which required behaviour is less familiar, this same increase in arousal can have negative effects. In fact we shall find that many of the questions a manager may wish to ask about group behaviour will inevitably be answered by 'it depends'. This is because the effectiveness of a group, whether it be measured in terms of individual satisfaction at work or in terms of task accomplishment, is dependent upon the complex interaction of a range of different factors. To help our understanding it is possible to group these factors into three broad categories: factors related to the individuals that comprise the group; those related to the context within which the group is operating; and those related to the dynamic processes involved, once a given set of individuals is working together in a given context. We shall focus on each of these in turn.

GROUP COMPOSITION

First, let us look at the number of individuals that make up the group, i.e. the *group size*. Here there are two forces which work in opposite directions. The larger the group, the greater the likely range of resources in terms of skills, knowledge, ideas, etc, but the more people working together the more difficult it becomes to organise them. Which of these forces has the greater impact depends upon the nature of the task. On additive tasks, where the end result is primarily a combination of individual output, group performance increases with increased size, although interestingly not at the same rate. In other words there is a diminishing degree of improvement for every additional member. On collaborative tasks, however, in which the group as a whole must accomplish the task with everyone working together, group effectiveness can be expected to decrease with increasing size. Here the optimum would appear to be between about five and seven people. The problem seems in part to do with the impact of size on member participation. Not only does the absolute amount of participation go down but perhaps, more significantly, the distribution of participation becomes less even. Some individuals feel a greater sense of threat or inhibition about contributing in a larger group than do others. And this inhibition has nothing to do with the potential value of his/her contribution. This means that not only may creative ideas be stifled but also critical evaluation of the ideas of more dominant members. This could be an important point to remember for any managers who find themselves chairing large meetings. Whatever the impact of group size on task effectiveness, its effect on member satisfaction seems to be clear, whether measured by how they report their feelings or by indirect measures such as absenteeism or turnover: *most people much prefer to work in small groups*.

What about the effect of similarities and differences between people? As might be expected, the more diverse task-related skills and abilities that members have the more productive they are likely to be. With regard to other characteristics, however, such as values, attitudes and interests, it seems that greater *similarity* leads to the formation of more stable groups and greater member satisfaction. But in relation to task effectiveness the picture is not quite so clear. There is some evidence to suggest that *difference* is preferable for purposes of problem solving. But it is not possible to make any clear generalisations. For this reason approaches which concentrate less on similarity and difference and more on *compatibility* may prove to be more useful. One such approach suggests that individuals vary in the extent to which they like to get involved in collective activities, the amount of control they like over and by other people, and how close to or friendly with other people they like to get. Here similarity or difference is less significant than compatibility. Thus, two people who are similar in their preference for close friendships might be compatible but two people who are similar in their high to control others will be incompatible. In the latter case their working relationship is likely to be effected by a power struggle. Not surprisingly, the evidence suggests that compatibility within groups lead both to greater task effectiveness and greater member satisfaction. The greater the degree of incompatibility the more likely it is that time and energy will be consumed by interpersonal problems. Along similiar lines, research into effective and ineffective management teams suggests that each person's personality suits them to some group roles more than to others. It also suggests that effective teams tend to consist of certain combinations of compatible roles. Putting these two findings together, considerable success has been claimed for the use of personality tests in selecting and building effective management teams. More will be said about group roles later.

THE WORKING CONTEXT

Let us now turn to the context within which groups operate. What can be said about the impact this has on satisfaction and performance? We have already seen how the nature of the task interacts with group size and individual characteristics to influence effectiveness. The nature of the task is also a significant factor in determining whether different styles of leadership are likely to result in group effectiveness. Such issues will be dealt with more fully in the next chapter.

All banks have rules either implicit or explicit, governing the behaviour of their employees with regard to where, when and how they work, the procedures to be adopted and methods and channels of communication. All of these are potential influences on the formation, development and effectiveness of groups. A considerable amount of research has been carried out to explore the effect of imposed communication channels, and the resulting networks, on such things as problem-solving effectiveness, member satisfaction and leader emergence. In particular, *communication networks* have been studied in terms of their degree of centralization. Thus the most centralized is one in which all communications pass through one person and there is no direct communication between other members of the group: the 'if you have anything to say, say it to me and I will decide what I tell the others' approach. The most decentralized is one in which nobody has any greater access to information than anybody else, and anyone can communicate to anyone else, i.e. there is a high degree of interconnectedness – the 'we are all in this together' approach. And of course there are approaches in-between. The findings from such research have been very consistent. On simple tasks, centralized networks are more efficient but on complex problem-solving tasks, decentralised networks are better. A leader is more likely to emerge in a centralized network. The greater the degree of interconnectedness, the higher the general level of satisfation in the group. The more central an individual's position in the network, the higher is likely to be that individual's personal satisfaction.

These findings can probably be explained by two factors. The greater an individual's access to information, the greater the sense of independence. Independence, being for the most part valued in our society, leads to greater satisfaction. On complex tasks, however, the central member of a centralised network is more likely to become overloaded by information and processing demands, so that the whole network becomes less efficient. In other words, the system suffers from the role overload of the central figure.

Patterns of communication are obviously related to physical setting. We have already suggested that group formation is influenced by physical setting. And this seems to be via the communications its facilitates or inhibits. Not surprisingly, for example, proximity is an important influence upon who will form groups with whom. But even when members of a group are all together in a single room, and so in theory can communicate equally with each other, the physical setting can still be influential. The seating arrangement affects both communication flows and the emergence of a leader. Thus, people sitting opposite each other tend to interact with each other more frequently than anyone else. And there is evidence to suggest that not only do people who perceive themselves as having high status in the group choose the most favourable seating position (e.g. the head of a table), but, perhaps more significantly, people who sit in such positions tend to be regarded by the rest of the group as having a higher status and so are reacted to accordingly.

In a sense, related to the impact of the physical setting, it is widely accepted that individuals and groups develop a proprietary orientation towards certain spaces which they will defend against 'invasion'. This has nothing to do with any formal rights of ownership they may have. The territory is simply occupied, either permanently or intermittently, by individuals or groups who then act as though it belongs to them. The smooth functioning of relationships is dependent upon the extent to which such territorial rights are respected. There are some ways of behaving which, although permissible on a person's own or perhaps 'neutral' territory, are inappropriate on others'. Infringements are likely to bring about a negative reaction. Where 'trespassers' are of high status this reaction is unlikely to be in the form of open resistance but the net effect is likely to be disruptive. The casual moving of a calendar, waste-paper basket or pot-plant may result in what seems like an 'over-reaction'. They could however be important territorial markers.

To some people such issues may seem like irrational nonsense which should be discouraged. But this leads us into another, perhaps less tangible, aspect of the context which affects the way groups operate, and that is the *organisational climate*. So, 'climates' which are typified by values which maintain that the only important relationships are those concerned with getting the job done, that effectiveness increases the more behaviour is rational and decreases the more 'emotionality' is displayed, are likely to involve rewards and punishments that serve to reinforce rational, non-emotional behaviour. As a consequence, overt behaviour is more likely to be based on ideas, while feelings for or about other people or the task will go underground. People will be rewarded for solely task-orientated behaviour and, being in competition for those rewards, will tend to sell their own ideas at the expense of others'. *Trust* will be low and the level of trust between superiors and subordinates affects the amount and quality of information flow between them. Low trust leads to poor information flow. Such climates have been termed 'defensive'. Communication is more likely to be distorted than in 'supportive' climates. These climates tend to be self-perpetuating. Defensive behaviours elicit defensive responses and *vice versa*.Obviously the manager, through his/her own behaviour will be an important influence on the climate that develops.

GROUP DEVELOPMENT

Implicit in the previous section is the idea that through time there are likely to be qualitative changes in a group's processes and the relationships between its members. A number of behavioural scientists have observed that groups seem to pass through a sequence of stages or phases of development, the dominant concerns within each phase being different from those in the preceding one. It has been suggested that broadly speaking there are four such phases each characterised by a dominant task issue and a dominant social issue.

The first phase has been termed 'forming'. In task terms this is a phase of orientation, establishing the parameters of the task and the availability of information and resources. In social terms this is a period of testing and checking out others while giving as little as possible of oneself away. There is a tendency to look to powerful individuals for guidance.

The second stage is 'storming', typified by emotional responses to the task and the demands it seems to be making on the individual. On the social dimension there is often polarisation and conflict around key interpersonal issues. Members seem to be expressing their own individuality.

In the third stage, 'norming', the group develops cohesion. New standards and new roles emerge and the emphasis is on harmony at all costs. Aspects of the task which have the potential for producing conflict are avoided.

In the final stage, 'performing', the task and social dimensions seem effectively to have come together. The group has established a flexible and functional structure of inter-related roles. Interpersonal problems have been sorted out and energy can be channelled into the task.

The model implies that groups must progress through each stage before they can reach effective performance. This progression, however, is not so straightforward and tidy as the description of the model might suggest. For this reason these phases of development are of significance to any manager, not just the one concerned with a group setting up 'from scratch' like a new section, special committee or working-party. Whenever there is some change in task, personnel or organisation, a group is in a sense exposed to some degree of reformation and as such is likely to regress to an earlier phase with its dominant issues and concerns to be dealt with anew. Sometimes old issues re-emerge without such reformation. It is likely in such cases that they have never been adequately dealt with but simply driven underground. Differences may have been suppressed or resentments ignored. Progression, in a a sense, will have been illusory. Finally, for some groups, progression is never completed. They get stuck in one of the phases, often in the constant battle of 'storming' or the unproductive cosiness of 'norming'.

Underlying the phase development model is an idea which has been suggested throughout this chapter: that *group effectiveness is dependent upon equilibrium between the task and social demands of group activity*. It also suggests that the nature and quality of interaction will change through time and that group members will become differentiated into identifiable roles. The particular role or roles that an individual plays in a given group will be influenced by a number of things: his/her position in the communication network; the kind of behaviour he/she typically displays with that group of people; his/her personality and abilities, and so on. The role an individual adopts in one group may be quite different from that played in other groups. As the group gains a history, it becomes more clear to its members what behaviour can be expected from each individual. The unexpected is discouraged and the roles become more clearly defined and more stable. The relative status of any particular role is likely to vary according to its relevance to the dominant group issue at any time.

Although there are a number of different ways of classifying the different roles and associated behaviours that might emerge within a group, they have in common the distinction made between those primarily related to task functions and those related to social, or group maintenance functions. In addition, it is suggested that some roles seem functional to the group neither in terms of task accomplishment nor in terms of group maintenance. These have been referred to as self-oriented roles. Here are some examples of possible roles and the behaviour typical of them.

A.   TASK ORIENTED ROLES

Initiator: suggests new ideas or changes in the way of doing things.

Information giver: offers relevant facts or relates personal experience which is pertinent to the problem.

Co-ordinator: shows or clarifies the relationship between various ideas and tries to pull suggestions together.

Evaluator: supplies standards of accomplishment and measures group progress.

B.   MAINTENANCE ORIENTED ROLES

Encourager: praises and supports the contributions of others, indicating warmth and solidarity.

Harmonizer: mediates differences between others and attempts to reconcile disagreements.

Gatekeeper: makes sure that those who want to contribute can do so and limits over-talkative members.

Commentator: calls attention to group processes, offering suggestions about problems they may be having in functioning.

C.   SELF ORIENTED ROLES

Aggressor: deflates others by expressing disapproval of their ideas, opinions or feelings or by attacking the group as a whole.

Blocker: is 'negativistic' and stubbornly resistant, constantly returning to ideas the group has already rejected.

Playboy: makes a show of lack of involvement by horse-play and raising irrelevant mundane issues.

Help-seeker: constantly attempts to elicit sympathy from others and depreciates self beyond reasonable limits.

Obviously there are many roles that may be played, and one member may perform several different roles during the life of the group. The point here however is the one of equilibrium. Problems of performance may be related to a missing role, that is, some important function in either the task dimension or the social dimension which is not being performed. The relationship between these two dimensions and the manager's role as leader will be explored in the next chapter.   .

In parallel with the emergence of a role structure, groups develop a system of *norms* which are shared rules or standards which designate what is acceptable and what is inacceptable in terms of member behaviour, attitudes and beliefs. They are usually accompanied by an accepted set of rewards and punishments associated with compliance or non-compliance. These may range from isolating deviants socially, through ridiculing them, to being openly offensive. This process of normative influence has been of considerable interest to behavioural scientists and has given rise to a wide range of research. Much of this has concentrated on the informal regulation of individual task performance and, in particular, the way this is often maintained at a level below what is possible, but within the general level of acceptability of management. But norms are not necessarily task-related. Some seem to be more oriented towards group maintenance. They might take the form of a private language, in-jokes or seemingly meaningless rituals. In terms of group stability they may be important in that they encourage solidarity by making the distinction between outsiders and insiders more clear and reinforce the system of roles, and perhaps, more importantly, the informal status and power differentials. As such it would be unwise for any manager to ignore them. Many an attempt to introduce changes has foundered as a result of doing so.

The nature and effect of this normative influence, however, is not uniform. First, there is a distinction between situations which are ambiguous and those which are not. In the former case conformity is produced by providing some certainty. In the latter, the individual is succumbing to the immediate social pressure to conform to the expectations of others. The significance of this distinction is that the effects of the former situation are relatively enduring, whereas the effects of the latter are confined to that situation alone.

There is also evidence that pressure to conform is not exerted evenly amongst group members. It seems that individuals can build up an 'idiosyncracy credit' which permits deviance from group norms in certain circumstances. This credit is related to status and the extent to which the individual has earlier conformed to the expected behaviour. Furthermore, it appears that individuals differ in their susceptibility to social influence. Thus the higher on self-esteem, assertiveness and intelligence and the lower on anxiety and authoritarianism, the less prone an individual will be to pressures to conform.

The general level of conformity within a group however is closely related to the level of *cohesiveness*. This is, in effect, the attractiveness of a group to its members – the extent to which they would make sacrifices to maintain its existence and their own membership of it. Not surprisingly, therefore, the higher the cohesiveness the higher the conformity, the social rewards for conformity being, by definition, more highly valued. General levels of satisfaction tend to be higher also. The relationship between cohesiveness and task performance however is not a direct one. Contrary to some assumptions, high cohesiveness does not *necessarily* lead to improved performance. The mediating factor seems to be the group's own norms for performance. Thus highly cohesive groups seem to be more effective at achieving whatever goals the membership establishes for itself but, as we have already suggested, these need not necessarily be in line with management expectations.

Summary

Throughout a career in banking, a manager is likely to be responsible for, and a member of, a large number of groups both formal and informal. Groups fulfil both important task and important social functions. They affect not only the way people behave but also the way they think and feel. As such, they are a significant influence on work performance and employee satisfaction. In either case, this may be enhanced or inhibited. Whatever the effect, it will result from the complex interplay of factors related to the group composition (size, personalities, similarities, compatibilities), the working context (task, communication structure, physical setting, organisational climate) and the processes of development (stage of development, roles, norms, cohesiveness). The effective manager needs to be aware of those group factors which are significant to his/her own work and to the work for which he/she is responsible. He/she needs an understanding of how they are likely to interact. And of course he/she needs to be able to do something about it. This chapter has been intended primarily as an aid to awareness and understanding. The action options open to the manager as a leader of working groups is dealt with in the next chapter.

Suggestions for Further Reading

This chapter has been based upon the vast body of research and theory concerning group behaviour as it applies to work in organisations. Those wishing to study that research and theory further can find much of it covered in more detail in the following texts:

Belbin, R. M., *Management Teams*, Heinemann, 1981.

Cartwright, D. & Zander, A., *Group Dynamics*, Tavistock, 1968.

Schutz, W. C., *The Interpersonal Underworld*, Science and Behaviour Books, 1966.

Shaw, M. E., *Group Dynamics: the psychology of small group behaviour*, McGraw-Hill, 1976.

Smith, P. B., *Groups within Organisations*, Harper & Row, 1973.

CHAPTER 6

Leadership

Philip Hodgson

Assistant Director of Studies, Ashridge Management College

The war hero leads his much reduced and tattered bank of tired men up the ridge to tackle yet another group of baddies. Our leader seems to lead a charmed life, the shells burst nearby, killing off one more of his loyal team, but our hero keeps going, leading his men finally to victory. The credits roll, the lights come up, the stirring music fades and we all leave the cinema pleased to have seen another example of leadership in action. But wait a moment, what has that sort of celluloid hero – where we all know that the script writer will ensure a happy ending – got to do with the kind of leadership that we see in businesses and other organisations in everyday life?

In this chapter I shall look at a variety of studies of what leadership is, review why those studies of leadership are important, and try to assess their value to existing leaders, potential leaders, and the led. There has been an enormous amount of research into leadership, and not all of it has been of direct value to the practising manager. Some writers have even suggested abandoning the concept of leadership altogether. However I feel that would be rather drastic, and would rob us of much useful and applicable work. But the subject is by no means fully 'sewn up', and the models, concepts and ideas that have so far emerged from the research are in no way comprehensive.

What is Leadership?

John Hunt[1] has said that leadership is ' . . . an outcome of a man or a woman's capacity to sense and prescribe what a situation requires and to encourage others to perceive and pursue that prescription.' He contrasts this with management, which he says is about keeping the show going. Some managers, he points out, are leaders whilst others are not, and some leaders make terrible managers. Some time ago it was said of an eminent man that he was an excellent and effective Cabinet Minister, but that was probably the only job he could do, and that most likely he would be hopeless as a manager! Professor Abraham Zaleznik[2] says that: 'the effective leader motivates people to create and follow new objectives. The effective manager motivates others and administers resources to ensure the company objectives are fulfilled.'

In both of these views the leader is a person with some kind of vision. He or she is looking beyond the immediate problems and other matters of concern, and is in some way communicating this vision so that followers can accept it as a real possibility – which is therefore achievable. Our war hero communicated the real possibility of storming the last ridge and his men followed him. On a world stage probably all the major leaders have had this ability to communicate and sell their vision of the future. Whether it is Churchill promising 'blood sweat and tears' or Hitler promising greatness for the Third Reich, or more recently Martin Luther-King with his 'I have a dream' speech, promising a new way of life for black Americans, all have somehow convinced their audiences that not only did they have a vision of the future which their followers wanted, but, more important, the great leaders knew a pathway to that dream. Let us now look at some studies of leadership and see how leaders find those pathways in practice.

Ohio Studies

Since the 1950s, Ohio State University has been conducting what is now one of the longest single studies into management and leadership. The general approach was to study managers and leaders at work and see if there were styles of behaviour which they used. They found that, of all the styles of behaviour which leaders used, 86% could be described as either *task oriented* or *people oriented*. Task oriented behaviour focused on getting the work done, and was concerned with deadlines, quality of product and efficiency. People oriented behaviour was concerned with the morale of the workforce and their commitment to the work and the organisation.

Some of the early and most influential work using this research came from Blake and Mouton[3] who drew a grid (Figure 1) with the dimensions of 'concern for people' and 'concern for production'. They then identified five main leadership styles within the grid of:

- 9.1 Maximum concern for production, minimum concern for people.
- 1.9 Minimum concern for production, maximum concern for people.
- 5.5 Halfway concern for production, halfway concern for people.

THE MANAGERIAL GRID

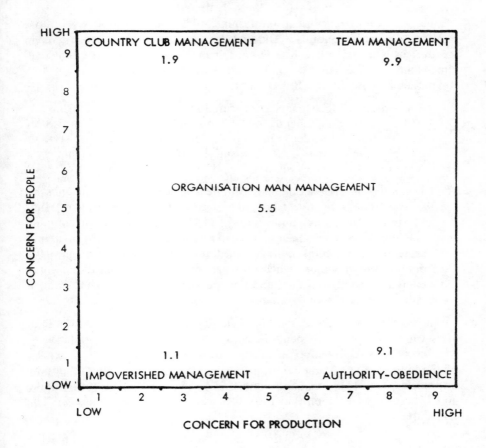

Figure 1

- 1.1 Minimum concern for production, minimum concern for people.
- 9.9 Maximum concern for production, maximum concern for people.

Blake and Mouton's training programmes have been widely used in this country, and have helped people to assess their existing style of management and identify ways they can adapt their style to the ideal style of the 9.9 manager. But the two-dimensional nature of the grid suggests that there is an ideal style where it is possible to combine maximum concern for production (or the task in hand), and maximum concern for people. Perhaps there are situations where it just is not possible to satisfy both these needs, irrespective of the leader's particular style preference?

Two other approaches since the original Blake and Mouton work have tried to answer this question. The first approach was developed by W. J. Reddin[4] in what he called his 'Three Dimensional Theory.' His first two dimensions are the same as Blake and Mouton – Task Orientation and Relationships Orientation. But to these he adds a third, that of:

> *Effectiveness.* Effectiveness is measured in terms of outcomes from the leader's work, and depends not only on the leader's style, but also on the situation the leader is in and the appropriateness of that style to that particular situation. Reddin suggests that no one leadership style is appropriate to every situation, and introduces the concept of:

> *Flexibility of Style* as a factor in effective leadership. Some jobs he says, require a relatively limited range of styles, others make 'High Flexibility Demands', and amongst those are high level or complex managerial jobs, non routine decision making jobs and jobs involving rapid environmental change. Reddin talks about strategies for organisational change which unfreeze the 'frozen organisation' which is characterised by its reliance on past rules and procedures and a reluctance to introduce change.

The second approach is called *Situational Leadership* and comes from Paul Hersey and Kenneth H. Blanchard[5]. Although they worked independantly of Reddin, they have developed his notion of flexibility one stage further, by taking into account the kind of subordinates which a leader might be responsible for. They produce a matrix with the same dimensions as Blake and Mouton, but they only identify four basic styles, see (Figure 2). The styles are:

Box 1 *Structured style*; where the leader takes responsibility for achieving the task, gives instructions, and generally refers the subordinate to rules, manuals and check lists.

Box 2 *Coaching style*; where the subordinate is asked how he would tackle a particular task, and his ideas are taken into account; but final responsibility for achieving the task still rests with the subordinate's boss.

Box 3 *Encouraging style*; may seem a little like the coaching style, but here it is the subordinate who has the responsibility for achieving the task. However, his boss does not expect that he can do it without some help, and will discuss how the subordinate will tackle the problem. The difference is that, with this style, the boss will expect his subordinate to be right most of the time and seldom need correction or guidance.

SITUATIONAL LEADERSHIP

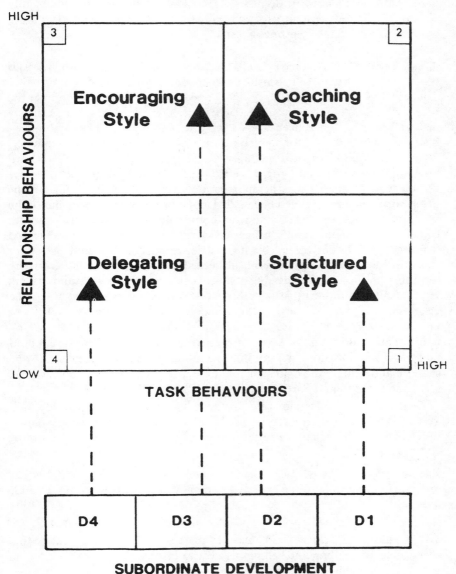

Figure 2

Box 4 *Delegating style*; is low on relationship and task behaviour, because the leader knows that the subordinate is well aware how to do the work in hand and doesn't need to discuss it. The subordinate is also competently able to take full responsibility for achieving the task to whatever performance criteria his boss might reasonably set.

The key point that Hersey and Blanchard make is to tie up the four leadership styles with four possible stages of development of subordinates. The levels of development, D1 to D4, are each best managed by one of the four styles, i.e. A D1 subordinate – where perhaps the person is completely new to the work, would need a box 1 or structured style; a D3 subordinate – who had been in the job for some time and only needed occasional guidance, would need a box 3 or encouraging style. Clearly, as Hersey and Blanchard point out, it is important for the effective leader to choose and have the flexibility to be able to use the appropriate style for each subordinate. The D4 subordinate (experienced and skilled in the task) would be very put off by a structured style being used, and would probably become very demotivated; equally the D1 subordinate (inexperienced and unskilled in the task) would feel very lost and uncomfortable if the delegating style was used.

The studies quoted above have all been done in America, and this may raise the question of whether the styles of American managers and leaders are the same as those in Britain? Some work done is this country by The Research Unit at Ashridge Management College[6] suggests that there are considerable similarities. The research was based on a proposal by Tannenbaum and Schmidt[7] which suggested that leadership behaviour could be seen as varying along a continuum, with autocratic management at one extreme and democratic management at the other. The more democratic the style, the more that subordinates are involved in taking decisions.

Four styles of leadership were distinguished in the Ashridge study, and you will see that they are very closely tied to the work done independantly by Hersey and Blanchard. The four styles are:

The autocratic or 'tells' style. The leader takes all the decisions and issues orders. His subordinates are expected to carry out these instructions without question.

The persuasive or 'sells' style. The leader still takes the decisions, but he will spend time persuading and selling his idea to his people.

The consultative style. The leader consults with his people before taking a decision. This style is in contrast with the previous style where discussion happens after the decision has been made.

The democratic or 'joins' style. The leader using this style works with his group of people to reach a decision by joint consensus and agreement.

The Ashridge work shows a strong preference for consultative style in British companies. However, the research also showed that managers were most commonly perceived as exercising autocratic or persuasive styles. Subordinates' attitudes on a number of important matters tended to vary depending on the kind of leadership style which they felt was being used on them. The most positive attitudes – which included the greatest degree of confidence in their bosses – were found amongst those who saw their managers as consultative. The least positive attitudes were found amongst staff who were unable to perceive any distinctive style being exercised by their superiors. The evidence obviously points towards the need for consistency in the leader's behaviour, so that subordinates know what to expect.

Action Centred Leadership

John Adair[8] who was a senior lecturer in Military History and adviser on leadership training at Sandhurst, developed what he described as a 'functional' approach to leadership. He argues that, for the most part, a group of people are assembled to tackle particular tasks, and one of the group will be designated the leader. The functional approach aims to take into account the three main areas of need to enable the group to achieve its task, these are:

(a)   *Task needs.*
The group needs to be quite clear on what tasks it is trying to accomplish, and be aware of and ready to implement the methods it is going to use.

(b)   *Maintenance needs.*
The members of the group must cooperate effectively if the group is to achieve its objectives. The group itself has a level of morale and motivation, which depends on all members.

(c)   *Individual needs.*
In the workplace, people have individual needs which may not be shared by the group as a whole. An individual whose needs are not being met by the group will withdraw from the group, thus reducing its effectiveness.

Adair believes that the leader's role is to appreciate that the three areas of need are dependant on each other, and to ensure that they are met. This doesn't mean that the leader has to do everything himself or herself; delegation is perfectly possible, but the leader is finally responsible. Adair stresses that failure to meet one of the needs will adversely affect the other two, and he concentrates on what leaders do, i.e. planning, initiating action, controlling, supporting, informing and evaluating.

What leaders do

In the last ten years, research seems to have moved away from the styles that leaders use and has tended to follow the line that John Adair pioneered with his Action Centred Leadership. But recent research has not just looked at what leaders do; it has also asked questions about a leader's background, upbringing, and what leaders feel to be important in helping them get to their present position.

John Hunt[1] found that people who made it to the top in organisations:

> have above average intelligence, but not too much above;
> are healthy;
> are from a middle to upper class background;
> have high power needs;
> are frequently the first born in their family, or at least were the first son.

Of course, just because they have made it to the top does not mean that they will be good leaders, merely that those people are in positions where leadership is vital.

Charles Margerison[9] published the results of questioning 244 Chief Executives and asked them what factors they felt contributed to their development. The top ten factors cited, with average scores out of 100, were:

1.	Ability to work with a wide variety of people.	78.4%
2.	Early overall responsibility for important tasks.	74.8%
3.	A need to achieve results.	74.8%
4.	Leadership experience early in career.	73.6%
5.	Wide experience in many functions prior to age 35.	67.6%
6.	An ability to do deals and negotiate.	66.4%
7.	Willingness to take risks.	62.8%
8.	Having more ideas than other colleagues.	61.6%
9.	Being stretched by immediate bosses.	60.4%
10.	An ability to change managerial style to suit occasion.	58.8%

As became clear from the Ohio studies, the ability to work well with people is of major importance, together with early responsibility, and a need to achieve results.

The route to the top of their respective companies involved on average:

Employment	in 2.9 organisations.
Jobs:	8.1 different roles.
Senior manager:	Average age of entry 32.
Chief Executive:	Average age of appointment 41.

Whether leaders are born or made, they are clearly well on their way at a fairly early age. Morgan McCall and Michael Lombardo[10] looked at what happened to promising young executives and asked the question: Why do some go on to make it right to the top, and why do others appear to get derailed on the way? They compared one group of 'derailed' executives with a group of 'arrivers' (i.e. those that did make it). They found remarkable similarities between the two groups. However, they did find four areas which distinguished between them:

1. Strengths become weaknesses. Loyalty becomes over-dependence, ambition becomes viewed as pure office politics and no-one trusts that kind of person.
2. Deficiencies eventually matter. The higher up a person goes the more they need all round skills (hence the concern in Margerison's study to gain wide experience in many functions before age 35), brilliance in some areas can mask mediocre performance in others. But at higher levels that mediocracy is more likely to be revealed.
3. Success goes to their heads. Those executives who had been told how good they were for some time sometimes got to a stage where they felt they could do no wrong. Once they had lost their humility, they were seen as arrogant, and people no longer wanted to work for them any more.
4. Luck. For a few unlucky executives, events conspired against them. They suffered from economic upheavals or were 'done in' politically.

McCall and Lombardo comment that they found very few leaders who could do no wrong. Both arrivers and derailed had plenty of faults but often these did not become apparent until fairly late in their careers. One person who coped with his flaws effectively would be distinguished from another who did not. It seems that part of successfully handling adversity lies in knowing what not to do. Lots of leadership behaviour patterns are acceptable to others; the key was in knowing which ones colleagues and superiors would find intolerable.

Alastair Mant, in his challenging book 'Leaders We Deserve'[11] takes a somewhat different line. He argues that, in the political arena at least, defective leaders do not arise by accident. They rise above their proper level of capability simply because they are filling a vacuum created by the indifference of abler people. Leadership as a process, according to Mant, is caused by following, and most people follow by instinct. For him, there are two very simple models of leadership. The first kind involves binary thinking, which he also describes as the 'raider' type. Raiders are associated with power, survival, conflict, win/lose, defence and raiding. The tertiary thinker, or 'builder' is concerned with authority, dependence, consensus, sharing, resolution, and building. The tertiary thinker as a leader will be concerned about the outcomes of his actions and how it affects the organisation. The binary thinker is mainly concerned about personal survival and opportunities for advancement. Mant says that the people who get to the top in public office tend to think in a binary fashion for most of the time, precisely because one of the best ways to prevail in competitive systems is to approach all activity in a binary/adversarial way. Mant's book like his previous 'The Rise and Fall of the British Manager'[12] is a classic of original thought.

The next book to be described has become a classic in its own right, and on both sides of the Atlantic too. This attractive original research, became bestseller within a year of publication and has been a major talking point in all kinds of organisation.

Thomas J. Peters and Robert H. Waterman[13] both worked for the McKinsey & Company consultancy. They reviewed a whole range of American organisations against a number of criteria based on growth and long-term wealth creation over a twenty-year period, and return on capital and sales. Starting with a fairly extensive list of apparently successful companies, they reduced the list by insisting on evidence that the company was not just good but consistently produced excellent results. Their book, 'In Search of Excellence' gives a detailed report on how those excellent companies operate, and in doing so reveals a lot about organisational leadership. They found eight qualities that emerged to distinguish excellent companies:

1. *A bias for action.* All the companies used an analytical approach to decisions, but were not paralysed by their analysis. A Digital Equipment senior executive is quoted as saying, 'When we've got a big problem here, we grab ten senior guys and stick them in a room for a week. They come up with an answer and implement it.'

2. *Stay close to the customer.* The organisations studied provided unparallelled quality, service and reliability, and in return got many of their best product ideas from their customers.

3. *Autonomy and Entrepreneurship*. An essential part of this is to encourage innovation at all levels and in all parts of the organisation. Peters and Waterman's original definition of excellence included the ability to come up with new solutions to organisational problems. In all of their companies, people have the autonomy to take initiatives and act entrepreneurially.

4. *Productivity through people*. Thomas Watson Jnr., the chairman of IBM talked about an inbuilt respect for the individual: Mark Shepherd, the chairman of Texas Instruments referred to every worker 'being seen as a source of ideas, not just acting as a pair of hands'.

5. *Hands-on, value driven*. Every excellent company studied was quite clear on what it stood for, and takes the process of shaping those values very seriously. But the values have to be right, and this tends to mean that they are not just to do with money but have broader implications. Philip Selznick is quoted as saying that companies – and most often leaders of companies – communicate those values not by formal memos, but by the indirect method of myths, legends and metaphors.

6. *Stick to the knitting*. The odds for excellent performance seem much better for companies that stay with the business areas that they know well. As the former chairman of Johnson and Johnson said, 'Never acquire a business you don't know how to run'.

7. *Simple form, lean staff*. Even the largest of the organisations studied, had simple structures. Few had massive corporate headquarters with vast central payrolls; many had a policy of splitting down any division that grew beyond a certain size.

8. *Simultaneous loose-tight properties*. The best companies were both centralised and decentralised. They centred around a few very strongly held core beliefs; all other aspects of the business would then be very decentralised with a lot of individual autonomy.

The political scientist James MacGregor Burns is quoted by Peters and Waterman as defining two kinds of leadership. The first he calls:

Transactional Leadership. This involves the building of coalitions; shifting attention within organisations so that new priorities get enough attention; being visible when necessary, and invisible when not; listening carefully and reinforcing words with credible action; being tough when necessary, and occasionally making use of power. Henry Kissinger called this the, 'subtle accumulation of nuances, a hundred things done a little better'.

The other kind of leadership that Burns identifies is *Transforming Leadership*. This kind of leader builds on people's need for meaning and institutional purpose. Often this kind of leadership has been most important to a company in its early stages. The transforming leader is less concerned with power, but far more concerned with purpose. This kind of leader will go to enormous lengths to demonstrate what he or she stands for, and will enroll followers into mutual support for a common purpose. Often the leader's style will be described as uplifting, inspiring, or even evangelising; certainly it involves discussions of what is morally right as far as the ultimate purpose is concerned. Howard Head, an inventor and successful entrepreneur says, 'you have to believe in the impossible'. At Hewlett-Packard one of the explicit criteria for picking top managers is their ability to engender excitement in their own staff.

Since 'In Search of Excellence' was published, a considerable range of research has been stimulated to enlarge, to confirm, to disprove, and to generally chew over the various points made in the book. It is now suggested that at least a dozen of the excellent companies described are now showing less than excellent results only two years later. Many have seen fundamental changes to their markets where strict adherence to Peters and Waterman's eight rules has not helped. For example, none of the rules emphasise the need to react to broad economic and business trends. But good management requires more than following one set of commandments. As Bob Waterman said, 'The book has been so popular that people have taken it as a formula for success rather than what it was intended to be. We were writing about the art, not the science of management.' Perhaps there is a need to see theories dismantled; perhaps some like to see the mighty fall, but whatever the merits and demerits of the book it has encouraged a revised interest in what is possible within organisations. Undoubtedly some of the orginally named excellent companies will falter and perhaps even fade, but then Peters and Waterman never said that those companies would go on for ever, merely that they seem to have been successful in the past. It is a point worth bearing in mind when looking at the British research done by Walter Goldsmith and David Clutterbuck and published under the title of 'The Winning Streak'.[14]

Their research followed very much the same lines as the American book, although they go a little further in naming names of those companies which they thought were not particularly excellent. In making their choice they say, 'We excluded subsidiaries, except as part of a group, and the banks (both because of their peculiar financial structure and the fact that none of the big clearing banks stood out for the calibre of its management).' Amongst a series of characteristics which were identified in successful British companies was the ' . . . ability to absorb and adapt management styles to their own circumstances . . . '. In all of the companies studied, certain issues mattered, and were seen to be of great importance, even if they were never clearly articulated. One of the issues that mattered was *leadership*.

Top management needed to be visible; they needed to have clear objectives; they needed to create an environment in their organisations in which managers could lead. Top management also have a clear vision of where their company is going, and they communicate that vision down the line to all their employees. And, significantly, that message is well received, because, in all the successful companies studied, managers down the line pinpointed effective leadership at chairman or chief executive level. As STC's Sir Kenneth Corfield puts it, 'Leadership here is all about talking to people'. The importance of the employee's view is emphasised by the work of Dr Richard Ruch of the School of Business at Ryder College, New Jersey. Ruch found that employees holding negative views of top management showed poor attendance, high labour turnover and higher than normal levels of industrial accidents and mental illness.

Warren Bennis[15] has argued recently that there are four essential competencies of leadership. He bases his ideas on the results of interviews with 90 leaders and their subordinates. Incidently his way of distinguishing between *leaders* and *managers* is that leaders are the people who do the right thing, whilst managers are the people who do things right. His four competencies are:

1. *Management of attention.*
Effective leaders draw people to them, by communicating a powerful focus of commitment. One such leader was described as making people want to join in with him by enrolling them into his vision. The word vision is used here not in the mystical sense, but in the sense of outcome or goal.

2. *Management of meaning.*
To communicate facts is very different from communicating meaning. Leaders communicate their vision in such a way that people can align themselves with it. People know what the leader stands for and can identify themselves with it.

3. *Management of trust.*
Bennis quotes a study showing that people would follow individuals they could count on, even when they disagree with their viewpoint, rather than people they agree with but who change their positions frequently.

4. *Management of self.*
Leaders know their skills and strengths and nurture them. They also never used the word failure. They admitted to making lots of mistakes, but they learned from them. A mistake was just a way of learning how to do it better next time. One leader is quoted as saying, 'Failure is impossible.'

Bennis suggests that modern industrial society has largely been oriented towards quantity rather than quality. Quantity is measurable, usually in money, but quality is something that has to be appreciated rather more intuitively and is much more to do with our feelings. It is our feelings that we use as a reference point when understanding meaning and value in our lives. The vision must have meaning and value if we are to follow it.

Leadership in Banking

Clearly the concept of leadership is not easy to pin down. The theories, findings and models of leadership behaviour cited above probably only cover part of the story. At one level, leadership is a practical matter of being visible, being clear on objectives and communicating them. But as many writers have said, you cannot become an effective leader just by following someone's checklist. But you can learn, and the last study quoted emphasised the idea that effective leaders were very optimistic about their ability to learn and develop.

How far can these theories and research reports be applied in the banking world? For me the best way of assessing these ideas is in the context in which banks operate, and that context has involved changes in three different aspects of society – economic, technological and social:

Economic. Banking was once an extremely stable area of employment. Employees joined a bank for life and although there was competition, it tended to be low key and certainly only between banks. In the last few years an unprecedented range of organisations have started competing with banks – some national, some multinational, some in the private sector and some in the public sector. This in turn has stimulated a considerably increased range of competition between the banks themselves, with extensive advertising campaigns, and greater pressures on managers in banks to keep in touch with the markets that they serve. Under these circumstances, leadership becomes so much more important, since change is seen as a threat by many people. This is especially so in organisations like banks where stability has been the norm for several generations. Helping organisations and their staff to cope with change must be a key challenge for leaders in banking. As Handy and Hepburn say in their study of Employee Relations in Finance[16] ' . . . the line manager will have to accept a greater responsibility for setting objectives, assessing performance, training, recruiting, communicating and handling local employee relations problems. Managers must become responsible for their own units not only in business, but also in people terms.' They go on to cite the case of the Jointly (management and union) Accredited Office Representative in a number of clearing banks, where managers now have to deal on a local basis with representatives of trade unions.

But the problem does not stop there, because as Bennis said, there is a big difference between doing the right things, and doing things right. Leaders in banking have to make major decisions affecting the future of their banks and the banking community.

Technology. The broadscale use of computer-based technology in banking has increased the speed at which information can be sent around the world and consequently has increased the pressure on managers to make decisions faster. As some of the studies cited above confirmed, autocratic decisions are much faster to make than democratic ones. The leader is faced with a trade-off between speed of decision-making and motivation of staff. And yet, in an environment which is rapidly becoming more and more computerised, the motivation of the staff must take on greater significance. Do banks run the computers, or do the computers run banks?

A second influence of new technology is the way it enables people to perform tasks single-handed which previously needed whole offices of clerical staff. The reductions of staff resulting from the increased efficiency which new technology allows, have obviously required careful handling to ensure that the organisation benefits. The people left in the organisation are now in a position to influence the resources and the public image of the bank to a much greater degree than previously. This side-effect of technology means that more responsibility gets pushed down the hierarchy to people who may need to develop their own leadership styles, since, although they may not have responsibility for many staff, their decisions may now have a significant effect on the bank.

Social. The previous two sections outlined some of the changes which not only banks, but society in general is going through. We are in an age of uncertainty. Uncertain levels of inflation, interest rates, exchange rates, together with political uncertainty in many countries of the world, and a very uncertain energy future means that there can be no guarantees given for the future of any organisation. This shifting ground emphasises the need for people with a practical vision of the future. As has been pointed out, the effective leader must not only have the vision but also be able to communicate it, and give it meaning, to the people who are going to help achieve it.

Are leaders born or can they be made? My answer to this age-old question is coloured by my experience in directing The Leadership Development Programme at Ashridge. We don't try to teach leadership – anyway most of the people who come on the programme are pretty effective already – but we can let people examine their leadership style and see for themselves the personal qualities which they have and which they can use to make them more effective as leaders. Certainly some people start off with a lot of advantages, but leadership is such a personal matter, that everyone can learn more because they can learn more about themselves.

The proof of the pudding is in the eating, and as a final word, who better to turn to than Robert Townsend whose pithy book 'Up The Organisation'[17] should, in my view, be required reading for everyone who works in organisations. He says, 'How do you spot a leader? They come in all ages, shapes, sizes, and conditions. Some are poor administrators, some are not overly bright. One clue: since most people *per se* are mediocre, the true leader can be recognised because, somehow or other, his people consistently turn in superior performances.'

The test of effective leadership must be as simple as that; whether in the banking world or any other organisation where people have to work together, the people working for the effective leader consistently turn in superior performances.

References
 1. Hunt, J., *Managing People At Work*, 1981, Pan.
 2. Zaleznik, A., 'Managers And Leaders: Are They Different?', *Harvard Business Review*, May-June 1977.
 3. Blake, R. R. and Mouton, J. S., *The Managerial Grid*, 1964, Gulf Publishing.
 4. Reddin, W. J., *Managerial Effectiveness*, 1970, McGraw Hill.
 5. Hersey, P. and Blanchard, K. H., *Management Of Organisational Behaviour: Utilising Group Resources* (3rd edition), 1982, Prentice Hall.
 6. Sadler, Philip., 'Executive Leadership', in D. Pym (ed), *Industrial Society*, 1966, Penguin Books.
 7. Tannenbaum, Robert, and Schmidt, Warren H., 'How To Choose A Leadership Pattern', *Harvard Business Review*, March-April 1958, 95–102.
 8. Adair, J., *Training For Leadership*, 1968, London: McDonald.
 9. Margerison, C. J., 'Leadership Patterns And Profiles', in *Leadership and Organisation Development Journal*, vol 1, No 1 1980, 12–17.
10. McCall, M. W. and Lombardo, M. W., 'What Makes A Top Executive?', in *Psychology Today*, February 1983, 27–31.
11. Mant, A., *Leaders We Deserve*, 1983, Martin Robertson.
12. Mant, A., *The Rise And Fall Of The British Manager*, 1979, Pan.
13. Peters, T. J. and Waterman, R. H., *In Search Of Excellence*, 1982, Harper and Row.
14. Goldsmith, W. and Clutterbuck, D., *The Winning Streak*, 1984, Weidenfeld and Nicolson.
15. Bennis, W., 'The Four Competancies Of Leadership', in *Training And Development Journal*, August 1984, 15–19.
16. Handy, L. J. and Hepburn, R., 'Employee Relations in Finance – New Challenges and Opportunities', in *Management Today*, May, 1985.
17. Townsend, R., *Up The Organisation*, 1971, Coronet.

CHAPTER 7

The Impact of Technology In Banking

L. D. Cowan

Director and Secretary,
Federation of London Clearing Bank Employers

Introduction

Banks are no strangers to new technology. For about 25 years computers have been used to process cheques and transfer funds; indeed, the rapid growth in business that has been a feature of the banking scene in recent years could not have been achieved without computers, and it is fortunate that the availabilty of large mainframe computers coincided with a significant development of the banks' business and the enormous amount of clerical work arising from decimalisation. Some idea of the level of activity in banking can be judged from a few statistics. For example, in 1982 the London clearing banks operated over 23 million current accounts and over 13 million deposit accounts through 11,266 branches. In the five years from 1976 to 1981 the annual cheque volume in England and Wales increased from 1,812 million to 2,511 million and a recent study by the Inter-Bank Research Organisation (IBRO) predicts that in 1996 the annual cheque volume could be a staggering 3,250 million. Banks were among the first organisations to use computers on a large scale and they have remained in the forefront of developments in data processing; banking as we know it today is totally dependent on technology. However, the volume of paper processed is only part of the story. Of as much importance to the successful operation of a bank is the cost of those transactions. As long ago as 1978 the then Price Commission reported on 'Banks: Charges for Money Transmission Services' and commented on the role of data processing in reducing or containing costs. These costs are significant and undoubtedly one application of technology in banking is to increase efficiency and reduce cost, especially the cost of money transmission services.

Computer technology has been of enormous benefit to the clearing banks, since without it their businesses could not have grown at the rate they have and remained viable. But at the same time technology has enabled others to compete with the banks in providing financial services to the public. This competition is not confined to other financial institutions such as building societies but also comes from non-financial institutions such as retail groups. For example, some large stores issue their own credit cards thereby competing with the banks in providing consumer credit, whilst others provide directly other forms of financial services. In turn, the banks need technology to remain competitive. Thus the available technology enables others to compete with the clearing banks whilst the banks themselves become more and more dependent on technology to remain competitive!

Technology and the impact it will have is undoubtedly the most significant factor affecting people working in banking today. This chapter examines developments in technology in banking and its implications for staff at all levels.

Developments in the Application of Technology in Banking

Banking, perhaps more than any other industry, relies upon the collection, storage, retrieval, assimilation and transmission of information. It is not surprising therefore that, in the late 1950's and early 1960's, the banks began to use large mainframe computers, initially for maintaining customer accounts. These computers were centrally located but, although customer account information was held in them, the computers were not on-line to the branches. This phase can be summed up as a period when the banks were basically doing the same things as previously but were now doing them in a different way. Large quantities of data were being processed centrally and there was a considerable flow of paper between the branches and the data processing centres (indeed, there still is). Although the money transmission system itself remained very much the same, its operation made use of technical advances in accounting and other machines. Increasingly these operated at very much higher speeds, using magnetic ink character recognition or optical character recognition to sort cheques. Today these machines can process as many as 2,400 cheques per minute. Obviously this greatly improved the throughput of work and eliminated much clerical and arithmetical effort, but the banking system itself was little changed. During the 1970's, improvements in micro-electronics enabled far reaching changes to take place in computing technology. Micro-computers were developed which were compact and versatile and which had relatively large memory capacity at a fraction of the price of their predecessors.

During this period the banks also benefitted from the improvements that were taking place in general office technology. Photocopying, electronic typewriters, improved telephone systems and, ultimately, word-processing were introduced with corresponding benefits – if little reduction in the volume of paper produced!

The first major change in the money transmission itself came in 1969 with the introduction of a system of making corporate payments through what came to be called Bankers' Automated Clearing Services Limited (BACS). The payment system used by BACS no longer relied on the exchange of paper but used instead the exchange of magnetic tapes which enabled funds to be transferred between banks or between branches by direct reading of the data contained on the tape itself. The system also enabled customers of banks to transfer funds between them by the same process. As the system developed, all credit transfers, direct debits and standing orders were put on to it. With the development of micro-electronics, cassettes or diskettes could be used as well as tape. Today, the system no longer requires the physical movement of magnetic devices but can effect payments through messages received via a telecommunications link. The impact of BACS can be judged by the number of automated payment transactions that pass through the system, now in the order of 12 million a week. In 1982 the total number of items processed was 544 million, more than ten times the number in 1969. BACS expects that in 1990 40% of all U.K. bank clearings will be processed by them compared with 20% at present.

The end of the 1960's marked the transition to the second phase of technological development in banking. In this phase, technology enabled the banks to provide many services to customers in an entirely new way as opposed to just doing the same thing, albeit in a different way.

The most obvious example of this is the credit card. Not only is this an alternative payment method to the cheque or cash, it represented a new approach to the provision of consumer credit. Today, credit cards provide credit in new areas of business, ranging from, for example, the payment of private school fees or private medical and dental bills and solicitors bills to such areas as local authority and water rates. The processing of credit card vouchers and payment arrangements, as well as the world wide authorisation systems used in credit card operations, have only been made possible by high speed data processing using large mainframe computers and a modern telephone system.

The second example of this phase of technological development is the introduction of automatic teller machines (ATM'S). These have been the spearhead of self service in banking. In Britain at present there are some 230 million transactions a year on over 6,000 ATM'S. There are 13.8 million card holders who between them withdraw almost £10 billion a year. The latest machines not only dispense cash but can give statements or balances, order cheque books and perform a range of other functions, including paying in. As individual banks agree arrangements that enable customers to use machines of other banks, and as the number of machines is increased and their reliability improved, ATM'S will become an increasingly popular aspect of banking giving the customer a more flexible service and also reducing the direct cost to the banks of each transaction.

A less obvious development but none-the-less one of the great significance is the introduction of counter terminals. There are two main categories. First, there are terminals located on the cashier's side of the counter, known as teller terminals. When a customer asks for a particular service the cashier inputs the necessary information directly into a terminal which may be connected to the back office of the branch or direct to a central computer. Apart from speeding up the service to the customer, time is saved in the work that is normally done after the branch has closed to the public. The second category is the customer terminal, located on the customer side of the counter. The customer uses the terminal to obtain the service he requires, using a magnetic card in connection with a personal identification number. In effect the customer is using technology to do some of the work done in the back office, eliminating the need for cheque sorting or manual cash paying out. Counter terminals are a logical extension of the back office terminal now found in all branches. Usually these are on-line to the bank's mainframe computer, although branch inputs are not always entered directly into the computer's main records. They are more likely at present to be stored in a separate file, the main records being updated from that file during batch operations carried out outside normal banking hours. More and more automation is being applied to other routine work of a branch, including dealing with securities and loan applications. Branch processors are now available that will compile the mass of information required to support business loan applications, eliminating much of the analysis work previously performed by bank staff. The purchase of stocks and shares is possible through bank-wide systems that can be connected directly to the offices of the stockbrokers which are now part of a number of major banks. The complexities of complying with, for example, the Consumer Credit Act 1974, will inevitably be resolved by computer programmes specifically designed to produce the increased information and documentation required by that Act.

Other changes have been taking place in the clearing system. In 1977 SWIFT (Society for World Wide Interbank Financial Telecommunications) came into operation. This is owned and operated world-wide by more than 1,000 banks in 42 countries and enables the electronic transmission of messages on virtually every aspect of international banking. It currently transmits over 7 million messages a month.

In 1984 CHAPS (Clearing House Automated Payments System) came into service, permitting countrywide electronic transfer of funds of £10,000 or over for same day settlement, with net outstanding balances settled daily through the Bank of England. This has reduced the volume of payments passing through the Town Clearing System, a process which involves the physical movement of cheques and vouchers between banks by messengers.

Future Applications of New Technology in Banking

Despite the above developments, banking still involves the massive distribution of paper and the handling of vast quantities of cash. It is therefore not surprising that futurologists speculate about the cashless society and the paperless office. Whether or not these will ever come about is a subject for considerable debate, but it is a safe prediction that cash and paper will be with us for a very long time to come. For all practical purposes thoughts of a cashless, paperless society can be ignored. Indeed, far from advancing towards the paperless office, computerisation seems to have been responsible for considerable growth in the amount of paper used in business today. Attempts will continue to be made to reduce the transmission of paper in banking but the forecast of annual cheque volumes of 3,250 million in 1966 is not exactly indicative of an imminent paperless banking system! An approach currently being developed uses electronic transmission of data instead of paper to effect payments. This is known as electronic funds transfer, or EFT for short. One application of EFT will enable shoppers to pay for goods directly at the point of sale through a system which will transfer the amount due from the bank account of the purchaser to that of the retailer: hence the expression EFT/POS – electronic funds transfer at point of sale. The system most likely to be introduced in the UK will use a plastic card containing an encoded magnetic strip which, when used by a customer of a bank in conjunction with the correct personal identification number, can activate a terminal at the counter or cash desk of any retailer using the system. A number of different systems are possible. The system may be on-line making the payment instantaneously or it may be off-line with batches of transactions being processed at the end of the day. Another possibility is to have an on-line system which checks at the time of sale that the cusomter has sufficient funds available to pay for the purchase but only debits his or her account at the end of the day. Another version uses a special plastic card in which a memory chip is embedded which is 'charged' with a certain amount of credit from which the cost of the purchase is electronically deducted at the point of sale. (It is in effect 'electronic cash'.)

There are a number of difficulties in introducing a POS system nationally. First, since retailers and other potential participants will not operate several systems, the banks and others involved have to agree collectively on the detailed specification of one system. Second, security must be absolute, not only to minimise fraud but to ensure consumer confidence in the system. Third, it must be foolproof technically and have 100% reliability. One only has to imagine the reaction in a major store on a busy Saturday afternoon if a technical fault were to put all of the tills out of action, even for a short period, to appreciate the importance of this. Fourth, there is the inevitable question of cost and, in particular, who is to bear the major cost of shop terminals and transmission time as well as of the computing and other technologies involved. POS is attractive to retailers. Used in conjunction with a laser device that reads a bar code on the product purchased and automatically inputs price and other information into the check-out terminal, it has great potential for speeding up checking out, thereby reducing queues. It can also simplify stock control and re-ordering procedures, eliminating a great deal of work. It can reduce the burden of having to handle large quantities of cash. POS systems will become a feature of banking in the UK. One survey has suggested that 80% of supermarkets and half of all department store cash points will be equipped with POS terminals over the next five years. The system could be applied to travel agents, railway stations, cinemas and restaurants as well as shops. Indeed, it can be used at most places where people buy things. But even if the introduction of POS systems is as widespread and as rapid as expected, they will make only a relatively small impact on the amount of paper moving through the UK banking system by the mid-1990s.

Another experimental development is home banking. This is a system which provides banking services through the domestic television set in conjunction with Prestel information systems. Although as yet these systems are at an early stage of development, it will be possible for a bank customer to use them to obtain direct, from the bank's computer, information about his account; to transfer money between different types of account; to pay bills, order and pay for goods and so on. The growth of home computers offers the prospect of a more sophisticated link which could be used to provide a wide range of financial services. Security is, of course, a major concern with any home banking system but significant advances in security systems have been made and as a result home banking is a development that can be expected to grow in the next few years.

A particularly significant development in the reduction of paperwork might well result from cheque truncation. At present, cheques are returned as part of the clearing process to the branch where the individual's account is held so that the validity of the signature on the cheque can be checked. Truncation seeks to transmit the relevant information electronically so making it unnecessary to send the cheque itself back to the branch, thereby eliminating the bulk of paper tranmission.

These are all developments in the area of retail banking but there are equally interesting developments in corporate banking. One example is electronic cash management or automated treasury management as it is increasingly being called. At the simplest level, this consists of an information link between the Treasurer's office in a company and the main computer of its banker. The treasurer can then be provided directly with up-to-date balances of various company accounts around the world, enabling him to switch money from one account to another electronically to take advantage of arbitrage, foreign currency exchange rate variations and other financial possibilities. At a more sophisticated level, not only is electronic payment possible but a range of decision support aids can be provided, including financial analysis and modelling. It is also possible to provide companies with a totally integrated treasury and accounting system as well as financial information retrieval. Other developments include foreign exchange dealing systems that record all transactions in detail as well as supplying information needed by dealers to make instant decisions and cross rate calculations.

Banks will also benefit from developments in technology that are not specific to banking. The ordinary office will become increasingly capital intensive incorporating the so called 'integrated electronic work station' whilst developments such as automatic translation phones, voice recognition systems and voice activated typewriters are of obvious application.

In summary, the application of new technology is taking banking into an integrated systems approach in which electronic data processing will inter-relate branch processing, ATM'S, on-line facilities, Point of Sale, home banking and credit and debit cards, as well as improved information to support management decision making. The main question is not so much what can be done as: what will customers find acceptable? What is the benefit compared with the cost and how long would it take to introduce those changes considered commercially advantageous? It is the rate of change more than the possible change that is of practical importance for staff working in the banks and it is the implications for staff of the above development that will now be considered.

Implications For Staff

NUMBERS OF PEOPLE NEEDED

Whenever the topic of new technology and its impact on staff is raised, the first concern normally expressed is in relation to employment. There is nothing new in fears about the impact of new technology on jobs. In the USA in 1934, one of the very first Gallup Polls asked people the reason for high unemployment. Most people blamed machinery. Another survey in Detroit in the 1950s asked people what they feared most. The majority put 'the Russians' first and 'automation' second. The Luddites are part of social history but concern about technology dates from much further back than them. For example, in 1397 a labour-saving device for automatically pressing pinheads was banned, and during the Middle Ages in England an Act of Parliament stopped merchants from setting up textile factories.

The available evidence to date indicates that computerisation has not reduced the number of people employed. In the London Clearing Banks the average number of persons employed in the UK increased from 195,863 in 1968 to 283,308 at the end of 1983. Despite the extensive application of technology referred to earlier in this chapter the number of staff employed has grown steadily. Of course, there has been a rapid increase in the volume of business carried out by the banks in this period. It is undoubtedly true that to cater for the same volume of business without computing, a much larger increase in staff would have been required. However, that begs the question whether it would have been possible to have coped with this level of business without computing. The situation is not unique to banking. A few years ago dire predictions were made about the impact of computers on the numbers of Civil Servants employed in the UK. Yet between 1970 and 1979 the number of major computer installations in the Civil Service rose from 107 to 140 and although the justification for each and every system was the staff saving it would make possible, in the same period staff in the categories most likely to be affected rose from 179,000 to 200,000. In the light of experience, therefore, why is so much conern expressed about the impact of new technology on employment? Part of the reason is the sheer scale of computing made possible by micro-electronics. As a result of technological development there has been a major reduction in the cost, size, power consumption and heat dissipation problems associated with earlier computers, as well as an improvement in performance and reliability. This has resulted in massive scope for innovation. It is therefore easy to talk about the micro-electronic revolution. Because offices in particular have been under-capitalised compared with, say, production units, scope for capitalisation of office work through the use of electronic systems is considerable. However, in reality we are not facing a revolution but a process of evolution. This does not stop some writers and commentators putting forward employment projections that are extremely pessimistic in terms of unemployment levels or from making alarmist projections about the elimination or de-skilling of a wide range of jobs.

Although there is no precise information available about the effects of new technology, one can reasonably point to a number of fallacies and weaknesses in many of the employment projections that have been made and can show basic flaws in the approaches used.

One can summarise the position by pointing to some of the reasons why the potential impact of new technology for altering jobs is likely either not to be realised at all or to take much longer:

1.   Just because something is technically feasible it is not necessarily economically viable and it is not necessarily inevitable that it will be introduced.

2. New developments take far longer in practice to introduce than is theoretically possible or is predicted by certain specialist commentators. It also takes longer to make changes to systems than it does to change products.

3. Dynamic elements arising from new technology are particularly difficult to forecast and an increase in productivity in service industries often leads to a greater variety of quality in the service provided rather than a reduction in numbers employed.

4. It is easy to emphasise the forces that cause change whilst ignoring the counter-pressures that slow it down.

In examining the likely rate of change in banking, it must not be forgotten that the industry has a heavy investment in people and systems as well as in an elaborate branch structure, and this level of investment limits the speed of change. New systems have to be introduced alongside existing ones and this often means greater complexity, cost and time in ensuring that the new system interfaces with existing ones. Furthermore, peoples' behaviour takes far longer to change than the time taken to introduce a new system or a new piece of equipment; it is one thing to talk about the electronic office but quite another to say how managers will overcome their present dependence on written material!

One of the most interesting of the numerous studies recently produced on new technology and employment is that by Mr. Amin Rajan of the Institute of Manpower Studies. In 'New Technology and Employment in the Financial Services Sector: Past Impact and Future Prospects' he develops the idea of 'moderators' that have to be taken into account when looking at the employment generation mechanism between new technology and jobs. These are the economic, social and organisational restraints which, at the very least, moderate or delay any adverse effect on labour of new technology and, in certain circumstances may even reverse it. His own forecast is that, although there will be a slowing down in the rate of increase of staff in the clearing banks compared with that experienced over the last ten years, there will none-the-less be a cumulative increase in numbers employed in the next few years.

A word of caution needs to be inserted when examining expected trends. The trends may be exactly right for the finance sector as a whole but there may still be a substantially different distribution of activity and services over the various institutions that make up the finance sector, including new entrants into the business of providing financial services. The clearing banks, for example, have no right to a particular share of the market. As technology reduces barriers to entry into financial markets, banks and others will have to work that much harder to maintain their present market share, let alone increase it. This will require first-class management and teamwork in the individual bank, for without it market share may well be lost to competitors; and although the market as a whole expands, an individual bank's activity level could still decline in the face of more effective competition.

If numbers of employees will not be dramatically reduced, the type of work performed will undoubtedly change. To take another analogy, the impact of technology in the transport industry has certainly led to a marked reduction of employment in shipping and in the docks. This has been more than offset by the remarkable growth of airlines and associated activities. However, many of the new jobs bear little or no relationship to those they have replaced. The potential that technology has for the creation of new services is considerable, and so it is more likely to lead to change in activity and to a change in the total level of service provided than to the overall level of employment.

In offices where past under-capitalisation compared with other sectors means there is considerable scope for the introduction of labour-saving equipment and for improved productivity, it is likely there will be a switch from unskilled to more highly skilled work. For example, certain relatively unskilled jobs such as filing clerk and accounts clerk are likely to be replaced by jobs requiring the manual dexterity and hand-eye co-ordination essential to keyboard skills. The critical question is whether the rate at which new and more highly skilled jobs are created will be greater than the rate at which unskilled employment falls, and the extent to which existing staff and new recruits can be trained to meet the demands of these new jobs. However, it does not necessarily follow that, where the activity and job content change, there will be changes in the qualifications or other features of the people required to perform the new job. For example, data preparation has changed out of all recognition since early forms of mechanisation such as Hollerith machines with their punched card input, or indeed the tape punching associated with early computers. It is doubtful if the type of person employed in data preparation today, or their educational qualifications, has changed at all. Machine operators working accounting machines in a branch of a clearing bank will have seen marked differences in the equipment they use, the speed with which cheques can be sorted, and the demands that the machines make. Very often the new machines are easier to operate than earlier models. None-the-less there has been no basic change in the type of person used to operate these machines.

In looking at the impact of technology on jobs, one has to be aware of the effect that technology has on the time discipline of individuals in relation to their job. Modern storage and retrieval facilities mean there may be much greater flexiblity as to when certain aspects of a job can be carried out. Many jobs that have been regarded as strictly sequential in nature and which have had to be done more or less continuously during the work period can now be performed in batches, completed work being stored and then processed at a convenient time, possibly after a branch or office has closed. Furthermore, instead of performing operations, employees are increasingly manipulating information about operations whilst computers do what was previously done manually. The flexibility that these changes permit is only just beginning to be appreciated but one effect will undoubtedly be an increase in part-time work. In the UK at present one in five of all those working in the regular, reported economy work part-time, often in a variety of patterns. Inevitably there will be an increase in this trend.

The other factor to be considered in looking at employment relates to comments earlier in this chapter on the high cost of money transmission services. The classic response to high cost in a service industry is self-service. There are countless examples of this. We take for granted self-service garages with hardly a thought about the electronics that make them possible. The growth of Do-It-Yourself shops and equipment hire shops is a response to high labour costs, and the advent of new materials has meant that many jobs previously requiring craft skills can now be performed by semi-skilled amateurs. Banking will be no exception to this tendency to self-service. Earlier in this chapter it was pointed out that self-service in banking has been spearheaded by ATM'S. This was a development primarily aimed at improving the flexiblity of the service to the customer but there is no doubt that other developments are bound to be introduced which will lead to more self service for economic reasons. This again will lead to changes in activity rather than to reductions in numbers of existing staff as banks expand their services into new areas of business.

Impact on Organisation

The organisational implications of technological change have yet to be fully realised but experience to date shows that new forms of organisation are often needed to resolve many of the problems found to arise with the introduction of new technology. The mere ability to obtain great quantities of information at high speed in a form suitable for direct use has implications for the decision-making processes in any business. The advance of technology results in new responsibilities and roles for technical, operational and administrative groups and increased dependence on support services. It may well have the effect of shifting some operational authority and power from line management to staff management because the latter control the computers.   Another effect may be to de-emphasise the importance of operations and give more power to the group responsible for the maintenance of the machine and its systems. In some of the sophisticated computerised systems now being developed, machines actually share with humans the control of the activities that take place in the organisation. The traditional form of organisation is based on inter-personal control; that is, some members of the organisation tell other members what to do. New technology introduces the idea of system control; the control the individual member has over the total achievement of the organisation is tied up with control exerted by the systems that have been introduced. Of course, ultimately both systems have human beings doing the controlling, but modern organisations highly dependent on new technology can increasingly be thought of, not so much as collections of people, but as collections of systems made up of human and non-human elements in which both influence to a different degree the outcome of their joint effort. Recognition of this has significant organisational implications.

In the first place, the relationship between man and machine is not straightforward. The first machines that were designed took no account of the needs of the humans who had to operate them. Gradually the science of ergonomics came into being 'fitting machines to the worker' and great progress was made in the design of machine controls and in methods of providing feedback from the machine and its processes to the operative. When mass production was introduced, assembly lines were designed that maximised production rates at theoretical levels which all too often failed to be met in practice. The production engineers assumed that people could be placed along the assembly line in some predetermined order and would then behave in some equally predetermined, pre-planned way. Unfortunately they didn't. Expressions like alienation, lack of motivation, limitation of output, withdrawal of labour became all too common. Ultimately researchers developed the concept of the socio-technical system, recognising the importance of introducing mechanisation without dehumanising work. This approach recognises that technicians can plan work in a way that maximises the effectiveness of the technical aspect of a system, but if the design of jobs and the methods of working ignore the human element the total may well function at well below the theoretical maximum. It may therefore be necessary to accept limitations to the technical system to accommodate certain human needs, but the final result will then be a more effective system overall. Although much of the work on socio-technical systems was done on assembly lines and in activities such as long-wall coal mining, the principle applies wherever man and machine are required to work together, including banking. The danger is that technical specialists will design systems solely with the aim of maximising that part of the total with which they are concerned, taking for granted the human input. Such an approach may lead to considerable problems and the lessons learnt elsewhere must be applied to the introduction of new technology in banking. This assumes, of course, that the introduction of new technology is actually planned. In reality there is a risk that technological change may be introduced in an *ad hoc* unplanned way. There are two quite separate forces at work; market pull and technology push. Developments usually come from a combination of both but it is necessary to be vigilant against introducing new equipment because of technological pressure unrelated to genuine commercial requirements. There is a tendency to want to introduce any development that appears to offer advantage provided financial or other resources permit. Not only must this not be done outside of an overall plan but it should be realised that the state of new technology today means that, instead of there being a surfeit of problems demanding technical solutions, in some activities there are multiple technological possibilities chasing relatively scarce applications. It is therefore essential to be quite clear about the objectives of the organisation, to define what information is required in the most cost effective way to achieve these objectives and to identify the problems or constraints that need to be overcome to do this. The technical specialists must then ensure that the best balance is obtained between the technical and social requirements of the new system.

The traditional form of organisation structure in banking is based on clear hierarchies in 'pyramid' form. This pattern is well suited to a business whose overall objectives can be broken down into a series of different tasks to be carried out at the various levels in the hierarchy, provided it is in a stable operating environment and the response time to the external environment is not critical. However, it is not so well suited to businesses in which technology is changing how they operate, and in which the information needed for decision-making is generated in a way that disregards the values of the established hierarchy. Systems based on new technology lead to an increased dependence on support services and staff and emphasise team work more than individual skills or status and position. Traditional hierarchies tend to support and give power, position, prestige and authority to older, experienced-based personnel, whereas in the new systems the younger, technical or professional person may be more important in providing solutions to operational problems. Traditional structures put great value on knowledge of the organisation and the particular company's business and such companies are often reluctant to recruit from outside on any scale. Technology-based organisations have key people whose career is based more on the technology than the particular company and who are thus much more mobile. Furthermore, they are likely to value wide experience, to look at challenges more in terms of particular projects than in terms of lifetime careers and be more concerned about getting out of date than about change.

The effect of changing to meet the needs of new technology may then result in tension and conflict which is nothing but a veiled expression of threats to traditional concepts of power and authority. Organisations will have to adapt to meet this challenge. Instead of vertical command with omniscience at the head they will need lateral consultation and joint decision-making. Jobs may lose much of their formal definition in terms of methods, duties and powers, instead of being related to a particular task immediately requiring attention. There is likely to be continual adjustment of tasks and structure through inter-action with others.

Earlier in this book, chapter 3, referred to the work of Burns and Stalker and their concept of mechanistic and organic (or 'organismic') systems. It is worth recapping the relationship between these in a number of key areas.

Mechanistic system	Organic system
• individual skills	• relationships between and within groups
• authority/obedience relationships	• mutual trust and confidence
• delegated authority and divided responsibility rigidly adhered to	• interdependencies and shared responsibility
• strict division of labour and hierarchical supervision	• multi-group membership and responsibility
• centralised decision making	• wide sharing of control and responsibility
• conflict resolution through suppression, or warfare	• resolution of conflict through problem solving

Banking seems to show the characteristics of a mechanistic system and this has worked very well in the stable conditions that have existed until now. However these conditions are changing and, as a result, the organisation itself will have to change. In predicting what that change will be it is reasonable to assume that banking will move much closer to the organic model in the future.

Recruitment and Promotion Prospects

Not only have recent years seen a substantial change in the technology employed in banking, they have also seen substantial changes in the division of labour which has particular implications for training. Although banks have always been fairly centralised, once they developed a national branch structure the relative importance of the Head Office function and the numbers employed there greatly increased. Over time, autonomy of the branches declined whilst the range and complexity of the financial services provided in conjunction with head office expanded. Recently some clearing banks have been moving towards what is known as 'satellite' banking. This means that in a particular geographical area there is a main branch which carried out the full range of banking activities with other branches in the area relying on that branch for specialist financial services which they no longer provide. Similar trends are likely in the future. As a result, some management positions that required a generalist banker approach will give way to more specialised posts. Clearly this has career development implications which, in turn, must be reflected in training practices.

In the clearing banks virtually all appointments are made from within, the philosophy being that any recruit is able to reach the highest levels of management on merit. Internal training programmes ensured that all staff received an all-round knowledge on most aspects of banking and the route to the higher levels was through the relevant professional examinations. This practice of promoting from within was not only confined to the mainstream activity of the bank but is also applied to other areas, including data processing. The approach became known as 'single tier recruitment'. Officially this approach still applies but there is now some change of emphasis in recruitment and it is likely to change formally in the not too distant future. The banks still recruit well qualified school leavers but there is more graduate or post-graduate recruitment for entry into special management development programmes. The trend in the future will increasingly be towards recruiting fewer, better qualified people who can expect accelerated promotion into the ranks of management if they are good enough, whilst the majority of other recruits are unlikely to move much beyond the clerical grades although there will be nothing to prevent them achieving higher promotion if they merit it. There is also another reason why single tier recruitment is likely to be abandoned in the future. School and college leavers today are far more familiar with computing and concepts of new technology than their predecessors but even so, there is likely to be a shortage of those able to cope with the demands that will be made by the management positions in banking in the future. Whether those who have the necessary abilities will be prepared to begin their careers by carrying out routine, low grade clerical work as at present must be open to question, particularly since other organisations in which they can commence their careers at a professional level will also try to recruit them.

In the large cheque-clearing departments staff need no particular qualifications and in some respects the work is not dissimilar to the routine, repetitive work found in manufacturing industry, whilst at the other end of the spectrum, highly qualified specialists are increasingly needed in specialist head office departments. Increasingly the banks will find it extremely difficult to 'grow their own' entirely and they will therefore need to compete for certain types of staff in the open market. The need for such specialists, many of whom will have data processing skills that are much in demand, will bring in individuals whose previous experience and work culture is quite foreign to banking and whose career aspirations will not fit into traditional banking patterns.

The effect that the career structure has had in banking is profound. Promotion has been the real reward for the bank employee. Loyalty to a career in the bank is fostered not only by the prospect of job security but by the prospect of promotion. Comparatively low earnings and status in the earlier years are balanced against the prospect of high earnings and responsibilities at a later stage. In practice, it is very difficult, if not impossible, to leave one clearing bank to join another. Thus overwhelmingly, possibilties for advancement are within the employee's own bank. However, changes in organisation and in the career structure are likely to put more value on the technical specialist. The concept of the all-round generalist banker that has existed for many years will break down as senior jobs are increasingly fragmented into a number of highly technical specialists. Many of those holding very senior positions in the future are likely to have extensive systems experience. Those with this type of knowledge and experience can be attracted to other industries; indeed, they may have come into banking from outside the industry and may move out of it again. This will make management development less predictable and will put more emphasis on the need to retain key people as well as the need to develop the skills necessary to recruit for senior positions, something the clearing banks have seldom had to do in the past. Change in the career pattern may have some marked effects. Once promotion prospects are perceived to have diminished, the natural tendency to ensure promotion by compliant and imitative behaviour could change and this may lead to more challenge from below in the management ranks or a less stable industrial relations environment at lower levels.

The impact of technology may also mean that significant competitive advantages may be gained by the employment of certain individuals, probably software designers, with exceptional talents. Since they will be in short supply, the traditional reluctance of banks to recruit from each other is likely to break down and they will then follow recruitment patterns widely practised in other industries. However, companies are in some ways like living bodies and some tend to reject 'transplants' from other organisations. Organisations' cultures vary quite considerably in their ability to absorb individuals from outside and the banks will have to learn how to modify themselves so they can introduce external talent effectively.

In some ways it is not difficult to see how many routine, relatively unskilled jobs could be changed by technology but technology will also affect more senior jobs too. The availability of more information on demand will enable loan decisions to be decentralised to a greater extent and credit scoring systems will be available which can automate many of these decisions. There will be emphasis on obtaining and checking information for input into databanks as well as updating that information. Experience shows that having more information available leads to even more information being required.

More and more information often seems to be required to do what you did before with less, and so the process of deciding what information is required and ensuring that it is available will become an increasingly important management task. Even so, computers are unlikely to provide all the information that is required and there seems always to be the need for human inputs with even the most sophisticated system.

New technology will change the content of managerial and other senior jobs and some activities will require more attention in future. More time will be spent on developing new services, marketing them and in finding new customers to take advantage of them. Technology will of itself create managerial demands as the banks themselves have to decide how to get a proper return on the ever growing capital investment they are making in new equipment and systems, whilst developing ways of deciding how to finance customers' investments in new technology and how to evaluate the soundness and potential return of such investments.

Training

Because promotion has been almost entirely from within, banks have had to invest heavily in training to support their policies of developing their own staff. They have some of the best training arrangements and facilities in the country. Not only will this investment continue but there will be even more emphasis put on training as the need to develop more specialists and up-date the skills of existing staff increases. Some things now learnt from experience will have to be taught systematically in the future. For example, much of the understanding of business and business accounts which leads to a bank manager's ability to judge a good business proposition probably comes from the time spent in the analysis and compilation of accounts in more junior positions as part of the process of preparing documents for approval of an advance. With the advent of the branch processor this work will be done by computer. How then will the bank manager of the future acquire this essential experience? Clearly it will have to be taught and to do this effectively will be a challenge that bank training departments will have to meet. No doubt other examples abound. Technology will undoubtedly lead to an increase in the number of training staff employed by the banks and training itself will make increasing use of new technology and computer aided learning systems. Although banks will still require in the future traditional skills and knowledge and the vital feel for a business, these will no longer be enough. Computer operations and new ways of processing and presenting information will be so vital to the day-to-day conduct of bank's business that the present division between data-processing skills, banking skills and management skills will become increasingly blurred. Eventually all senior managers in banking will be as familiar with data-processing and information technology as with traditional banking subjects. Banks will have considerable opportunity to reassess their information systems and will be able to change decision-making structures to take account of new business opportunity and challenges. This flexiblity will require a high degree of management ability as opposed to administrative skills. Progress in the bank will therefore go to individuals with significant managerial ability, data-processing knowledge and experience as well as banking ability. Managers at every level will be their own computer operators using a computer terminal as naturally as today they refer to a customer file or to a report. All of these developments have significant training implications and effective training can only grow in importance to the banks as a result.

Trade Union Considerations

Trade unions understandably have a concern about the impact of new technology on their members. Job losses, job design and content, health and safety, the implications for the working environment, involvement of employee representatives in management decision-making and ensuring their members gain improved terms and conditions of employment are areas in which the trade unions are actively interested to varying degrees.

Generally, in banking the trade unions are not against new technology as such. However, they do want the benefits of the technology to be shared against any threats that technology may present. Sometimes it appears that unions are taking an extreme position which no management could ever accept. This is particularly so when unions claim that technology should be used to reduce working hours, increase the length of holidays or reduce the retirement age to an extent which cannot possibly be justified in any commercial setting. Some unions also appear to be deliberately fuelling the worst fears of their members by making extreme predictions about the dire consequences of new technology. It has to be recognised that unions seek to achieve a number of objectives. High on the list of these objectives is recruitment of new members. Many of the extreme statements made by unions about technology aim to frighten non-members to such an extent that they will join a trade union to gain protection. Such tactics often prove to be counter-productive.

Unions approach the subject of technology in a number of ways. First, they seek to establish consultative or, if they can achieve it, negotiating committees, at which management regularly discusses and possibly has to seek agreement on all aspects of new technology. Although it is right and proper that any management should consult with employees on matters that affect them, it is hard to see how any employer can put himself in a position where unions control the rate at which he introduces something as essential to the viability of his business as new technology. Second, unions may seek a formal signed agreement with an employer covering the introduction of new technology. This will almost certainly seek a commitment that there will be no involuntary redundancy as a result of the introduction of new technology. It is unlikely that an employer who had seriously thought about the implications of such a commitment would be prepared to give a blanket or unqualified assurance on this. In practice it is often impossible to isolate the factors that may lead to any particular situation and it is not always clear whether the need to change manning levels is due to new technology, changes in the market, economic factors or some other cause. Usually an employer will only be prepared to go as far as to say that he will take all steps possible to minimise or avoid the need for involuntary redundancy and this may be modified by including some minimum notice period, or other time, following an introduction of new equipment, during which no manning levels would be reduced.

Third, unions will normally seek some involvement prior to the introduction of new equipment and for an opportunity for employees to be involved in planning prior to its introduction. They are likely to want to have a say in the design of the work place, including minimum standards concerning the environment in which new equipment is used. Fourth, although employers should be anxious to avoid the restrictions that are associated with anything that resembles paying for change, trade unions can be expected to seek a commitment that their members receive financial rewards and perhaps longer holidays or shorter working hours in return for co-operation with the introduction of new technology and such claims will have to be dealt with.

Some of the above points are not contentious and will be willingly accepted by most employers. However, no employer is likely to put himself in a position where the introduction or the operation of new technology can be vetoed by unions. In practice the weakness of a trade union's position in trying to enforce unreasonable demands in relation to new technology lies in the fact that the vast majority of staff welcome new technology and find that it actually makes work less arduous.

Although trade unions are aware of and are concerned about a number of problems related to the introduction of new technology, they recognise that total opposition to technological change is not feasible. Generally they accept that an increase in their members' standard of living is dependent upon harnessing technological development. Thus, rather than outright opposition, the trade union concern is to ensure that technology is introduced at a pace at which its social impact can be fairly spread and to ensure that the benefits of new technology accrue to their members. They also realise that in a competitive environment, failure to keep up with advances made by competitors will of itself result in job losses that could be significant in scale.

Finally, a major concern of a trade union is to increase its membership's education regarding technology, not so that they become computer experts but rather to make as many of them as possible aware of the effects of technological change and the benefits trade unionists should expect to obtain from new systems at work. They are also concerned about possible changes in career structures previously mentioned in this section. They are concerned that fewer employees will need higher levels of qualifications, that staff might suffer a reduction in the skills they need and that some jobs could be de-skilled. The approach by the employer should recognise that technology is not a potential battleground between management and employees and their representatives. It is an area of potential positive co-operation. But employees do have genuine concerns and these must be brought into the open, fully discussed and all possible reassurances given in a spirit of openness. Managers should also recognise that if technology is to be of benefit, employees must share in that benefit to a reasonable extent.

Health and Safety

In introducing any new equipment it is necessary to consider the health and safety implications for those working with that equipment. Although one often associates questions of health and safety at work with possible external harm involving accidents, the questions that arise with new technology in banking are very different. Generally banking does not involve work with mechanical components; thus the risk of external physical injury caused by coming into contact with the dangerous part of a machine is far less than in, for example, manufacturing, agriculture, mining or fishing. This type of risk to one's safety therefore is not great in banking except in very special areas. Risk to one's health is a different consideration however. This has to be considered in terms of physical factors or ergonomic considerations relating to the equipment used and to posture and the repetitive nature of work as well as psychological factors associated with noise, organisation of work, rest breaks and facilities.

The most widely used piece of equipment associated with new technology is the visual display unit. Consideration of the luminance or brightness of the characters upon the screen is important. These must be bright enough for easy legibility yet not so bright as to cause undue tiredness to the eyes of the user. Flicker is another consideration as is the contrast between the colour of the screen and the colour of the characters portrayed upon that screen. The shape of the characters projected on the screen and the number of dots which make it up can affect legibility. The most important point in relation to character generation on a VDU is for the contour and the character to be as sharp as possible to permit the eye to focus properly. This is both a function of the original design of the equipment and the age and state of repair of the cathode ray tube itself. Regular maintenance of VDU's is important.

If the above points have not been properly considered, it is possible that users may develop eye strain, headaches and stress related symptoms. Keyboards of a visual display unit also need careful design and positioning and this requires certain ergonomic principles to be taken into account. The ambient lighting around VDU screens has to be arranged so that it does not reflect off the screen and dazzle the user of the equipment. Unions often pursue the question of eye tests for those working with VDU's either as part of general safety requirements or as a voluntary measure on the part of the employer. The reaction to this varies from employer to employer but many will arrange eye tests for staff prior to their starting work and at regular intervals thereafter. Unions frequently claim that if needed, eye glasses should be provided by the bank at its expense.

Any activity which is staffed with numbers of young women and which involves a high level of usage of electronic equipment is bound at sometime to be subject to concerns about possible hazards to unborn children. In recent years there have been a number of such concerns expressed about visual display units and terminals. These have been the subject of the most rigorous examination by occupational health specialists and scientists in a number of countries and have convincingly been shown to be entirely groundless. None-the-less, purely emotive doubts may still exist and some employers have recognised this and stated that expectant mothers who are at all troubled at the thought of working for long periods with VDU's may be moved to other work for all or part of the working day where this can reasonably be provided.

Other important considerations affecting health and safety of employees at work cover the design of chairs, desks and counters, particularly where staff work at a work station which requires a different posture for different functions. In some countries problems have been found resulting from work involving rapid repetitive movements such as performed by typists, key-punch operators and VDU operators. This may lead to condition known as tenosynovitis but it can be avoided by job rotation and changes in routine. Occasionally problems of noise arise with some equipment. Printers, for example, can produce a particularly irritating noise; so can photocopiers. This means care when selecting the equipment and in designing the environment in which particular items are operated. It is important that, when new technology is introduced in the workplace, there is scope for proper breaks from the work and often facilities such as rest rooms and refreshment machines are provided to ensure there are no grounds for allegations of physical or mental stress at the place of work.

Other considerations to be taken into account include such things as heating, humidity, ventilation and dust and the use of chemicals at work.

The above are only some of the considerations that need to be taken into account when introducing new equipment and this is a subject about which specialist advice is needed at the planning stage.

Conclusion

A short chapter such as this can do no more than indicate some of the changes that are likely to take place in the available technology, the applications of it in banking, and the possible implications of staff. It is tempting to think that as time goes by the position will become clearer. This is not likely to happen; the rate of growth of technology is such that more and more possible applications are appearing all the time and, as a result, the future position actually becomes less clear and less predictable all the time.

It is important to recognise that we are not at some fundamental crossroad in our industrial history; we are in a process of evolution. Rapid it may be, but none-the-less it remains evolution and we can look at present and future developments as part of a continuum. A major consideration in this is the slowing down effect on change of the investment the banks have made in staff, buildings and capital equipment. This means that the impact of technology on staff will take place at a much slower rate than some forecasters predict, and at a pace where the change and the impact can be managed.

However, the introduction of technology must be planned and the social implications of new methods of working built into the design of the systems of the future. Technology will then remain the servant of man; rather than man becoming an unwilling slave of technology.

CHAPTER 8

Communications and Participation

Leif Mills

General Secretary, Banking Insurance and Finance Union

Banking is one of the key sectors of the British economy and it is essential that there should be an effective system of communications and participation throughout. That, of course, is easy to say but can be difficult in implementation – an effective system of communications and participation depends upon the purpose of it as viewed by the various parties, the size of the individual banking institution, the degree of unionisation and the internal organisational structures of those institutions. Because of the nature of banking business, the question of confidentiality of information as between competing banking institutions is also an important aspect.

Generally, all political parties in the country are committed to the aim of an expanding economy, the hope for full employment for all those seeking work, and the involvement of the community to achieve these ends. No reasonable man would gainsay the worth of these ends. It is when one comes to translate these broad strategic aims to particular items of policy, that contentious and indeed emotive debate takes place. It is easy to generalise about the macro economic state of the nation and, indeed, many do so who pay little attention to the micro economic state of the particular company or institution in which they are involved.

Involvement of Staff

There are few industrialists or financiers who would not concede that the well-being of their particular enterprise in part depends upon the involvement of their staff in the future of that enterprise. In a crucial sense, this is what the whole debate on communications and participation is about: *how does one achieve the involvement of people, and more particularly in what way does one achieve it?* It is when one makes that crucial jump from macro economic generalisations to micro economic application that the problems of communications and participation become both pertinent and difficult.

In the UK's financial sector it is more important than ever that those who work in it should appreciate both the strategic aims of the financial institution by which they are employed, but also should be involved in how those aims are practically going to be achieved.

The classic argument against central state interference in any activity is that those nearer to the ground both know the position better and will do it anyway. The reality of the situation belies this: the degree to which there is effective communication and participation in the financial sector or indeed almost any other sector of the British economy, is appallingly low, particularly when compared to that existing in our major economic competitor countries. Perhaps part of the problem is the *confusion over the purpose of participation and communication.*

In a sense, debate about the involvement of employees in the management of institutions has in turn been over-shadowed by political expressions as to the ultimate purpose of that involvement.

The UK's financial sector is a large employer of labour. The London clearing banks alone employ over 280,000 people. The Scottish clearing banks employ some 24,500. The TSB Group employ just under 20,000 and there are a host of other financial institutions, finance houses, international banks, insurance companies, insurance brokers and many others. If one takes the definition of banking, insurance and finance in line with the Department of Employment's Standard Industrial Classification, the number of those employed is $1\frac{1}{4}$ million. This includes a number of people in bill-broking, estate agencies, various firms of accountants as well as the mainstream areas of what is traditionally regarded as banking, insurance and finance. A realistic figure, though, for those in the 'mainstream' is some 8–900,000. This is the figure which the TUC's Committee on Financial Services has adopted as the realisable potential in trade union terms of all those who work in the financial sector.

The finance sector is, therefore, by any definition, a large employer of labour and is increasingly so. It may well be that future employment is directly affected by the application of technology. Up until now, the effect of technology has been that banking business can expand with a lesser increase in staff than would otherwise be needed. In ten years' time there could well be a decline in numbers involved. But even so, the total numbers employed will still be large. It is accordingly crucial that there should be an effective means of communication to and from those who are employed and participation by those who are employed in the objectives of those institutions.

As well as the size of the institutions concerned, the other significant factor affecting any debate at the moment about communications and participation, is the *structure* of those institutions and the changes taking place in that structure.

Communications

At the turn of the century communications presented relatively few problems as the function of all banks or insurance companies was clearly defined and understood and the size of individual institutions was relatively small. The banking mergers in the first two decades of this century made the problem more acute. The banking mergers of the late 1960's and early 1970's increased this problem. The expansion of banks and insurance companies into each other's business and indeed new areas had meant an increase in size of the institutions with the impersonalisation that goes with this.

It is now no longer possible to draw a clear distinction between what is a bank, an insurance company, a finance house or even a building society. After all, banking insurance broking subsidiaries are now important in the insurance broking world. Lloyds Bank is the biggest estate agent in the country. Building societies are direct competitors for deposits and offer a range of special savings and deposit accounts. Insurance companies are merging and competing with banks through the issue of unit trust linked bonds and deposit schemes for the money that would previously have gone straight to a traditional bank. With the abolition of single capacity dealing in the Stock Exchange, banks are now buying significant shareholdings in stockbroking firms and – when the regulations are relaxed – will undoubtedly buy majority shareholdings in those firms. The trend of all these changes is for banks and others to become more akin to the German type of universal financial institution – an institution offering a wider range of services in the attraction of deposits, the lending and the saving of money, and in other areas such as the provision of finance for house building.

It is not surprising in view of all this that the need to involve staff in the objectives of the institutions – and to be actually aware of those objectives – takes on an increasing importance. Unfortunately, given the state of political debate in the UK, important subjects seem to have a temporary life-span in terms of public interest. In the mid-1970's employee participation was very much a live issue. It is now very much dormant.

The veto by the British Government in the Council of Ministers of the EEC of the Vredling Directive, has been largely ignored in the media and elsewhere – and yet such a fundamental expression of political opinion would have led to extreme concern and indignation some ten years ago.

The view of BIFU is quite clear. The UK's financial sector is important in terms of the country's economy, its growth, its future prosperity, and in terms of numbers of people currently employed and those who will be employed in the future. It is therefore vital that there should be an effective system of communications and participation throughout the banks, finance houses and companies that make up that financial sector.

At the moment it is not happening. The current Government's view is in general one of opposition to formalised procedures for communications and participation, and it would appear that it was because of that that the Government vetoed the Vredling Directive within the EEC process. However, it would seem that British participation within the European community does represent the best immediate hope of getting something done on this subject because if it were left to the individual managements within the financial sector, then inactivity would be the order of the day.

Participation

There have been many formulae put forward on communications and participation, varying from mild forms of consultative committees and house magazines – together with such items as profit sharing – through to the other end of the spectrum of organised union committees and, in some cases, workers co-operatives.

Partly because of our membership of the European Economic Community, the subject became a real one in the mid 1970's. The UK Government in August 1975 announced their decision to appoint a Committee of Inquiry '. . . to advise on questions relating to representation at board level in the private sector'. This Committee, under the chairmanship of Lord Bullock, reported in January 1977 and enjoyed the unfortunate distinction of producing a report that was roundly attacked before it had even been published. It was perhaps one of the most leaked committees there has been since the War. In essence, its recommendations were for a statutory right to a ballot to allow participation in private sector companies employing 2,000 people or more. It did so through the medium of a formula of equal employee and employer representatives on a board of directors, with a third element being those from outside. It also made the valid point that employee representation was best effected through organised employees – that is, trade unions.

It was clear at the time that, given the parliamentary position of the Government – and the attitude of all parties to the report – that it would be a difficult task to translate the Bullock recommendations into practice. My own union at the time agreed in Conference that the Bullock Report represented a significant move in the right direction. We also made the crucial point at the time that employee participation at board level in private sector companies was only the icing on the cake and that it should only come about providing there was an effective structure and participation in financial institutions at national, regional and local level in all the many decision-making processes that were appropriate for participation.

It was a pity then and it is a pity now that so much of the debate on participation has centralised round the concept of board membership, when really that by itself is meaningless unless there is an effective system of participation throughout the company.

At that time, significantly, the minority report to Bullock had an even less favourable reception than the majority report. The three minority signatories to that report naturally criticised the original terms of reference to the Committee (with indeed some justification), made a number of rather superficial comments about the majority proposals being 'the thin end of the wedge' and stated that their proposals indicated 'a method of infiltration which could eventually lead to trade union/worker control' – although this does seem to ignore the whole ethos behind the majority report. In particular, the minority report advocated a two-tier board system, but then stated that none of their proposals should apply in the financial sector because of the alleged aspect of confidentiality.

The Bullock Report was laid to rest. In its place the Government issued a White Paper in May 1978 on industrial democracy. This was subsequently translated into a Bill. It carried forward much of the original Bullock proposals but did make the basic change of proposing a two-tier board system instead of the unitary board systems favoured by the Bullock Committee.

The White Paper received the same hostile reaction as the majority report of Bullock had received. At the time – June 1978 – the Director General of the Institute of Directors commented on this by stating ' . . . let us mark the White Paper on so-called 'industrial democracy' for what it is – the high-jacking of the nation's wealth-making vehicle by the trade union movement and let us resist it with all the strength we can muster'.

The Bill lapsed with the election of 1979 and since then the impetus for any statutory form of participation has come from the European Economic Community.

EEC Measures

The two measures from the EEC on participation which have caused comment and concern, are the *Draft Fifth Directive* from the Commission and the *Draft Vredling Directive*.

The Fifth Directive was first issued in 1972 and it currently proposes that in public limited companies of 1,000 employees or more, the employees should have certain statutory rights to influence decisions taken by the Board of Directors. It does not propose a form of workers' control, but does propose that all member countries of the EEC should be required to adopt one of the four different systems of employee representation ranging from worker directors to schemes that could be negotiated through collective bargaining.

The Fifth Directive has been likened to the Loch Ness Monster in that both are sighted only occasionally and then seen to disappear without trace. Both are the subject of periodic publicity and each is then the subject of speculation and argument as to what its shape and direction is.

It is unclear whether the Fifth Directive will pass the crucial hurdle of the Council of Ministers and then be adopted within the EEC member countries.

The Vredling Directive was originally aimed at multinational companies, but now its scope is wider and it would apply to any company which has at least 1,000 employees employed within the EEC as a whole even if the base of the company is outside the EEC. The aim of the Directive is to give employees rights on information and consultation and in particular to -

(a)   general information on the company as a whole to be given on an annual basis;

(b)   specialised information prior to any major decision taken by the company which is liable to have a serious effect upon the employees;

(c)   prior consultation on any such major decision, with the management and the company being obliged to defer any actual decision for at least 30 days to allow for that consultation to take place.

It was that Vredling Directive which the UK Government opposed but which was supported by the other countries.

There are three basic trade union attitudes in the UK to the whole question of particiation.

One is outright opposition as it would cut across the traditional – and in my view somewhat archaic – symbolic confrontation of union and employer in collective bargaining.

The second is that participation should be welcomed to the extent of having 50% plus membership on boards of directors of companies, which would then be taken as the first step towards workers' control of those companies.

The third view is the more realistic one in that there is a case – and an urgent one – for more consultation and participation and that, as far as membership of boards of directors is concerned, this should mean limited participation together with an underlying network of participation at regional and local level.

The trade union attitudes will vary according to how one defines the purpose of participation. If the purpose is eventual workers' control, then clearly the second option is that which those concerned will support. If the purpose is to continue what is increasingly an old-fashioned type of collective bargaining, then the first option would be supported. However, if the purpose is to make staff aware of what their managements are doing, both tactically and strategically, and to ensure that staff are motivated to support those objectives and can have an input into how those objectives are developed, then the third option is that which is preferable.

An example of effective participation in banking in our experience has been in the trustee savings banks.

The Trustee Savings Banks

The TSBs have undergone a fundamental transformation in the last ten years, both in internal structure and from being deposit-taking institutions into lending banks with all the functions that modern commercial banks have. Some twenty years ago our participation in the TSBs was through the medium of collective bargaining at national level with the TSB Employers Council and then at local level with the individual 83 banks. Following the 1976 TSB Act and the reduction in the numbers of individual banks to 17, so our involvement increased – and it was important that this should be so in order that staff could be fully involved in the transformation of the TSBs from being a public sector body whose funds were deposited with the National Debt Office and whose investments and securities were strictly limited to gilt-edged, into being one which can operate in the market as much as any other commercial bank. Accordingly, in addition to national negotiations with the TSB Group, we established with the management Joint Consultative Committees in each of the constituent banks.

Our own union structure was changed to conform with the bank structure through the medium of Regional Committees. The Regional Committees corresponding to the individual banks elected members to a National TSB Council; the Regional Committees also had representatives directly on the individual bank Joint Consultative Committees.

The process has been taken further with the restructuring of the TSBs into four banks – Northern Ireland, Scotland, England and Wales, and Channel Islands. England and Wales and Scotland are clearly the two biggest and the ones in which we are directly involved (in addition to the Channel Islands).

Although the banks have been amalgamated and many functions centralised, there is still, though, a case for regional consultations and, whereas under the old system there were 11 constituent banks in England and Wales, with corresponding Joint Consultative Committees, there are now going to be six Regions and each of those Regions will have a local Negotiating Committee which will deal with particular issues relating to that Region in the bank and also act as a means of consultation and participation. Similarly, in Scotland there will be one Local Negotiating Committee covering the four Regions of the TSB Scotland.

In addition to this, we still negotiate at national level with the TSB Group and through a number of national sub-committees. We also have a Consultative Group consisting of the Chief General Manager, the General Manager TSB Scotland, and the General Manager Personnel. The union's senior lay and full-time officials in the TSBs are also members and are kept fully briefed and also involved in the structural changes to the TSBs, the timescale for parliamentary legislation to complete the process of turning the TSBs into an ordinary commercial bank, the speed and type of introduction of new technology, and the new services which the TSB Group is continually offering to its customers. Points that are raised in this Consultative Group can then be referred back to the union's own structure or alternatively to the Board of the TSB Group.

We have been pushing for an extension of this through the medium of membership of the Central TSB Board and also the boards of the constituent banks. We believe that this would be helpful and in a sense be a practical symbol of full employee participation at all levels. We are still pushing for this – two or three representatives on the board of the constituent banks at national level – and will continue to do so as the new TSB legislation goes through Parliament.

However, the above is an example and while our attitude to communication and participation in the TSB is very much one of practicality, nevertheless trade unions as a whole have still not defined their attitude because of this basic difference as to the purpose of effective communication and participation.

At the 1984 TUC a motion was passed without dissent which stated –

'Congress notes that workers facing redundancy or privatisation have no legal rights in the events of closure, change of ownership, privatisation/contracting out/hiving off, to compel employers to disclose information, and that this deficiency seriously affects the ability of unions to prepare realistic alternative costings and plans.

Congress notes the progress made on the draft European Directive on informing and consulting employees in multi-plant and multinational companies which has become known as the 'Vredling Directive'.

Congress regrets the role played by the Conservative members of the European Parliament and their political allies in watering down the original proposals in the European Parliament but recognises that the final compromise agreed between the Commission and the Parliament represents a step forward in enabling workers to gain access to information and for unions to have enhanced consultation rights.

Congress condemns the actions of the British Government in vetoing the proposals in the Council of Ministers and similarly stopping the Commission's recommendations on shorter hours of work. Congress calls for a campaign by the Movement to reverse these blocking moves by the British Government.

Congress believes that a statutory right to trade union access to all relevant data, including such information as comprehensive details of transfers, company output, balance sheets, sales and customers, and detailed contract tenders is indispensable and calls on the General Council to press for its early introduction.

In many ways TUC motions are designed to get maximum unity to a form of words rather than define clear objectives.

Progress in the EEC

In most of our fellow member countries of the European Economic Community there is, by statute, provision for employee participation in both public and private sector companies which include financial institutions. A similar position exists outside the EEC in respect of Norway and Sweden.

In Sweden, for example, company law states that at least two staff representatives should be appointed to the unitary boards of each bank – not branch – employing 50 or more staff.

The experience of employee participation both within and without the EEC in Europe, has been twofold: first, it has resulted in more awareness of the staff and their unions of the strategic decisions and problems facing the managements of financial institutions; second, it has not resulted in any of the prophesied fears of inability to manage, or union takeover of management functions.

One of the problems, however, that has beset legislation on participation in the UK is the somewhat false argument of whether participation should be through trade union channels or on an individual basis. In Norway, Sweden and Denmark this is not a problem in banking because the trade unions there have a membership of some 85–95% and therefore employee representation invariably means union representation. A lesser position exists, for example, in the Netherlands and West Germany. It is interesting to note, however, that in West Germany, the majority of those staff elected to serve on the supervisory boards of companies are themselves union members in spite of the fact that trade union membership generally in West Germany is lower than it is in the UK – and in banking terms, considerably low.

One of the objections to employee participation at board level is that it would inhibit management of banks and other financial institutions from discussing their future strategy because the union members could belong to a union which is involved in competitor banks and companies. There has been real apprehension about this, but the experience of European countries would point to the fact that in practice this fear has not been realised.

Indeed, the so-called problem of confidentiality exists anyway. My own union deals with a whole range of banks and financial institutions and we are necessarily privy to certain strategic plans of one bank which could not be disclosed prematurely to a competitor. That confidentiality on the part of the union has always been observed and it is only a difference of degree and not of substance to follow that line of multi-bank/union involvement to one of employee participation where members of a board of a bank are also members of a wider union.

This is not to pretend that all employers in these countries are euphoric over statutory employee participation nor that there are other problems arising from this. In West Germany, for example, only public companies are able to raise equity funds in the share markets and to become a public limited company means that the statutory regulations on participation would apply. Partly because all German Plc's are required to let their employees nominate at least one-third of the Supervisory Board – apart from the statutory regulations concerning the necessity for Supervisory Boards themselves, for annual accounts to be testified by an independent auditor, and for an annual report to be published – there is a tendency for owners of small and medium-sized companies to regard a Plc as a rather unattractive form of company organisation. In some cases, therefore, companies will establish themselves as private limited companies even though the marketability of its equity is consequently much reduced.

This is perhaps a problem more in Germany than in the UK where there is, in any event, a much different attitude to gearing than there is in the UK. The proportions of debt to equity in most German companies is significantly higher than it is in the UK.

On the other hand, it must be said that German companies which do have employee participation on Supervisory Boards do not express themselves in any way as disenchanted with the result. They would be concerned if half employee representation on the Supervisory Board led to either deadlock or union control, but the current position of shareholders' representatives having the final say has allayed any such apprehension.

We firmly believe that there should be participation at all levels of every type of financial institution, particularly banks, and that this should embrace membership at board level – i.e. some two or three persons elected onto the board of each bank who would be so elected through union channels.

The argument could become one of whether such persons would be representative. However, we continually have to remind ourselves that we do not live in an age of Athenian democracy but one of representative democracy, and that those elected to positions of responsibility must be responsible themselves to the body that elects them and this can only be done in a structured sense. In terms of employee representation, that structure exists within trade unions.

It is arrant nonsense to suggest that appointing certain of the general management of the banks as Executive Directors is in some way a substitute or alternative to employee participation. It is equally nonsensical to suggest that having individual members of staff serving on the board is somehow a credible solution to the problem of participation. After all, to whom would such people be responsible?

Accountability

Of course, this question of *accountability* is more readily solved in a position where trade union membership represents by far and away the vast majority of the employees of the bank. It should, however, not be taken as a reason for not doing so where trade union membership could well be under 50% of a bank's employees.

Much depends upon the state of unionisation within a company or institution. Where there is no trade union at all then a company can institute employee participation with employee directors, but the basic problem would remain: to whom would those employee directors be accountable – apart from the board – and how could such an unstructured system operate effectively? Where a number of unions are organised in a company or institution – and this is a problem particularly mentioned in the Bullock Report – then perhaps a joint union panel could nominate those concerned for participation and possibly board directors. This would be clearly unsatisfactory but in a sense is part of the price for the existing union multiplicity that exists within companies today.

Where there is a single trade union operating in a company or institution (and this applies in many banks at the moment) then there are two schools of thought: first, that an employee participation structure including employee directors should run parallel with a union structure. This to my mind is both cumbersome and divisive and could well lead to, at worst, rivalry between the two structures or, at best, some confusion between individuals trying to perform two basic roles within different structures; second, that an effective system of participation should only operate if union membership is above a certain level – otherwise there should be a dual system as referred to earlier. To my mind, again this is confusing and possible divisive.

The most obvious course would be to accept that where a trade union has a negotiating agreement within a company or institution then that trade union should be the vehicle for an employee participation structure. The actual percentage of trade union membership would be irrelevant for this purpose because the issue of whether that trade union is recognised for negotiating purposes will have been dealt with by the management concerned when agreeing to the original negotiating agreement.

Purpose of Participation and Communications

There is then the whole question of the purpose of participation and communciations.

The purpose of participation is to involve people in decisions; and the purpose of communication should be to keep people involved as to what decisions are contemplated and what the effect of those decisions is likely to be.

Some banks in the UK at the moment have a structure of Consultative Committees or staff communication meetings whereby directives from Head Office are discussed at local level and a feedback is then given from local level to Head Office. Clearly, there is nothing wrong *per se* in such committees or meetings provided that their terms of reference are clearly defined and also that they are not used as a substitute for participation. Participation, after all, does mean having some positive influence in the decision-making process.

All too often, bank views on consultation and participation have consisted in telling their employees – often through the union – of what they are intending to do.

In fact, effective communication and participation does mean impinging directly on management decisions *before* they are finally reached. This may well be intolerable to certain bank managements, but the corollory is clear in that such a system does place responsibility on the participants themselves.

Our central view is that there should be an effective system of consultation and participation at all levels of a bank or other financial institution – this means at local, area/regional level, culminating in a national level. This has worked in the Trustee Savings Banks and this could work elsewhere. We believe that the ultimate expression – the icing on the cake – should be two or three members on the boards of the banks concerned. We readily accept that having board members by themselves without the underlying sub-structure of participation is worse than useless.

Indeed, one of the problems with the original British Steel Corporation experiment of Worker Directors was that the individuals concerned had no role or function to play in any part of the corporation. Unions distrusted their role and they themselves were unsure of it.

In Williams & Glyn's Bank we had for some years, a system of Consultative Committees at local level and regular discussions at central level with the bank on its plans.

At the same time as this, both in Williams & Glyn's and in most other banks, we have also extended the area of Negotiating Committee. It is now common for there to be negotiating committees – and subsequently union committees which correspond to this – for specialised groups in the bank such as trustee and tax staff, data-processing staff, secretarial staff, technical and services staff and many others. That structure of committees in itself is important and such a structure can be used to consult and communicate what is happening in specialist divisions and companies of banks. At the end of the day, though, there should be a co-ordinating body at central level and this is what is often lacking.

Our experience also shows that, in some cases, managements of banks try – albeit disingenuously – to use the network of consultative committees/staff communication meetings as an alternative channel for the views of their employees on matters which should ultimately be the subject of collective bargaining. It is all very well to accuse unions of being unsure of the real purpose of communications and participation: it is a fair point to make that many bank managements themselves seem to be ambivalent about the purpose at the moment.

The experience of some of our colleagues in Scandinavian banking unions on employee participation – particularly at board level – is that they have secured more information about the future plans of the banks and as a consequence have participated in the likely effects of such plans, and their views have been taken into account before final decisions are made. A particular example of this was in a major Scandinavian bank over the siting of a computer centre – its move away from the head office of the bank – and the timing and practicality of such a move. This does place an onus on the employee directors to report back to their union structures and it also places a responsibility on the unions to accept the consequences that flow from certain board decisions.

Of course, it would been entirely wrong for employee directors to get involved in board decisions about the level of pay increases that might result from collective bargaining. On the other hand, it is eminently sensible that employee directors – and through them the unions to which they report – should be aware of the balance sheet of the various banks and the effect of pay claims and settlements on the balance sheet and, above all, on banking profitability.

The content of participation does involve an awareness of all aspects of a bank or company or institution and the effect of its existing operations and, more importantly, its proposed operations.

In recent years much of the debate of communications and participation has centred around the introduction of new technology. If there are two issues on which trade unions are more concerned than any other today in the UK, they are the unemployment level and the economy as a whole, and the effect of technology – and the two are related.

New Technology

We receive a certain amount of information at individual bank level and at inter-bank level on technology and the development of CHAPS II, electronic funds transfer/point of sale, cheque truncation, and many others: and indeed we cannot complain at receiving such information nor would we seek to do so. However, the problem occurs of receiving information as to what is *actually* being done and the repercussions of this upon individual banks and their staffing and branch structures.

We have consistently argued as a union that each bank and financial institution should conclude a *new technology agreement* with us which allows for a proper procedure for the introduction of technology to be discussed with the union and its effects to be negotiated as they concern staff, their jobs and career prospects. With limited exceptions we have not yet got over the hurdle of convincing bank managements that such technology agreements will not infringe their right to manage, but will in fact make the introduction of technology more well-received, will allay apprehensions and will be done in a fashion that could benefit the staff, the bank and the customer.

Training

The concept of involvement in board decisions involves a responsibility on the part of employee board members to be conversant with all major aspects of the board's deliberations. It would be foolish merely to have employee directors to be devoted exclusively to particular items affecting the employment conditions of employees. Equally, it would be naive to assume that employee directors could be as fully conversant with all the financial aspects that concern a board as are some of the other board members. However, some *training* in the scope and function of a board – particularly the financial structure of the company – is essential.

Equally, it would be important at the lower levels of the company for there to be effective training on the wider aspects of the company, its range of products, new services it is developing, new types of technology that are available to it, its relationship with other companies or institutions in the same field, the effect of legislation upon board decisions – all of these are matters which do require training in order to assist some knowledge of, as well as involvement in, decisions which are taken in the consultative process.

Conclusion

Our general concern as a union is to ensure that the City of London retains its pre-eminence in the world's money markets and as the world's financial centre. Our concern is also that British banks should be profitable and provide an increasingly better level of service to customers. It is equally our interest that this can be done while staff benefit from all the changes that are taking place and are not adversely affected by technology, branch network reviews or changes in bank functions.

Communications and participation are essential if that aim of the City of London pre-eminence and banking profitability is to be maintained, providing that it is equally accepted that the staff themselves have a legitimate function and role in the achievement of those ends through their union.

CHAPTER 9

Organisation Development and the Management of Change

Allan P. O. Williams

Director of the Centre for Personnel Research and Enterprise Development,
and Reader in Organisational Psychology,
The City University Business School, London.

Introduction

Organisations need to adapt to their changing environments. Companies operating in a fiercely competitive market or in a technologically changing society can no longer rely upon the past successes of passive evolutionary change; their management must increasingly think in terms of active planned change. However, everyone who has been involved in planning and implementing change, whether in the context of mergers, consultative systems, appraisal schemes, methods of work, or range of services, will be only too familiar with the problems accompanying change efforts.

One of the most valuable contributions of the behavioural sciences has been to help in the process of developing theories and models relating to planned change. Organisation development (OD) is a label which has come to be attached to a particular set of strategies for effecting change within social systems. This chapter attempts to introduce readers to some of the concepts and activities in this field.

SYSTEMS PERSPECTIVE

A system has been defined as: 'An orderly grouping of separate but interdependent components for the purpose of attaining some pre-determined objective'.[1] A bank is a system which is designed to achieve certain goals through the provision of financial services in a socially responsible manner. The value of adopting a systems perspective in studying organisational change is that it highlights certain properties which enterprises share with other living and social systems.[2]

First, systems thinking reminds one that an organisation is an *open* rather than a *closed* system, that is, it is dependent upon the environment for its growth and survival. Thus, in the process of achieving its formal goals, a bank will in effect be:

- importing energy from the environment in the form of labour, materials, finance, equipment;
- transforming this energy into financial services;
- exporting these services into the environment;
- re-energising itself with further resources from the environment.

If an institution's goals, characteristics and services are not as well matched to its environment as those of a competitor, then this will be reflected in profits, market share, recruitment and retention of talented staff, labour disputes, and so on.

Secondly, systems thinking draws attention to the propensity of organisations to maintain equilibrium. Change implies a temporary state of disequilibrium and therefore tends to arouse resisting forces. Because an organisation consists of several inter-related sub-systems, resistance is not only encountered from the sub-system which is the main target for change, but also from other sub-systems trying to maintain the status quo. What can one learn from the behavioural sciences which help in the trouble-fraught task of managing change?

Resistance to Change

Resistance is as natural a characteristic of social systems as pain is to the body. The problem, therefore, is not how to overcome resistance but how to prevent it. The concepts of motivation and social norms are helpful in this context.

Motivation. Motivation implies that people have biological and psychological needs which they seek to satisfy. Through experience, individuals learn to identify situations where need satisfaction is achieved; once rooted to these situations, they are often reluctant to exchange security for insecurity.

Unfortunately change is associated with uncertainty. For many employees, and their union representatives, uncertainty threatens the continued availability of traditional sources of need satisfaction (e.g. job security, high salary, career prospects). Being a target for change, therefore, arouses anxiety in the individual and generates resistance against the initiators or agents of change. It is significant that *people involved in the planning and implementation of change show little subsequent resistance*; they have had after all the opportunity of influencing decisions so as to safeguard their sources of need satisfaction, and at the same time they have directly learned about the objectives, methods and predicted outcomes of change. In other words, *participation in change reduces uncertainty*.

Social norms. Through learning experiences in the family, at school and so on, an individual comes to be socialised within society; he or she comes to acquire beliefs, attitudes and values, characteristic of that culture. Socialisation reduces uncertainty by making individuals reasonably predictable to others, and thus facilitates productive interactions.

In common with other social systems, an organisation's stability and effectiveness depends upon its ability to socialise. It is through this process of organisational socialisation that individuals learn about the goals of the institution they have joined, the preferred means of achieving these goals, the responsibilities and behaviour patterns of the roles they are entering, and other 'norms' which are used to guide and maintain the identity of the organisation and its constituent parts.

The relevance of organisational socialisation in understanding resistance to change arises from the fact that *every technical or structural change has social implications.* These are obvious when role relationships change, that is, new working groups are formed and old friendships and statuses are affected. But they are less obvious in the actual processes of introducing change. A manager may successfully introduce a new method of work within his branch, whereas a head office consultant may fail in the same branch. The different results may simply reflect the fact that the manager was sufficiently familiar with the relevant 'social norms' operating within his branch so that he conformed to them in introducing change, whereas the consultant unknowingly violated these norms. In a classical paper on overcoming resistance to change,[3] the main theme is that people who resist are often not resisting technical change as such, but *the disturbance to established norms* governing social relationships.

If this contributory factor of resistance to change is to be minimised, a number of things suggest themselves including:

1. As far as possible introducing change through normal channels so that social norms are likely to be adhered to.
2. Using internal rather than external consultants since they are more likely to be aware of the characteristics of the social system to be changed.
3. Selecting line staff to be trained as internal consultants (they would probably have undergone similar socialising experiences as their 'clients').

4.   Ensuring that external consultants either work closely with an internal partner who can compensate for their cultural deficiences, or receive appropriate socialising experiences before actively intervening in any part of the social system.

A 3-Step Model of Change

A diagnostic framework which has proved useful in understanding and successfully introducing change is the unfreezing/changing/refreezing model of the change process which is attributed to the American social psychologist, Kurt Lewin.[4] Such a model is of practical value in drawing attention to the importance of each link in the chain of activities and helping people to become better change agents or managers of change.

Unfreezing. Before certain changes can be successfully introduced into an organisation, appropriate structures, procedures or norms have to be *unfrozen.* Unfreezing takes place when sufficient forces for change are generated so as to overcome an organisation's equilibrium-maintaining characteristics. These forces can be in the form of external pressures resulting from loss of market share to competitors, union militancy, depressed economic climate, government legislation and so on; or internal pressures resulting from high rates of turnover and absenteeism, low morale, or internal disputes.

In the face of these various pressures, organisations may take various actions which augment the unfreezing process. These may include changing the top management team, commissioning an attitude survey, or embarking on an organisation development programme.

Changing. The unfreezing process encourages people within an organisation to consider alternative structures, procedures and norms in the hope that a more effective manner of maintaining the system's equilibrium will be found. It is at this stage that actual change takes place according to specified goals and selected strategies. Basic principles can be learnt as to when, for instance, people-orientated strategies are likely to prove more successful than structure-oriented strategies, and power-based better than collaborative-based strategies.

Refreezing. This is the phase during which change is stabilised and integrated into the rest of the system. Poor integration increases the probability that rejection will take place once the special forces behind the change are removed; as when the consultant withdraws, additonal resources temporarily allocated to facilitate change are no longer available, and powerful internal sponsors of the change take up new appointments.

Training courses aimed at changing management style are the most notorious examples of change efforts which fail to cope with the refreezing phase. Individuals may find that their attitudes and behaviour are unfrozen and change during the favourable learning conditions of a course, but when they are back on the job and become subjected to the previous forces (assuming that their job and boss have not changed), their old behaviours are likely to re-assert themselves. While the individual's behaviour was temporarily changed, corresponding changes to the social system to which he belongs did not take place, and effective refreezing of his or her newly learnt behaviours were prevented from occurring.

Applying the model. One of the directions in which banking institutions are slowly moving is toward greater genuine consultation of staff over matters which affect them and their jobs. Let one assume that the top management of a bank wishes to strengthen evolutionary change by a planned effort involving the implementation of new structures. According to the 3-step model, in order to have a good chance of succeeding, existing structures, procedures and norms relating to consultation would have to be *unfrozen*. This means that individuals and groups who are capable of resisting change in this area have to perceive for themselves the deficiences in current practice. There are many techniques for tackling this problem, and some will be described later under 'Organisation Development'.

If top management has already decided that structural changes will have to be made in order that the objectives of greater consultation are achieved (e.g. improving decision-making with respect to quality and commitment, improving communications and staff morale), then decisions have to be made relating to the detailed form of these structures and to their subsequent introduction. A *change strategy*, relying more on the exercise of power rather than on collaboration, could be effective where the social system regards the exercise of such power as legitimate, and where there is a clear structural solution which has been shown to be effective elsewhere. If these conditions are not present, or if the power approach is inconsistent with the changes being proposed (such as in the present example), then a more collaborative approach is called for so as to prevent insurmountable resistance to change at a later stage. A collaborative approach means that all parties, who have the power to make any new changes succeed or fail, should have the opportunity to influence the design of the proposed structures.

If the unfreezing and changing phases have been appropriately dealt with, then the task of integrating any resultant change becomes easier. But the need to take further action to facilitiate the *refreezing* process remains. Assuming that the changes introduced involved managers holding formal monthly meetings with their staff, then the sort of actions that would help integration are: ensuring that the formal reward system takes into account a manager's performance at this task; management giving due weight to recommendations coming from these meetings; training programmes reinforcing the potential value of such meetings, and helping in the acquisition of appropriate skills; monitoring the success of the meetings, and modifying their rules so as to enable them to achieve their objectives more effectively. With respect to the last point, it is worth mentioning that there is nothing like the success of a new procedure to ensure its integration into a system, but success may have to be gradually attained through a process of experimentation.

The discussion on resistance to change, and the unfreezing/changing/ refreezing model should have helped (i) to clarify the value of a systems perspective when initiating and managing change, and (ii) to highlight certain conceptual frameworks with a view to improving one's skills in managing change. The next section on Organisation Development goes a stage further, since it is not only concerned with the *processes* of change already discussed, but also with the *goals* of change (i.e. the direction in which organisations should develop).

ORGANISATION DEVELOPMENT

Organisation Development (OD) is a term applied to certain types of planned efforts at bringing about organisation change. The trend has been to use OD to refer to a wider and wider range of efforts at planned change, with the result that its definition and boundaries have changed over the years. Briefly exploring the history of OD is a good way of starting to learn about this relatively new grouping of knowledge and techniques.

In the 1960s there appeared several influential publications which laid the early foundations for OD as an applied behavioural science. In the main the authors were organisational psychologists such as Bennis,[5] Schein,[6] and Blake and Mouton[7] who were: (i) heavily influenced by the human relations perspective, the learning potential of T-groups (aimed at increasing sensitivity and awareness), and general systems theory; and (ii) dissatisfied with current achievements in bringing about organisational change. It is therefore not surprising to find that the early orientation of OD practitioners was to try *to change social systems rather than individuals, to use non-directive and collaborative methods* in bringing about change, and to favour humanistic value systems. Values influencing these practitioners included: the development of human potential, opportunity to influence work environment, and appreciation for the unique and complex needs of individuals.[8]

This orientation has led to the development of sophisticated social inventions for intervening directly into organisational processes (e.g. survey feedback), and to the development of alternative roles for the consultant or change agent. The classical consultant role is that of 'expert'. In this role, the consultant diagnoses the problem and prescribes a solution. A second role is that of 'teacher', where the consultant is primarily concerned in disseminating knowledge selected on the basis of being appropriate for a given situation. A third role is that of 'counsellor', where the consultant adopts a joint problem-solving approach with the client. It is this latter counselling-type role which many behavioural scientists have found conducive to change; it reduces resistance, generates commitment for solutions to problems, and is compatible with humanistic values. Not surprisingly therefore this is the role most often used in OD interventions.

While this orientation to OD remains strong, it is only part of the subject matter. As a result of contributions made by practitioners and theoreticians who were more concerned with the influence of structure and technology than with attitudes and processes, OD has blossomed into a more interdisciplinary approach to planned change.[9]

What formal definition is OD given? One often quoted in textbooks is the following:

'OD is a method for facilitating change and development in people (e.g. styles, values, skills), in technology (e.g. greater simplicity, complexity), and in organisational process and structures (e.g. relationships, roles). The objectives of OD generally can be classifed as those optimising human and social improvement or as those optimising task accomplishment or more likely some blend of the two'. (Friedlander & Brown, 1974, p.314).

Using the framework implied in this definition, we can identify the basic types of OD interventions – *'process-oriented'* and *'technostructural'*. The former is primarily directed at attitudes, values, norms, goals, and relationships influencing behaviour. The latter is primarily directed at technological and structural variables influencing behaviour. Let us explore these types of interventions and their associated theories and technologies in more depth.

Process-oriented interventions

A bank, or one of its units, may feel that it is not effectively solving certain persistent problems (e.g. low productivity, low morale, poor communications). In this situation, an internal or external process-oriented OD consultant will try to help 'clients' to develop and implement effective solutions, not by telling them what they ought to do, but by helping to create better problem-solving conditions.

The consultant's assumptions of conditions necessary for effective problem solving will be influenced by certain behavioural science theories.[6] Three basic assumptions are likely to be: (i) the sharing of information is valuable, particularly when such information has remained unshared in the past (ii) confronting and working through differences among people who work together can enhance collaboration; (iii) participation in decision making can lead to increased commitment.

Group development. Within the context of a management team, the OD intervention technique which the consultant may use to bring about more open, confronting and participation problem solving behaviours could be some form of *group development* or *team building*. This would involve the consultant collecting data about the way in which the management team conducted its meetings, feeding back the data to the team, encouraging the team to examine the norms governing its behaviour, and encouraging them to plan and implement changes to enhance their effectivness as a decision-making body.

Intergroup development. Often the creative and productive energy of an organisation is sapped by intergroup suspicion and the unfavourable image which different parts of an organisation have of one another. The consequences of such attitudes are poor cooperation and communication. Such problems may be experienced between different departments, districts, or between central and local head offices in a bank. They may also be experienced by different parties in a merger situation.

Mergers create all sorts of human problems relating to job tenure, career prospects, working relationships, and conflicting managerial styles. An OD intervention programme designed to help effective problem solving in this situation could very well involve a consultant collecting data from each party about those factors which are perceived as aiding or hindering cooperation; and also data relating to their perception of each other. The data is fed back and shared in confrontation meetings which are designed to form a basis for problem solving (but not increased conflict or the display of defensive behaviour).

Total Organisation Development

The initial OD intervention is where the total organisation is the target for change. The most famous example of a packaged programme which attempts this is Grid OD (Blake & Mouton).[7] However, a currently more favoured approach is 'survey feedback', and so this is the technique we will use to illustrate total OD interventions.

Attitude surveys are no strangers to the banking industry. They have been used as general diagnostic tools for identifying and clarifying potential problems, and as a way of assessing attitudes and opinions towards specific issues such as preferred forms of representation. When an attitude survey is the basis for an OD intervention, it is referred to as 'survey feedback'.[10] In survey feedback the diagnostic data is not simply presented to top management (as is usually the case in the traditional attitude survey) but selectively fed back to all organisational groups participating in the survey. As with group and inter-group development, survey feedback encourages the norms of openness, confrontation and participation in the organisation's problem-solving processes.

The most influential model of survey feedback has been the one devised by Mann.[11] Diagnostic data is initially fed back to the top management team, and then down the hierarchy through the medium of successive teams. Each team sees the data for that part of the organisation for which it is responsible and for comparative purposes may be shown the average data for all teams at the same level in the hierarchy. At such feedback meetings the appropriate superior takes the chair, the data is discussed, plans for desirable changes are made as are plans for introducing the data at the next level. The consultant may attend some of the meetings as a 'resource' person.

Survey feedback does seem to be quite a powerful OD technique for stimulating an organisation into successfully resolving certain types of problems. This is not surprising in light of the earlier discussion on resistance to change, since: (i) it operates through the existing authority structure and is therefore less threatening to those in power; (ii) it allows all levels to be involved in planning changes affecting themselves; (iii) survey data is relatively objective and seen to be directly relevant to problems affecting staff; (iv) group meetings and the use of comparative data help the unfreezing process and the search for alternative solutions to problems; (v) the group approach also helps to increase the commitment of individuals to action plans, thus contributing towards refreezing.

The strengths of survey feedback can also be its weaknesses. There is evidence to suggest that survey feedback is unlikely to be instrumental in bringing about any significant structural change, and that the changes which do occur are likely to be either cosmetic or temporary. But these are criticisms which have been levelled at process-oriented interventions in general.

Techno-structural interventions

Planned attempts to change technological and structural variables can only justifiably be thought of as falling within the OD field if the methods employed in planning and implementing these changes are consistent with the open and participative methods referred to in process-oriented OD. Thus, structural change which is unilaterally imposed by management in an office (whether with or without the help of a consultant) should *not* be labelled OD.

Technostructural interventions can be sub-divided into two main categories: (a) those which are primarily concerned in improving the match between people and jobs, and (b) those primarily concerned in improving the match between organisations and their environments.

Person/job development. Many influential motivation theorists have criticised the person/job relationship which the majority of working people experience. Herzberg, for instance, has argued that large categories of jobs should be redesigned or enriched so that they provide incumbents with increased opportunities for experiencing job interest, responsibility and achievement. He has demonstrated that enriched jobs can lead to greater job satisfaction, better quality work and increased productivity. Others have attempted to show that, by applying principles of 'good' job design, it is not only the individual and the employing organisation who benefit, but society in general through an improvement in the overall mental health of its working citizens.

Planned change which tries to develop person/job relationships for groups of employees in the direction of good job design as defined by motivaiton theories, and involves interested parties (management, union representatives, and the workforce) in the planning and implementation of change, is likely to be referred to as an OD programme. An example of such a programme has been described by Buckingham;[12] job enrichment principles were applied in re-structuring the role of foreman in nine factories in the tobacco manufacturing firm of Gallaher Limited.

Another influential model in job design has been the *autonomous work group*. The theoretical basis for this model has come from the work of behavioural scientists at the Tavistock Institute of Human Relations in London. They have shown that in designing new technical systems, organisational structures are often adopted which ignore the needs of the social system. The consequent mismatch between technical and social systems adversely effects job satisfaction and performance. One way in which the needs of the social system can be catered for is to organise work around autonomous work groups, that is, groups which are:

1. Allocated meaningful units of work (e.g. servicing *all* the needs of a client or assembling complete television receivers).
2. Given significant autonomy or responsibility in carrying out their task (e.g. determining their own work pace, distributing tasks among themselves, carrying out their own quality control).
3. Composed of individuals who are compatible with each other (e.g. come from similar backgrounds, and share common interests).

There may only be certain situations where the autonomous work group model is likely to represent a superior form of organisation than, for instance, the assembly line model. But there are examples of its successful application in many different industries, suggesting that type of work and technology are constraints but not determinants of organisational structure. In other words, management have far greater choice in how work is organised than they are prepared to believe. Although the most publicised use of autonomous work groups has been in manufacturing industry (e.g. Volvo), there are numerous examples in service industries. Butteriss[13] for instance, describes how one British insurance company successfully introduced this form of organisation for some of its staff in order to try and improve efficiency and flexibility.

Many other studies could be referred to here, although some of these may be discussed in the literature under the label of 'quality of working life' or 'QWL programmes' rather than OD.

One of the main differences between QWL and OD is that the former has developed into a more powerful ideological movement concerned in changing the quality of working life of the average factory and office worker, and has sought action at national levels rather than limiting itself to change programmes at the organisational level. In recent years, the main QWL thrust within the United Kingdom has been provided by the Department of Employment through the Work Research Unit and the Tripartite Steering Group of Job Satisfaction.

Organisation/environment development. As a result of studies conducted by behavioural scientists in the UK and US, contingency theories of organisational design are having an impact on management thinking. These theories indicate the structure and climate (i.e. style or characteristic ways of operating) which is most appropriate for an organisation if it is to succeed in a particular type of environment.

In their classic study of the electronic industry in Scotland, Burns and Stalker[14] found that the less successful organisations tended to be 'mechanistic'. More successful organisations tended to be more 'organic'. (See Chap. 3) The explanation put forward for these findings was that the rapidly changing nature of the environment in the electronics industry meant that organically structured organisations were more successful because of their superior speed in adapting to change.

A refinement of the organic/mechanistic model has come from the work of Lawrence and Lorsh[15] who have further elucidated the complexity of the interface between an organisation and its environment. They have drawn attention to the fact that different parts of an organisation may interact with quite different environments. Thus, a more organic structure and climate may be appropriate for the R & D department or the marketing department, but the production department may achieve greater success with a mechanistic structure.

Ideas relating to organisational structure are primarily the concern of senior management. This means that an OD programme which is aimed at developing a better fit between an organisation (or parts of it) and its environment has to start at the top. Again, what determines whether a programme of organisation/environment development can be classifed under the OD umbrella will depend upon the methods applied in planning and implementing the changes involved.

Intregrated Approaches to OD

So far OD activities have been described as process-oriented and techno-structural. This method of presentation was chosen because it reflects the history of OD, and differences in the orientation of OD practitioners. OD practitioners do not disagree over the problems which need to be solved, but over the means of solving them. The process-oriented practitioners will expect appropriate techno-structural changes to follow their interventions, and the techno-structural practitioners will expect changes in processes to follow their interventions.

In terms of earlier discussions on systems thinking, resistance to change, and the unfreezing/changing/refreezing model, one would predict that OD activities which adopt an integrated approach to change (i.e. focus on both process and techno-structural variables, and adopt a system-wide perspective) are more likely to succeed in achieving their objectives. In practice this ideal approach is difficult to achieve unless: (a) the sponsors of an OD effort occupy positions of sufficient power and authority to encourage an integrated approach, and (b) they have some clear goals of the direction in which they would like to see their organisation move.

With respect to the goals issue, some behavioural scientists have developed theoretical frameworks describing ideal organisational systems which are conducive to the long-term survival and growth of organisations. Thus McGregor's Theory Y has provided an integrative framework (internally consistent) for many change programmes, as has the participative management or System 4 framework of Likert.[16] An informative account of applying the latter has been written by the Chairman of the Harwood Corporation, following the takeover of an ailing competitor (Marrow et al, 1967).[17] The new owners initiated planned change activities in order to move the acquired company from an authoritarian System 1 climate to a participative System 4 climate. This overall goal was successfully achieved over a two year period, and follow-up research seven years later indicated that many of the changes were durable. The significance of this study is that planned change took place along several dimensions, including: work flow, training (technical and leadership skills), payment systems (in negotiation with a union), and increased participation in decision making and problem solving at all levels.

One of the problems with better known behavioural science frameworks which help to provide an integrative philosophy is that they tend to imply that all organisations should move in the same direction. Thus Theory Y is better than Theory X,[18] System 4 is better than System 1, a 9.9 managerial climate is better than a 1.9 or 9.1 climate (Blake & Mouton)[19] organic structures are better than mechanistic ones, and so on. Given the underlying democratic and humanistic values underlying the work of behavioural scientists in the West, and the typical rate of environmental change, this is not surprising. Caution must however be exercised in generalising from these models, as indicated by contingency theorists.[20]

An integrative framework which is less likely to fall into this trap is the socio-technical model of the Tavistock Institute, which aims to achieve joint optimisation of technical and social systems within work settings. The approach is much less ,'packaged' than others, and its flexibility is more likely to accommodate the interest and power of unions in planned organisational change.

Evaluation of OD

How valuable have OD models and strategies been to those organisations which have been influenced by them? It is impossible to give an unequivocal answer to this question because of the difficulties of conducting valid research, and because there is no such thing as *the* OD approach. OD has become a mix of technologies and theories. However, on the basis of the less-than-ideal research which has been conducted and the scholarly reviews written, it is possible to make a number of tentative generalisations.

First, process-oriented approaches (e.g. team development, survey feedback) appear to produce positive effects in terms of attitudes, job satisfaction, and organisational climate. These in turn may lead to reduced levels of labour turnover, absenteeism and role stress. But these approaches are unlikely to bring any significant changes in structure.

Secondly, techno-structural approaches which focus on designing jobs (e.g. job enrichment, socio-technical systems approach) are, similarly, likely to show favourable results in terms of increased satisfaction and work climate. In addition, favourable effects on quality and productivity are more likely to be demonstrated than process-oriented approaches.

Thirdly, instead of thinking in terms of process or techno-structural approaches, we should adopt a more integrated approach. In other words, combine the strengths of the process approach (which is likely to minimise resistance to change); with the strengths of the techno-structural approach (which is likely to bring about more significant and lasting change).

Fourthly, OD strategies are often slower to bring about change and are potentially more meek in their impact than alternative strategies. This is not surprising given the democratic value system underlying OD.

Conclusions

Within the context of organisation development British banks have not been innovators, or if they have, then they have shied away from publicity. This means that there is a paucity of banking material for illustrating the application of principles and methods touched on in this chapter. Reasons for the apparently low level of innovation can be explained in terms of: (1) the largely bureaucratic and mechanistic structures of major banks; (2) the dependence upon trained bankers rather than specialist staff in managing the personnel function; (3) the relative stability of the banking environment in the past, and (4) the existence of a loyal and captured workforce resulting from the concept of a lifelong career and a paternalistic philosophy.

However, many of these factors are changing. New specialists, such as computer staff, and their unions, can wield disproportionate power within the banks. The complexity of managing the modern enterprise has increased the need for more sophisticated approaches to management training and development, and the recruitment of professional staff in this area. The banking environment (e.g. competition, technology, customers) is changing much more rapidly than before. Political and economic forces have significantly reduced a bank's discretionary powers in rewarding and dismissing employees. It is becoming increasingly difficult to preserve the notion of lifelong careers in a single institution.

This means that banks, along with other organisations, are going to find themselves becoming more concerned in the future with the business of managing change. If they want to minimise some of the problems which manufacturing industry has encountered, then they must learn (1) to mechanise without dehumanising the person/job relationship; (2) to introduce changes without alienating the workforce and their union representatives; (3) to embark on planned change programmes before they are forced into unplanned change by the onset of crises. This chapter has tried to draw attention to some of the concepts, methods, and sources of knowledge which may prove useful in this task.

References

1. Mockler, R. J., 'The systems approach to business organisation and decision-making', *California Management Review*, 1968, 11 (2), 53–58.
2. Katz, D., & Kahn, R. L., *The Social Psychology of Organisations*, 1978, Wiley, 2nd edition.
3. Lawrence, P. R., 'How to deal with resistance to change: retrospective commentary', *Harvard Business Review*, 1969, 47 (1), 6.
4. Lewin, K., 'Frontiers in group dynamics', *Human Relations*, 1947, 1, 5–41.
5. Bennis, W. G., *Organisation Development: its Nature, Origins and Prospects*, 1969, Addison-Wesley.
6. Schein, E. H., *Process consultation: its role in organisation development*, 1969, Addison-Wesley.

7. Blake, R. R. & Mouton, J. S., *Building a Dynamic Corporation through Grid Organisation Development*, 1969, Addison-Wesley.
8. French, W. L., & Bell, C. H., *Organisation Development*, 1978, Prentice Hall, 2nd edition.
9. Friedlander, F., & Brown, L. D., 'Organisation Development'. In Rosenzweig, M. R., & Porter, L. W., *Annual Review of Psychology*, 1974, 25, 313–341.
10. Williams, A. P. O., & Woodward, S., 'Attitude Surveys'. In Williams, A. P. O. (ed), *Using Personnel Research*, 1983, Gower.
11. Mann, F. C., 'Studying and creating change'. In Bennis et al, *The Planning of Change*, 1961, Holt, Rinehart & Winston.
12. Buckingham, G. K., Jeffrey, R. G., & Thorne, B. A., *Job Enrichment and Organisational Change: a study in participation at Gallaher Ltd.*, 1975, Gower Press.
13. Butteriss, M., 'Work restructing in financial operations', *Journal of Building Society Institute*, 1976, 30 (117), 9–12.
14. Burns, T., & Stalker, G., *The Management of Innovation*, 1966, Tavistock.
15. Lawrence, P. R. & Lorsch, J. W., *Organisation and environment: managing differentiation and integration*, 1967, Harvard Business School.
16. Likert, R., *The Human Organisation*, 1967, McGraw Hill.
17. Marrow, A. J., Bowers, D. G., & Seashore, S. E., *Management by Participation: creating a climate for personal and organisational development*, 1967, Harper & Row.
18. McGregor, D., *The Human Side of Enterprise*, 1960, McGraw Hill.
19. Blake, R. R., & Mouton, J. S., *The Managerial Grid*, 1964, Gulf.
20. Morse, J. J., & Lorsch, J. W., 'Beyond Theory Y'. *Harvard Business Review*, 1970, 48 (3), 61–68.

PART II

STAFF POLICY AND ADMINSTRATION IN BANKING

Introduction

From the preceding chapters depicting some of the organisational and motivational problems which are inherent in the management of people, the book now moves on to some of the practical issues of staff policy and administration.

Manpower planning in aggregate must clearly be a fundamental activity for any large-scale organisation which seeks to match its anticipated demand for various types of skill with the supply of suitably qualified and experienced men and women. Malcolm Bennison outlines the mechanics of manpower planning and offers step-by step guidance in establishing company manpower maps, trends, flows and planning models. He shows how wars, changes in commodity prices and exchange rates can cause difficulties in managing economies, which in turn affect the growth rates or organisations and make manpower planning, as a purposeful, on-going activity, imperative. But the process is not easy. Long-term plans based on approximations and probabilities, must inevitably be flexible. 'Effective manpower planning is more the product of monitoring analysis than it is of accurate forecasting.'

Quantitative and qualitative targets must be set. The age, sex and skill distributions of the employed population must always be taken into account to guarantee a bank's pool of talent and provide career avenues for its staff. Decisions relating to the selection of personnel and reviews of their performance are therefore crucial.

Brian Stone devotes his chapter to the approaches which might be taken to personnel recruitment and selection, and relates these approaches to the broad requirements of manpower planning. At the same time, and in detail, he outlines the construction of job specifications and interview plans, drawing attention to the 'criterion problem' in personnel selection and the need to identify reliable predictors. The criterion is that which is to be predicted.

Personnel selection must therefore focus on identifying the skills and attributes conducive to successful performance on the job. The snag is that criteria are not static, but change over time. Success on one job does not necessarily mean success on another; there is a world of difference between the skills required to be a competent clerk and those required to be a competent manager. Selectors must therefore decide quite carefully what it is they are looking for and know how to go about it – 'the selection process is to match the candidate to the job.'

The author describes the main techniques: interviews, panel interviews, tests and group assessment methods. He draws attention to the persistent problems of interview assessments – questions of reliability, validity and errors of judgement – and shows how their worst efforts might be mitigated.

All human judgements are essentially subjective. Therefore determined attempts must be made to achieve uniformity and consistency. In matters of employee appraisal and counselling, these claims come to the fore. Tony Jackson provides a comprehensive account of this area. He considers the main methods of reviewing staff performance, potential and rewards. He analyses the conflicts often endemic in appraisal systems, arising from fallibilities in judgement and the disparate objectives which such schemes are designed to serve. Computer print-outs can reveal the distribution of assessments across an organisation and highlight deviations in standards. Common standards in the pursuit of equity must be coupled with a clear determination of the performance criteria which are actually relevant. Some schemes lend themselves to greater objectivity – such as Management by Objectives. Here again there are pitfalls. Perhaps it is in the area of employee 'counselling' that most improvements can be made. Dr. Jackson sees counselling as a means of helping employees to make decisions about goals and to solve their own problems.

Training in making appraisals, and in counselling, are obvious, if sometimes neglected, responsibilities. Staff training is a very practical activity in all organisations. Three chapters are devoted to the education, training and development of staff in banking. Training, however, may only be one possible solution to an organisational problem. Since the training function is so well established in banks, it is a not uncommon assumption, but sometimes an erroneous one, that problems of staff performance necessarily lend themselves to a training solution. In fact, the root cause of performance which is below par may stem from environmental or motivational factors. Keith Hillyer gets to the nub with the key question: 'Could they do it if their lives depended on it?' Mr Hillyer talks mainly about the technical training of bank staff, but his analyses of training criteria, behavioural objectives, standards of performance and measurements of training effectiveness have much wider implications. He also discusses the application of learning theory to the design of industrial and commercial training programmes, and he points out that training is not simply a matter of courses but also of planned experience and job rotation since the emphasis is on learning rather than teaching. Above all, the training and development of individuals must be systematic and geared to specific objectives.

In the following chapter, Mr. Hillyer moves on to discuss the training and development of managers. He seeks to reconcile the needs of the organisation with those of the individual. He distinguishes between management training and management development. This chapter emcompasses technical knowledge, social and leadership skills, methods of inculcating these, and concludes with an overview of popular management training approaches. He also puts the case for 'self development'. He quotes Carl Rogers: 'I have come to feel that the only learning which significantly influences behaviour is self-discovered, self-appropriated learning.'

Eric Glover explores the role of professional education in banking, its origin, aims and trends. Whilst, he notes, that during the first hundred years of the Institute the main aim was to improve standards through educational programmes, the emphasis during the next hundred years will veer more towards the banker's need for career-long education. Mr. Glover traces changes in the educational system, particularly in business studies qualifications, and shows how these have become reflected in the Institute's role as a 'qualifying' association.

Overall, the chapters in this section are concerned with some of the mechanics of human resource management in large-scale organisations. The procedures outlined are all part of the central activity designed to ensure that the right kind of people are in the right place at the right time. Such policies are very much concerned with organisational survival and growth.

CHAPTER 10

Manpower Planning

Malcolm Bennison

Associate Director, Institute of Manpower Studies, University of Sussex

INTRODUCTION

'It is an ill wind that blows nobody any good' so the proverb says. The recession which began in 1980 as the first edition of this book was printed was indeed an ill wind which has blighted the lives of many families and individuals. Yet its impact has spurred on the development of the tools and techniques of manpower planning. In 1980 they had been tried and tested in a small number of organisations and found to be effective. Five years on they are deeply embedded in a hundredfold more organisations and the banking organisations are avid users of them. By 1980, there were already two increasing and convergent pressures on organisations to adopt a longer-term approach to the management of manpower.

Organisations have become more complex, requiring a wider range of specialist skills in their employees. It is more difficult for a bright young person to enter an organisation at the bottom and train in all aspects of the organisation before being given an executive role. Banking in particular has needed to employ computing and telecommunications skills in order to cope with the automation of its basic processes. When skills are needed but take a long time to acquire, organisations often respond by creating new career streams. In doing so the size of the manpower management problem is considerably increased.

Employment legislation has greatly increased in recent years. Since the loss of full employment in 1974 there has been an emphasis on the protection of employment. It is now extremely difficult to reduce the size of an organisation quickly and cheaply. Time can be bought by generous redundancy payments, but the impact of legislation has been to slow down the process by which an organisation can reduce its numbers. Those responsible for managing manpower must begin to look further ahead in attempting to forsee manpower problems. This is especially true of organisations in which a major part of the total costs are manpower costs.

The new skills, with their long training requirements, slow down the speed of replacement of employees. The impact of legislation equally slows down the ability to reduce the size of the organisation. Together, these considerations increase the pressure on organisations to look ahead, to attempt to plan manpower on a longer-term horizon.

The pressure on organisations to survive through the recession by ensuring that manning levels are held at their most economic is an obvious one and explains some of the increased interest in manpower planning. But this short-term negative reaction does not offer a complete explanation. The majority of the work currently being done in organisations is more positive and long term. Some banks are turning to manpower planning to help them set recruitment levels that ensure that a continual flow of well qualified people are entering their organisations. They realise that success in ten to twenty years' time comes from todays recruits. Others are exploring their career management problems. Todays promotion blockages, many now realise, are the direct result of ill-prepared early retirement schemes implemented to help survive the recession. There is now an active manpower planning unit in most banking organisations exploring these issues to develop more appropriate policies.

The Concept of Manpower Planning

No system of manpower planning exists. No set of rules can be written for an organisation to follow on in taking its manpower decisions that will lead to the ideal Manpower Plan. No single mathematical manpower planning model is available that, given the right data, will solve an organisation's manpower problem. The reality is that a collection of techniques and models exist which, if used within a relevant approach to manpower problems, will help in the taking of improved manpower decisions.

The basic concept is a simple and practical one. Do not attempt to plan in too detailed or rigid a manner. The 1970s showed the futility of highly detailed plans which calculated turnover rates to the fourth decimal place. These types of plans survived during the 1960s because a failure to achieve plans resulted in, at worst, a profit reduced from excellent to very good. They were completely unable to cope with the fluctuations and uncertainties of the 1970s when business futures were at the mercy of oil crises, rapid inflation and wild exchange rate fluctuations.

The only successful way to plan in an uncertain world is to examine a number of scenarios of the future, asking questions like 'what happens if Home Banking takes off in the next 5 years?' and analysing its effect on levels of manning, levels of recruitment, rates of promotion etc. The concept of a map of manpower decisions has been found to be a viable one for organisations.

The map brings together the decisions – i.e. the level of recruitment with the factors that influence it, the number of jobs expected in the future, the number of people expected to leave the present complement and the way that it is intended to replace them, by promotion from within or by recruitment externally. For each of the factors it is important to look at a range of future possibilities. To take the previous example, say three different levels of take up of 'Home Banking' could be postulated which would necessitate different numbers of employees and so lead to different numbers of recruits. As the future unfolds it is monitored and when it becomes clear how home banking is taking off the level of recruitment can be tailored accordingly. The organisation can manage uncertainty better if this concept of manpower planning is followed.

The Approach to Manpower Planning

Although no system of manpower planning exists, it is possible to describe a systematic approach. The elements in the approach need to be considered in looking at all manpower problems, but the degree of detail necessary and the complexity required will depend very much on the situation of the organisation and the type of problem under consideration. Flexibility, not slavishness, is required in utilising the approach.

The approach begins by identifying the manpower decisions that have to be made by an organisation in managing its manpower. The effect on the decisions of such important factors as the future expected size of the organisation, the levels of wastage, has to be evaluated and allowances must be made for changes in the factors. It is important to establish those critical levels for each decision that cause a change in policy. The final part of the approach is to monitor the organisations's progress, comparing the current situation and its expected future with the critical levels for the decisions, to establish when policy changes are necessary.

Drawing the Manpower System

A diagram showing a pattern of boxes and flows representing the way that manpower behaves in the organisation is the key to identifying manpower decisions. An example of such a diagram is that in Figure 1.

Wherever there is an entry point into the organisation, a decision is required; what level of recruitment is needed to fill the number of expected jobs and allow for wastage? Where two types of manpower can be considered for the same job, decisions must be taken as to how much of each type of manpower will fill these jobs. For instance, bank managers could be drawn from the assistant bank manager level in the organisation, or perhaps they could be recruited from other banks. Decisions concerning rates of promotion can only be evaluated by separating the organisation hierarchically into groups of jobs between which there is a sufficiently great step for it to be considered a promotion. In Figure 1 the decision points can clearly be seen.

Determing the levels of recruits into this system is a manpower decision. The level of recruits needed will depend on the number of jobs that the organisation intends to have in each of the boxes in future years. If the organistion is growing, recruits will be needed to sustain the growth.

People leave organisations by either retirement or wastage. These, too, must be estimated to calculate the number of recruits needed to sustain the organisation at its current level.

The choice of how the organisation replaces people who leave, or fills extra jobs resulting from growth, will also affect the number of recruits. Filling all the extra jobs and replacing vacant posts at branch manager level by recruiting managers from other organisations will reduce the number of recruits required, since recruits will now only be required for the levels below manager.

Drawing the manpower system for the current situation helps the understanding of the crucial manpower issues and identifies critical decision points. The technique is equally useful when employed to illustrate a hypothetical situation such as a bank deciding whether it should develop an accelerated stream for promotion to bank manager. The manpower system drawn to represent this situation could appear as either of the two following situations. Figure 2(a) illustrates a policy of selecting The 'fast track' potential managers from existing trainees, giving them special training, appointing them to chief clerk positions after training and expecting them to compete for positions at assistant branch manager and branch manager levels. Figure 2(b) is an alternanative policy of recruiting young people with potential for branch manager, giving them special training and reserving a specific number of posts at chief clerk and assistant branch manager level before they compete for branch manager vacancies.

Drawing the alternative manpower systems in this way helps to emphasise visually the *policy* differences in the mind of management.

Early Warning of Manpower Problems

Adding easily obtainable data to the manpower system and drawing the boxes and flows in scale to each other brings the manpower system to life.

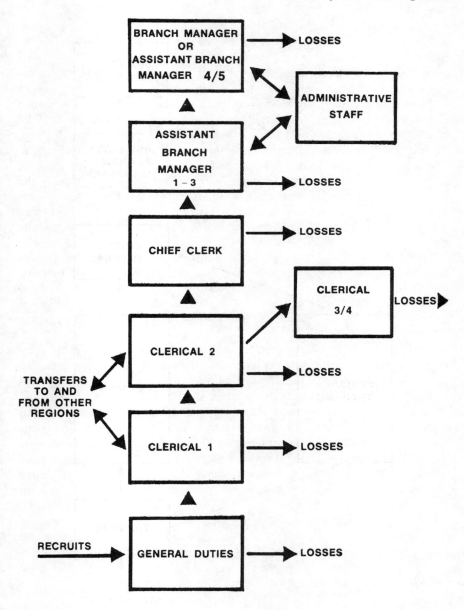

Figure 1 Typical Bank Manpower System

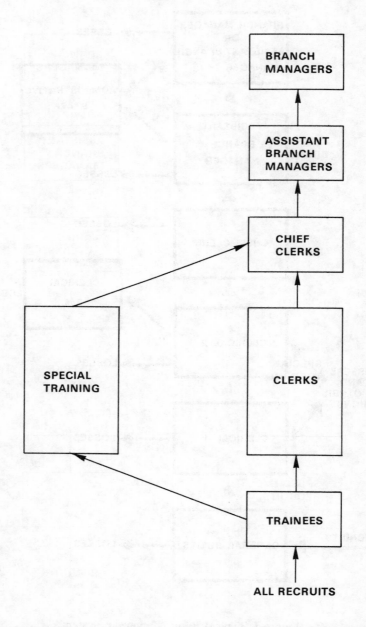

**Figure 2A Bank Manpower System showing accelerated training
for some recruits**

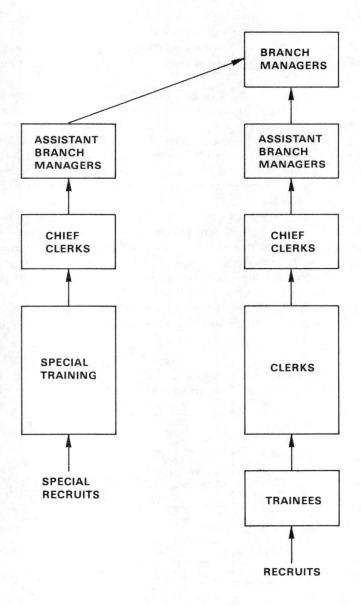

**Figure 2b Bank Manpower System showing separate recruitment
stream with accelerated promotion to manager**

The regional personnel managers of one of the banks were not particularly concerned at the following situation (Figure 3).

On the other hand, they readily understood why the average age of the chief clerks had fallen so much when the same data was presented as in Figure 4.

It was clear that the addition of new functions in the bank's activities had led to a growth in the assistant branch manager posts. The traditional route to assistant branch manager was from chief clerk. Rapid rates of promotion had followed, all the experienced chief clerks were now assistant branch managers and had been replaced by younger clerks. The regional personnel managers commented 'no wonder personal relationships have deteriorated in the bank, the steadying influence stemming from the long experience of our chief clerks has been lost!'

Excessive turnover levels show up very clearly when the system is drawn to scale and a year's flow is depicted on it. In the organisation opposite (Figure 5) everyone tolerated the high turnover rates amongst trainees but drawing it to scale caused management to investigate why.

They could see that they were getting no value for almost one third of the recruits who were leaving in the first year.

The age/grade distribution of employees or the length of service/grade distribution is easy to obtain and will give a vivid picture of the experience

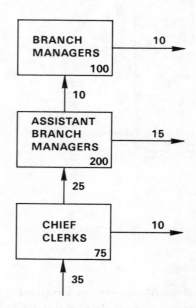

Figure 3 Manpower system traditionally drawn

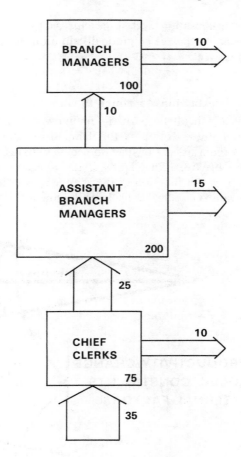

Figure 4 Manpower system drawn to scale

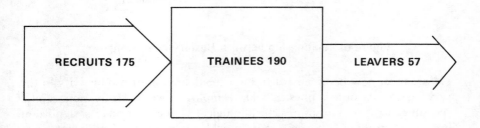

Figure 5 Manpower system to scale showing excessive wastage

profile of the organisation and some clue as to the general outlook for careers. In this bank, the age by grade distribution shows how inexperienced are branch employees.

Estimating the Demand for Manpower

One of the most difficult tasks of the manpower planner is estimating the demand for manpower. In reality the demand for manpower is a function of the way an organisation's business objectives change and how manpower relates to the objectives. In Figure 6, the relationship of manpower to business objectives is a function of the change in productivity and how this might be constrained by social considerations and affected by external events.

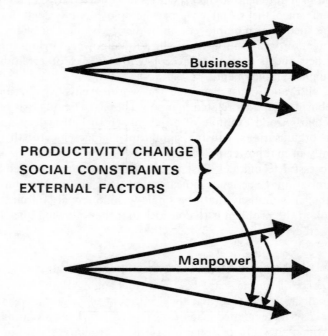

Figure 6 Relationship between Business and Manpower

Care must now be taken not to limit the definition of productivity to the very narrow one of how physically hard employees work. Motivation, capital spending, work organisations, technological change, all have a significant impact on productivity, some more quickly than others. The first step in arriving at future numbers to be employed must be to assess how much productivity will change within the relevant time period.

Amin Rajan of IMS has recently analysed the banks' view of their business over the next few years[1] and concludes that three issues will govern future employment. The obvious one is how business prospects and the market will change. The second concerns what form the branch network will take as a result of current rationalisation plans, and the third speculates on what input of the new technology available is to be applied.Weighty questions indeed, and unlikely to be answered accurately enough for detailed manpower plans. The proposition that a practical manpower planning system must focus on how to help management *change* policies in a way that is appropriate to changing conditions is strengthened by this uncertainty.

A more difficult assessment is to estimate how far the available level of productivity can be realised, since it may be constrained by social factors. In a period of high unemployment, efforts are directed to keeping people in employment since the social cost of unemployment is high. Legislation inhibits the shedding of employees and other legislation provides subsidies to encourage an organisation to retain its manpower. Organisations often feel that their social duty is to accept a lower level of profitability and maintain higher employment.

Finally, allowance must be made for world events which significantly affect the business and its related manpower levels. The oil crisis of 1973/74 is a particularly good example of an event which had a deep and lasting impact on organisations, causing significant changes in growth rates and consequently in manpower policies.

Few successful techniques exist to estimate the manpower requirements of an organisation. Experience indicates that there are so many facets to the problem that it is unlikely that one single technique will be found. A good way to look at the problem is to consider that the following questions need to be answered.

What Level of Manpower can the Organisation Afford?

Different costs of business are continually changing both in their rate of inflation and the percentage that they represent of the total cost. Latterly, manpower costs have inflated faster than most other costs. Situations quickly occur in which the rate of inflation turns a profitable situation into an unprofitable situation. Close attention must be paid therefore to the level of manpower that the organisation can afford. Many organisations have developed statistical measures for relating manpower to business parameters. These statistics vary with the organisation. Some of the more popular ones are:

- added value per employee
- wages and salaries as a percentage of gross sales revenue etc
- sales per employee

They are used to monitor the changing relationship between manpower and the business and to help assess when action is required to reverse an unsatisfactory trend. This method provides an excellent means of testing how realistic are the bottom-up forecasts. It can be used as a measure of the gap that exists between the 'grass roots view' of the organisation's manpower needs and the way its financial future appears. Used in this way, the measure is helpful to the senior managers of the organisation in assessing the direction of their manpower and financial policies.

What Level of Manpower Should We Require?

When organisations go from growth to contraction they often become unbalanced in the proportion of people employed under different activities. It is easy to estimate the number of people required in the 'direct activities' of an organisation; in banking this would include the people who deal with the accounts of customers. It is much more difficult to estimate the number of people in the 'overheads' and specialist service functions. When an organisation contracts, the latter tend to stay at their previous levels and the relationship between the direct and indirect staff gets more heavily weighted in favour of the indirect staff. Organisations find this a particularly difficult problem to deal with. Some have used 'zero-budgeting' and 'base-case' techniques effectively in coming to a much more realist view of the levels of manpower needed for current activities.

How do we take into account current trends in the labourmarket and the other factors that affect manpower?

The rate of technological change in organisations appears to be increasing rapidly. The advent of the micro-processor offers the opportunity to increase productivity very significantly. This is not only true of manufacturing industry, but it is also true of organisations that operate large clerical systems. Word-processors, real-time accounting systems and the transfer of information between computers using advanced telecommunications systems, promise a great deal.

Rajan in his study suggests that the following questions are uppermost in policy makers minds. How will ATMs and counter terminals affect business and manning levels? Will locating them in shops, offices, factories and public places attract a wider customer group? Can the range of services provided by ATMs be expanded to include accepting deposits, fund transfers between accounts and hotel and airline bookings. How quickly will the chequeless society come about? The answer to this question depends on innovations in three key areas: communication, electronic transfer at point of sale and 'home banking'.

In answering these questions, the organisation is thrown back on its own subjective assessment of their impact. There is too little experience of such technology from which new levels of productivity could be calculated and the extent to which the available productivity can be implemented is difficult to assess, since social constraints apply.

Answering the preceding questions is extremely difficult for any organisation. They raise deep divisions of opinion amongst managers since they involve subjective judgement. Experience indicates that three to four years is needed before a process, designed to answer the questions, becomes understood by managers in the organisation. Even then an *honest* attempt to answer each of the questions will only produce a less uncertain view of the future.

An organisation must not expect to be able to forecast its future demand for people accurately, but it is possible to understand the way that manpower relates to business objectives. Given this understanding, an organisation can hope to react to changing events with a degree of success. Monitoring becomes equally as important as forecasting.

Estimating the Outlfow from the Organistion

Employees leaving the organisation are one of the main driving forces of manpower planning, since replacing them may involve promotion from the level below and ultimately recruitment of someone new into the organisation. It is important, therefore, to measure and predict the outlfow.

For practical purposes two types of outlfow must be distinguished, retirement and natural wastage.

Retirement can be predicted with a reasonable degree of accuracy. Normal retirement rules are a function of age or length of service or a combination of both. Once the rules and the ages and lengths of service of employees are known, retirement can be predicted. Sickness, death and the wish of some employees to retire early, will affect the prediction. One organisation was astonished to find that only half of its employees within ten years of retirement survived to their official date of retirement!

Natural wastage is much more difficult to predict. The traditional measure, the crude or BIM (British Institute of Management) wastage index, the number of employees leaving during the period, calculated as a percentage of those in employment at the start of the period, is misleading. Recent research has shown that wastage is strongly linked to length of service: employees with short service and younger employees are much more likely to leave than any other groups. Unless the length of service and/or the age structure of the organisation is taken into account the crude wastage index can give the wrong impression. Figure 7 illustrates the problem.

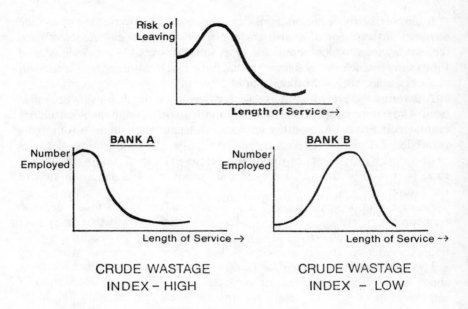

CRUDE WASTAGE   CRUDE WASTAGE
INDEX – HIGH   INDEX – LOW

Figure 7 Relationship between Wastage and Length of Service

Two banks, A and B, have been found to have the same wastage behaviour. That is, when the numbers leaving are compared by length of service in each of the two organisations, we find the same pattern, illustrated by the top diagram in Figure 7. However, most Bank A employees have low lengths of service so, since the highest risk of leaving occurs with low length of service, the numbers of leavers from Bank A will be high. On the other hand, Bank B will have a low number of leavers since it has few people with short service and most of its employees have medium and long lengths of service and their chance of leaving is low. Calculating crude wastage indices for both A and B Banks will produce very different rates, yet the wastage behaviour of the two banks is identical.

This explains why attempts to run an organisation down by natural wastage are often disappointing. When an organisation stops recruiting, the number of people with short service decreases, they leave and are not replaced. The people left have lower chances of leaving and therefore the number of leavers reduces. The measure and prediction of wastage must take into account the length of service structure of the organisation.

The *external labour market* has been found to be an extremely important factor in understanding natural wastage. Comparing patterns of wastage for the same occupations over a period of time shows that there are considerable variations in the pattern of leaving from one year to the next.

A number of other factors affect levels of wastage. Among these must be included different occupations, whether an employee is in his, or her, first job, the age of employees, and travel to work patterns.

Over the last five years research work done by Dr Andrew Forbes of IMS in association with the Midland Bank has resulted in techniques which help an organisation explain and forecast changes in the level of its labour turnover. The research[2] showed that a mathematical relationship could be evaluated between the monthly level of labour turnover and the following variables:

> State economy and labour market as represented by unemployment or vacancies.
> Relative pay between the bank and its competitors for labour.
> The proportion of staff below age 25.
> The number of recent recruits.
> The month of the year for which labour turnover is to be forecast.

This enables a bank to look forward in time and, having made projections about levels of unemployment or vacancies, relative pay, the proportion of employees below age 25, recent recruitment levels etc., estimate the likely level of labour turnover. Consequently decisions on levels of recruitment can be made with more confidence. The following diagram shows the labour turnover rates experienced by the Midland Bank between 1971 and 1982.

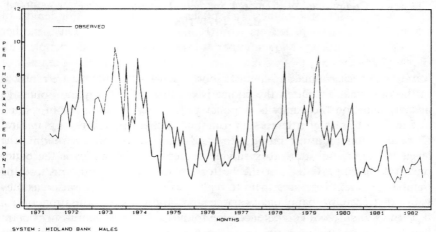

Figure 8 Midland Bank Turnover 1971–1982

The large drop in labour turnover during 1980 can clearly be seen. Figure 9, the next diagram, shows how closely the level of labour turnover calculated by the relationship matches that which was experienced.

This research work has been repeated in other banks and organisations and the same type of relationships have been found. Current work is concentrating on assessing how well the forecasts made using the techniques are working out a practice.

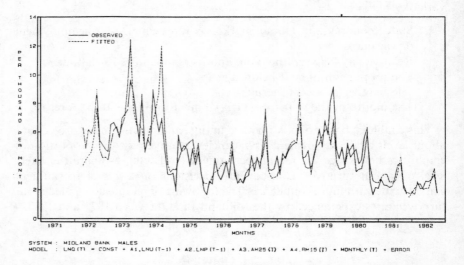

Figure 9 Comparison of predicted and actual labour turnover for Midland Bank 1971–1982

Replacement Policy

Manpower decision-making cannot ignore the ways that people are replaced in the organisation. Often the choice is prescribed by company policy. In one organisation there may be a policy only to recruit direct from school, and to fill jobs at higher levels by promotion. Other organisations may have a combination of direct recruitment and internal promotion to different levels in the organisation. It is difficult to decide which policy is the better one. Taking employees in at the bottom of the organisation and training them, subsequently moving them to higher levels in the organisation as they gain experience, probably enables an organisation to have a tighter control over the standards of competence of employees. External recruitment often benefits an organisation in that those recruited contribute new ideas developed in different circumstances. Only subjective assessment can really determine which policy is best in which situation. It is important, however, to evaluate different combinations of these since they affect the manpower decisions significantly.

Data on the types and quantities of people recruited from year to year are normally relatively easy to get, but those concerning promotion present a greater problem. Few organisations have records which summarise promotions from year to year. Often such information is limited to that which can be found in dossiers of individuals and as such is difficult to summarise. It is necessary to be able to estimate the proportion of people who reach different levels in the organisation and the time taken to reach those levels. They can be estimated from simple data relating to age, length of service and grade, using techniques such as career progression diagrams of the kind shown in Figure 10.

The career progression diagrams in Figure 10 summarise the promotion policies for an organisation for two different groups of staff. They are obtained by taking a snapshot of the relationship between how long employees have been in a career stream and how far up the organisation they have progressed. Length of time in the career stream can be measured by age or length of service and progress up the organisation by grade, salary band, job evaluated points, or simply using judgement to group together jobs at similar levels.

Each line on the chart represents the boundary between two grades. By examining the slope of the line, the age or length of service where significant changes in slope occur and the percentage of employees who are below a grade boundary at retirement, much can be deduced about the promotion policy followed by the organisation.

In career stream 1 all employees will reach senior manager before they retire and, on average, they will achieve promotion through the grades into management at about 30 and senior manager at about 40. In contrast, the employee in career stream 2 has much lower prospects of promotion. Only 40 per cent. of employees in this career stream are likely to achieve promotion to senior manager before retirement.

Drawing the Manpower Map

At this point in the approach the manpower system has been defined, an estimate has been made of the numbers of people needed by the organisation to meet its objectives, rates of outflow have been measured and the replacement policy operated by the organisation has been assessed. The remaining task is to bring these factors together in a way that helps decision-making.

In practice, three steps are necessary: the determination of the practical limits of variation for the factors, the use of techniques to quantify the relationship of the factors to the decision, and the assessment of the critical levels for each decision.

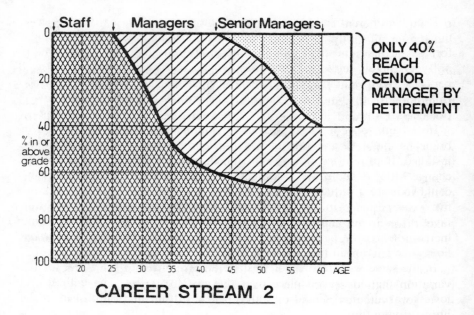

CAREER STREAM 2

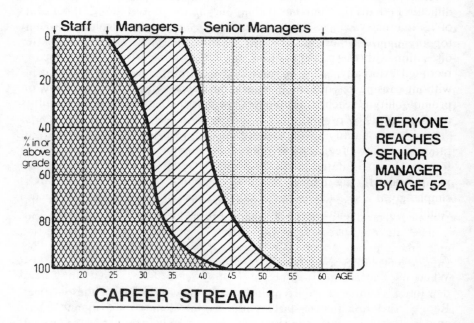

CAREER STREAM 1

Figure 10 Career Progression Diagrams

Each factor is looked at to determine the practical limits within which it might vary over the period under consideration. This is important. A single forecast of the number of jobs the organisation needs in five years time is not very useful, neither is it to state that the rate of growth expected is 2 per cent. and to examine one per cent. on either side as a sensitivity analysis. In looking for the limits of variation it is essential to find limits that have a practical meaning.

In a bank, one of the influences on numbers of employees needed in branches could be the rate at which teleprocessing of accounts can be installed. If current technology is assumed, perhaps branch numbers would change little. A subjective assessment of the impact of full teleprocessing could indicate a reduction in numbers of 2 per cent. per annum over the five year period. On the other hand, corporate planners assess, given favourable circumstances, that re-entry into house purchase finance would increase staff by 2 per cent. per annum. These are examples of practical limits of variation in factors.

In the same way, records of wastage are examined to get a feel for the variation that has taken place over the past five years. The highest and lowest wastage rates found over that period of time are established as the limits of variation.

Attempting to assess the variation in replacement policies is much more difficult. Perhaps the bank has had a policy in the past of filling 70 per cent. of its internal vacancies at manager level by promotion from below and topping up the other 30 per cent. by direct external recruitment. After discussion with the personnel function it is estimated that the proportion recruited externally could be expanded from 30 per cent. to 50 per cent. without causing resentment from amongst current staff before a limit on promotability is reached. Employees are pressing for the bank to fill all its manager needs by promotion from below.

A way of quantifying the relationship between the numbers employed, rates of outflow, replacement policy and manpower decisions has to be found. The quantitative methods normally used are called mathematical manpower planning models. Essentially the logic by which they operate is simple: given a set of rules and a calculator, a child of average intelligence could obtain the same results as the computerised model.

A Simple Example

When he was at the Institute of Manpower Studies, Jonathan Casson developed a simple example to illustrate the use of models[3]. The Ruritanian Republic has lost a considerable number of battles recently. A tribunal of enquiry has investigated the situation, shot a number of senior generals and decided that the problem lies in its manpower policies.

THE MANPOWER SYSTEM

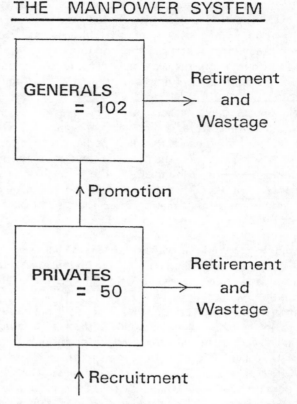

Figure 11 Generals and Privates – Manpower System

Over the years its manpower system has evolved until the point illustrated in Figure 11.

There are only two significant manpower groups, Generals and Privates, with a marked preponderance of the former; there are double the numbers of Generals (102) to Privates (50). A replacement policy ensures all vacancies at the General level are filled by promoting Privates, who are in turn replaced by recruits.

The tribunal has decided that the basic fighting ability of its army must be improved and that it can be achieved by reducing the number of Generals and increasing the number of Privates. It intends to achieve the change over a five year period and has set a target of 96 Generals and 58 Privates by the end of the next full year.

The Staff Officers of the Ruritanian army have examined the policies and have summarised them in Figure 12.

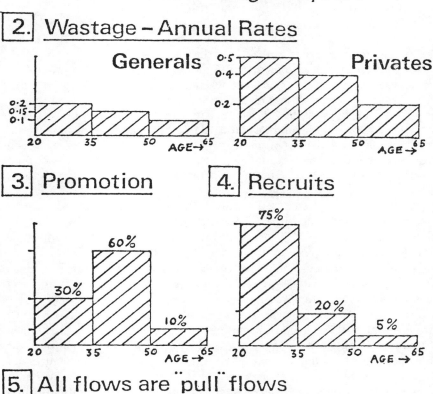

Figure 12 Generals and Privates – Summary of Policies

Currently, Generals and Privates retire automatically at the age of 65 and this has been confirmed as the best policy. There is a considerable annual wastage of both Generals and Privates, which also reflects, in the much higher rate for Privates, the tactical plans adopted by Generals, of leading from behind. Records show that around half of the Privates aged between 20 and 35 will fail to survive to the end of the year. They also show that the rate has fallen by age 50 when only about 20 per cent. will fail to survive. In contrast, this 20 per cent. level is the highest rate of wastage for the Generals; their rate also decreases with age and by age 50 only 10 per cent, will be lost in a year.

The manpower system shows that vacant posts at General level are replaced by promoting Privates. The career progression diagram shows that the age range 35–50 provides the majority of the promotees, about 60 per cent, with about 30 per cent. of the vacancies filled by Privates below 35 and 10 per cent. being filled by veteran Privates aged over 50.

The prime recruitment need is for young men, and so 75 per cent. of all vacancies among the Privates will be filled by recruits aged 20 to 35 with the remaining 25 per cent. spread over the age range 35–65.

The Staff Officers have noted that all flows are 'pull flows': a promotion or recruitment can only take place when there is a vacancy to be filled, Privates being 'pulled' up to General to fill a vacancy caused by retirement or wastage. Push flows, the other case, happen when a promotion occurs to the next level on attainment of a standard of performance in the lower level, or as a result of a policy to promote, say 10 per cent. of the lower level each year; people are 'pushed' to the next level irrespective of vacancies. 'Pull' systems are often called 'renewal' systems and 'push' are referred to as 'Markov' systems.

This is important since it determines the method of operation of the model: in a 'pull' system the model commences its calculations with the higher levels, for a 'push' system with the lower levels. Where the system is mixed, special rules apply.

The first task is to calculate, for the General level, the vacancies caused by retirement and wastage, to adjust this figure by the growth factor, and then to calculate the required replacements to meet this target.

The starting stock of Generals is examined for the number of retirements; two Generals will become 65 during the year. The wastage rates are applied to the remaining stock to generate the likely wastage, 14 in total over the three age bands, leaving a stock of 86 after wastage and retirement. Since the target size for the end of the year is 96 Generals, 10 vacancies will need to be filled by promoting Privates. Applying current policy, this would entail promoting three Privates below age 35, six between 35 and 50 and one above age 50. If there are enough Privates to promote, this would increase the number of Generals from 86 to 96. The final calculation is to adjust the age distribution to allow for the passage of one year. Figure 13 details the above calculations.

This process is repeated in Figure 14 for the Privates. The wastage rates are applied to the starting stock and 22 vacancies are forecast, leaving 28 out of the original 50 Privates. Ten Privates have to be promoted to General and it is most important to check that, after wastage, sufficient remain in the age ranges for promotion. The stock of Privates is now reduced to 18 and there are sufficient to promote to General. Since the target figure for the end of the year is 58 Privates, 40 will have to be recruited. Having chosen

GENERALS

Start size = 102
Target size = 96

Starting Stock. =102

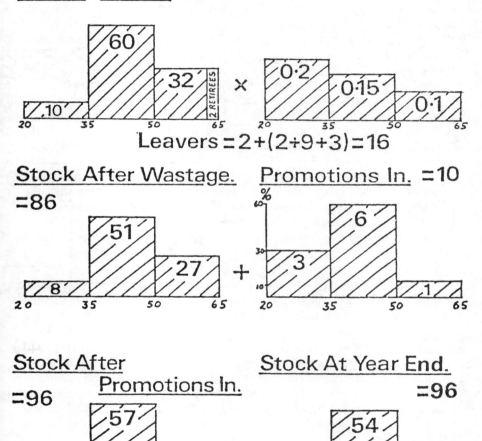

Leavers = 2 + (2÷9+3) = 16

Stock After Wastage. =86

Promotions In. =10

Stock After Promotions In. =96

Stock At Year End. =96

Figure 13 Generals and Privates – Calculations for Generals

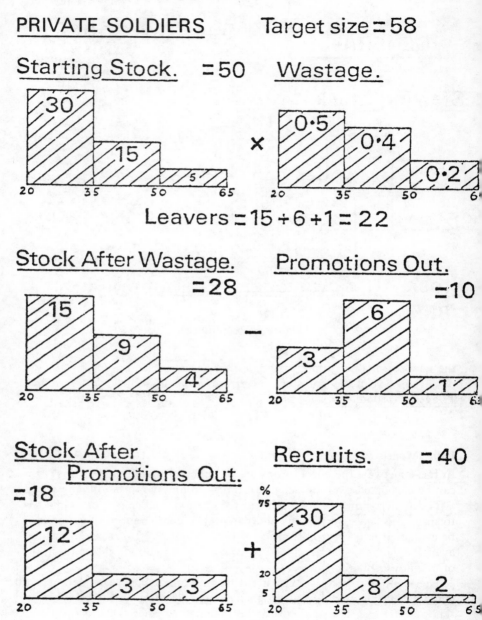

Figure 14 Generals and Privates – Calculations for Privates

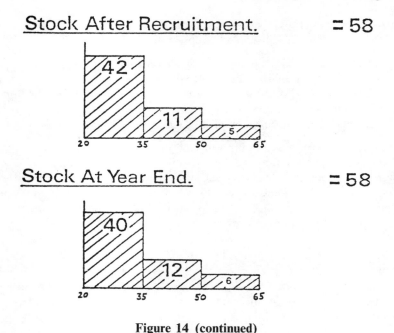

Stock After Recruitment. = 58

42
11
5
20   35   50   65

Stock At Year End. = 58

40
12
6
20   35   50   65

Figure 14 (continued)

the new recruits according to the desired age range and adjusting for the passage of a year, the final stock of Privates is 58, 40 in the lower age range, 12 aged 35–50 and six aged 50–65.

Using Models

In the same way, the effect of any set of policies on any manpower system can be calculated over any length of time – in any organisation, any bank.

The models, however, use sophisticated methods and computer techniques to speed this process up: many alternatives and combinations of factors can be evaluated in a very short space of time. Models of this type are readily available, having been developed by organisations who are in the forefront of manpower planning.

The manpower map is constructed by running a suitable model on any combination of factors to assess their combined effect on the decision. In this case the decision that has to be taken is whether the organisation's traditional policy of filling its bank manager vacancies by promotion from within will need to be changed over the next five years.

The starting point is to complete a series of runs of the model. Three factors are believed to be important: the expected number of jobs over the next five years, the rate of outflow and the replacement policy itself. A first run could assess the number of likely promotions if:

> the number of jobs increases by 2 per cent per annum;
> the additional staff are required to staff up the home loans new venture;
> the present level of outflow remained over the five years at the highest rate found in the previous five years;
> and the organisation filled all its vacancies by internal promotion.

For the second run, the assumption that the number of jobs would increase by 2 per cent. per annum could be dropped and an assumption of zero growth in numbers put in its place. This would reflect that the additional staff needed for the 'home loans new venture' would be offset by savings made by installing teleprocessing equipment. The runs would be repeated until all possibilities were exhausted.

Anticipating Difficulties

The final aspects to be considered in order to evaluate the decision on whether the current promotion policy will need to change, stems from an assessment of the combinations of policies which could cause serious difficulties for the organisation. It is important to assess where these lie and examine the consequences. One such difficulty could arise when the number of promotion opportunities is greater than the number of promotable staff.

Alternatively difficulties could occur when the level of promotion falls to such a low level that staff are demotivated. This level is extremely difficult to arrive at even subjectively, but nevertheless it must be assessed.

From these kinds of analyses, certain strategies will show up as being more manageable than others, so too will potential 'bottlenecks' (e.g. an appropriate rate of promotion to fill expected management posts resulting from expansion) and potential human relations problems (e.g. frustration of unpromoted staff resulting from lack of organisational growth). Completing a series of runs of the model in this way pinpoints the pitfalls.

The purpose of these models is to draw a picture of the relationship between critical decisions and the factors that affect them. This can be used in conjunction with careful monitoring of the way the factors are changing so as to develop new policies to meet difficult situations.

Effective manpower planning is more the product of monitoring analysis than it is of accurate forecasting.

References

1. Rajan A., *New Technology and Employment in Insurance, Banking and Building Societies* Special report, Institute of Manpower Studies Series, Gower Press 1984.
2. Forbes A. F., McGill D., *Understanding Wastage* Institute of Manpower Studies, (Report CN426) 1985.
3. Bennison M., Casson R. J., *The Manpower Planning Handbook*, McGraw-Hill, London 1984.

CHAPTER II

Recruitment and Selection

Brian Stone

Senior Lecturer, Manchester Polytechnic

Personnel represents a high and increasing cost to any organisation, and in particular to banks, in which it represents a large proportion of costs, and which banks have been traditionally reluctant to reduce in conventional manners, such as by schemes of redundancy. Furthermore, at present a career in banking is structured, as organisations are structured, so that people progress in terms of increasing complexity of work and necessary skills. For these reasons accuracy in recruitment selection, and indeed in selection at organisational levels other than at recruitment, is vital.

The Manpower Plan

The process of recruitment should begin at the Manpower Plan, which will represent a focused concentration on those parts of the corporate strategy which concern staffing, and which have clarified manpower objectives. The Manpower Plan will have enabled the organisation to determine areas where there are likely to be shortages due to internal supply factors such as planned corporate changes, career progress and management development, retirement and redeployment. It will also have considered such extraneous factors as population changes, technological advances, projected governmental policies and local variations.

A recruitment programme will be derived directly from these determinations, in the form of an *action plan* in which the number and type of staff to be recruited, trained and developed, will be specified. In the ideal organisation this will be communicated to the personnel staff not just periodically but by constant update; and there will be clear and comprehensive communication also on the company's recruitment policy in terms of internal *versus* external selection, tiers of recruitment and the importance or otherwise of outside experience, and the calibre and level of staff needed to fulfil future staffing needs as circumstances and forecasts change.

The UK clearing banks have tended to recruit at very specific tiers:

School leavers at 16 years old, usually with a specified minimum number of 'O' levels (normally 4 including Maths and English)

School leavers at 18 with 'A' levels

University and Polytechnic Graduates on leaving college for one of two intial destinations: to branch or departmental banking on a general graduate training scheme, or to departments to utilise their academic speciality in a technical field such as computers or economics.

Post-experience recruits at all levels, from typists to senior executives, who have an expertise gained in other organisations and which the bank itself cannot provide via internal recruitment, such as tax officers with Inland Revenue experience.

People to fill specific vacancies where particular physical or practical chacteristics or abilities are needed, such as messenger or catering staff, or drivers.

There is a tendency among bankers to refer to one- or two-tier recruitment as the subject of debate: this normally refers to obtaining staff for branch banking, and whether or not to recruit one tier with career ambitions on to a path which leads upwards, and another for specific low-grade clerical tasks on a flat career path. While, as has just been suggested, bank recruitment is in fact already multi-tiered, this debate has validity, and many believe that the clearing banks are causing present and potential career dissatisfaction by persisting in a policy of recruiting overqualified staff for simple clerical tasks in a era when career advancement is less rather than more likely than in the past. Where two-tier schemes are operated, of course, fair practice would require a workable system of transfer as staff develop and grow, so as not to lose potential managerial talent in a bureaucractic trap of tier rigidity.

Definitions

At whatever level of entry, people are usually recruited either for specific jobs or for development programmes such as Graduate Trainee Schemes. The personnel staff will either have, or will draw up, a specification for the job for which staff will be needed. At this point it might be useful to propose some definitions:

JOB ANALYSIS is the process whereby the facts concerning a particular job are worked out or discovered; these facts are then recorded on either a JOB DESCRIPTION or a JOB SPECIFICATION from which will be derived a PERSON SPECIFICATION.

A JOB DESCRIPTION is an outline in general terms of the activities, tasks and responsibilities involved in a job: it is a written statement of job content.

A JOB SPECIFICATION is more detailed, and will specify additional factors and supplementary information on the methods of performing the job; skills and knowledge required.

THE PERSON SPECIFICATION lists the characteristics or abilities or training needed to perform the job competently, and will be used as the basis for selection.

Job Descriptions and Specification

Job descriptions will specify first the purpose of the job: why it exists at all, its overall targets and ideal achievements. This is not the same as a summary description of the work involved, although it is occasionally difficult to separate content from purpose: the purpose is the reason for the job. The job's dimensions will often come next, i.e. the size and scope of the work where that can be specified. In the case of a branch manager, this could relate as much to the branch itself as to the work, since it would include information on the number of accounts, the size of the branch, the present resources and lending figures, and the number and grades of staff at the branch.

The nature of the job and its responsibilities will follow, under broad headings. Where the facts can be quantified, they should be, and where responsibilties are limited, the limits should be clear. In this section, or one associated with it, it will be apparent to which functions the job-holder is accountable and for what. It is useful to note constraints in terms of resources, time and staff which surround the job. These sections are usually produced in a narrative form to provide a clear and complete description of the job involved. They will usually imply, or better state, criteria by which performance on the job is to be judged.

To this document and any associated, detailed specification, is added the expertise and experience of Personnel and in-line staff to produce a specification of the main abilities, skills and characteristics of a person performing the task. The job-specification refers to the job, and the person specification to the kind of person who will perform it well. It is this document which is the keystone to the next stages in selection. Frequently it is cast in the form of the well-known 'Seven Point Plan' designed by the National Institute of Industrial Psychology under the following headings:

Physical Make-Up:	Attributes of health, appearance, speech, physiology required by the job
Attainments:	Education, experience, training needed to begin the tasks involved
General Intelligence:	Amount and power of reasoning ability necessary

Special Aptitudes:	Mechanical ability, spatio-temporal relationships, artistic, verbal or numerate talents
Interests:	Relevant to the job, such as outdoor activities, maintenance/repair, problem-solving hobbies etc.
Disposition:	Dependability, acceptability to the kinds of people contacted, courage, flexibility and the like
Circumstances:	Family and home background, financial circumstances if appropriate, mobility.

There are other classifications which are sometimes more appropriate such as the Munro-Fraser five-point plan, which looks at Impact on People, Qualifications, Brains and Abilities, Motivation and Adjustment. These 'plans' also form the basis for further stages in the selection process such as advertisements and interviews, as we shall see later in this chapter.

So far, then, the organisation has determined its needs in terms of future supply of manpower, has detailed the areas in which it will experience those needs, has analysed the work involved in the jobs to be filled, specified precisely the tasks which make up the job, and specified the qualities needed by the person to fill it. It has, in fact, determined the demand side of its manpower equation. It must now look to supply.

The Recruiting Process

We have examined the sources from which banks recruit, and we shall therefore go on to deal briefly with methods of tapping those sources to obtain the best material for future bank staff. Advertising, to begin with, will make the bank's needs known to the labour market, and, if well done, will tap the needs of the candidates in that market to attract them to the bank. It has been said that the perfect job advertisement attracts the single perfect candidate to the job advertised, and nobody else. In reality, of course, while the advertisement needs to be sufficiently specific to filter the total market, leaving those who apply to be at least close to the ideally qualified applicant, there will usually be either too few candidates (filter too fine) or too many (mesh too wide)' What is usually sought is a short list from which a closer selection can be made.

To do this, the advertisement should list essential qualities from the person specification, some of the principal benefits offered in employment, the organisational position and context of the job, the paper qualifications or alternatives acceptable, and the procedure for application. It would need to appear at appropriate times in well-selected media – when and where the best candidates would read it, of course – and it would need to be designed and presented in a way commensurate with the status of the job and the advertising organisation.

In addition to press and broadsheet or poster advertising, the banks produce brochures aimed at different levels in the recruitment market, principally for school leavers and for graduates. While obviously broader and more detailed than advertisements, nevertheless the same types of heading and production standards would feature in such publications.

Brochures are by nature expensive to produce, since they are both reflective of the quality of the organisation and intended to compete in presenting the bank's image among just such publications from direct competitors. Their effectiveness should therefore be carefully monitored.

The response to the advertisement is the first in-house filter, and it is not difficult, if the criteria for selection are reasonably clear, to cut down the list of applications at this point. Some organisations set great store by the letter in response to the advertisement: its physical presentation, the paper on which it is written, the handwriting, organisation and content, the apparent attitude towards employment with the particular bank concerned. The inclusion of a well thought-out and produced Curriculum Vitae is sometimes regarded as advantageous to the prospective candidate in recruitment to more complex jobs.

An application form will be sent to the appropriate remaining candidates. As a document which represents the bank, this form should also be well designed and presentable. More importantly, it should be seen by the designer as a vital filter in the succession of refining devices for the selection of the right employee. It must request information of an administratively mundane but necessary type, such as name, address, age and so on; but it should also result in revealing insights into the character and personality, skills and experience of the candidate. The degreee to which probing questions are asked at this stage will depend on the importance and complexity of the job, but in a market where supply exceeds demand as is so frequently the case with the better jobs in banking, there is no reason to avoid discriminating between potential candidates at this stage. Again, the pattern suggested by five or seven point plans can be used to design parts of the document.

In addition to probing questions, there is much to be said for freehand statements from the candidate, in which they are broadly required to fulfil many of the demands of the Letter of Application, sometimes requested as a supplementary document but easily included on an application form so as to enable the information to be processed in a standard manner, albeit via subjective judgements on the part of the reader.

The First Sift

This reader will in fact be the Recruiting Officer, given different job-titles and status by different banks. His (or her) responsibility is essentially to compare such evidence as he has of the applicant's suitability against criteria for selection for the next stage of recruitment. These criteria will be more or less explicit to the recruiting officer, depending on how sophisticated the organisation is, and presently range from an intuitive, experience-based knowledge of the contemporaneous work of the branch clerk to a full job-description and personnel specification. It is after this filter process that the final stage of matching supply to demand will be reached, and selection made, by means of interviews, panels, assessment centre techniques and tests, or a combination of these.

The Interview

At all levels, the commonest form of final filter is the *Personal Interview*. The widespread use of the interview may be difficult to understand if viewed dispassionately since it is so fraught with unreliability. To begin with, there is the problem of whether the process of interviewing is an effective filter: like the propitiation of the divine spirits, it is a ritual that nobody is prepared to dispense with in order to see whether its absence will be disastrous.

Secondly, the training and development of *recruiters* should be carefully done, using both internal and external training sources. Their performance and effectiveness in their work should also be monitored. But however well it is done, and however professional the interviewer is, the interview is by definition an interpersonal interaction; and therefore in addtion to interview validity (whether it in fact measures what it purports to measure) there is also interviewer reliability (whether the assessment is accurate and consistent) to consider, in examining the usefulness of interviewing in selection. The diagram below will indicate some of the influences affecting the match-up at interview between the criteria for selection and the characteristics actually possessed by the candidate.

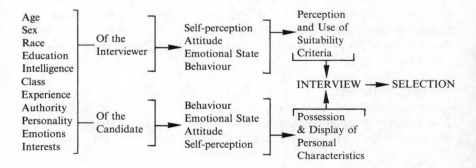

In addition to these simple personal interaction factors affecting the outcome of an interview, there is also the matter of the degree and extent of the interviewer's specific training in Personnel Management (overall expertise in the matter of personnel selection and its place in the organisation), in Recruiting (the entire process to which this chapter refers), and in Interviewing (impartial expertise in determining the quality and quantity of information necessary in the face-to-face process, and techniques for obtaining that information).

Despite the increasing sophistication of training in Personnel Management, and in the subject itself, nevertheless many organisations still staff their Personnel Departments with a majority of line staff either in transit from one job elsewhere in the organisation to another, or on finite temporary secondment. Indeed it would probably still be difficult to find departments where there is a preponderance of trained professionals, or a multitude of staff possessing the qualifications awarded by, or having attended courses approved by, the Institute of Personnel Management. In many cases a few week's formal training is regarded as sufficient, the remainder of expertise being gained on the job. The clearing banks may be among those who are exceptions to these observations (it may be of interest to the Institute of Bankers, possibly, to survey the matter). In any case, the point made is that the training of the interviewing staff would affect the outcome of interviewing as a selection technique.

Finally, before examining personnel selection techniques, there is the matter of '*the Criterion*', a measure of how good a worker is. In fact, in selection, we are interested in *predictors* with relation to *criteria*, that is, measures of current quality related to predictions of future quality: how good are the candidates now and which of their qualities can we use as indicators to predict how effective they will be in the future? We are after all not usually just selecting them for the present job, but for some future fulfilment of more advanced job requirements. For perfection, an organisation would examine long-term ideal criteria for success, and attempt to make predictions as to the currently-possessed characteristics of the candidate in terms of the probability of their meeting such criteria. It would then validate its selection methods by checking selected candidates against those targets, and, naturally, adjust its selection techniques accordingly if necessary.

Selection Techniques

In recent years a great deal of work has been done on *Interviewing Techniques*. Many academic and commercial courses now include modules in which it is intended that the student/trainee improves interviewing methods and effectiveness. One way of developing interviewing skills is to examine this interpersonal interaction by contrasting it with simple conversation. Any training which includes the following, and uses sophisticated techniques to develop skills under these headings, would help the trainee to make better use of the interview as a selection method:

OBJECTIVES	In an interview, objectives are specific and explicit, and the expert interviewer can and does specify, in writing if necessary, what it is hoped will be achieved by the end of the interview.
PLAN & STRUCTURE	Unlike a casual conversation, an interview should be planned and structured. In particular, the opening (brief, confident and personable) and the close (short, firm and reassuring) can be planned, as well as the questions to be asked.
TENSION MANAGEMENT	There is a tension based on the importance of the outcome, on the formality, and on the fact of self-exposure, which interviewers should manage, and be trained to manage, to their advantage. Occasionally the correct thing to do will be to reduce that tension.
ROLE	There is an interviewer and an interviewee: the former should ensure that this distinction is clear and preserved by engaging in behaviours which indicate the relative authority between themselves and interviewees who tend to be more receptive if the interviewer is in charge though not dominant or aggressive.
INVESTIGATION	Interviews are always investigatory (otherwise they become speeches). The distinction and selection between open and closed questions, listening and sustaining, noting and recording techniques can all be learnt and improved, remembering that the objectives of selection interviews always include the gathering of enough personal information to make selection *decisions*.
SITUATION	Obvious though it may seem, care should be taken to 'stage manage' the interviews: seating to suit the purpose; adequate light, heat, air; no interruptions or distractions; all necessary documentation to hand.

Finally it is conventional to note that the interviewer is presenting the face of the organisation, and in banking as elsewhere the standards of personal presentation of the interviewing staff will be seen by the candidate as reflecting those of the organisation. Professional recruitment staff also bear in mind, at this point above all, that *the selection process is to match candidate to the job*, immediately and for the future. This includes giving candidates a clear and full opportunity to consider whether the post offered is correct for them in their own view as well as that of the organisation; and the interview is often the stage at which candidates are offered realistic information about the work and the organisation, and almost invariably given the opportunity to ask their own questions.

Panel interviews differ only in the number of interviewers and the resultant extra pressure on the candidate. This method does give the opportunity to a number of additional assessors to judge the person being interviewed, and for questions to be asked and information obtained in the special field of expertise of each panel member. It also allows for a measure of discussion of the candidate by a variety of partners in the selection task, based on one set of data. While it is therefore economical of time and possibly rich in specialist judgement, it could be argued that the pressure on candidates of being outnumbered can act to discourage free response on their part; and unless for a specialist post, a one-to-one interview would be equally successful.

At this point in the selection procedure *Tests* are sometimes used, to assess the potential ability of the candidate to perform the tasks specified by job analysis. These can be divided roughly into achievement, aptitude, intelligence, and personality tests. Tests of achievement are those in which the current ability is assessed, such as typing exercises or oral language tests. Tests of aptitude measure the possession of certain faculties which in the future enable the tasks to be performed, such as those used to judge whether people have the fine manual skills necessary in certain electronic assembly work, or for such work as computer programming: there are some quite sophisticated tests for this, and these are certainly used by bank personnel departments to select computer staff. At the clerical level in banks, there is some use of these for specific jobs; and although there is also considerable dependence on the State examination system to judge the clerical ability of candidates for branch banking jobs, there are moves to test the literacy and numeracy of prospective clerks independently. Managerial aptitude is also tested by such exercises as 'in-basket', critical thinking tests, group decision-making exercises and tests of intelligence.

The last-named are of course problematical, if only because it is difficult to persuade psychologists to define 'intelligence', although most would recognise that the intuitive definition of an intelligent person is one who analyses and solves abstract problems accurately and quickly. Intelligence tests examine verbal/education ability, in which the comparing and contrasting of words and their meanings are central; and also numerical ability, in which various mental or arithmetical questions are asked, and also kinaesthetic/motor questions, posing problems comparing sizes and shapes, and dealing with time and space. Appropriate use of these tests would depend on the user's objectives, their understanding of the test, and the judicious assessment of the results with relation to the job.

A test is a standardised instrument – in terms of the test items and in terms of the scoring. Any test results must be scaled against the performance of representative and relevant groups of people, i.e. interpreted against a Norm Group. In other words, all test results must be expressed in meaningful terms in the context in which they are given. 'Seventy-five out of one hundred and fifty' is less meaningful than (say) 'seventy-five is equal to the mark scored by the top 20% of all candidates'. The 'Population' against which an individual's scores are compared is important. Norm-lists giving such comparisons are available whenever tests are administered. Several norm-lists may be available for any one test, e.g. for particular age groups, for an occupation, for the industry/organisation, or nationally. In test manuals, norms are expressed in different ways and their interpretation requires familiarity with certain statistical concepts in order to understand the diverse ways in which norms can be produced.

Personality tests are even more complex to discuss, because personality is at least as difficult to define as intelligence, and it is outside the scope of this chapter to enter a detailed discussion of this. Personality tests such as the 16PF (one of the most popular) ask the candidate to answer a large number of questions about how they think they would behave in certain situations, and present the results in terms of scores. Experts in the use of the results can then predict the likelihood of the candidates' success in given occupations.

The *Assessment Centre* approach, increasingly popular though certainly not new, is both an extension of the personality test and also usually includes some of its mechancial techniques as part of the process. The Assessment Centre is used mainly for more advanced selection, such as graduate recruitment or management development programme selection. It consists essentially of a period of 24 hours or more during which, usually at a confined location, the behaviour is observed and the achievements and aptitudes of a group of candidates are measured by a group of assessors. A variety of exercises, activities and tests are employed, and the social behaviour of those under scrutiny is also recorded and judged. Once again, the success of the technique is dependent on the clarity of the assessors' objectives, the appropriateness of the tests to the prospective work, the validity of those tests and the skill wherewith they are applied, and the calibre of judgement of the assessors.

For certain complex posts there are multiple stages in the process following application: for example, more than one interview, or interviews followed by an assessment centre session, or an additional panel interview. After whatever procedure is regarded as appropriate by the organisation for selection to the post in question, a decision is made, and each company will have its own checks and authorisation systems to conform or adjust the decisions made by the personnel operations staff. The selection process includes notification of the candidates of their success or failure, and a proper system will include methods of doing this, and promptly: there are organisations which delay notification an inordinate length of time, and which even have the discourtesy to omit to notify unsuccessful candidates at all. Not all successful candidates will accept the post, by the way, and reserve-lists are sometimes needed to ensure that the right number of posts are filled.

The bank of today would be scarcely recognisable to the clerk of fifteen years ago, and it would not be unreasonable to surmise that changes taking place in society and in technology now will make the bank of fifteen years hence equally unrecognisable to today's clerk, who if recruited now will expect to be near branch management level after about that period. As long as the banks continue to recruit for a lifetime career, then, they must be looking to attract and select the people who will manage the bank of 15–20 years hence.

To do this effectively they should be engaged in the creation of managerial scenarios, and deriving from those the characteristics they feel the manager will need. They should deduce logically the predictors in the medium and short-term which will indicate whether prospective candidates will possess those characteristics, and devising and using selection methods to test the candidates' suitability in those terms. They might be starting from both ends, as it were: more or less sophisticated models of future society in general, and commerce and industry in particular, for a horizontal view; and easily derived suppositions about what the microchip-based machines will remove as necessary human tasks at the other, to look vertically at the organisation.

The banks may also find, indeed are already finding, that staff trained outside the bank are not only essential in specialist areas, but can be used in branch banking too. There are already hints that this concept is becoming current, and transfers into branch banking from other areas, indeed from outside banks, while not commonplace, have nevertheless occurred in all major banking corporations (as indeed bank personnel are beginning to discover that they might have a market value outside the safe walls of their traditionally birth-to-death employers). Management development programmes have probably now succeeded in indicating to trainees that what the banks are now seeking are not bank managers, but managers (of banks), and recruiting philosophy and operations will now move to selecting, as career-path recruits, not clones of the current bank clerks but ones demonstrably capable of following paths towards a future management job possibly radically different from today's manager.

It is to be hoped, indeed expected, that someone in some department is engaged in futurology of this nature, and communicating the findings to the banks' decision-makers, otherwise those on the shop floor of recruiting and selection for advancement are carefully and professionally moving their banks along a false vector.

Implied if not overtly stated in this chapter is the importance of trained professionalism in a bank's selectors. As in any other organisation, the training of personnel staff is as vital as training for other support services and as training for line people. A sound set of selection staff will possibly be a balanced mix of career personnel staff and line staff on short or longer terms with the personnel operations department; but each will have a carefully planned, executed and monitored continuous training programme. Either included in or additional to this will be methods of inculcating as clearly as possible visions of the future so that each selector can maintain perspicaciousness in his selection of staff for the bank of the future.

Necessarily condensed, this chapter cannot have covered the ground completely, and further reading would be necessary to gain a fuller view of the subject of recruitment and selection. Most good books on general personnel will include chapters on the subject; and the brochures issued by the major banks for the recruitment of general staff or of graduates provides an insight into their recruitment philosophy and practices. These are normally available from the banks' personnel managers, for serious enquirers. Employees of banking or other corporations interested in furthering their knowledge of the subject would also be well-advised to examine examples of the company's job-description (possibly their own) and to consult their Personnel Departments about their use of these and person-specifications in recruitment and selection, both for entry into the organisation and for management development. Study of the company's application forms would also help to indicate what the organisation seeks and how it goes about finding it. Examples of Job Descriptions for an Assistant Manager and for a Securities Clerk are shown in Figures 1 and 2 (reproduced by kind permission of the Royal Bank of Scotland).

Further Reading:

A classic work in the field of industrial psychology is *Industrial Psychology*, by Milton Blum and James Naylor, NY, Harper and Row, (1968), which contains valuable if complex work on selection criteria, interviewing and testing. *Psychology for Managers*, by Cary Cooper and Peter Making,

London, MacMillan (1984) contains a good deal of up-to-date material on the same subjects, among others. For the interpersonal skills involved in the interviewing process the reader will find valuable a book by O. Hargie, C. Saunders and D. Dickson, called *Social Skills in Interpersonal Communication*, London, Croom Helm, (1981).

Figure 1 Job Description – Assistant Manager

DOMESTIC BANKING

Job Title: Assistant Manager

Reports to: Manager

PURPOSE

Ensure the efficient organisation and performance of the routine work of the branch, subject to the direction of the Manager.

DIMENSIONS

Resourses	£
Advances	£
Total Number of Accounts	
Number of Current Accounts	
Staff	Manager, Assistant Manager and 5 Clerks

NATURE AND SCOPE OF POSITION

Although all the work of the branch is under the responsibility of the Manager, it is the duty of the Assistant Manager to free him of as much of the routine work as possible.

The incumbent organises and supervises the work of the staff under the guidance of the Manager. The Grade 3 clerk attends to the preparation of securities in addition to a number of general offices duties, including some counter work. One of the Grade 2 clerks is responsible for the correspondence and branch statistics and returns. Another Grade 2 clerk acts virtually as a full-time cashier, and the two remaining clerks operate the computer terminal and attend to the junior work in the office.

Apart from supervising the routine work of the branch, the Assistant Manager is responsible for the counter service. He ensures that there is sufficient cash to meet day to day requirements, and that the counter is adequately staffed. A proportion of his time is taken up by either acting as a cashier or dealing with customers' problems or queries referred to him by junior cashiers.

The checking of securities and foreign work in the office are dealt with by him, which require a certain amount of technical knowledge, although problems of a highly technical nature are referred to the Manager or, if necessary, to specialised departments at Regional Office.

Constant consideration has to be given to the question of staff training. The incumbent has to ensure that members of the staff are given the opportunity to do varied jobs in the office and he also provides some training in such areas as the more routine foreign and securities work.

Human relationships are of prime importance. It is essential that the service to the customers is courteous and friendly and it is also important to maintain a good staff relationship.

The incumbent has some authority to agree to requests for overdraft facilities up to a maximum limit of £   , but requests for amounts above this would be referred to the Manager or, in his absence, to the branch department at Divisional Office. Within this lending limit, up to £   may be unsecured. The Assistant Manager has a Personal Loan limit of £

It is essential that the incumbent keeps himself informed about any decisions taken by the Manager as he takes charge of the branch in the Manager's absence.

PRINCIPAL ACCOUNTABILITIES

1.   Provide a good service to customers by efficient organisation and supervision of the work of the office, subject to the direction of the Manager.

2.   Promote good customer relationship by providing a good counter service and by dealing efficiently with their securities and foreign problems.

3.   Increase the efficiency of the office by effective staff training.

4.   Ensure that branch records are adequate to provide information and returns to Divisional Office.

Figure 2 Job Description – Securities Clerk

JOB DESCRIPTION FORM (GRADES 1–4)

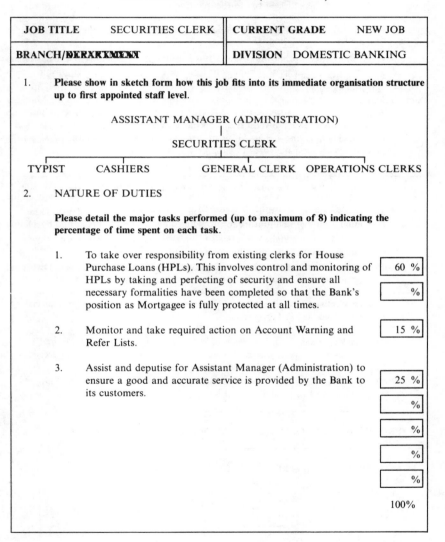

JOB TITLE	SECURITIES CLERK	CURRENT GRADE	NEW JOB
BRANCH/~~DEPARTMENT~~		DIVISION	DOMESTIC BANKING

1. **Please show in sketch form how this job fits into its immediate organisation structure up to first appointed staff level.**

ASSISTANT MANAGER (ADMINISTRATION)
|
SECURITIES CLERK

TYPIST   CASHIERS   GENERAL CLERK   OPERATIONS CLERKS

2.   NATURE OF DUTIES

Please detail the major tasks performed (up to maximum of 8) indicating the percentage of time spent on each task.

1.   To take over responsibility from existing clerks for House Purchase Loans (HPLs). This involves control and monitoring of HPLs by taking and perfecting of security and ensure all necessary formalities have been completed so that the Bank's position as Mortgagee is fully protected at all times.

60 %

%

2.   Monitor and take required action on Account Warning and Refer Lists.

15 %

3.   Assist and deputise for Assistant Manager (Administration) to ensure a good and accurate service is provided by the Bank to its customers.

25 %

%

%

%

%

100%

Figure 2 (continued)

3.	**With whom and for what reason does the job holder have contact with people other than colleagues in the branch or department**.
	Contact with Solicitors, H M Land Registry, Building Societies, Insurance Companies etc., regarding HPLs.

4.	**What experience will the average job-holder (e.g. the present one) have had before taking on this job?**
	A good working knowledge of all aspects of Branch Banking is required and in particular it is essential to keep abreast of the Bank's requirements and various legal requirements in taking a charge over property. The average job holder would need at least 5 years service before attaining these qualifications.

5.		**Please outline the most complicated decisions required to be taken by the job holder.**
	a)	Appreciate the significance before release of deposit monies and completion monies for property transactions.
	b)	Have an understanding of financial commitments on personal and family budgets before recommending loan facilities.
	c)	In the absence of an Advances Department be satisfied that various security conforms with Bank's requirements.

6.		**In what ways and to what extent can mistakes in this job involve delay or financial loss to the bank and and its customers?**
	a)	Lack of understanding of detailed procedures can result in an unsecured HPL position or at least greatly weakened security following recent legal decisions in this area.
	b)	Lack of proper direction and advice to junior staff could affect the Branch's image and lose profitable business.

APPROVED BY JOB HOLDER ..../MANAGER .... DATE................

EVALUATION COMMITTEE USE ONLY

EXPERIENCE	[ ]	SUPERVISION	[ ]
COMPLEXITY	[ ]	LOSS	[ ]
DISCRETION	[ ]	CONTACT	[ ]

TOTAL　　=　　GRADE

AUTHORISED...................................DATE....................................

CHAPTER 12

Performance Appraisal, Counselling and Management by Objectives

Tony Jackson

Senior Lecturer in Occupational Psychology,
Henley – The Management College

Despite what organisations do to their employees, rather than because of what they do, individuals manage to progress and learn within the job context. Systems to formalise people's development have been part of most organisations' personnel procedures for decades. But the emphasis which these systems have had has changed dramatically over the last ten to fifteen years.

The Dictionary definitions of 'appraisal' revolve around the ideas of evaluation and price fixing. Historically that possibly explains its usage to describe a method designed to provide information for the organisation for various purposes.

The objectives of any appraisal scheme revolve around direct and indirect advantages for the organisation. Direct advantages include such things as the provision of better information for administration decisions and manpower planning, etc; indirect ones refer to the enhanced performance and commitment of employees, plainly of benefit to the organisation.

The inherent shortcomings and inconsistencies of traditional techniques have been, and are being, acknowledged. This has led to the emphasis being portrayed in this chapter, that of *developing* the performance of an employee in the current job as opposed to attempting to *assess* that performance. Employees are, therefore, moving towards being active agents, rather than the passive agents of yesterday, in determining what will happen to them.

Purposes of Appraisal

When a company introduces or proposes an appraisal scheme, the underlying aim is to increase the effectiveness of the organisation's human resource as a whole. All activities in the scheme can be directly or indirectly tied to this. That is not to say that some parts of the scheme will not also result in personal benefits to individual employees, but organisations will not normally devise schemes with these as end objectives in themselves.

Within the context of a straightforward appraisal scheme most organisational purposes are concerned with establishing controls or, perhaps, bringing about change. From this, therefore, a number of major purposes emerge. First the evaluation of staff (i.e. place a value on) – in these terms the scheme is used to allocate rewards, share out bonuses or other perquisites on as fair a basis as possible. Secondly, the scheme can provide an audit of the skills and knowledge of the employees. Here we are concerned with people's current and future work potential with its obvious links into the planning activities, e.g. manpower planning and training needs analysis of the organisation. Thirdly, it is also of some importance to those organisations where mobility is expected of staff. In such cases it can prove a useful record for an incoming manager, to review the strengths and weaknesses of the staff of the branch or section etc. Finally, as a record of decisions made; the system can be used as a check to see what is happening within departments.

These purposes may not always be explicitly enumerated. Moreover, they may overlap, merge and even conflict with one another. When a categorisation is attempted, three main groups emerge: allocation of rewards and benefits, *the reward review*; improvement of current job performance, *the performance review*; prediction of the level and type of work which the individual will undertake in the future, *the potential review*.

These three activities overlap and interlock to a certain extent, and, despite a recent contrary view[1], the evidence suggests they should be separated in practice. At least one reason for this is that the techniques, procedures and information required to achieve each, are not necessarily the same.

Depending on the orientation and ambition of an appraisal scheme, an employee's interests can be served in one or more of the following ways. First, the satisfaction of the need for feedback on the individual's performance, including how well regarded is the person's work. Secondly, the knowledge that decisions on salaries, promotions etc. are as equitable and unbiased as possible. Thirdly, an opportunity to participate in decisions affecting the employee's own work. Fourthly, career counselling and planning with their possible outcomes of increasing motivation and optimism as well as, perhaps, commitment to the organisation.

Individual performance can be enhanced in three major ways. First, performance improvement can be enabled, i.e. by the provision of feedback on past performance and by clarifying requirements for the future. Secondly, such improvement can be assisted by such means as coaching the employee's on the job behaviour and by means of regular monitoring of achievement against objectives. Thirdly, by enticing improvement, for example by tying together individual performance and discretionary rewards.

Conflicts in Performance Appraisal

Often it is not the objectives themselves which are in conflict in performance appraisal schemes. Rather the methods which are used to achieve the objectives may carry inherently conflicting aspects, e.g. when the process is used both to inform the appraisee of an assessment made, as well as to provide help in improving job performance. It is the combination of judgemental with counselling activities which is at the heart of such conflict. Specifically when an employee is undergoing some form of evaluation there is little likelihood that that appraiser could simultaneously be viewed as a helper, there to assist in problem diagnosis and future development.

Formats of Appraisal

Given the multiplicity of purposes of appraisal it is understandable that there is a larger number of techniques available to help both record occurrences and focus attention on pertinent aspects. Such techniques would include:

1. *Checklists*: lists of characteristics against which the appraiser judges the appraisee's performance. The characteristics may be derived from job descriptions, personality traits or attitudes, e.g. leadership, decision making, initiative, dependability, etc.
2. *Activity Sampling*: a self explanatory term; the appraiser reviews performance by looking at just a small part of the work undertaken during the year.
3. *Objective Measures*: includes such things as the number of items sold, the number of units processed, time taken to perform a specific task, etc.
4. *Subjective Measures*: systems using these are more concerned with the quality of performance, i.e, how well the appraisee has worked, than with the quantity.
5. *Critical Incidents*: involves interviewing a number of people in the department about what they consider to have been difficult problems or incidents. Full details are noted, and trends and common factors are sought. From this analysis performance measures are derived.
6. *Comparisons*: in which the performance of one person is compared with that of one or more similarly employed people.

7.   *Ranking*: involves ranking, in order, one appraisee against another. It is a system which is most often used to allocate reward or merit payments. Ranking can take one of three formats. First, alternation, in which the 'best' and 'worst' employees are placed on the list, then the next 'best' and 'worst' and so on until a full ranking is obtained. Secondly, by paired comparisons, in which all members of a department are compared, one at a time with all other members; the end result being a ranking for that department. Thirdly, a forced distribution. Here the basic assumption is that in any group of people there will be some who are very good, some who are very poor performers, and a majority being in the middle ground. Each appraisee is assigned to a point on the distribution in such a way as to cover the spectrum, i.e. poor to good performance.

8.   *Scales (graphic or numeric)*: ask the appraiser to look at the appraisee's performance on certain behaviours and rate it on a scale. For example:

sets priorities and objectives

I ---------I ---------I ---------I ---------I
1   2   3   4   5
always   never

9.   *Questionnaire*: consists of a series of bipolar statements concerned with performance. The appraiser has to score the appraisee's performance on all statements or some subset of them. A typical banking example would be:

meets deadlines I -----I -----I -----I -----I does not meet deadlines
                1   2   3   4   5

In this instance the statement is a simplified one. The respective poles may contain the following behaviours; meets deadlines, consumes work, manages additional tasks despite being overloaded, assists others, linked with; does not meet deadlines or deal with additional tasks, does not assist others.

10.   *Written Statements*: involves recording the individual's performance verbatim on the form. There is usually some stimulus sentence to help the appraiser focus on specific areas, e.g. 'in considering the main tasks and responsibilities of the position, what have been the difficulties and problems that have been encountered?'

Most forms use amalgamations of these different formats, especially the combination of questionnaire and written statements.

These can be looked at under three main headings – personality, results and behaviour based appraisal.

Personality-Based Appraisal

This requires the identification of qualities, traits, attitudes, etc. thought to be necessary for effective performance, and against which employees are rated. It is when the list of prescribed characteristics takes shape that its problems become quite obvious. Such a list might include emotional make up, interests, values, motives, knowledge, skills and aptitudes, as well as the 'character' aspects such as resourcefulness, initiative, loyalty etc.

Regretfully there are problems with such words. First in defining them, especially given that different people will attach widely different meanings to each word. And in any case, psychologists have difficulties agreeing definitions for trait characteristics. How much less of a chance do managers, who use the words in less precisely defined contexts, have of agreeing meanings across a range of situations.

Secondly, determination of which traits are more important in a particular job is rarely researched. Often what occurs under these circumstances is some kind of summation of scores on the various factors, which lends a spurious credibility to the process. Regretfully, such scores are meaningless.

Thirdly, and perhaps most importantly of all, whilst the application of traits may be useful in providing predictions vis-a-vis future career paths and plans, they are of little value in the feedback of performance to assist employees to improve in their current job. They give no indication as to which actions are appreciated, which are depreciated. But worse, personality, be definition, refers to relatively enduring characteristics of the individual, implying an inability to change. In any case there is an ethical consideration: should managers be asked to attempt to change aspects of an individual such as personality? When all is said and done employees are paid to behave, to perform not to *be* something.

Results-Based Appraisal

The reference here is to the outcomes and consequences of an employee's actions. Naturally, criteria may vary widely depending on the individual's role in the organisation. In a sense such measures are a summary or index of organisational outcomes for which an individual is at least partially responsible. Such criteria often form the basis of Management by Objectives programmes (see separate section below).

In brief, there are problem areas with such schemes. It is difficult, for example, to obtain cost-related measures especially for white collar jobs. Even when feasible measures can be devised they are likely to be affected by factors over which the individual has little or no control. Such measures also assume that the type and amount of resource allocated to each employee is the same. Finally, but not least importantly, results often get fed-back to employees too late for them to have any reinforcement value to performance; and it is important for the feedback to be not just as precise and as personal as possible, but also to be proximate to the behaviour giving rise to the result.

Behaviour-Based Appraisal

These measures encompass what an individual actually does whilst working. The theory is that such measures should define precisely what employees have control over and relate to how they are to attain those targets they have been charged with reaching. Whilst personality may explain or clarify why a person does something, and results may indicate the consequences of the action, behaviour is at the heart of an employee's controllable actions.

To measure performance the last decade or so has seen developments in Behaviourally Anchored Rating Scales (BARS). Based on a development of the critical incident method, they require an analysis of the components of job performance. Similar behavioural items are grouped into a yardstick against which employees' performance will be compared.

Such measures require both time and effort to distil. Even the simple noting of critical incidents over a period of time can become a major chore. Moreover, whilst the actual recording of the incident might get close to objectivity, the decision as to what is critical is, by definition, subjective. Worse, outstanding behaviour, if not critical to performance, may not be recorded.

In summary then, results factors are arguably of greatest significance for that is what is paid for. However, the fact that results may be one or more steps removed from what the individual actually does must be borne in mind. Personality factors are of little direct relevance and are perhaps best used predictively (and possibly even better to be left in the hands of a psychologist). Their common use, therefore, should be precluded. Whilst practical difficulties are argued against behavioural measures, these are now being overcome and so the arguments against their use are less strong. The emphasis has to be on what is observable and can be of use as feedback, not what is to be inferred, or is unchangeable.

Problems

Whatever the format and purpose of the system, there are a number of problems of which the people running the system should be aware. These problems can be classified into four major categories, technical, administrative, social and forms.

Technical problems include such items as halo (conversely known as the cloven hoof effect), bias, labelling and central tendency. Halo is well known, but worth a brief revisit anyway. It is the tendency to assume that because someone is neat, tidy, smiles readily and agrees with all that is said, then he or she is also honest, intelligent, full of initiative and has powers of leadership. Confidence tricksters rely on this human failing of judging the whole from seeing a sample. 'Labelling' is a not dissimilar phenomenon. If someone is labelled as being clever or a high flyer then others look, albeit subconsciously, for those behaviours which confirm the label. Under these circumstances other inappropriate behaviours are overlooked or ignored.

With appraisal formats which have rating scales as an integral element there is a tendency, 'the central tendency', to mark around the average. In those cases where the left hand column carries the same poor (or beneficent) label, there is a tendency for raters to proceed down a single column.

Administrative problems include such items as time, paperwork, user training and confidentiality. Whilst these almost speak for themselves one or two key points should be made. By time, for example, is meant the amount of time which is taken to operate the system. The managers may expect preparation, interview and writing-up time for each person in the department. With eight or more people this exercise could have an apparently disproportionate encroachment into the managers' time for actual work. The paperwork too may be so elaborate that it requires a great deal of time. Specific skills may require training with its obvious disruptions within the organisation. Confidentiality raises all sorts of issues such as where should information be located, who can access it etc.

Social problems are less easily seen or described but they will include such things as alienation and the maintenance of mediocrity. The former often comes about because people do not understand the system which is being worked, or have never seen any changes or action resulting from the appraisal system. Maintenance of mediocrity refers to many managers' inability to grasp the nettle of dealing with subordinates' actual performances. Also, the system may produce rigidity, primarily through the need managers may feel to *control* rather than *change* behaviour.

This leads into the consideration of what must be considered as two major problems: that of *setting common standards* and *defining criteria*. In any organisation system where different managers are looking at performance, there are bound to be wide differences in their views of similar behaviour. In other words, even at the descriptive level we will find quite startling differences across the organisation. When we attempt to display standards in the form on which the appraisal is to be recorded, then these are open to alternative definitions by different managers. Indeed should the criteria then be judged on a poor, average, above average, excellent – or some such – scale, we exacerbate the problem of getting a consensus across the organisation as to the precise level of performance which falls into each of the categories. In other words even the more apparently objective formats are riddled with subjectivity.

Finally, *the form*, on which the kernel of the appraisal is captured, provides a source of problems. In essence the problem reduces to one of research, or rather lack of it. Many organisations do not undertake sufficient research to decide what should appear on the appraisal form. Often identical forms are used across a wide spectrum of jobs and levels in the structure of an organisation, assuming that the skills and knowledge requirements are at least similar. In a sense, even worse, it assumes that the jobs themselves are not dynamic, i.e. they remain stable in content and context over time; a somewhat ill-founded belief in the majority of cases.

Who is the Appraiser?

A question which is of major concern, because one of the implications of the answer is: 'who should appraise the appraisee?' Thus in the Civil Service the manager prepares a written report on the subordinates in the department. These reports are sent on to his or her own manager who is the one who will carry out the appraisal. The subordinate will also prepare for the interview using a similar form. In essence, the system has a certain objectivity attached to it. However, the 'grandfather' figure may have little or no contact with the appraisee, except for the annual appraisal. All the information is filtered through the subordinate's immediate manager.

Some systems demand that the peer group, i.e. one level of managers appraise one another. Such appraisals tend to be honestly, perhaps even 'brutally', carried out. But they do deal well with on the job performance to bring about performance improvements.

In other instances, subordinates carry out the appraisal. A number of organisations utilse this method. The problem is finding a format which will allow for useful feedback to be given but without pinpointing specific individuals. One organisation, for example, uses questionnaires the results of which are fed back to the manager anonymously. The manager too, fills in the questionnaire, as to where he or she believes the subordinates will place their rating. It has been found to be quite a powerful modifier of behaviour.

There are organisations in which a centralised function undertakes the appraisals (e.g. personnel), others use external assessment procedures such as assessment centres. Such practice is prevalent at the more senior levels in some organisations.

However, the one favoured by most organisations is the subordinates immediate boss. This manager is in the best position to be able to judge performance against a wider context. Moreover, there is likely to be at least daily contact between them, and possibly a very close working relationship, putting the manager in a very good position to discuss actual job performance.

Management by Objectives

Few organisations claiming to have MbO (Management by Objectives) system actually do. The major aspect which is lacking is the concept of a two way flow in the objective-setting exercise itself. But first a description of what is popularly named MbO.

In essence the chief executive will determine the organisation's objectives both for the longer and shorter term. A full consideration of possible constraints which will act to inhibit achievement of these targets, as well as determining criteria against which successful achievement of targets will be measured, will be undertaken. A meeting will be then arranged with the executive's reporting managers to discuss and agree targets, constraints and measures for each subordinate. This process is continued down the organisation by each of these managers with their respective subordinates. As time progresses review meetings are also held at each level to check progress and make any alterations which may be necessary.

As this description implies, providing all employees share in the common goal and have a common commitment, then MbO works well. Duplication of effort can be substantially reduced and delegation is actively encouraged by this system.

Some managers do have difficulty setting objectives mainly because they get overly concerned with numeric measurement. However, in some areas, e.g. sales, production etc. objectives can, by and large, be easily set, even in numeric terms. In others it will be less easily accomplished, but the important aspect to stress is that the need is to have objectives which are neither too easily nor with great difficulty, achievable.

The procedure for objective setting has advantages. Attention of both manager and subordinate is focused on the specific need of the job. The subordinate's targets will be specific and personal. As well, to the extent that the subordinate has had some say in the agreement of targets, then commitment is likely to be higher.

Usefully, any review of a previous year has to begin with a reference to the original objectives. This is especially helpful, in pulling concentration away from recent events and so helps in a review of the whole year. The system should also enable subordinates to obtain a more composite view of the organisation so they can judge better where their own contribution will be, or has been, fitting. Moreover, because there is a concentration on success measures, subordinates are better placed to monitor and control their own performance.

There are, of course, disadvantages. There is an explicit assumption that both manager and subordinate are parties to the agreement of objectives, yet many organisations claiming to have an MbO system leave no room for manoevre by the subordinate on whom a set of objectives is fixed. Under these circumstances many of the claimed benefits of MbO fade away. Often target setting is carried out in a mechanistic and overly numerical way. Too, there is an inherent danger that the objectives will be seen as limiting freedom. Organisationally there can be major difficulties when an MbO system is taken from one part or division of the organisation to another, even when based on initial success in the first case.

The appraisal and MbO systems have many similarities and may often be mistaken for one another. Common to both is the basic meeting – reviewing the past and planning the future. Within the context of MbO, however, there is an assumption that meetings are dependent on each other, both in time and as a continuous chain starting at the top of the organisation. It also assumes a formal sharing of objectives between manager and subordinate. MbO may also generate masses of paperwork.

On the other hand appraisals can occur at any time, without the necessity of waiting for the chief executive to begin the process. The objectives being discussed and set can be both unique and personal and, perhaps most importantly, without reference to the objectives of the appraising manager. Generally speaking, a much wider range of styles of undertaking an appraisal is tolerated than would be in the case in MbO.

There has been much praise and criticism noted about MbO systems. By and large it works well in areas such as production and sales where output is measurable. It can be made to work in service or non-profit functions, too. But it takes effort, an effort which has not always been forthcoming.

Context of Performance Appraisal

Appraisals must always take note of the context within which the employee performs the job. In these terms, assessments are to be made taking into account controllable outcomes attributable to the employee's behaviour, not to other's actions or job technology. Indeed, performance deterioration may be due to other organisational factors such as political battles, poor resources, insufficient information, etc. The reverse, performance improvement, may have similar causal factors.

Once it has been established that a specific performance is due to factors internal to the individual as opposed to externally (i.e. to others, or the organisation, or changing technology), then action must be seen to result from the appraisal. This may take the form of an initiation of change, but whatever the action, it must be visible. A belief that the organisation does not 'do its bit' is one of the greatest discouragements to the employee.

Overtness of Appraisal

Involvement of the appraisee in the process still varies from total involvement to non-involvement. The appraisee's involvement, therefore, lies on a dimension which at one extreme includes not knowing the appraisal has occurred, to the other extreme of full participation with mutuality of goal setting, and will take in at the intermediate stages awareness without involvement. formal notification of a decision made and so on.

There are arguments both for and against giving notice or feedback to the individual. If instead we relate these to the objectives of the appraisal the case is clarified.

First, if performance improvements are required, feedback, as precise as possible, is vital. Covert schemes cannot cope with this aspect. Secondly, if assessments are the order of the day, then the evidence suggests these are fairer if carried out and justified with the person being assessed. Though there is a tendency in such systems for some managers to inflate assessments in order to avoid confrontations. Thirdly, if improved manager-subordinate relationships are being looked for, then participation is vital.

Covert appraisals are most useful when dealing at a planning level in the organisation where assessments and performance predictions are sought. Though there is a strong counter argument to this case which will be explored later. To return to the argument, secrecy can legitimately be justfied on the grounds that employees may see honest potential assessments as 'promises' when these are in reality merely explorations of possibilities. Covert appraisals are, generally, less time-consuming and easier to operate.

Appraiser Limitations

Most of us have our limitations and it is easy to expect too much of managers, who have many and diverse pressures to contend with. Most limitations can be alleviated either (or both) through a soundly designed scheme or, more importantly, a thorough and relevant training scheme. But neither of these can hope to contend with and overcome all problems.

A common problem is for the appraiser to dwell on trivial or unimportant aspects of the appraisee's behaviour. In such circumstances the whole degenerates into a 'nit picking' exercise. This situation is aggravated if the appraiser does not have a full understanding of the appraisee's job, and can only identify superficial components of it. The employee's reaction is most likely to be defensive, making open and constructive dialogue difficult to develop.

Secondly, there is a tendency to accept the first satisfactory explanation for performance symptoms, rather than to pursue diagnostically what may be a much more complex situation. Too often this is due to either conflicting priorities, or pressures placed on managers.

However, perhaps the major problem is concerned with the different standards of different managers, which raises the spectre of incomparability between their respectvie reviews. In general it is not that groups necessarily feel unfairly treated by their individual managers. Indeed, managers are often seen as being fair and consistent to their subordinates. The problem rather lies in how one group compares itself with another group under a different manager. Some departments will have more competent staff than others, and, because there is a not unnatural tendency to appraise relatively, those employees having less competition from colleagues may benefit (financially or in some other way), at the expense of those in a department where competition is more fierce.

Inconsistencies, of course, apply not just between different managers, but also with the same manager with different subordinates. The reasons are as varied as the people concerned, better knowledge of one, personal relationsips, timing of the appraisal (e.g. during heavy or light managerial work load).

Many of these can be, at least in part, overcome by having a good monitoring system. The advent of computers makes this totally realistic today. For example, one of the major clearing banks evaluates the evaluations made by managers in two ways. First to check for consistency of spread across different areas of the five point rating scale (which forms one part of their appraisal). The usual bias emerges for them as for most other organisations, i.e. most people perform better than average. In the second place a department can be given a comparison of its rating of its own appraisees compared with ratings given across the whole organisation. Areas of concern can thus be highlighted and appropriate remedial action put in train.

Intentional Abuse of the System

Systems, once in existence, may be exploited by those for whom that system was built to help. The type of abuses being considered here are especially aided by those schemes concerned with evaluation as opposed to those having a development or coaching orientation.

First, then, the subordinate who is highly regarded may receive poor evaluations simply to stop any chance of being promoted out of that department. Alternatively, in a salary orientated review this type of person may receive a high rating to attract a large bonus or merit award to prevent his or her wishing to leave the department or company.

Conversely, a poorly viewed subordinate may be given a low rating to create frustration and cause either voluntary or involuntary dismissal. Or such a person may be given high ratings to ensure promotion to another department.

Occasionally, the abuse takes the form of taking the easy way out. As a good generalisation, many managers find it difficult to face people with their poor performance. Hence the recent proliferation of literature in this area. Such evaluations, i.e. giving higher ratings than performance would indicate, could, perhaps, be justified where it leads to improvements in performance. The problems arise when such ratings percolate through the department, for once the equity of the system is faulted then the integrity of that system fails and cannot easily be regained.

Of course, it may be that, in order to show the department up in the best possible light, a manager rates all subordinates highly. Third party monitoring may effectively stop these kinds of occurrences.

Such practices are not direct consequences of the design of the scheme, but arise as a result of other situational factors, such as connections with the reward or career progression systems. The problem, organisationally, is that this type of political manipulation, when (*not* if) observed by employees, undermines their confidence in the scheme.

Looked at in a slightly difference light, it may be that the ability to manipulate the system implies there is some form of control being left in the manager's own hands. The problem is that once established, such practices are diffiult to eradicate.

Counselling

Essentially this is a method of helping employees to make decisions about goals. The normal pattern of interaction is a one to one basis; alternatively co-counselling, where individuals having similar problems come together to share views and perspectives on how to deal with them, can be used.

The chief aim of counselling is to obtain an understanding between the two parties which patently necessitates the building of trust between the people involved. However, it also involves the conquering of interpersonal anxieties and emotional blocks which may be present. The process is subtle and requires high level interviewing skills of a form slightly changed from any other type of interview. The greatest danger in counselling is that the interview session itself drifts away from a common sense approach into emotional complexities, and thus exacerbates the problem under discussion.

A fundamental point about counselling is that there are many situations in which all an individual needs to know is that someone else agrees with him, or at least shares his view or will support him in a plan of action. In this sense counselling may be an indispensable skill to managers.

It could be expected that, as managerial skills in problem solving increase, and as these skills are added to the total experience of the organisation, fewer problems should occur. At least those problems which do occur should be solved more easily. In other words, as the body of managerial experience grows, the reality of business life should grow closer to management plans and forecasts. This does not appear to be the case. Managers would argue that their problems are increasing both in number and complexity. For example, the microchip may well handle the new industrial revolution, but it will also bring many managerial headaches. The electronic office will still require an old fashioned medicine cabinet for the asprin.

It might be helpful at this stage to look at the kinds of problems which face managers. They appear to fall into two major categories, technical and human. Of these the human category still comes a poor second in the world of business. Promotions to executive posts are usually made on the criterion of technical ability. This is particularly true in the professions. Scientists, engineers and accountants, for example, having a long and exhaustive training in a particular technical discipline, tend to judge people's performance on the basis of their technical skills. Yet commonly, as people move through the organisation they become less and less involved in technical work and more involved in the human aspects of management.

An added difficulty in trying to predict when people problems will arise is that quite naturally, situations are judged by people's own standards. Thus, if one employee is happy with a particular situation then his or her belief will be that everyone else will be. This thought brings to light the first rule for the solution to a person's problem. Simply, it is necessary to acknowledge that if a person says they have a problem then a problem exists. We are too prone to dismiss, or make light of, problems which others believe they have.

Clearly we could delineate three areas which may be the root cause of problems. First, when people feel their pay is inequitable for the work they do and the responsibilities the job carries. This feeling may include not only underpayment, but also overpayment. Secondly, the nature and content of the work itself: is it too easy or too demanding? Thirdly, the capacity of the individual to carry out the work he or she is given to do. More problem areas could be delineated such as interpersonal conflict, underestimation of their own abilities, etc. However, the important aspect to note is that each of these gives cause for a person at work to feel dissatisfaction and, therefore, to have a personal problem.

In any organisation which wishes to use counselling there is one major need. Approaching the manager on any sort of delicate matter opens up two possibilities. First that the information may not be treated confidentially and, secondly, that it may be used in a damaging way against the subordinate. In other words there must be a good climate within the organisation for counselling to be effective.

Effective Counselling

What are the major elements of effective counselling? The first thing to look at is the prime aim of counselling, which is to *help the individual discover* the solutions to his or her own problem. This statement is probably contrary to a manager's natural inclination, which is to give advice. A non-directive approach to counselling is essential, not simply because of any unwillingness to use authority, but rather because it is in line with the reality of human behaviour. People become committed to a particular decision or course of action when they have made up their own minds and personally believe that it is the right thing to do. Whilst money, conditions and the type of work are all contributory factors to the motivation of people at work, the essential factor is the personal commitment which a person brings to that work. It then becomes 'my work' and counselling is a way of acknowledging this process and attempting to work with it.

Counselling also results in the realisation that what is right for one person is not necessarily right for another. What is important to the individual may not be so to someone else. Counselling is based on the recognition of an individual's autonomy and of the potential power possessed by that person. It attempts to realise and release this power, rather than to deny it or fight it.

Counselling involves a number of elements. The most important is that of *listening*. It is not a passive activity. Karl Rogers coined the description 'active listening'. It implies doing something positive rather than simply refraining from talking.

Secondly, the problem as presented has to be reviewed. It can be difficult to start a counselling interview and much depends on the relationship which already exists between the manager and subordinate. From the subordinate's viewpoint, the more serious or delicate the issue to be raised, the more difficulty will be found in saying it. Consequently, the first words are unlikely to be a full statement of the problem. Rather, socially acceptable and generalised words will be chosen.

Thirdly, the manager must attempt to find the 'core' problem. This follows naturally from understanding the dynamics of the 'presenting' problem. Within the words used during the early part of the counselling interview, there are clues or linkages which point to the essence of the problem. At the core there will be something that is concerning the subordinate personally and proximately.

Fourthly, managers need to be able to recognise and allow for feelings to be admitted. Problems invariably have feelings associated with them. Those that are purely technical do not require counselling. They can be solved by factual analysis. It is the emotional content which can cause the difficulty for managers, both in its exploration and recognition.

Fifthly, there is one thing which is almost invariably guaranteed to stop effective counselling; that is *criticism*. When people feel criticised they feel threatened. And the automatic reaction to that is either flight or fight, i.e. the person threatened operates defence mechanisms for protection against the perceived threat. The climate of openess and trust essential for effective councelling is lost and will take a long time to re-establish. However, it does depend on how precisely and constructively that criticism is effected by the manager as to whether it has deliterious effects.

Sixthly, whilst there is a major concern to help people to solve their own problems, the situation is rarely clear cut. Moreover, although there is no one formula for any interview, and especially a counselling one, there are stages in its progress which we can analyse. Again, these may neither be so clear cut nor may they follow in this precise order, but they include: the presenting problem, the core problem, discovering why it is a problem, exploration of feelings, examining possible solutions and alternatives, recognising their implications and deciding on a course of action (or no action).

Finally, the direction has to be chosen. Counselling could be described as an exploration. In which case, there is some necessity too for the counsellor to steer the interview in the right direction, i.e. a direction leading to the resolution of the problem. But which is the right direction? Inevitably the counsellor's choice of response takes the discussion into one or another area. The session may go down a dead end. In this case all that is lost is a certain amount of time. Much worse, in terms of its effects, is an inappropriate questioning style which can enlarge something of little significance into something of importance. Resolution of this pseudo-important matter brings little benefit and leaves the real problem untouched.

In essence, what the effective counsellor does to combat this problem is to continually construct mental hypotheses and use these as a basis for giving a direction to the discussion. The importance of the word 'hypothesis' cannot be over-stated. It is a temporary and tentative explanation which seems to fit the facts as they have thus far been explored. It may be changed in the light of new and different information. This seemes to go against the idea of listening and giving our full attention to the individual being counselled, yet in essence, the skilful interviewer will be able to switch into this mode of thinking, with practice. That part of the brain which is continually computing facts and feelings which are being heard tests them against tentative hypotheses which are being formed. This leads the interviewer to take the line of approach which enables the person being counselled to explore and examine some particular aspect of the situation and perhaps gain knowledge and insight about him or herself. The ensuing conversation may then confirm the counsellor's hypotheses and so enable them to go further down that particular avenue. If, however, the opposite happens, then that idea is rejected and a search made for another which is more probable.

The counsellor, therefore, needs an understanding of human behaviour and especially an awareness of the range of human feelings and emotions. With broad insight into all the kinds of factors which are likely to be contributing to the problem, then wide-ranging hypotheses can be constructed which are more likely to be helpful in leading to the core of the problem.

Why, then is counselling so important within an organisation? Organisations require efficiency at all levels and a continual awareness of minor changes. So which areas within the organisations contribute dramatically to its ability to respond quickly and appropriately to market changes and so on? Undoubtedly one key area is the manager–subordinate relationship. It is a common experience that every manager has an effect on the performance of subordinates and the way in which their work is carried out.

Final words

It is important that any appraisal system should support the organisation's strategic objectives. If an organisation wishes to have an integrated human resource management system which has a capacity to support its business plan, then some form of appraisal is not merely an option, it is a necessity. Its inputs are so vital, that, if undertaken ineffectively, the overall human resource management system is destined to be ineffective.

At least two perspectives must be accounted for in assessing any perform-ance appraisal scheme; first the effectiveness as judged by appraisers and managers, secondly as judged by appraisees and subordinates. Ideally, the performance appraisal should satisfy the needs of both. To meet the employees' needs it must help them to know the organisation's official view of their work, their chances for advancement, salary increases and perhaps most importantly, the ways they can improve their performance to meet their own and the organisation's goals better. To meet the goals of an organisation, performance appraisal must help the organisation to utilise the skills of its employees, and to motivate and develop them to perform effectively.

Finally, it should be remembered that it is always dangerous to accept a system which works well for other organisations. Organisations are like poeple: they are unique. Indeed, a comment from a senior personnel director responsible for the manpower across a wide range of functions in a large organisation, each function having a different appraisal scheme, was asked how he coped. He answered simply 'If the people concerned with the system are happy with it and know how to work it, then I will find ways myself to extract the information which I require from their system'.

References
1. Lawler, E. E. III, Mohrman, A. M. Jr., and Resnick, S. M., Performance Appraisal Revisited., *Organisational Dynamics*, 20–35, 1984.

Recommended Reading

Anstey, E., Fletcher, C., and Walker, J., *Staff Appraisal and Development*, Allen and Unwin, London 1976.

Ilgen, D. R., Peterson, R. B., Martin, B. A., and Boeschen, D. A., 'Supervisor and Subordinate Reaction to Performance Appraisal Sessions'. *Organisational Behaviour and Human Performance*, 28, 311–330, 1981.

Meyer, H. H., Kay, E., and French, J. R. P., *Split Roles in Performance Appraisal*, Harvard Business Review, Jan–Feb, 1965.

Randell, G. A., Packard, P. M. A., Shaw, R. L., and Slater, A. J., *Staff Appraisal*, I.P.M., London 1978.

Stewart, V. and Stewart, A., *Practical Performance Appraisal*, Gower Press, Farnborough, 1974.

CHAPTER 13

The Principles of Training and Learning

Keith Hillyer, JP, FIB

Freelance Consultant;
Formerly Group Training Manager National Westminster Bank

'When will they ever learn, when will they ever learn?' You may remember that refrain of the popular song of a few years ago: 'Where have all the flowers gone?' It emphasised the futility of war and the failure of each new generation to learn the lessons of earlier conflicts.

It is this emphasis on *learning* (i.e. what the learner does) as opposed to *teaching* (i.e. what the teacher does) which most marks the changes in education and training in recent years. Before turning to training and its methodology, therefore, we should spend a little time examining how learners learn.

Learning Theory: Although the words 'Learning Theory' are written and spoken frequently, the fact is that there is not one separate theory of learning but a number of theories which have been developed over the years. We will look briefly at some of these and, later on in the chapter, when we turn to various methods of training, we will see how these methods have been influenced by the various learning theories.

Learning is 'a relatively permanent change in behaviour that occurs as a result of practice'[1]. It is not an event, therefore, which happens of its own accord or without prompting. The learner may wish:

> to acquire or develop *knowledge* in a particular area.

The reader of this book will, for example, be hoping to improve his knowledge in the field of 'Management and People in Banking'.

> to acquire or develop a new or existing *skill*.

In the business field, the learner may wish to improve his skill in interviewing techniques, negotiations, computer operation or programing. In the recreational area, he may wish to learn to swim, ride a bicycle or improve his golf. It should be noted that the majority of skills also have a knowledge element.

to change his *attitude* to a particular topic

It is unusual for a learner to identify his own need to change an attitude or approach, though his attitude is a frequent problem for the trainer. A lack of confidence or commitment by a learner can be a barrier to the acquisition of knowledge or skills and this must be dealt with if learning is to take place. It is an important and frequently neglected area. 'Education does not consist merely in adorning the memory and enlightening the understanding. Its main business should be to direct the will'.[2]

Learning takes place within the trainee. It is not possible to observe this, although we can see training being applied to him. We must infer from systematic observation made both before and after a learning experience that a consistent change of behaviour has occurred.

Some Learning Theories

Psychological theory of human behaviour has developed in the last hundred years. Many of the theories overlap, but all provide some help to the trainer as he struggles to effect that 'relatively permanent change of behaviour' which we have already mentioned.

Lunzer[3] has suggested two helpful ways of classifying the various theories. First, he distinguishes between the *behaviourist* and the *cognitive* theorists. The behaviourists treat learning as the link between a stimulus and a response. This is written symbolically as S–R. The cognitive theorists emphasise the part which the brain plays in that period between a stimulus and a response. They stress that the experiences, attitudes and perceptions of the learner will all modify his reaction.

The second major division concerns the view taken of the stimulus. There are those who regard an external stimulus as essential to the elicitation of a response whilst others maintain that individuals are activated spontaneously and if no stimuli are present in the immediate environment, then these will actively be sought.

This two-by-two classification should not be taken as other than very general and simplistic. There are intermediate stages between the extremes and the demarcation lines are flexible.

The Behaviourists

J. B. Watson (1878–1958), was probably the first of the behaviourists or connectionists. After many observations of both animal and child learning, he concluded that stimulus–response (S–R) connections are more likely to be established the more frequently or recently an S–R bond happens.

E. L. Thorndike, of the same period, laid emphasis on the reinforcement of the S–R bond which comes from a pleasing or gratifying outcome. This became known as his Law of Effect. Unsuccessful attempts at solving a problem are unlikely to be repeated but successful ones will be repeated until the response takes place wherever a similar problem appears. I. P. Pavlov should be mentioned, since he is probably the most widely known of workers in this field. However, his work is not of great practical use to the trainer as it was principally in the physiological field. His experiments with the salivation reflex of dogs are perhaps the most well-known.

In contrast to Pavlov, the work of the American psychologist, B. F. Skinner, is very relevant to training and training methodology, particularly as his theories form the basis of programmed learning instruction. Skinner developed Thorndike's Law of Effect by maximising rewards during learning. He introduced many very small steps, known as frames, by which the learner derived satisfaction through making many correct responses. A long chain of satisfaction through correct answers is known as *continuous reinforcement*. However, it is observable that satisfaction wanes if rewards are continuous but that enthusiasm can be regenerated by rewarding at irregular intervals. This is known as *intermittent reinforcement* and will be very familiar to those who gamble on fruit machines. There is an excellent lesson here for the tutor in the classroom and, incidentally, for the working manager as Blanchard and Johnson have pointed out[4]. Whilst in Pavlov's conditioning the stimulus was provided externally, in Skinner's work the stimulus depends on producing a reward through an accidental behaviour initially which later becomes intentional. This has become known as *operant conditioning*. It will be apparent that both types are fundamentally learning by trial and error.

The Cognitivists

One of the fundamental problems of the learning theories which we have outlined so far is whether the actions of such a complex animal as a human being can be adequately explained by analysing very small portions of behaviour. The cognitive group of psychologists would say that an individual's perception of a situation must be taken into account in attempting to explain his behaviour. M. Wertheimer, who founded the school of Gestalt psychology with Köhler and Koffka, was certainly of the view that the behaviourist approach clouded the understanding of human behaviour and instead he concentrated on perception. The Gestalt school is, however, best known for its work on insight or intuition, that sudden realisation of the solution to a problem which we have all experienced. 'Eureka' cried Archimedes when the idea suddenly came to him of a method of detecting the adulteration of the gold for Hiero's crown. Another important name is that of E. C. Tolman, who suggested that it was not 'S' connecting with 'R' which leads to learning, but that all behaviour has a purpose leading towards a particular goal. This behaviour is based on cues and previous experience. The expectations of his environment which the individual has acquired from present and earlier perceptions are modified in the light of new experiences, and this is the learning.

D. A. Kolb[5] illustrates the theories of the cognitive school by means of his learning loop.

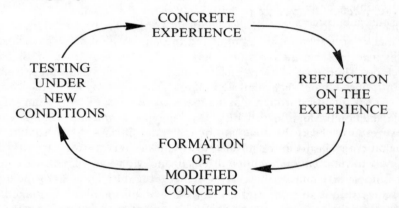

He showed by practical experiments on this theoretical model that some people are more comfortable or competent at one particular part of the cycle. Mumford and Honey[6] developed a Learning Styles Questionnaire which helps identify an individual's own preferred style of learning. These styles are defined as:

Activists	– who enjoy the here and now, are dominated by current experiences.
Pragmatists	– who are interested in experimenting with new techniques.
Reflectors	– who like to stand back and observe, to collect data and think.
Theorists	– who like to analyse and synthesise to produce models and systems.

It will be seen that not only is it helpful to the trainer to have knowledge of the preferred style of trainees when arranging training experiences but also it is useful for the individual trainee when planning activies for his own self-development. This work is particularly useful in the training of managers, since they bring to a training course a wealth of practical experience. If the trainer can arrange opportunities in brief times away from the job for managers, first to reflect on their experiences and compare them with those of colleagues and, secondly, to consider relevant theory, then the managers may form new ideas and translate these into practical action for their job.

There are two other wide areas of approach to the problems of learning which have developed in recent years which we should mention briefly.

The advent of computers and the study of the ways in which they process information led to comparative studies in the field of automatic communication and control in living bodies, an area known as Cybernetics.

Others have worked at the categorisation and classification of educational and training material. This practical approach is of much help to trainers and the publications of Bloom[7], Belbin[8] and Gagne[9], for example, though very different in their approach provide helpful tools for the practising trainer.

Development of Training in the Banks

Have you ever met a bank apprentice? Some of today's senior bankers will remember some of the generation before them who referred to themselves proudly as 'apprentices'. Although not formally 'bound apprentice' as was the Lincolnshire poacher, the use of the term provides an interesting insight into the attitude to work and training in the banks of those days. In fact, in the Middle Ages, when most the the population were illiterate, the only way to learn one's trade was through being instructed by a skilled man.

This method of receiving direct instruction on the job from a skilled instructor has therefore, a long and honourable history and is still the principal means by which most people in banks, and indeed throughout industry and commerce learn their jobs today.

In the period after the second World War there was, in this country, a growing discontent with vocational training and the apprenticeship system. Concern was expressed about the plight of those who failed to obtain an apprenticeship. The length of the apprenticeship period was also widely questioned. This anxiety resulted in the appointment of the Carr Committee, which reported in 1958.[10] Though the report dealt mainly with craft apprentices, it did identify a number of problems of general application. It recognised that 'more attention could profitably be given to methods of training' (para 62). In addition, as Perry[11], points out, 'there was an oblique reference to the absolute and vital need to ensure that training must have the support of all levels within the company, from the Chief Executive downwards, if it is to be carried out in an environment which will ensure success'.

This point was emphasised by Edwin Singer[12], who wrote:

'Training and development is a continuous process which flourishes best when the overall environment is such that managers are known to be interested in the development of their staff. This means that they should be as interested in people as in money matters. The application of well thought out routines and the exercise of sound judgement are essential for the functioning of any bank but these are insufficient if they are not accompanied by a positive interest in the development of the staff who perform much of the day to day work.'

Legislation

A strong lead from the centre was, however, needed and this was provided after several years of national debate by the passing of The Industrial Training Act 1964 and the first Industrial Training Board, for the Wool Industry, was announced in June of that year. By 1969 there were 27 boards set up under the Act and three voluntary boards, including one for the Insurance Industry. It was the early intention that there should be a statutory board for the Banking, Insurance and Finance Sector. However, this did not materialise because of a change of government policy at that time.

The Industrial Training Act has since been modified by the Employment and Training Act 1973 and the Industrial Training Boards were placed under the wing of the Training Services Division, one of the two arms of the Manpower Services Commission. Changes in government strategy over the last year or two have resulted in the demise of many of the ITB's and only a handful remain. New programmes in training are to be supplemented through the MSC, particularly in the area of the transition from full-time education to work.[13]

The impetus to training generally given by the 1964 Act, however, had a major impact on training in the banking industry through the tremendous advancement in training technology which it inspired and its emphasis on the importance of *training the trainer*. This improvement of the quality of training was timely, for jobs everywhere, not only in banking, were changing rapidly. In branch banks in the past it was often the boast of the manager that he could do any job in the office and, in walking about his branch, that he could lean over the shoulder of any member of his staff and help with any problem which might be troubling. The advent of the computer changed all this, and the drastic revision and reduction of the book-keeping systems, whilst ridding us of many dull routine jobs, meant that many new skills were introduced. New jobs were created for bankers to tackle. Data processing, perhaps, provided the greatest range, but work study, marketing, management information systems and many others all widened the scope of technical training.

Those trainers who concentrated exclusively on the knowledge and skill elements of the new job soon found that the most difficult problems lay elsewhere in the attitudinal area. They discovered that many of the older generation of bankers resisted the introduction of new methods, preferring the tried and tested ways which they had learned as 'man and boy'. Since those days, of course, the pace of change has accelerated and much attention is currently paid to the management of change (see Chapter 9).

An increasing welter of legislation bore down on the banker in the fields of employee relations, company law and consumer credit, whilst the Finance Acts necessitated lengthy annual appraisal, not only by the domestic banker, but more particularly by his colleagues in the trustee and income tax fields.

Learning and the Learner

As we have seen, there has been a considerable amount of study in the field of human learning and this has had a tremendous impact on those who design and deliver training. Much greater emphasis is now placed on the learner and the conditions under which he learns. Account is taken of the educational level of the learner and his age. Great care is needed in training and retraining the older worker to ensure that the methods selected are appropriate to the trainee's earlier experiences.

The learning must be carefully designed so that it:

stimulates the learner to want to learn;

keeps him active;

maintains his interest through experience of a number of learning methods;

presents the material logically and provides practice in whatever is being learnt.

Training

We must now ask ourselves the question 'what is training?'. Training has been defined as 'the systematic development of the attitude/knowledge/skill behaviour pattern required by an individual in order to perform adequately a given task or job'.[4]

1. The development of the training is 'systematic'. Whilst the ordinary dictionary definition of 'systematic' in its sense of 'methodical' and 'found or done according to a regular plan' is correct, the word is now also used by trainers as descriptive of the trainer's approach to a problem.

2.   The types of behaviour required are divided into the areas of knowledge, skill and attitude. The work of Bloom[7] and Belbin[8] is of particular practical importance here. Bloom categorised educational objectives into various levels in the cognitive, affective and psycho-motor domains, whilst Belbin, who identified five basic types of learning, leads the trainer by means of an algorithm to the appropriate training method.

3.   The purpose of training is to improve performance in a job. This may seem a trite and unnecessary comment. However, the simple questions asked of oneself or even more advantageously of the tutor at the end of a training session of any kind, 'Has this helped me to do my job better?' and 'What shall I now do differently?' can still, all too frequently, be answered negatively. Those activities arranged under the guise of training which cannot demonstrate subsequent improvement in performance in the job should be closely questioned.

The Systems Approach to Training

The seven steps of the Systems Approach to Training[15] are set out in the diagram. Before considering each step in detail we should note two features. First, steps two to six are enclosed in a box. This is the pure training area. Step 1 is concerned with establishing whether training needs to be done, and step 7 reviews the worth of the training. It can be seen, therefore, that the final word on steps 1 and 7 will be that of the line manager. Steps 2 to 6 will however be the prerogative of the trainer. Secondly, it will be seen that there are a number of dotted lines labelled 'feedback'. This shows how information obtained at later stages in the training cycle is fed back continuously to keep the training relevant and up-to-date. The rapidly changing environment and working systems make this a most important feature of the whole approach.

STEP 1 – IDENTIFYING THE TRAINING NEED

Problems which may need a training solution are presented in many ways:

- changes in legislation.
- changes in systems.
- changes in services provided.
- inadequate performance ... ... and so on.

If people are not doing what they should be doing in a job, it may be right to provide some form of training. But there may be other causes. A key question often is 'Could they do it if their lives depended on it?' An

The Systems Approach to Training

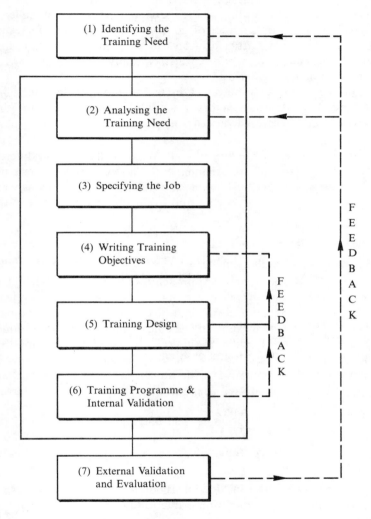

affirmative answer means that the problem is unlikely to yield to a training solution and that other areas should be explored.

Two main alternative problem areas are environmental and motivational. For example, we have all experienced the problem of trying to settle quietly to a job which needs our undivided attention for an hour or two in surroundings which bring constant interruption from callers or telephone. It is not lack of training which prevents us from doing the job but the environmental restrictions.

Again, some tasks are not seen as being of importance, of providing satisfaction for the job-holder or of being rewarding. Indeed, some tasks are seen as being very unrewarding to the individual. The roles of Collector of Taxes (such as VAT) or enforcer of government regulations, for example, are unlikely to be seen as particularly rewarding or satisfying to the individual banker. The trainer must, therefore, watch carefully for motivational factors which may be hindering performance.

The aim then in the early stages of discussion and investigation will be to identify and eliminate other factors which inhibit performance and then to concentrate on the performance deficiency.

STEP 2 – ANALYSING THE TRAINING NEED

The primary purpose of the training needs analysis is to determine the central nature and content of the job covering:

> the main job objective;
>
> the conditions under which it is performed;
>
> the responsibilities involved.

Methods employed may include structured interviews, questionnaires, work diaries or observation of experienced job-holders at work.

STEP 3 – SPECIFYING THE JOB

The end product of the analysis should be a *comprehensive specification for the job* which goes into more detail than the kind of job specification normally used in recruitment and grading.

A training specification should describe clearly:

> what the trainee will have to do after training;
>
> what judgements he makes;
>
> what factors he takes into account.

Moreover, it must be continually updated to cater for any changes which may occur in the job.

A job specification must include information on the important aspect of the job and will itemise some or all of the following:

> exact job title;
>
> numbers carrying out the job;
>
> job objectives – main and subsidiary;
>
> job performance standards;
>
> tasks – main and subsidiary;
>
> physical, social and psychological conditions under which the job is performed;

responsibilities;

difficulties;

irksome tasks.

Having arrived then at what the trainee needs to know and what skills he needs to acquire, the next step is to examine the current performance of the trainee so as to arrive at a statement of the exact training needs.

Job needs → trainee's present state → training need

STEP 4 – WRITING TRAINING OBJECTIVES

Good training objectives are central to good training. Objectives written in behavioural terms, observable actions described by an action verb, are the essential basis on which good training is organised.

The end results to be achieved must be quite unambiguous. You may remember Alice's conversation with the Cheshire Cat:

'Would you tell me, please, which way I ought to go from here?'

'That depends a good deal on where you want to get to,' said the Cat.

'I don't much care where,' said Alice.

'Then it doesn't matter which way you go', said the Cat.[16]

We must state with accuracy and precision what direction we wish our trainees to take. We do this by means of a training objective.

Each *training objective* is made up of three parts and should specify the:

performance – what the trainee has to be able to do;

conditions – under which the performance has to take place;

standards – the level of performance expected.

When writing objectives the trainer will use precise words describing observable actions, i.e. behaviours, for example:

list;

discriminate;

describe;

state;

identify;

contrast.

Other words may lead to misunderstandings as to the precise training and are best avoided, for example:

grasp significance of;

appreciate;

understand;

be aware;

discover;

become skilled in.

Some examples of training objectives are given below. The reader may care to identify the words which apply to the component parts of each objective, i.e. performance, conditions and standards.

1. The trainee cashier will be able to count with 100% accuracy 100 clean £5 notes in 35 seconds.

2. Given a list of products with a maximum of eight digits and a rate of interest for each, be able to convert to a sterling amount using interest tables provided. All answers to be correct to the nearest penny.

3. Given the set of guidelines issued during the course, the student will have prepared:

   a set of plans for improving the performance of his unit;

   a plan for presenting, gaining acceptance and implementing his plans,

   to the satisfaction of his line manager.

STEP 5 – TRAINING DESIGNS

The exact content of the training programme is now determined by *training design*. A learning analysis is carried out which:

breaks down the identified training objectives into enabling objectives. These are objectives which are subordinate to the training objectives and set out in greater detail what the trainee must learn and do in order to satisfy the requirements of the training objective;

determines the methods and media to be used. Because everyone has his own style of learning the training designer must choose the method most appropriate to the subject to be covered and to the people being taught. The selection of the appropriate methods is based on the categories of learning identified during the learning analysis. If training is to be effective then the training methods have to fit the circumstances. Careful consideration needs to be given to choosing the media which will best support the methods and style of learning already identified;

identifies the type and place of tests and assessments throughout the training programme where appropriate.

STEP 6 – TRAINING PROGRAMME AND INTERNAL VALIDATION

The Training Programme will determine the form of the training, for example:

a formal course;

on the job training;

personal modules;

distance learning packages.

It is inevitable that at this stage an assessment of overall cost in terms of tutors, equipment, space, time and materials will have to be made. This assessment may reveal that compromises will have to be accepted, and conflicting priorities resolved. It could also highlight the need for additional facilities and increased resources.

Whatever form the training takes, it has to be validated internally. That means answering the simple question, 'Has the training done what it set out to do?'

Internal validation involves checking whether the training has achieved the training objectives which were specified at the outset.

Here the importance, as was mentioned earlier, of describing what the trainee will be able to do in observable actions becomes obvious. Consistently applied throughout the training period internal validation will not only check on the effectiveness of the training but will also provide data on which any necessary changes or improvements can be made.

STEP 7 – EXTERNAL VALIDATION AND EVALUATION

External Validation is concerned to check that the change of behaviour effected by the training:

accurately matches the requirements of the trainee back at the job and,

continues in the real-life situation away from the training. There is a need to guard against the occasional boss who says, 'Never mind what they taught you on the course, this is the way we do it here'.

Evaluation looks at the training as a whole and its value to the organisation as a whole. It is concerned with:

the cost-benefit of training in monetary terms;

the perceived value and usefulness from the point of view of the people involved and the work they do.

At all stages, the Systems Approach to Training provides for feeding back into the loop information which will improve what is done. It relies, however, on the understanding and full co-operation of the line managers who are responsible for sending their staff.

They must:

carefully select them in accordance with their needs and any training criteria laid down;

brief them on what they are expected to learn and debrief them afterwards;

help them to put the training into practice in the work-place as soon as possible after the training is completed, so as to reinforce what has been learnt.

Training of Training Staff

The importance of giving a thorough training to training staff is becoming increasingly recognised. As the Chairman of the Manpower Services Commission has said, 'Properly organised training promotes job satisfaction and contributes to the efficiency . . . and profitability of any organisation'.[17] The banker who spends a spell as a tutor or trainer in his bank will bring with him to the job a good knowledge of banking and its services and, having successfully mastered a series of posts in the line, will have the trust of those for whom he will work as a trainer.

If he is to be competent in his new role he will need to learn about learning, and the design, implementation and evaluation of many forms of training. He may find himself involved in any or all of four types of training activity as the Training of Trainers Committee points out.[18]

. . . a direct training element where he will be engaged in the preparation for, and the giving of, direct instruction.

. . . a planning and organising element in which, in addition to supervisory skills, the trainer will need to acquire special techniques, e.g. job and skills analysis, to enable him to identify training needs.

. . . a determining or managing element in which at senior levels the trainer will need to be in touch with the plans and policies of his bank and aware of the systems and legislative changes which will have an effect on the bank's business.

. . . a consulting and advising element. Part of the trainer's role which is not always recognised is that of the consultant or catalyst. He will work informally in a number of ways to facilitate improvement in performance. For this role he will need a high level of inter-personal skills.

The Future: Influence of the Computer

The computer has had, and is having, its effect on training as in so many walks of life. Many readers will already have experienced some form of instruction in its use and this will increase rapidly over the next few years. We should therefore be clear as to the the meaning of some of the terms used.

Computer Managed Instruction is the use of a computer to design individual instructions for students. Directing them on a training route tailored to their requirement. It monitors students progress and provides reports on the use of training facilities.

Computer Assisted Instructions is using a computer as a teacher or tutor.

Computer Based Training is using all methods of training as appropriate, including the two computer methods mentioned.

Training may be given by computer using the large on-line systems now in use in the majority of banks. Some banks are, at the time of writing, conducting quite large-scale experiments in mini-computer systems and, with the multitude of micro-computers on the market, we shall inevitably see these used also. Development costs are substantially more than traditional methods, though savings on implementation could outweigh these in the long term.

The Future: Legislation

The first edition of this book mentioned the changes in bank work as a result of EEC legislation and this continues, though not quite at such a pace as was originally expected. Article 118 of the Treaty of Rome still stands and will, in time, no doubt, make its own impact as it works to 'the promotion of close collaboration between member states in the social field, particularly in matters relating to basic and advanced vocational training'.

Conclusion

It has become increasingly evident during the last few years that high quality training administered by competent trainers can have a substantial impact on the effectiveness of an organisation.

Training is no longer seen as an optional extra but as providing a direct contribution to improving the performance of bank staff to the greater profitability of the institution they serve and to their own personal potential for advancement.

References
1. Hilgarde, E. R., Atkinson, R. C., and Atkinson, R. L., *An Introduction to Psychology*, New York, 1971.
2. Joubert, J., *Pensées*, 1842.

3. Lunzer, E. A., *The Regulation of Behaviour* vol.1 Staples, London, 1968.
4. Blanchard, K., and Johnson S., *The One Minute Manager*, Fontana/Collins, 1982.
5. Kolb, D. A., and Fry, R., *Towards an applied theory of experiental learning of group processes*, (ed Cooper, C. L.) Wiley, 1975.
6. Mumford, A., and Honey, P., *The Manual of Learning Styles*, Maidenhead, 1982.
7. Bloom B. S., (ed) *Taxonomy of Educational Objectives*, Longman, 1956.
8. Belbin, R. M., An Article in *Industrial Training International*, April 1969.
   see also –
   C.R.A.M.P., *A guide to Training Decisions – A User's Manual*, ITRU Research Paper, TRI, Cambridge.
9. Gagne, R. M., *The Conditions of Learning*, Holt, Dinehart & Wilson, 1965.
10. *Training for Skill – Recruitment & Training for Young Workers in Industry*, Report by a sub-committee of the National Joint Advisory Council, 1958, HMSO.
11. Perry, P. J. C., *The Evolution of British Manpower Policy* (para 229), 1976, BACIE.
12. Singer, E., *Bankers Management Handbook*, Chapter 30, McGraw-Hill Book Co. (UK) Ltd., 1976.
13. *Training for Jobs* Cmnd. 9135 HMSO, Jan 1984.
14. *Glossary of Training Terms*, Dept. of Employment, 1981.
15. Much of this section is taken from *Systems Approach to Training*, an internal publication of National Westminster Bank, March 1984.
16. Carroll, Lewis, *Alice's Adventures in Wonderland*, Chapter 6.
17. O'Brien, R., Forword to the 1st Report on the Training of Trainers Committee 1978.
18. *Ibid*, Appendix 4b – Core.

CHAPTER 14

Management Training and Development

Keith Hillyer, JP, FIB

Freelance Consultant;
Formerly Group Training Manager National Westminster Bank

The basic purpose of a Management Development Unit is to assist with the achievement of the business objectives of its bank. To this end it will have an input into all policies involving the human resources of the business. These will include manpower planning, organisational development and succession planning. The Unit will also advise on all matters which affect the performance of staff, including recruitment, appraisal, pay, deployment, training and industrial relations.

The Unit will be functionally responsible for career progression, professional education and internal and external management programmes.

The corporate plan of the bank and its short and long-term strategies will be dependent on a manpower plan, indeed will have been modified by the present and future availability of the human resources needed as shown by that plan.

No one bank has objectives identical to another. But they are different in other ways also. The McKinsey 7–S framework highlights seven interdependent variables of an organisation. These have been further developed by Peters and Waterman.[1] The variables are:

structures of the organisation;

strategy – its business aims;

systems;

shared values – the culture of the bank;

skills;

style of management;

staff.

It will be seen, therefore, that no management development programme can be the same as another, however superficially similar the organisations appear. It is apparent, also, that to be effective the management development unit must have the backing, support and understanding of the top management of the bank, have access to managers at all levels and be privy to the present and future plans of all divisions and departments.

As we have seen, management development will have an important input into many areas of operation. These will include:

Planning	– the short and long-term plans of the organisation will be affected by the present and future supply of managers and their level of competence and expertise.
Recruitment	– the attraction of staff of the right qualities in the right numbers.
Appraisal	– the identification of individual potential and monitoring of performance.
Development & Training	– the design and implementation of complementary programmes to meet both individual and group needs.
Career Progression	– the movement of managers to provide for their development needs by appropriate experience.
Industrial Relations	– the agreement of conditions of service to ensure the retention of sufficient management talent.

Most of these areas are covered in detail in other chapters of this book, but it is the duty of management development to assist the general management in ensuring that *all* the various policies relating to the human resources of the bank are linked to the overall business strategy.

Management Training

We have seen in the previous chapter that *training* has been defined as 'the systematic development of the attitude/knowledge/skill behaviour pattern required by an individual in order to perform adequately a task or job.[2] The focus of *management training*, therefore, will be on the manager's job and the individual tasks which make up that job. Through appropriate analytical techniques the trainer will identify as objectively as possible those behaviours necessary for competent performance. He will then devise ways acceptable to each individual manager, in which these behaviours can be practised and improved.

There is not a simple dividing line between the 'task' orientation of management training and the 'person' orientation of management development. A great part of the early years of a banker will be devoted to tasks to be completed to firm deadlines. The cash balance, the out-clearing, the cheque payment, the head office and government reports and returns, all impose strict deadlines. It is understandable, therefore, that the application to the urgent task in hand imposed by these strictures inclines a young banker to a task orientation, sometimes to the neglect of the consideration of human needs. Training for supervision and management, therefore, frequently has a large bias towards inter-personal skills to correct the imbalance created by work experience.

Management Development, on the other hand, has a much wider and less specific range. 'Special Education for upper management most often involves the concept of broadening. It is not expected to change personality. It is generally directed at building strength on strength and not repairing weakness.'[3] Management development focuses on the individual manager rather than on the job which he is doing.

Management development, however, in looking to the future need of a manager, may identify deficiencies of knowledge and skills in modern management techniques and arrange for appropriate remedial training or educational experiences.

Why is Management Development Needed?

The majority of managers in the United Kingdom receive no education in management. With the rapidity of change in the economic, technological, social and legislative areas the modern manager increasingly needs a solid professional base of knowledge and skill in the art of management. This professional base is in addition to the knowledge and skill required for the purely technical side of the job.

The modern manager needs a firm core of theory in accountancy, economics, marketing, computing and the behavioural sciences. He must learn, too, the techniques and skills based upon these theories if he is to be effective.

The major banks in this country all have senior managers with responsibility for ensuring that the managers and potential managers of their banks are subject to appropriate training and developmental experiences to fit them for their present and future roles. But this is an expensive operation and is not, or should not be, applied indiscriminately.

Who Should Participate in a Management development Programme?

The brief answer to this question is, of course, every manager and member of the staff who has the potential to reach management. Individual needs, however, will vary widely, as will the investment of time and money which the individual's bank will judge to be necessary and appropriate.

Compromises will invariably be made between the present operational needs of the bank, the training and development needs of staff members to meet the demands of the future and the individual career aspirations of individuals.

Some operational managers give the impression that they believe that the personnel department should produce instantaneously the quantity of staff at particular levels, with the appropriate experience, personaility, knowledge and skills to pursue any project which they advocate.

On the other hand, some individual members of staff seem to believe that a bank should be able to provide a series of jobs at regular intervals, and of increasing responsibility, so as to fulfil what they perceive to be their ultimate potential.

The persuasive powers of the management development unit are frequently put to the test in these circumstances.

Consider the lop-sided pyramid in the diagram.

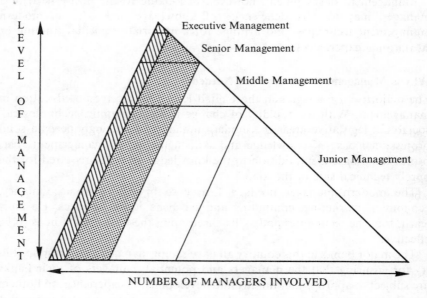

It can be seen that large numbers of managers progress to junior management only. Others, during the same number of years, achieve middle, senior or executive levels.

Fewer managers achieve the higher levels, but their responsibilities are greater, their posts include oversight of a larger part of the bank and they tend to spend comparatively shorter periods in appointments on their way up the ladder. For all these reasons their bank is likely to invest greater sums in their training and development.

The early identification of those with potential to achieve senior posts is, therefore, vital, as has been pointed out earlier in this book.

What is Management and what does a Manager do?

A great deal of the literature on management originates in the United States where, with some notable exceptions, there is a tendency to hide simple messages under a cloud of high-sounding phraseology. We are not, however, without devotees of that particular cult in the United Kingdom. Alistair Mant quotes[4] a UK management organisation's definition of management activity: 'Responsibility for judgement of the decisions in effectively planning, motivating and controlling operations towards known objectives attained through efficient co-operation of the personnel concerned.'

Let us be clear, then, about what precisely we are discussing. Mant gives three meanings of the word management:

Management I   = ACTIVITY of running things; work
Management II   = IDEOLOGY of management; values, assumptions.
Management II   = PEOPLE: a body of 'managers' paid to run things.

In this section we are looking at his Management I – the activity of running things – what a manager actually does that can be observed.

Think of the manager who is closest to you in your organisation. How does he spend his day? In interviewing, telephoning and dictation? These can be seen to be activities of management relative to controlling, organising and planning that part of the business for which he has responsibility. But is he managing when he is presiding over a staff meeting, or making a presentation to a departing colleague? Is he managing when he is strolling about the office apparently passing the time of day with his staff or meandering slowly round a business exhibition, or attending a Rotary Club lunch?

Henry Minzberg[5], in a study of managers at work, found many common characteristics in a selection of managers across a broad spectrum of commerce and industry:

> unrelenting pace;
> brevity, variety, interruption;
> preference for line action;
> listening and talking more than reading and writing;
> a network of contacts, a 'controlled disorder' between his own organisation and others.

He identified ten managerial roles which cluster around three main headings – inter-personal, informational and decisional activities.

They are:

Interpersonal roles

1.   Figurehead – the formal representative of the organisation at formal and social occasions
2.   Leader – the supervision, training and encouragement of staff. The monitoring of the work-flow.
3.   Liaison – the contacts which a manager builds across and outside the organisation which are not strictly within the formal organisational structure.

Informational roles

4.   Monitor – collecting and analysing information of relevance to his field of operation
5.   Disseminator – the communication to others in his organisation
6.   Spokesman — communication of information to others outside his organisation

Decisional activities

7.   Entrepreneur – seeking to take advantage of external conditions to improve the operation of his unit
8.   Disturbance handler – the resolution of problems hindering the work-flow
9.   Resource allocator – deciding which of his staff will get what resources. In essence, the setting of priorities.
10.   Negotiator – smoothing the progress of his own unit by arranging trade-offs with others.

You may find it helpful to consider each of these roles in turn in relation to the manager whom you considered earlier. Which of the fragmented activities which were identified can be placed in one or more of the ten roles listed?

What makes a Successful Manager?

When carrying out research preparatory to revising the management training of my own bank, I asked this question, amongst many others, of a wide variety of people. These included bankers at all levels of the organisation as well as many non-bankers. The replies could be placed into three broad groups. There were those who said, 'Good managers are born, not made.' They contended that if people were selected who had the right qualities they would be successful in management. A second group emphasised that experience was the key factor. 'The only way to learn to be a good manager is by sitting in the chair and doing it,' they said. A third group, prodding me firmly in the ribs with a forefinger, said, 'You've got to give them more and better training.'

Of course, there is an element of truth in each point of view, though each raises further questions. What are the 'right' qualities needed? Can we afford the time and expense of learning solely by experience? 'Experience is a good teacher, but she sends in terrific bills.'[6] What precise training is needed?

Burgoyne[7] and others found that only a small portion of managerial skills can be traced back to innate or parental sources. Most learning comes from work and other events and experiences not specifically designed for learning purposes. However, they also found that deliberate education and training activities have a significant part to play in the development of effective managers.

Their work produced a particularly useful list of eleven qualities of a successful manager and it can be seen that whilst some are innate, others may be taught or learnt from appropriate experience.

Knowledge

1. Command of the basic facts — the organisation, its goals and plans, who's who, own job, targets, etc.
2. Relevant professional knowledge — technical knowledge

Skills

3. Continuing sensitivity to events — perceptive and open to information, facts and figures, and feelings of other people.
4. Analytical, problem-solving, and decision/judgement-making skills —
5. Social skills and abilities — inter-personal skills, communicating, delegating, persuading, selling, etc.

Personal Qualities

6. Emotional resilience — maintains self-control yet gives, to some extent, under stress and strain.
7. Pro-activity — inclination to respond purposefully to events, rather than merely responding to demand. An initiator.
8. Creativity — ability to come up with unique new responses to situations.

9.	Mental agility	– ability to grasp problems quickly, to think of several things at once, to see quickly the whole situation (rather than ponderously ploughing through all its components).
10.	Balance learning habits and skills	– independent learners, not passive – cabable of abstract thinking as well as concrete practical thought.
11.	Self-knowledge	– his goals, values, strengths and weaknesses.

Earlier in this chapter the reader was asked to make a comparison between a manager known to him and Minzberg's managerial roles. Burgoyne's list of qualities of a successful manager provide a useful opportunity to review one's own capabilities. How does the reader rate him or her self on each of the qualities? What is being done or can be done to improve any found to be low scoring? There are a number of publications which will assist[8] in this process of 'self development'.

Self-development is an integral and important part of management development. It is the pro-active person, the initiator, the independent learner who will develop most rapidly and, as a result, receive, the support and help of his bank. Many would agree with Carl Rogers who wrote, 'I have come to feel that the only learning which significantly influences behaviour is self-discovered, self-appropriated learning.'

Management Development and Training Methods

If we keep in the forefront of our minds the overall objective of management development, that is, the achievement of the bank's overall business objectives, we shall see that the multiplicity of management development activities fall into a number of categories:

activities which effect the bank as a whole – its culture, climate and values, that is the development of the organisation as a whole;

activities which attempt to improve the overall knowledge and skills of all those employees;

training and developmental exercises to improve the level of knowledge or skills of particular groups or grades of staff, their teamwork or inter-personal skills, for example;

development programmes for individuals which may be intended –

to improve their professional or general level of education;

to fit them for a present or future post;

to remedy the lack of some particular skill or experience.

A number of these activities have been covered in some detail in other chapters of this book. It is, however, useful to examine them from the Management Development and Training aspect. The management development and training managers of a bank have a wide range of methods available to them. They will select them in accordance with their view of the organisational, departmental or individual needs.

A description of a number of methods, which are known to be used in the banking world, closes this chapter. The list is by no means exhaustive, but it is unlikely that present-day members of the staff of a British bank will not experience many of them during their careers.

On the Job Training Experiences

Action Learning: In the chapter on the Principles of Training and Learning we mentioned (in Step 7 of the Systems Approach to Training – External Validation) the importance of ensuring that the behavioural change induced on an off-the-job course is continued back in the work-place. This is known to the trainer as the problem of '*transfer*'. Action Learning overcomes this difficulty by forming small groups, often from different organisations who work on current problems of their own organisation with the help of a supervisor and a set advisor. The latter is often an academic with access to resources which may be of use to the participants. The system was developed by Reg Revans.[9] In essence it creates a climate of self-help so that participants may learn by doing.

Coaching: Most senior bankers, when discussing their careers and the various factors leading to their success will, almost invariably, name a manager under whom they served as having taught them the most about the practice of their job. These named individuals seem to be natural coaches. They realise the importance of helping their subordinates to approach current problems in a systematic way. They lead them through the various stages of the definition of the problem, the consideration of relevant factors, the generation of options available and their evaluation. They continue to guide with the selection of the preferred solution and the design of the action plan necessary for its implementation.

Not everyone feels comfortable in the role of coach, though its importance is increasingly emphasised in the formal management programmes of many banks.

Job Rotation: By the rotation of jobs, individuals can acquire new knowledge and skills. This, however, must be carefully planned and the participants fully briefed on the opportunities of the new experience. Job rotation is often used in banks, by the frequent attachment of branch managers and staff to specialist functions – for example, advances, personnel and marketing – at area, district or group offices. The concept of development by this method is sometimes extended by attachments to other companies or the Civil Service.

Formal Off-The-Job Training and Development

Internal Courses: All the major banks run formal courses at residential or non-residential training establishments and staff colleges. There is naturally a tendency to cater for the type of programme which is needed by large groups of staff and the total cost represents the major proportion of the training and development budget.

The courses are mainly of two types. Those which aim to improve the knowledge and skills of the participants in the technical side of their work, for example, advances, marketing and international busines, and those which concentrate on general management.

In addition, the larger banks now also train their own specialist staff in such fields as data processing, personnel, trustee, and others where large numbers of specialists are employed.

External Courses: It would be difficult to find a business school or management department of a university in this country which is not regularly patronised by a major bank. The management development department selects managers to attend these courses, and their selection is based principally on the individual's needs as seen by the department, but a tremendous benefit to the bank as a whole comes from the wide variety of experience which the participants bring back the effect of which is slowly disseminated throughout their organisation. There has been an increase in recent years of the use of European and American business schools and universities which also contribute to the broadening of the individual and the enrichment of his bank.

Institute of Bankers: The important role played by The Institute of Bankers, in both the professional education of bankers through its formal educational system as well as its more general developmental role through its other activities, must be emphasised. Local Centres' activities, summer Schools, lecture and library services, all play their part. A separate chapter by the Secretary General of the Institute covers, inter alia, educational courses in the management field.

Training and Development Methods

There is a wide variety of training and development methods, modules, theories and so on. The following are a selection of some of the more common in use by the major UK banks.

Action Centred Leadership: This is taught, or perhaps a more appropriate word would be learnt, on short courses of a few days duration. It was developed by John Adair[10] and is based on three functional areas of leadership, all of which must be taken into consideration if the leadership is to be successful. The three areas are those of individual needs, task needs and group needs. This form of training is essentially practical in approach and is given a major impetus in this country by the Industrial Society. The under-lying theme is often illustrated by the diagram:

Assertiveness Training, which has been around for about twenty-five years, [11] received a new stimulus from the Equal Opportunities Commission. There was a demand from women for the provision of training in techniques which enabled them to attain their rights without behaving in a masculine and aggressive way. The methods concentrate on establishing the objective which the participant required from a business encounter and teaches how to obtain this by quiet persistence. It is, of course, equally appropriate for both sexes.

Brainstorming was developed by Alex Osborn[12] just before the second World War. It is one of a number of techniques to develop creative thinking and is based on the assumption that, not only are two heads better than one, but several heads are even better. Under a trained leader, a group attempts to solve a specific problem. Ideas, however fanciful are called out and recorded and members of the group build on the suggestions. No criticism is allowed during the short creative period, but later a full analysis is made and frequently a practical solution to the problem is produced. The solution often has its basis in what was originally a quite bizarre or outrageous suggestion.

Case Study: Probably the most common of all management teaching methods.[13] The case study, which originated at Harvard Business School, consists of a description of a business problem. It is normally a disguised real-life situation of an organisation, or part of it. Students attempt to solve, by discussion, the problem which has been posed. Presentations of group views are often followed by further refinement of solutions in plenary session.

Case studies vary widely in size and complexity and may run for a few minutes only or take up a whole course. The focus on the identification of the real problem in a situation is a particularly valuable attribute of the case study method. 'It isn't that they can't see the solution, it is that they can't see the problem,'[14] applies in many areas and at all levels of management.

COVERDALE TRAINING

Coverdale Training[15] is one of a number of training methods or approaches which concentrate on the identification of the strength of the participating individuals and their improvement rather than in the eradication of faults. Groups are given small tasks to complete, but the aim of the training is not the successful completion of the task but a demonstration of the way in which group members interact. By reviewing how they prepared for the task and carried it out, the group acquires a greater knowledge of human behaviour which they can develop in practice in their management job.

DISTANCE LEARNING

Readers will be familiar with correspondence courses in which students work on a portion of text and then submit to a test based on what they have learnt. This concept has been considerably widened in the past few years and now embraces the type of course available from the Open University. It is now possible to study some management topics by this method. The absence of a tutor whilst the student is working means that the material has to be of the highest quality. The embodiment of sophisticated technology has brought with it first-class methods of monitoring and of progress control.

LIFE ORIENTATION

Two American psychologists, Stuart Atkins and Allan Katcher[16] developed this package which, as we have seen with other methods, concentrates on building and developing the strengths of managers.

Atkins and Katcher say that managers fall broadly into four categories which the call: *supporting–giving, controlling–taking, conserving–holding* and *adaptive–dealing*.

The supporting–giving manager's basic approach is to work conscientiously and provide excellent service. He is idealistic, loyal and helpful and always eager to please.

Any strength, however, which is over-played, say Atkins and Katcher, can become a weakness. Idealistic may be impractical, trusting may become gullible, and so on.

A controlling–taking manager is confident, risk-taking and forceful. Under pressure he may become domineering, arrogant and impatient.

A conserving–holding manager is practical, economical and thorough; He may, in excess, be stingy, stubborn and unfriendly.

The adaptive–dealing manager is people-oriented. He is flexible, enthusiastic and tactful. He may become unrealistic, childlike and placatory when under stress.

A manager's most preferred style or combination of styles is identified by means of a short questionnaire and in subsequent discussion he gains insight not only into the effect of his own behaviour on others but also into ways of influencing colleagues, subordinates and superiors.

MANAGERIAL GRID

Robert Blake and Jane Mouton[17] developed the managerial grid, which is another method to help managers understand their managerial style and that of others with whom they have contact. The grid is fully described in Chapter 6 and referred to again in Chapter 9.

As in the other methods we have mentioned, the focus is first on the individual manager and then on his relations with others, both inside and outside his work team.

OUTWARD BOUND TRAINING

Many banks send younger members of their staff for leadership training at special centres in lakeland or mountainous areas. Outward Bound[18] courses are physically demanding and very intensive. Participants carry out tasks in small groups, perhaps involving rock-climbing or canoeing. There are briefing and de-briefing sessions carried out with experienced instructors and individuals learn a great deal about their own strengths and weaknesses. They develop confidence and self-reliance and learn the importance of the correct use of inter-personal skills in achieving objectives.

SENSITIVITY TRAINING (T-GROUPS)

This form of experienced-based learning[19] was very popular with trainers in the sixties, though not with many of their students who frequently resented the unstructured approach and the apparent minimal participation of the tutors.

More recently, the value has been appreciated of allowing a small group, over a period of time, to analyse its own feelings, reactions and behaviours. This type of training is now fairly common and may be found as one of the themes running through a management programme, or as a concentrated two or three day event. Its great strength is that participants take responsibility for their own learning, and the skill of the tutor will be in his ability to help people to be open and honest about themselves and to focus participants' minds on to the real issues and the group's inter-action.

References

1. Peters, T. J. and Waterman R. H. Jr., *In Search of Excellence*, Harper & Row, New York, 1982.
2. *Glossary of Training Terms*, Dept. of Employment, 1981.
3. Glickman, Hahn & Ors., *Top Management Development & Succession – an exploratory study*, Collier Macmillan, 1978.
4. Mant, A., *The Rise & Fall of the British Manager*, Macmillan Press, 1977.
5. Minzberg, H., *The Nature of Managerial Work*, Harper & Row, New York, 1973.
6. *Naked Truth & Veiled Allusions*, Minna Antrim, 1902.
7. Burgoyne, John and Stuart, Roger, 'The Nature, Use & Acquisition of Managerial Skills & Other Attributes', Centre for the Study of Management Learning, Univ. of Lancaster, *Personnel Review*, 5.4.76.
8. Pedlar, M., Burgoyne J. and Boydell, T., *A Manager's Guide to Self-Development*, McGraw-Hill, 1978, is based on the eleven qualities listed in the text.
9. Revans, R., *The ABC of Action Learning* (2nd Ed.)., Chartwell-Bratt, 1983.
10. Adair, J., *Action-Centred Leadership*, Gower, 1979.
11. Smith, Manuel J., *When I Say 'No', I Feel Guilty*, Dial Press, New York, 1975.
12. Rawlinson, J. G., *Creative Thinking & Brainstorming*, Gower, 1981.
13. Erskine, J. A., Leenders, M. R. and Mauflette-Leenders, L. A., *Teaching with Cases*, Univ. of Western Ontario, 1981.
14. Father Brown in Short Detective Stories – *The Point of a Pin*, by G. K. Chesterton, 1927.
15. 'The Basic Philosophy of Coverdale Training' in *Industrial & Commercial Training*, Vol. 8, No. 1.
16. Atkins, Stuart, *The Name of Your Game*, Ellis & Stewart Publishers, Beverly Hills, 1981.
17. Blake, R. R. and Mouton, J. S., *The New Managerial Grid*, Gulf Publications, 1979.
18. 'Management Development Using the Outdoors', *The Training Officer, Vol. 16, No. 10, 1980*.
19. Smith, P. B., *Group Process & Personal Change*, Harper & Row, 1980.

CHAPTER 15

Professional Education for Bankers

Eric Glover

Secretary-General,
The Institute of Bankers

Professional Education, in the sense in which the term is used in this chapter, is more highly developed in the UK than anywhere else in the world. My purpose is to explore its role in banking – its aims and origins, its function and development in recent times – and to look at the current trends which will affect its future.

Aims and Origins

The body most closely concerned with this area of banking – The Institute of Bankers – was founded in 1879, for much the same reason as many other professional bodies appeared at about the same time: to improve standards through education programmes geared to the needs of the occupation concerned. Whether banking is or is not a 'profession' does not greatly concern us here, though the question has often been debated elsewhere. It depends entirely on how you define 'profession', and in this context the word is used to refer to an established occupation for the practice of which a formal course of learning is normally required.

Banking itself, as the history of the Institute's first 100 years shows,[1] was hardly regarded as a full-time occupation at all until late in the 19th century, so one could hardly accuse the bankers of the day of delay in establishing a formal organisation. The Institute had three main objects:

(i)   to facilitate the consideration and discussion of matters of interest to bankers;

(ii)   to afford opportunities to its members for the acquisition of a knowledge of the theory of banking;

(iii) to take any measures which may be desirable to further the interests of banking.

These objects have remained the same since 1879 though the means of fulfilling them have changed frequently and considerably. In this respect, the Institute is unlike some of the other professional bodies, which have, for instance, shed their qualifying role and concentrated entirely on post-qualifying education. Whatever the precise role of the Institute at any time, however, the objective of banking education has always been the same – to produce good bankers. Of course, education can never replace the lessons of practical experience, and it is very closely linked with training – indeed in the more practical subjects it is hard to distinguish between the two. For our purposes, however, education is that which provides the foundation of principles on which a career is built, whereas training is more specific, related to the technical and management need of particular employers. The definition of education as 'that which remains when what was learned has been forgotten' is worth thinking about.

Functions and Development

THE QUALIFYING ROLE

From its earliest days the Institute established levels of attainment for the award of its qualifications, and it was left mainly to individuals, to an association which has always emphasised personal achievements, to find ways of reaching them. Of course employers have always had a strong incluence, in providing incentives to qualify, through their interest in curriculum content, and in recent years by providing tuition, especially in the form of revision courses for the practical subjects.

But professional education in the UK has always been (more than purely academic learning) a matter of self-education, in that time for study has been limited, while the student's main concern has been to earn his living and acquire practical experience. Tuition material has not always been ideal; opportunities for the exchange of ideas have sometimes been restricted (especially for those in remote places), and the incentives for qualifying have not always seemed sufficiently attractive. In no other major profession has this 'voluntary' aspect of the qualification been so evident as in banking, in that the Banking Diploma has never been a 'licence to practise', as qualifications are, for instance, in medicine, the law, and some branches of accountancy. The background to the banking qualifications, then, has always been a particularly strong combination of two of the most important features of professional education – the union of theory and practice, and personal commitment by the individual.

The qualifications have changed over the years, as the business of banking itself has changed, though the basic structure has remained the same: a foundation of general commercial subjects, followed by a study of those aspects of the subjects most closely related to banking, with a final test in the application of the theory to practical problems. In the early years some of the subjects were more general than would be found in today's curriculum, since many young bankers had left school after only a few years' schooling. They therefore often lacked some of the basic skills which today one hopes (sometimes in vain) to find imparted by the primary and secondary schools. This description of the qualifications will start by looking at the reasons for the syllabus content, and then examine the changes made in recent years following the work of the 'Wilde' Committee, which carried out one of the most thorough reviews of the Institute's work in its first 100 years.

CONTENT

The business of banking, more than ever today, cannot easily be related to one area of knowledge. To be a successful banker one must be able to draw on many different skills as well as having the right human and intellectual qualities to start with. A reasonable level of numeracy is important as a basis to that understanding of accounting statements which is essential for anyone who is to be involved in lending. It also helps to be able to apply some of the simple statistical techniques and, in the early stages of the young banker's professional education these numerate skills are often taught at the same time as the principles of accounting.

The next vital ingredient would be a knowledge of economics, for two main reasons:

(i)   to understand the part in the economy which is played by the bank for which he works;
(ii)   to appreciate his customers' problems.

Perhaps equally important, though harder to define precisely, is the need for the banker to be able to demonstrate to his customers – actual and potential – that he has a sound grasp of economic developments, and is therefore one whose advice about likely future trends should be listened to with respect. He would be a poor banker indeed who could not make some informed comment in answer to his customers' questions about stock market movements, the reason for exchange rate changes, and rises and falls in interest rates. To satisfy this last requirement he needs to be well versed in monetary economics so that he can explain the relationships between the banking system and government in matters of monetary control.

With his knowledge of accountancy and economics, he is in a better position to undertake credit analysis, to look at the balance sheets and profit and loss statements of would-be borrowers, and to calculate the appropriate accounting ratios which indicate the state of health of the business. He will also be aware of the assumptions on which the accountancy principles are based, and will know something of the reasons for current cost accounting, to allow for inflation, (a problem which is highly relevant also to the banks' own balance sheets; those who aspire to management will certainly need to know something about the banks' needs to maintain the value of their capital base). When he has completed his analysis of the accounts, however, he still needs to rely on his economic expertise to satisfy himself that the business concerned will do sufficiently well to ensure that the bank's money, and the interest which it attracts, are both safe.

The banker must then ask himself about the legal implications of the business he is conducting. This is not to suggest for a moment that he may ever be tempted to indulge in any doubtful practices which could land him in gaol. He is however vitally interested in decisions in legal cases which could affect the value of the security against which he has made an advance; and in rules which determine the circumstances in which he can discuss business with prospective customers. The banking qualifications therefore set out to give him a background knowledge of commercial and banking law.

The last – and some would argue the most important – area of basic education covered in the qualification has always been a study of language. It might be referred to as 'Business English', but in recent times the term 'Communications' seems to have become the more popular word. Yet the aim is the same: to improve the ability of the banker to express himself effectively in his dealings with both customers and colleagues. It is sometimes argued that, in view of the number of years which present-day recruits have spent at school, compared with their predecessors of a few generations ago, this concern with our native language on the part of a professional body is unnecessary; in my experience most employers, bankers and others, would not agree.

These basics have always appeared in the Institute's qualifications, and the structure of basic background followed by the more relevant theory and completed by the exercise of practical applications has proved itself to be sound. We shall however see that some major changes to this general concept have been found necessary.

TUITION

Before exploring the need for change, a word about tuition. Traditionally, professional education was built on study in the individual's own time, often through attendance at further education establishments (hence the growth of the 'night schools'), but in many cases too on the use of correspondence courses or simple textbooks. The Institute of Bankers has always favoured good quality oral tuition, and in 1926 established a system of recognition which encouraged colleges in England and Wales to offer classes for young bankers. In return for providing tuition of a satisfactory standard, the colleges were able to set their own examinations in the Part I subjects (as assessed by the Institute's own 'moderators'), thus giving college teachers an additional interest in the courses they were conducting. This scheme has now been overtaken by developments which will be described later – and which are themselves run on similar lines – but for 50 years served banking education well. Many young bankers have relied on a mixture of oral and postal tuition, provided by both public and private enterprise, but the most notable development of the last 20 years has been the increase in the amount of direct tuition for the examinations offered by the banks themselves, largely through revision courses for the Part II subjects held at their own training centres. Such courses have helped to improve the pass percentage markedly in some subjects, and have also generated a spirit of corporate loyalty in individual banks, through the desire to overcome the common enemy – the examiner.

For many candidates, however, the main incentive for completing the qualification was a negative one: the knowledge that without it the chances of promotion to management would be greatly reduced. There have also, for many years, been financial inducements for completing the examinations, but these have been of minor importance compared with the prospect of promotion.

The Need for Change

For various reasons, banking education has enjoyed a boom in recent years: the business of banking itself has expanded rapidly, and the expansion has been accompanied by an increase in the number of staff, despite technological developments (the clearing banks in the UK now employ over 280,000 people); the banks themselves have placed more emphasis on qualifications; and there has been rapid growth – for much the same reasons – outside the UK. Why then have there been so many changes in banking education in the last few years?

THE WILDE COMMITTEE

When the WIlde Committee (named after its Chairman, Derek Wilde, who was the Deputy Chairman of Barclays Bank) was appointed to carry out a review[2] of the Institute's work in 1972/73, there was apparently no pressing need for reform. Membership of the Institute and entries for the examinations were at record levels, and local centre activities (largely for qualified members) were enjoying a good level of support. There were however already signs that changes would be needed soon if the qualifications were to continue to provide the right professional service for members.

In the first place the banks themselves, especially the larger ones, had been greatly widening the range of their activity, both in their lending operations and in the extent of financial services generally. Bankers whose bread and butter had been lending to personal customers and to small businesses found that they now needed to know a lot more about such services as instalment finance, leasing, factoring, taxation, investment management and even the travel business. At the same time, the bank's international business was becoming more and more important, making an increasing contribution to profits. Such changes in the nature of the business suggested that the existing Banking Diploma, though providing an excellent background of commercial education and insight into lending techniques, needed reinforcement.

RECRUITMENT

Equally important have been changes in education and their effect on bank recruitment. During the 1970s there was very rapid growth in the numbers entering higher education in Britain, and by the early 1980s there were about 750,000 students in full time or sandwich higher education courses – about four times the number in the early 1960s. For an industry which had relied mainly on intake at the same age level (16/17 years) for staffing at all levels, the message was that some rethinking of recruitment policy would be necessary. If the banks wished to recruit 'career' staff with the same level of ability as the old 'school certificate' intake (now GCE 'O' levels) they must now look to those with 'A' levels and degrees. In general, boys and girls who do well at school (academically) go on to further studies, and are not available for employment. Admittedly, a few years ago, when it was harder to recruit good staff than it is now, the banks and other employers were accused of enticing young people away from the university and polytechnics. Yet the trend continues towards more full-time education, and those responsible for recruitment must recruit at the higher age levels if they are to find people of the right calibre to fill managerial jobs in the future.

A further change in education of great relevance to banking studies is the growth of business education in the public sector, especially in Britain, through the National Awards in Business Studies. These awards are widely available at different levels with a variety both of subjects to choose from and of courses (full time, day release, evening and so on), and offer a broadly based business qualification, with the prospect of some specialism, to those who expect to follow a business career, but who are not yet committed to a particular industry or employer. (These awards are now controlled in Britain by the Business and Technical Education Council, whose courses relate closely to practical business problems).[3]

EMPLOYMENT ATTITUDES

Perhaps partly as a result of these changes in educational opportunities, attitudes of young people towards employment have altered also. School-leavers no longer expect – as they did say 30 years ago – to join the staff of a large company and stay there for 40 years or more. They are prepared to try a number of jobs, and want to keep their options open – including their educational ones – while they do so. This sort of mobility is naturally more noticeable at times of full employment, and the recruitment difficulties of the early 1970s were eased, for the banks and other employers, by the recent recession and by technological progress leading to a reduction in the number of staff required. In other countries where the Institute's influence is strong, banking has often grown so rapidly in recent years that the demand for competent staff has been intense, and those who have completed the banking qualifications have had a wide choice of employment.

Nature of the Changes

The Institute's response to these influences was to change both the structure and the content of the qualifications and, in conjunction with the banks, to develop a pattern of tuition which emphasised more clearly than ever the importance attached to professional education by the employers. What follows is an outline of the main features of the 'new' three stages, highlighting their advantages compared with the 'old' Banking Diploma (see Appendix A).

1. FLEXIBILITY

To allow for recuitment at different ages and different educational levels there are now several entry points, and the various levels of qualification correspond more closely with career prospects. At the same time, a route to the top has been kept open for any new recruit who has a minimum of four 'O' levels or the equivalent, including 'O' level English, since there has always been a strong tradition in banking that the 'late developer' should be given every opportunity – a belief which has been fully justified by the excellent performance in the professional examinations of some of those whose academic records at school were mediocre.

2. VARIETY

In each stage it is now possible more than previously to vary the content, according to the specialist needs of candidates. Of course it is not possible to cover the 200 or so different services offered by the major banks but the candidate is now introduced to the range of facilities offered by his employers, and thereby becomes better able to cope with enquiries which need to be referred from his customers to the bank's specialist departments. International trade continues to be a separate subject, for the reason referred to earlier, and has been joined by *investment*, which was not previously part of the curriculum at all. The other newcomer is *The Nature of Management*, which deserves more than a passing mention since the introduction shows clearly a change of mind about the role of the examinations.

Traditionally, the Banking Diploma concentrated on the techniques of banking, starting with the background knowledge described above, and moving on to a detailed consideration of practical problems, often requiring the application of a number of skills for their solution. Bank training had much the same emphasis, with particular attention being paid to the understanding of customers' accounts. In recent years the balance shifted as employers everywhere paid increasing attention to the management of people. Perhaps the change has been most clearly seen in the relative importance attached to the work of personnel management. The personnel manager's job was often poorly regarded and poorly paid in the 1960s, yet in recent years the salaries of personnel specialists have risen faster than those in other sectors, and many companies which did not previously have staff specialists at all now employ them as senior directors. The reasons for this change of attitude are stressed in other chapters of this book.

For banking – still an extremely labour intensive industry – the personnel function is as vital as in any other sector, and the attention which is now being paid to it in the training and education of future managers (which in this context means anyone who may have supervisory responsibilities) was overdue. In the Institute's qualifications two papers are concerned:

(i)   *The Nature of Management*, which aims to give students an understanding of the techniques of management, and of human behaviour, both in banking and in other business;

(ii) *Human Aspects of Management* – very much the subject of this book – which is concerned with both general principles of managing people and with the particular problems of banking (see also later under Financial Studies Diploma).

Both these papers, then, are a recognition of the importance placed by employers on knowledge in these areas, both for the management of their customer's business and for the efficiency of the banks themselves. It is only fair to add, though, that the secondary banking crisis of the 1970s, caused largely by poor lending to the property sector, led to some misgivings that the broadening of banking education and training in this way may have been achieved only at the expense of neglecting vital technical areas. It could just as easily be agreed that it was a failure to learn the lessons of economic history which was to blame, rather than intelligence of accounting ratios.

The Financial Studies Diploma

From the Institute's educational policy review there developed a quite new qualification, the Financial Studies Diploma. Originally envisaged as an integral part of a three-stage structure leading to Associateship, it has now become, in the main, an extra qualification for those who are already Associates and who wish to undertake further studies. It is a mixture of advanced banking and 'management' subjects, and is designed to lead to a degree-level qualification for those who are expected to reach senior positions in their banks. (See Appendix B). There has been a most encouraging response, with a record number of over 850 candidates for the 1984 examinations, most of them being Associates who have recently reached management, or are just about to do so.

Marketability

No apologies are offered for the use of this term – it expresses the point perfectly. One of the complaints about the old style Banking Diploma was that it meant little to people outside banking – very few bankers, after all, used to leave banking for other occupations. (Only a few years ago, a speaker at a senior Institute gathering expressed the view that his bank regarded it as 'a failure' if any of their managers left to work elsewhere). We have already noted earlier the growth of business studies qualifications in the public sector, and one of the aims of the new arrangement was to make the best use of these, by linking them to the Institute's own awards, at two levels. The first part of this policy was carried through, and many candidates in the UK use a National Level Certificate in Business Studies to satisfy the Stage 1 requirements. For Stage 2, the link was not easy to achieve, in view of the need for a high degree of specialist content and for consistent standards of achievement which could be relied upon world-wide; the Institute therefore decided to concentrate on its own examining system for the final subjects.

Innovation

The content of qualifications at all levels is reviewed regularly to ensure that it is relevant to current needs. Thus minor changes to Stage 2 subjects occur almost every year, and recent additions to the Elements of Banking syllabuses in Stage 1 should ensure that future candidates for the more practical Stage 2 subjects are better prepared.

Developments in financial services, however, sometimes mean that more radical steps are needed, and during the 1980s two further qualifications have been introduced – a Credit Card Certificate, for staff employed in a specialist but rapidly expanding sector, and an International Banking Diploma, which shares five 'core' subjects with the 'domestic' version, and also contains three specialist papers (the first examinations in these papers, for candidates enrolled on a pilot course, were held in April 1985). Other options may be introduced if there is sufficient demand.

Tuition

One effect of the partial switch to the public sector has certainly been a change in tuition habits. The major banks in the UK – and some elsewhere – have all agreed to grant study leave for those taking the qualifications, and it is usually a condition that the students concerned should attend college classes, for either a full-day or a half-day per week. The result has been a considerable shift from evening classes and correspondence courses to daytime tuition, emphasising even more strongly to both candidates and teachers the commitment of the banks themselves. As a result, we can expect a greater understanding of the subjects studied, especially as candidates are given increased opportunities to discuss practical problems. The improved provision for study leave has certainly had its effect on the quality of recruitment, as careers advisers, and young people and their parents are impressed by the greater opportunity offered to obtain a worthwhile qualification.* Those who have already obtained qualifications in higher education – especially graduates – are more attracted to a structure which gives them credit for their previous attainments.

Outside the UK it has been difficult to make the transition to the new scheme of things: college tuition is not so widely available, banks are even less able to allow study leave, and the general level of education on entry is often lower. There has been, however, a very rapid growth of interest in UK qualifications, as more and more indigenous staff have been required to fill jobs in often expanding financial centres (especially in the Far East), and employers become even more aware of the need for good levels of education. It is significant that the first ever course for the Financial Studies Diploma was held in Hong Kong, the Institute's largest local centre, from 1977 to 1979.

The new subjects have created a need for new textbooks, and The Institute of Bankers has itself undertaken many recent publications which are directly

---

*   Indeed, there have been complaints from the educationists that the prospects are too attractive: young people are entering employment rather than going on to higher education. Is this such a disaster?

relevant to both Stage 2 and to the Financial Studies Diploma. All of these have been produced in addition to regular publications such as examiners' reports, which indicate the sort of answers expected in the examinations and the examiners' assessment of the results achieved.

Liaison with teaching institutions which offer banking classes (about 400 in England and Wales alone) has greatly increased the burden on the officers of the Institute's local centres, and it is a tribute to the enthusiasm of these volunteers that they have coped so well with such major changes.

Although the emphasis has been on oral tuition, many candidates have used correspondence courses, and have often achieved excellent results, including winning some of the top prizes. To help improve the quality of the tuition offered, The Institute of Bankers has had, since 1968, a recognition scheme for correspondence courses, which has kept the tuition material offered up to date, and has maintained the standards of personal tuition and of assessment.

Examinations: The Assessment of Performance

It would not be appropriate here to discuss the many different theories and techniques for the assessment of professional knowledge. The main method for qualifying bodies in the commercial sector has usually been a written paper, under strict supervision, over a period of three hours or so. In the Institute's own examinations the tradition has been maintained, with a variation in the last paper of the Financial Studies Diploma, where a list of topics is published well ahead of the examination.

In the public sector examinations, results are based on a combination of assessment during the course and on final written examinations, a system which increases the subjective element, but guards against a freak performance, one way or the other, in the examination itself. Objective testing, which requires 'yes/no' answers to a number of stated alternatives, increases the burden on the examiners who set the papers whilst making the task of the markers easier. It is claimed that it is a more accurate way of measuring basic knowledge than the essay-style answer which is usually required. This may be so, but for an industry which depends so much on good written communication, both with customers and within the bank, the traditional essay still has a lot to recommend it.

Post-Qualifying Education

So far this chapter has dealt with that part of professional education which attracts members in the first place – the need to acquire a formal qualification as an almost essential condition for promotion. The pressure on young bankers to do this has been great and the average age for completing the Banking Diploma has steadily dropped to about 25 overall, with the UK figure slightly lower. This means that the average banker expects to have about 35 years of his career ahead of him after he has completed his qualification, and during that time his knowledge of current theory and practice will need constant up-dating. At a time of much less rapid change than today – 100 years ago – this need was recognised by the Institute's founders, who made 'the consideration and discussion of matters of interest to the profession' the first of the Institute's objects. It is still the most important object, in view of its concern with the banker's whole career, and is the area in which further expansion of the Institute's work is most likely.

What sort of activities are involved? To some extent it is a matter of making the banker aware of changes which are taking place in those subjects which he has studied in preparation for the Banking Diploma – new legislation, for instance, or changes in accountancy practices.

Much of the Institute's work for the qualified member is devoted to just this function. It is however in the areas of practical banking where the issues are not so clear cut – in what might loosely be termed the 'management' areas rather than the 'technical' ones – that the greatest value lies. It is likely that individual banks will each react in much the same way when confronted with a legal decision which affects the value of their security; and will have the same attitude towards inflation-adjusted profit statements from their corporate customers. In other areas there is far more room for doubt, and the provision of a forum for discussion is more valuable.

It may be argued that this area of staff development is adequately taken care of in the largest banks, by individual bank training programmes supplemented by external courses at business schools. Excellent though many of these are, however, they do not provide fully for the exchange of ideas about problems of mutual interest which is a feature of so many Institute activities.

PUBLICATIONS: LOCAL CENTRES

As a basis for continued learning about the financial world, the Institute provides all its members with a monthly journal, and publishes numerous works which are relevant to both qualified members and students. In the last three years, six videos have been produced in collaboration with a polytechnic as aids for banking teachers. The Institute's library provides a full service to those engaged in financial research, and is frequently called on to advise bankers outside the UK who are concerned with setting up a similar facility. It is an age, however, when people expect to learn by a variety of means, and the Institute's local centres were formed as an answer to this need. Some of them have existed for two-thirds of the Institute's history, and their influence now extends well beyond the UK, as centres have been formed in Africa, the Mediterranean and the Far East. These centres provide a mixture of academic and social events, but their main purpose is to keep Institute members at all levels in close touch with new trends in banking, and many of them enjoy excellent support. Evening lectures by top bankers and other professional speakers remain popular, but programmes also include seminars, discussion groups, quizzes, industrial visits and joint meetings with members of other professional bodies. One of the most imaginative local centre-based Institute activities of recent years has been a computer-based Banking Game, involving 125 teams each year in a competition designed to illustrate some of the problems and decisions involved in the running of a bank branch. As an example of an exercise which requires cooperation between people from different banks, and which promotes learning by participcation, it would be hard to beat.

POST-EXPERIENCE COURSES

Reports on management education in the UK, published in the 1970s, indicated a continuing lack of external management courses designed for those working in financial services (indeed for those in services generally: the emphasis has usually been on the problems of manufacturing industry). External courses have been acknowledged as a better way of broadening the horizons of management staff than 'internal' training. Away from the presence of their colleagues and superiors from the same bank, people express themselves more freely and are likely to gain a broader view of the business in which they work and of other businesses which they exist to serve.

The Institute has attempted, either on its own or in conjunction with universities and business schools, to satisfy some of this need by offering courses in subject areas which have not been adequately covered elsewhere: for example, 'Strategic Planning for Financial Institutions'; 'Analysis of Business Performance'; 'The management of Human Resousres in Banking'. These one-week courses have been supplemented more recently by one and two-day seminars, sometimes run jointly with other institutes ('Banking and Insurance'. 'Credit Analysis and Risk Appraisal'), and ranging over several technical and management themes. A joint venture with the International Chamber of Commerce resulted in two one-week seminars in the late 1970s for bankers of more than 50 nationalities, including a majority from the developing countries. In 1981, courses in lending were held in the Gulf (Bahrain and the Emirates), and were immediately successful, demonstrating a need for the knowledge which could be passed on by senior Institute members. The scope of these courses has been extended, and they are now well supported also in the Far East, Africa, and the West Indies.

The Institute's largest venture in this area of work is the International Banking Summer School, now in its 33rd year and attracting regularly over 200 bankers who are destined to reach the highest levels of management. The Cambridge Seminar, which was started in 1969, is also designed for the high fliers, and provides a unique opportunity for about 100 middle management executives (mainly bankers from UK and other European countries, but also now including a number of their contemporaries from other parts of British industry) to discuss some of the most topical issues affecting banking. There is a great deal of cachet in being selected to attend one of these courses, and in any influential group of bankers almost anywhere in the world there will be at least one former member.

As one of the ways of celebrating its centenary in 1979, the Institute endowed a research fellowship, which *inter alia* should help to improve communications on matters of common interest between banking and the management education institutions. The relationships which have already been created should thereby be strengthened further. Study tours – to examine the banking systems of other countries – have been held successfully in recent years and are likely to increase in importance.

The future

The future of professional education in banking is likely to be increasingly in post-qualifying activities. Qualifications will continue to be important, and will change in ways similar to those described earlier – by the introduction of new subjects and adjustments to existing ones – in line with the needs of the business itself. Methods of tuition will change – one hopes for the better – as candidates who have grown up with modern technology expect more stimulating ways of learning. More and more people, however, will study business subjects full-time before they start their careers, so that over the longer term we can expect a decline in the demand for at least some part of the professional examinations in banking. Other professional bodies share this view, and indeed one of them, the British Institute of Management, has dropped its qualifying role completely.

This view of the future – of banking education as a career-long activity rather than as a single act of salvation – seems to be shared by the Institute's members themselves. Because once they have completed their qualifications, they are not forced to remain members in order to practice their trade (as they would do, for instance, in law, medicine and accountancy). Yet the great majority of them do remain members, because they value the educational benefits which they continue to receive. If we add to these the social benefits which grow with increasing wealth and leisure, then there seems to be every reason why professional education, in the way it is provided by The Institute of Bankers, should continue to flourish.

References
1. Green, Edwin, *Debtors to their Profession: A History of The Institute of Bankers, 1879–1979*, 1979, The Institute of Bankers.
2. The Institute of Bankers: Educational Policy Review; A Report by the Wilde Committee, *The Institute's Future Role as a Qualifying Association*, 1973, The Institute of Bankers.
3. *Higher Education into the 1990s*, 1978, Department of Education and Science.

APPENDIX TO CHAPTER 15

(A) The Educational Structure

Entry Level	STAGE 1	Usual Study Period	Award
4 O-levels, or equivalent, including English Language	a) BTEC National Award in Business and Finance† (or overseas equivalents),	2 years	BTEC National (or local diplomas and certificates)†
1 or more A-levels plus O-level English Language or equivalents	b) The Bankers' Conversion Course	1 year	None – course gives right of entry to Stage 2

Entry Level	STAGE 2	Usual Study Period	Award
Stage 1; or recognised degree or professional qualification*	Part A - Three papers Part B - Three papers Part C - Two practical papers	3 years	Banking, International Banking, Trustee Diploma (leading to AIB)

Entry Level	FINANCIAL STUDIES DIPLOMA	Usual Study Period	Award
Recognised degree or professional qualification*	(for Direct Entrants) – Two special papers plus background reading	1 year	None
AIB; or successful completion of direct entry papers	**Diploma** (six papers)	2-5 years	Financial Studies Diploma (Dip. FS)

† Candidates for the BTEC National *Certificate* (viz. the part-time qualification) must take the National Award in Business and Finance, Finance Core with units Elements of Banking 1 and 2.
* Of a standard and content acceptable to The Institute of Bankers.

APPENDIX TO CHAPTER 15

(B) Financial Studies Diploma

Object

To provide a degree-level qualification in banking and management subjects for those who are expected to reach senior management levels.

Regulations

Entry Requirements:

Either:

  1.   Banking or Trustee Diploma of The Institute of Bankers

or:

  2.   Recognised degree or professional qualification* – plus a preliminary course of background reading and two introductory papers (see below).

Content

Introductory papers (seen entry requirement 2 above):

(a) Banking:
     The Monetary System, International Trade and Bank Services; Accountancy and the Banker.

(b) Trustee:
     Trust Accounting†;
     Practical Trust Administration†.

†   Common to the Trustee Diploma.

Section 1   PRACTICE OF BANKING 3
               or
               FINANCIAL MANAGEMENT (TRUSTEE) 1
               HUMAN ASPECTS OF MANAGEMENT
               BUSINESS PLANNING AND CONTROL

Section 2   MARKETING OF FINANCIAL SERVICES
               PRACTICE OF BANKING 4
               PRACTICE OF BANKING 5
               or
               FINANCIAL MANAGEMENT (TRUSTEE) 2
               FINANCIAL MANAGEMENT (TRUSTEE) 3

All papers will be examined by the Institute.

*   Of a standard and content acceptable to the Institute.

PART III

EMPLOYMENT CONDITIONS AND INDUSTRIAL RELATIONS

Introduction

This section is devoted to employment conditions, industrial relations, collective bargaining, negotiations, the structure of payment systems, employment legislation and the emerging role of women.

Ironically, bank executives by background and history are often less interested in the problems of industrial relations than their counterparts in industry. Yet the institutions and procedures of industrial relations, collective and individual rights at work, and the economic and political environment in which banks have to operate, have a direct and pervasive influence on life in the banks. Lack of interest on the part of bank executives in the realities of the employment world must surely be myopic. Even line managers, whose prime job is to lend money and promote the bank's services, cannot for long remain immune from the implications of industrial relations, which is the fabric of their organisation, and still remain successful.

Professor Kessler opens the section by discussing the concept of an industrial relations system and the nature of conflict. 'It is as important for the management to realise that some conflict of interest is inevitable as it is for unions and their members to realise that there are certain common interests', and that collective bargaining has long been considered the best method of resolving differences of interests, or as 'a rule-making process by joint regulation'. The content of collective bargaining, the author points out, need not be confined to pay, but may be extended to include manning levels, job demarcation, and pace and distribution of work, discipline and promotion. 'Indeed, it is difficult to set a theoretical limit to the subject area'. Conversely, 'it is also natural for management to want to maintain as much freedom of action as possible'.

This chapter explores the traditional system of collective bargaining, the roles and status of the parties concerned, substantive and procedural rules and recent developments that have taken place in the various levels of bargaining. The author considers questions relating to the extent of the bargaining unit, appropriate bargaining agents and the coverage of collective bargaining. Moreover, collective bargaining is set in a wider industrial relations perspective – an economic, social, technological and legal environment.

Sheila Rothwell and Tim Morris continue the theme. They examine the industrial relations system which obtains in banking in the UK, national and domestic bargaining machinery and problems of representation. They discuss the consequences of the Federation of London Clearing Banks' invitation to Dr. Johnston to carry out an enquiry into the problems of staff representation, and the subsequent rejection of a call for amalgamation. Many people argue that a solution should be found – if only from the point of view of objective logic. The close-knit nature of the industry and the homogeneous nature of its staff point inevitably to a single union structure, however much autonomy may be provided to its constituent parts. With internecine rivalries removed, trade union officials and lay representatives would be free to concentrate on the development of participative activities which increase their influence beyond the field of wage bargaining. The authors conclude their chapter with a review of comparable practices in international and overseas banks.

John Waine follows with an analysis of financial reward systems and salary administration. He provides a detailed account of job evaluation methods and emphasises the prerequisites of job analysis and the establishment of 'benchmarks'. The objective is to construct an equitable payment system reconciling internal differentials and external relativities in salary levels and to create a sensible salary structure. Finally, he concludes with a note on salary costing and budgeting.

Women now form the majority of employees in banking. Marjery Povall traces the trends in women's employment, but notes that despite some significant shifts, 90% of women are employed in secretarial and clerical jobs. Attitudes may be slow to change, but certain Acts of Parliament have been designed to help – Equal Pay, Sex Discrimination, Employment Protection. How successful have they been? The author draws on relevant research studies and points the way towards positive action programmes.

Employment legislation is here to stay – and it takes many forms. Legislation has circumscribed managers' freedom to act. Uninformed managers may well be troubled and bewildered by laws and codes of practice which have made their jobs more difficult, but in some senses managerial courses of action have become less ambiguous. Jane Welch translates legal technicalities into plain language. She highlights the main issues regarding contracts of employment, disciplinary and grievance procedures, sex and race discrimination, maternity rights, unfair dismissal, redundancy, health and safety, trade union membership and disclosure of information. She provides a very practical guide for the busy manager. 'If employers are in sympathy with the spirit of law, they are much less likely to infringe the letter of the law'.

CHAPTER 16

Industrial Relations Systems and Collective Bargaining

S. Kessler

Professor of Industrial Relations, The City University Business School

This chapter starts with a brief consideration of the concept of an industrial relations system and the nature of conflict in order to put collective bargaining in context. It then proceeds to outline the nature of collective bargaining, in particular that it is a process for the joint determination of the rules concerning the employment relationship. Next it looks at the development of the traditional system of collective bargaining in the UK and then at the changes which have taken place, in particular, with regard to the level, content and coverage of collective bargaining. Finally, it considers the environmental factors which influence the process of collective bargaining, in particular, economic, technological, social and governmental factors.

THE CONCEPT OF AN INDUSTRIAL RELATIONS SYSTEM

It may help to put collective bargaining in context to consider first the concept of an industrial relations system. According to Dunlop,[1] in each country there is an industrial relations system which is sub-system of the wider economic, social and political system. Every industrial relations system involves three groups or parties – first, employees and their organisations, secondly, employers and their organisations, and thirdly, Government and government agencies concerned with the workplace and the work community. The first two groups might be considered as the primary parties. Overall the system creates a complex of rules to govern the workplace and work community and these may take a variety of forms and be created in a variety of ways, for example, unilaterally (particularly by employers), by agreements, statutes, and by custom and practice, but their essential character is to define the status of the parties, to govern their conduct and to determine rewards and obligations.

The rules are fundamentally of two kinds. First, *substantive rules* which determine terms and conditions of employment and secondly *procedural rules* which establish methods and procedures for reaching substantive agreements and resolving disputes about them. Some substantive rules may be determined by the Government, for example, a national minimum wage, minimum holiday entitlements, maximum hours of work, and so might certain procedural rules, for example, limitations on the right to strike. In Britain, however, the main method of determining the rules has been by the primary parties through the process of collective bargaining.

The parties do not of course operate in a vacuum but within an environmental context which includes economic, technological, political and social factors. These factors are discussed later in the chapter. The subject matter of industrial relations therefore involves studying each of the parties to the system, their relationship and interaction with each other against the environment in which they operate. The particular relationship with which industrial relations and collective bargaining is concerned is of course the employment relationship.

It should be noted that the concept of an industrial relations system is one which can be applied at different levels, in particular, first at national level so that it makes sense to talk about the British System of industrial relations, the German System or the American System. Secondly, it can be applied at industry level so that one can say that there is such a thing as an industrial relations system, for example, in the Banking Industry, in the Electricity Supply Industry and in the Engineering Industry. Thirdly, the concept can be applied at company and plant level. At each level the primary parties are present, they create substantive and procedural rules and they operate within a complex of environmental factors. It is well established that some industries and some firms are more strike-prone than others and that the quality of industrial relations varies from industry to industry and from company to company. The reasons for this are to be found partly in the history, culture, and environment in which the particular industry or firm operates.

Finally, a word needs to be said on the question of conflict. Fox[2] has argued that two views may be taken of the enterprise. First the *unitary* view, that there is one source of authority and one focus of loyalty, and that the enterprise is a team striving jointly towards a common objective. Secondly, there is the *pluralistic* view, where the organisation is seen as 'a pluralistic society containing many related but separate interests and objectives which must be maintained in some kind of equilibrium'. There is also a third view – the *radical* view[3] which believes that conflict is endemic, denies any common or related interests whatsoever, and believes that conflict can be overcome only by a complete change in the structure of society.

If the pluralistic view is accepted it follows that some degree of conflict is inherent in the very nature of industrial organisation. It is then as important for management to realise that some conflict of interest is inevitable as it is for unions and their members to realise that there are certain common interests.

Insofar as this proposition became accepted, then *collective bargaining* became increasingly considered by many as the best method of resolving differences of interest.[4] This perspective has been termed 'liberal collectivism' – 'liberal' in the sense that the role of the State was limited, and 'collective' in that the parties were free to organise and engage in collective bargaining. Liberal collectivism developed during the late 19th century and for much of the 20th century as opposed to the earlier perspective of 'liberal individualism' or 'laissez-faire' whereby it was believed that everything should be determined by the free play of the market, that employment contracts were freely entered into by relatively equal people, capable of pursuing their own best interests, and that any combination would adversely affect the free market mechanism which if left to itself would ensure the greatest possible good for all. In the late 1960s and 1970s there developed a greater degree of Government involvement, for example, through Incomes Policies and through the establishment of tri-partite mechanisms involving Government and employers and employee representatives which has been labelled 'corporatism'. By the 1980s it was clear that corporatism was in retreat and that we might be returning, not necessarily to liberal collectivism, but to individual liberalism or neo-laissez-faire.[5]

The Nature and Theory of Collective Bargaining

Collective bargaining is a method of settling the pay and conditions of employment of employees. It is the term coined by the Webbs, pioneers in this field, to describe the method which seeks to settle pay and conditions by a bargain in the form of *an agreement* made between employers or associations of employers and organisations of employees. The classical view would consider it therefore as simply the collective equivalent and alternative to individual bargaining. It was a method developed by workpeople in order to enhance the weak bargaining power of the individual employee vis-a-vis his employer.

The more modern view of collective bargaining as propounded by Allan Flanders[6] however sees it as much more than the collective equivalent of individual bargaining. Flanders saw collective bargaining as essentially a *rule-making process by joint regulation*. As such one needs to compare collective bargaining, not with individual bargaining, but with other forms of rule-making processes, for example, unilateral determination by employers or statutory regulation. Collective bargaining is distinguished from these by the authorship of the rules, namely the fact that the rules are jointly determined.

Flanders views on the nature of collective bargaining coincide with those of a number of other writers. Chamberlain & Kuhn[7] argue that there are three theories of the nature of collective bargaining. First, the *marketing theory*, where collective bargaining is a means of contracting for the sale and purchase of labour. Secondly, the *governmental theory* which sees collective bargaining as a form of industrial government, its main function being to lay down the rules and establish the machinery for the making, interpretation and enforcement of rules. Thirdly, the *managerial theory* which sees collective bargaining as a method of management and stresses the functional relationship between unions and companies: they combine in reaching decisions on matters in which both have vital interests. Chamberlain & Kuhn do not suggest that these three theories are clear-cut and mutually exclusive. Partly they reflect different stages of historical development. Thus early negotiations were mainly a matter of fixing terms for the sale of labour (the marketing theory) – later came the need for settling disputes on these and other issues between the parties, which sometimes took the form of setting up joint bodies – the basis for the governmental theory. Finally, when eventually agreements were made which entered into the internal decision-making processes of a business enterprise, there was a basis for the managerial theory.

Flanders thought that the *managerial theory* was the most useful one to pursue, for the marketing theory only covered economic relationships while the governmental theory was too limited, being concerned only with procedural rules to the exclusion of substantive ones. A modern theory of collective bargaining has to recognise that it is a *process for regulating labour management as well as labour markets*. It is not just a process for determining economic relationships but managerial relationships as well, so that collective agreements may also seek to regulate the exercise of managerial authority in deploying, organising and disciplining the labour force.

The Development of the Traditional System of Collective Bargaining

Collective bargaining machinery developed in Britain during the nineteenth and first part of the twentieth century from local to district to industry level. Typically, negotiating machinery at industry level comprises representatives from an employers' association on one side and representatives from a trade union or unions, sometimes combined into a federation, on the other side, for example the Engineering Employers' Federation and the Confederation of Shipbuilding & Engineering Unions and, in the clearing banks, representatives of the Federation of London Clearing Bank Employers and representatives of The Banking Insurance and Finance Union (BIFU) and the Clearing Banks Union (CBU).

Essentially, industry-wide collective bargaining arrangements were established voluntarily, some, for example engineering, on an ad hoc basis, while many others owed their origin to the Whitley Committee, established in 1916, which recommended the establishment in each industry of a National Joint Industrial Council. The Government accepted the recommendation and encouraged the establishment of such Councils. Although a number fell into disuse or were abolished in the depression following the First World War there was a revival during the Second World War and there are some 200 Councils in existence today – partly in the public sector, including local and central government and the Health Service, but also in parts of the private sector.

Finally, mention should be made of Wages Councils, for although these have been established by law, owing their origins to the Trade Boards Act 1909, they have some of the characteristics of voluntary collective bargaining arrangements. Thus they involve negotiations between the two sides of the industries concerned with a view to reaching agreement. The main differences are, first, that they include in their membership independent persons, appointed by the Department of Employment, who in effect have a casting vote if there is disagreement between the two sides; and secondly, that decisions reached by Wages Councils are legally binding and enforced by the inspectorate of the Department of Employment. At the end of 1983, there were 25 Wages Councils, for example in retail distribution and hotel and catering, covering nearly 3 million workers. Wages Councils are generally found in areas where trade union organisation is weak and where the danger of exploitation is thought to be particularly likely,[8] but at the time of writing the Government is considering their future.

In most industries there are agreements laying down the procedure to be followed for discussing and settling disputes which may arise at industry or plant/company (i.e. domestic) level. It is common for procedures which apply to disputes arising at the level of the plant to provide for a number of stages of discussion before the machinery is exhausted at domestic level. It is then usual for there to be recourse to the external stages of the industry-wide agreement either at local/district level or at industry level or both. As regards disputes which are industry-wide in scope, there may be no more than one stage of procedure, for example, discussions at a national conference or on a National Joint Industrial Council. However, in a number of industries, there is provision for voluntary conciliation and/or arbitration, normally with the agreement of both sides. Disputes procedures usually provide that there should be no strikes or lock-outs until the agreed procedure has been exhausted.

If one were to describe collective bargaining institutions in this country at the end of the Second World War, one would say that essentially they consisted of a series of industry-wide negotiating arrangements and industry-wide procedures for settling disputes which started at domestic level, and if not solved at that level, progressed to district and industry level. Negotiations did not primarily take place at domestic level, only consultation and the interpretation of industry-wide agreements. Such a description would, of course, have been an over-simplification. For example, in most piece-working industries, domestic negotations were common and some large firms were not members of employers' associations, preferring to conduct their own negotiations. However, there would be sufficient truth in such a description to illustrate the enormous change which has taken place in our collective bargaining institutions in the post-war decades; above all the growth of collective bargaining at domestic level – either within the individual plant or at company level.

CHANGES IN THE TRADITIONAL SYSTEM – 1945/79

In this period there were a number of significant changes in collective bargaining that we need to consider. First, there was its development at plant and company level; secondly, there was the changing content of collective bargaining; and thirdly, there was the growth of trade unionism, particularly among white collar workers.

Levels of Collective Bargaining

Collective bargaining takes place at a number of different levels. Negotiations and agreements at industry level are still a central feature of British industrial relations, despite the growth of domestic bargaining. These agreements normally fix rates of pay and basic conditions of employment, such as hours of work, holidays, and overtime premia. However, in most of the private sector the rates of pay fixed by industry agreements are now minimum rates, below which pay determined at plant or company level must not fall. On the other hand, other terms and conditions of employment fixed at industry level tend to be treated as standard, that is to say to be applied without variations in individual companies and plants. In most of the public sector, rates of pay determined at industry level still tend to be standard rates.

Because industry-wide agreements normally lay down only minimum rates of pay, there is plenty of scope for bargaining at company and plant level. Some large firms prefer to be outside employers' associations and to conduct their own negotiations on an entirely independent basis. Such non-federated firms, for example Ford and Vauxhall, thus have their own negotiating procedures and make their own agreements with the unions. These may resemble national agreements where the bargaining unit is the entire company and the company agreement provides standard pay and conditions for all the firm's establishments in different parts of the country. But this is not necessarily so. Many companies, including very large ones, such as G.E.C. and Unilever, prefer to treat their different plants, subsidiaries or divisions as separate bargaining units. At company level, bargaining is usually carried out by union full-time officials, or a negotiating team consisting of officials and shop stewards. At plant level, bargaining is mainly carried out by shop stewards. Such bargaining may be for the whole plant with management negotiating with joint shop steward committees or it may be 'fragmented' bargaining with different work groups or departments within the plant. However, in the decade following the Donovan Commission Report[9] of 1968 with its criticism of 'informal, fragmented and autonomous bargaining', there was a considerable restructuring and formalisation of plant level bargaining. Survey evidence on the extent and nature of collective bargaining institutions at establishment level are contained in Brown (1981)[10] for manufacturing industry, and in Daniel & Millward (1983)[11] for manufacturing, the public sector and the private service sectors.

The major direction of change was unquestionably the *growth in the importance of domestic bargaining* and most firms of any size now have their own domestic negotiating arrangements (and disputes procedures) resulting in their own distinct pay structures. There are a number of reasons for this. First, and perhaps most important, was the achievement and maintenance of full employment during the first three decades after the Second World War. This on the one hand gave bargaining power to work groups and on the other hand meant that employers had to compete for labour and directly or indirectly pay more than the industry-wide established rates. Secondly, the development of modern management techniques, including personnel management techniques, meant that companies wanted to make better use of their own manpower resources, and this meant freedom from the constraints of industry-wide agreements and the tailoring of pay structures to the needs of the individual firm or plant. Thirdly, the more rapid development of technological innovation again necessitated greater flexibility at company level and freedom from the constraints of industry-wide agreements. Finally, there was the effect of social changes in society as a whole whereby people wanted more direct influence in determining matters which affected their well-being.

The Content of Collective Bargaining

The second major change was the extension of the content, subject matter and scope of collective bargaining. Collective bargaining in its early days was concerned primarily with pay and basic conditions of employment. Since then in many industries, and companies and plants, it was gradually extended and might well include not only wages, hours of work and other conditions of employment such as holidays, sick pay and premium rates, but such questions as manning, job demarcation, the pace and distribution of work, discipline and promotion. The extent to which this happened varied from industry to industry and from firm to firm, but the trend was unmistakable. Indeed, it is difficult to set a theoretical limit to the subject area of collective bargaining, although the attempt is often made by management anxious to preserve its prerogatives. Trade unions, in exercising their own functions, necessarily limit the managerial rights of employers, and any managerial decision which affects the well-being of their members is of concern to trade unions.

In banking, the subject matter of collective bargaining has been clearly defined. Thus the Industry's procedural agreement states that it applies to the following terms and conditions of employment;

'i.   The basic minimum and the standard maximum of the salary ranges of clerical grades 1–4 or their future equivalents. (Note: the ultimate maxima of these ranges are determined at domestic level).

ii.   Age related salaries for clerical grades 1 & 2 – or their future equivalent.

iii. The length of the basic working week and the length of the basic working day.

iv.   Overtime rates and qualifying periods for the payment of overtime working.

v.   Holiday entitlement for staff paid in accordance with (i) above.

vi.   Territorial allowances.

vii. Any national clerical Job Grading Scheme for clerical grades 1–4.

viii. Minimum Managerial Salary.'

Such precision is not necessarily true of all British industry. It is natural for unions to want to influence decisions which affect the well-being of their members, such as the introduction of new machinery and changes in manning, although whether this is best achieved by collective bargaining, consultation or participation is another question. It is also natural for management to want to maintain as much freedom of action as possible. However, it is important to note, that the widening content of collective bargaining owed less to union national policy than to reactions to employees 'on the shop floor' to matters which directly affected them.

The Coverage of Collective Bargaining

The third major change was the growth of trade unionism, particularly among white-collar employees, and hence in the coverage of collective bargaining.

The Growth of White-Collar and Manual Unionism in Great Britain 1948-1979[12]

	1948	*Union Membership (000s)* *1968*	*1979*
White-collar	2062	3056	5125
Manual	7056	6637	7577
Total	9118	9693	12702
		Union Density* (%)	
White-collar	33.0	32.6	44.0
Manual	50.3	49.8	63.0
Total	45.0	42.7	53.6

*   Union density is the number of members as a percentage of the total number of employees.

It will be seen from the above table that between 1948 and 1968 white-collar trade union membership grew by 1 million employees or by 50%, although white-collar union density did not increase. In other words, the growth in membership increased proportionately with the growth in white-collar employment. However, in the period 1968–79 white-collar union membership increased by a further 2 million – or by two-thirds – to over 5 million employees, and white-collar union density increased very substantially indeed from 32.6% to 44.0%. This latter period saw a very significant growth in manual union membership and density, so that overall trade union membership increased by some 3 million and trade union density increased from 42.7% to 53.6%.

White-collar unionism, in particular, developed in parts of the private sector, it already having been well established in much of the public sector. This growth was not just horizontal in occupational terms, for example, among clerical workers, but also vertical, up the occupational ladder, for example, to foremen, supervisors, technicians, and in some cases, managers and the professionally qualified. With the growth of white-collar unionism came the demand for recognition and collective bargaining rights. This sometimes resulted in resistance from employers, including some who had long recognised manual unions,[13] in the belief that their relationship with white-collar workers was in some way special and that trade unionism and collective bargaining were therefore inappropriate.

Among the questions which needed to be answered were: who are the *appropriate bargaining agents* and what are the *appropriate bargaining units*?

With regard to the former, the choice may be between a staff association and an external trade union, between a purely white-collar union and the white-collar section of a manual union, or between different white-collar unions. With regard to the latter question, it is the norm for British indusry to have separate bargaining units or negotiating arrangements for manual and white-collar emloyees and indeed for there often to be sub-units on a geographical, and particularly on an occupational, basis. Thus skilled manual workers may negotiate separately from semi-skilled, and unskilled and clerical workers separately from supervisors or technicians. While it is important for bargaining units to be agreed which genuinely reflect common interest groups, too great a fragmentation can clearly cause major difficulties.

As mentioned earlier, a detailed picture of the extent of collective bargaining is given in the Daniel & Millward Survey taken in 1980, which covered establishments employing 25 people or more. This showed that, overall, 67% of establishments recognised at least one union, with the public sector reaching virtually 100%, private manufacturing 68% and private services 42%. Unions were more widely recognised for manual workers than for white-collar workers and there was a much greater degree of recognition in the larger establishment, for example in establishments of 1000 plus, 94% recognised manual unions while in establishments of 25–49 less than half did so. The above figures on recognition are in accord with data from the 1978 New Earnings Survey which showed that the proportion of full-time employees reported to be affected by some form of collective agreement in that year was 70% for all industries and services, 69% for manufacturing, 40% for the private service sector and 92% for the total public sector. It will be noted that the number of employees covered by collective bargaining machinery is much greater than the number of trade unionists, for generally speaking, collective agreements are applied by employers to all their appropriate employees, whether or not they are members of a trade union.

THE ENVIRONMENT AND CHANGES SINCE 1979

Collective bargaining, no more than industrial relations in general, does not take place in a vacuum. Environmental factors need to be considered for they have a profound effect on the two main parties – employees and their organisations and employers and their organisations – and relationships between them. The key environmental factors may be grouped in a number of ways and we here consider briefly economic and market factors; government and the law; technological factors; and social factors. Environmental changes since 1979 have been very great indeed and so have been their effect on industrial relations in general and collective bargaining in particular.

Economic and Market Factors

The overall state of the economy clearly has an influence on collective bargaining, some of the key factors being the movement in the cost of living, the state of the labour market, and the rate of economic growth. Of at least equal importance is the economic environment at the level of the industry and individual firm. Thus the nature of the firm's products and its product markets, whether the firm is expanding or contracting, its profitability and productivity, the proportion of labour costs to total cost, are all key variables.

The change in the economic environment since 1979 has been profound. There has been a massive increase in the number of registered unemployed to more than 3 million with real unemployment even higher. The number of employees in employment between 1979 and 1984 fell by about 2 million and a marked change in the structure of the labour force has taken place. It is true that changes in the structure of the labour force have been proceeding for some time but these changes were greatly accelerated during this period. Thus, most of the decline in employment has been in manufacturing industry whereas employment in the service sector has remained fairly stable. There has also been a relative growth in the employment of white-collar workers, women and part-time workers.

The effect of mass unemployment and the fall in the number of employees in employment has been first a dramatic fall in union membership of more than 2 million by 1983 from its 1979 peak. Secondly, there has been a marked decrease in union bargaining power and in some cases a marked weakening of the position of shop stewards. In some industries and companies this had led to what might be termed an employer's counter offensive. In terms of the topics discussed above, this has manifested itself particularly in a reduction in the scope and content of collective bargaining, or put another way, in a re-assertion of managerial prerogatives. With regard to the level of bargaining, there have been no signs of any change in the trend towards plant/company bargaining. On the contrary, even in the public sector there are indications that in some areas the Government is encouraging a degree of decentralisation.

Government and the Law

Our traditional system developed on the basis of voluntary collective bargaining, that is to say without legal compulsion on either side, and collective agreements were not legally binding. Statutory developments essentially took the form of removing legal obstacles to collective bargaining and to trade union organisation and practice. The traditional role was thus one of minimum interference, although the State did gradually provide services to assist in keeping the peace, such as voluntary conciliation and arbitration services and a minimum protective role in certain aspects, for example, in the Wage Council industries and in Safety and Health.

In the mid-1960s and the 1970s there was much greater government intervention. Two major changes were the growth in statutory individual rights, for example, with regard to unfair dismissal, minimum notice, redundancy payments, maternity leave and equal pay (see Chapter 20); and secondly, the development of incomes policies by both Labour and Conservative Governments, with collective bargaining taking place against the constraints of incomes policy.

The changes in the political environment after 1979 have been as profound as the change in economic environment. The Thatcher Government has ended the post-war consensus and is committed to a free market approach, to monetarism, to reduced public expenditure, to privatisation, to no incomes policy (except through the exercise of cash limits in the public sector) and to reducing the power and influence of trade unions whom it sees as restricting the free play of the market. It has ended successive post-war government's commitment to full employment, arguing that government cannot achieve this, but can only create the environment in which employment might flourish, for example, as a result of reduced inflation, higher profitability and lower real wages.

Most of the Government's measures have had a detrimental effect on trade union organisation. Restriction of space prevents an elaboration of these measures but special mention must be made of the changes which have been enacted in Collective Labour Law. In this area the government has proceeded in stages and to date we have had The Employment Acts of 1980, 1982 and the Trade Union Act, 1984. The first two Acts combined severely restrict the immunities of unions and their members if they take certain kinds of industrial action, in particular picketing away from the workers' own place of work and most forms of secondary action. Further, by changing the definition of what is a trade dispute, more limitations have been imposed. Restrictions have been placed on closed shops which are likely to make them unenforceable, and clauses in commercial contracts which seek to make union membership a condition of the contract have been made void. The Government has also repealed Schedule 11 of the 1975 Employment Protection Act and rescinded the Fair Wages Resolution both of which provided some protection for the relatively lower paid. The Government is also considering the possible abolition of the Wage Council system. Under the 1984 Trade Union Act, individual ballots have to be held before industrial action can be officially called, if such action is to attract immunity, and individual ballots have to be held for the election of union executive members and on the question of whether unions should have political funds or not. Further restrictive legislation is likely.

Technological Factors

The state of technology and the nature of technological change are clearly of significance. A high degree of mechanisation or automation, for example, may mean a low proportion of labour costs to total costs and make it easier for employers to concede pay demands than would otherwise be the case in a labour intensive industry. It may also mean higher productivity per man and may also greatly enhance the bargaining power of particular groups of employees. On the other hand technological change may result in the threat of redundancies, weaken the bargaining power of other groups of employees, demand new skills and disturb existing pay differentials.

The rapid development of new technology in recent years has led unions, because of fears of unemployment, to press for shorter working hours, longer holidays, and earlier voluntary retirement. Unions have also pressed for technology agreements which have sought to provide, for example, improved job security, greater disclosure of information, increased consultation and opportunities for re-training.[14]

Social Factors

We have already mentioned changing social attitudes as being a factor in the growth of workplace bargaining and in extending the subject matter of collective bargaining. Changing social attitudes are unquestionably of key importance for, in the last resort, collective bargaining is concerned with people and their lives – not just at the place of work, but as a whole, for a person's income determines his life-style and that of his family. A whole host of factors, including full employment, the spread of education and the growth of the media, changed social attitudes in the first three post-war decades. There was for example, a greater challenging of authority, a desire to have more say in matters affecting one's life, demands for equal opportunities, rising expectations of a higher standard of living and increasing comparison of rewards between industries and occupations. These all fed into the subject matter of collective bargaining. The extent to which these social attitudes have permanently altered in the changed economic and political environment of the 1980s remains to be seen.

Conclusions

In this chapter we have looked at the nature of collective bargaining and at the development of its institutions, procedures and practices over time. We have tried to show how it has evolved and changed, in particular with regard to its content, coverage and level. The environment in which it operated has always been of crucial importance and of outstanding significance was the emergence and maintenance of full employment for some three decades after the Second World War. Following this, 1979/80 marked the most significant turning point of all and collective bargaining in the 1980s has to be viewed in terms of a drastically changed environment.

With high unemployment and changes in the structure of the labour force leading to greatly reduced union membership, with adverse legislation, a hostile Government and more rapid and sweeping technological change, there can be no doubt that unions have been on the defensive and are likely to be so for some time to come.

Management, for its part, under competitive pressures, has been taking more positive steps to increase productivity and to reduce costs. Different employers have developed different strategies which have been discussed by Sissons.[15] The most common strategy has been the re-exercising of managerial prerogative and a restriction of the scope and content of collective bargaining. This process in some companies has often gone along with an extension of joint consultation, partly through traditional joint consultative committees but also increasingly by other means such as quality circles and briefing groups. There is perhaps a growing realisation that worker co-operation is required to meet the challenges of the future and that what has been called 'macho-management' is not sufficient.

A number of other writers[16] have discussed the changed industrial relations scene of the 1980s, and one of the major questions often raised has been whether the changes that have taken place are of a permanent or temporary nature. Only time will tell.

References

1. Dunlop, J., *Industrial Relations Systems*, 1958, Holts.
2. Fox, A., *Industrial Sociology and Industrial Relations*, 1966, Royal Commission Research Paper No. 3, HMSO.
3. Fox, A., 'Industrial Relations: a social critique of pluralist ideology' in J. Child (Ed), *The Business Enterprise in Modern Industrial Society*, 1969, Macmillan.
4. It was described as such by the Whitley Committee Report, 1917; the Donovan Royal Commission, 1968, *In Place of Strife*, 1969; the 1971 Industrial Relations Act, and The Code of Industrial Relations Practice, 1972.
5. For a discussion of such industrial relations perspective, see G. Palmer, *British Industrial Relations*, Chap.2., 1983, Allen & Unwin.
6. Flanders, A., *Management and Unions*, 1970, Faber & Faber.
7. Chamberlain & Kuhn, *Collective Bargaining*, 1965, McGraw Hill.
8. The Employment Protection Act, 1975 provided for the possibility of establishing a statutory joint industrial council to replace a wages council in order to facilitate the transition from statutory regulation to voluntary collective bargaining.
9. Report of the Donovan Royal Commission on Trade Unions & Employers' Associations, 1968, HMSO.
10. Brown, W., (ed), *The Changing Contours of British Industrial Relations*, 1981, Blackwell.
11. Daniel, W. W. & Millward, N., *Workplace Industrial Relations in Britain*, 1983, Heinemann.

12. Bain & Price, 'Union growth; dimensions, determinants and destiny', in G. S. Bain (ed), *Industrial Relations in Britain*, 1983, Blackwell.

13. See Commission on Industrial Relations annual Reports (HMSO 1969 to 1974). Small and medium-sized firms also often argued that trade unionism was inappropriate to their special circumstances.

14. Webb, T., 'Union Tactics for the High Technological Age', *Personnel Management*, May, 1983.

15. Sissons, K., 'Changing Strategies in Industrial Relations', *Personnel Management*, May 1984.

16. For example: Roberts, B. C., 'Recent Trends in Collective Bargaining in the UK', *International Labour Review*, May–June 1984.

    Brown, W. & Sissons, K., 'Industrial Relations in the Next Decade', *Industrial Relations Journal*, Spring 1983.

    Bright, D., Sawbridge, D., Rees, B., 'Industrial Relations of Recession', *Industrial Relations Journal*, Autumn 1983.

    Brown, W., 'British Unions: new pressures and shifting loyalties', *Personnel Management*, October 1983.

Chapter 17

Industrial Relations in Banking

Sheila Rothwell,

Director, Centre for Employment Policy Studies, Henley Management College,

and
Tim Morris
Lecturer in Industrial Relations, London School of Economics

In the broadest sense industrial relations is concerned with the whole range of influences upon the relationship between employer and employees, including law, pay structure and strategies and the various methods of resolving disputes, or conflict. In the banking industry the terms and conditions of the majority of staff are fixed directly or indirectly by collective bargaining, right up to relatively senior levels of management. This chapter will therefore concentrate upon institutions of collective bargaining, particularly focusing upon the clearing banks, and examine the structure of negotiations as well as the parties involved. It will explore how the procedures governing the conduct of bargaining have changed, and the way these have impacted upon the outcome of several issues. It will also look at how the relationships between the parties have developed since the collapse of Dr Johnston's proposals to establish a merger between the rival unions, in 1980. The final section will consider the pattern of industrial relations in international banks in Britain and in other parts of the world, and the extent to which they are influenced by national traditions and practices.

Institutions and Parties
Since 1968 the English clearing banks have come together to fix the pay and conditions of their clerical staff by negotiation with trade unions. Similar arrangements were introduced in Scotland in 1970 and the membership of

each federation of employers was initially determined by ownership and participation in the respective clearing systems, thereby excluding other retail banks. Subsequently the constitutional guidelines of the English Federation have been relaxed but until now no other retail banks have been offered the opportunity to participate. Yet the clearers' settlements significantly influence the levels of pay and conditions elsewhere in the banking and finance sector. Institutional developments in the clearing banks therefore have broader repercussions as well

It may seem perplexing that the banks choose to fix the terms of employment of their staff collectively yet in the market place they are in competition for business. There are certain advantages in employers combining in factor markets in some conditions. First it should be noted that the banks are labour intensive organisations with up to two-thirds of their total operating costs being attributable to staff salaries, pensions and other benefits. The maintenance of common pay rates minimises the possibility of competition. The importance of minimising labour costs is therefore crucial to profitability but the demand for staff is usually strong both because of the turnover of existing staff and because the expansion of business has led to an overall growth in the size of the banks. Twenty years ago the English clearing banks employed 145,000, but at the end of 1983, total employment was over 280,000. If they can establish common rates of pay the banks will minimise the risk of competition for labour pushing up the price, and this holds true even in conditions of relatively high national unemployment. Operating in unison also reduces the risk of a single bank being 'picked off' by union action and the employers being exposed to a constant round of pay demands, as has happened in other industries with more decentralized bargaining when product and labour markets were more buoyant. Co-operation thus offered strength and greater predictability for the banks. This was important, not because bank unions are highly militant (they are not), but because the persistence of divided representation has created a situation of competition between the unions which is reflected in the bargaining process. To some extent this was overcome when national arrangements were instituted in 1968 by the creation of a joint staff side. Formal co-operation between the unions did not eradicate the underlying competition between them however, and the joint staff side broke up in 1977 to be succeeded by separate negotiations.

Trade Union Growth

Banking is almost unique in its particular form of divided representation. By itself multi-unionism is not unusual, because historically different groups of workers have become organised at different times and usually by groups catering for them specifically. Where unionism is more orderly, as in West Germany for instance, this is because the structure was imposed at a certain point by the State – in the German case after the Second World War. In Britain the first groups to organise were craft workers in the early 19th century, followed later by the less skilled manual workers and finally white collar staff including bank clerks. Unionism in banking really became established during and after the First World War with the growth of the Bank Officers Guild, the forerunner of the present day finance sector union, the Banking Insurance and Finance Union (BIFU), and with the emergence of the internal staff associations in each of the larger clearing banks, nowadays grouped as staff unions in the Clearing Bank Union (CBU).

Nationally, statistics of trade union membership growth and of trade union density (the proportion of employees who are union members) have shown considerable fluctuations. During the 1980s membership and density have fallen fast. Steady growth has however still been maintained in membership in the 'insurance, banking and finance' industry sector as a whole from 137,000 members and a density of 38.9% in 1948 to 395,000 members with 54.8% density in 1979, reflecting the continuing growth in employment. BIFU is one of the few TUC unions not to have lost members since 1980.

The special form of multi-unionism in banking is based on the rivalry between BIFU and the staff unions for members and dominance in bargaining. Other unions have been able to overcome institutional divisions by agreeing to co-operate in joint working arrangements, nationally in confederations and at the work-place, by establishing joint shop steward structures. In banking such co-operation has consistently been undermined by the differences of ideology, methods and principles of organisation. To understand this the historical origins of each type of body must be considered.

1. BANKING, INSURANCE AND FINANCE UNION

Originating as the Bank Officers Guild in England and the Scottish Bankers Association in Scotland, this body was founded in response to a number of factors common to staff in all the clearers concerning changing conditions of work. High inflation, unmatched by pay rises during the First World War, was one. Historically therefore the Guild made its appeal to all grades of employees in all of the banks. Out of this grew the union's demand for collective bargaining at a national level with a coalition of the banks, and this remained the traditional principle of the union until very recently.

Ideologically BIFU has consistently been more in the mainstream of trade unionism, although it has a relatively moderate image. Since 1940 it has been affiliated to the Trades Union Congress and its General Secretary now has a seat on the General Council. It is not affiliated to the Labour Party though. As an example of its moderate image, BIFU has long favoured the use of third parties to resolve disputes through arbitration, an uncommon policy among British unions. On the other hand it has not been averse to taking industrial action, once a secret ballot of the membership had indicated a majority in favour, and recently altered the rule book to facilitate authorisation of such action by the union's executive. While the number of strikes in banking has been low compared both to manufacturing and to the public sector, the union regards its ability to take industrial action as a crucial indicator of its independence from the banks. Membership willingness to take action appears to have increased since the late 1970s.

It was only in 1979 that the banking union changed its name to BIFU. From 1946 to that time it was called the National Union of Bank Employees and the new title formalised the broadening of its horizons across the whole finance sector. Although the English clearing banks remain the largest group of members in the union it has become one of many sections which often have different problems and priorities. As an indicator of this heterogeneity it is notable that English clearing banks membership constituted 85% of total membership in 1945 and 49% in 1983.

BIFU's organisational structure, like many other '*externally*' based unions has developed from a geographic regionally based branch system to one that is now regional, sectional and workplace based. The highest policy making body of the union is the Annual Delegate Conference to which delegates are elected by branch members. Conference determines policy for the forthcoming year, but the day-to-day running of the union is in the hands of the National Executive Committee, of which the General Secretary is an ex-officio member. He, like other full-time national officers, is appointed, not elected, and on a life-time rather than fixed term basis. Some changes in his position are likely, under the Trade Union Act 1984, which requires perodic election of all voting members of a union's Executive Committee.

2. CLEARING BANKS UNION

In 1980 after the collapse of Dr Tom Johnson's efforts to draw BIFU and the staff associations together, the latter decided to take up the proposals for an industry wide body called the Clearing Bank Union. With BIFU's refusal to participate, the problem of division remained however, and the CBU is in many ways an extension of earlier loose confederations of the associations, such as the CBSA (Confederation of Bank Staff Associations).

The staff unions which now constitute themselves as divisions of the CBU have sustained many of the principles of *INTERNALISM* by which they have traditionally distinguished themselves from orthodox unions.

To take account of the varying membership needs and interests, the union's constitution has since the late 1970s been amended to make provision for more sectional autonomy. The current sections are English Clearing Banks;

Scottish Banks; Trustee Savings Banks; Yorshire Banks; International Banks; Finance Houses; and Insurance. Each section has its own annual conference and committee; and within each, members in each institution (e.g. Standard and Chartered Bank within the International Bank Sector) have their own elected executive committees, annual meetings, and varying branch structures. Occupational structures are also important and there are separate 'Computer' and 'Technical and Services' Sections, although these staff are also represented through their Institutional sections. The union has 'union membership agreements' (whereby union membership is a condition of service for all employees) only in the Yorkshire Cooperative, and Trustee Savings Banks. Changes may however be made in the light of the new balloting requirements of legislation which came into force in 1984. BIFU has sole bargaining rights in most of the International Banks, Scottish Banks and Williams and Glyns.

Internalism is not an elaborately developed theoretical concept but is more pragmatically derived from the experience of the associations. So again it has to be understood in the light of the associations' development. One of the important components is a stress on a representative relationship which is exclusive to a single employer. In contrast, most TUC unions (in the private sector at least) have regarded reliance upon a single employer as likely to reduce their independence, all resources being tied up with the fortunes of a single enterprise. Yet the associations, emerging around the same time as the BOG, were in part a reaction to the Guild's industry-wide aspirations. Favouring a structure which was internal to their respective banks, they reasoned that banking was a life-long career (for male staff), that inter-bank recruitment did not occur and that systems of management, job organisation and pay did vary to a degree between each bank. There was thus no basis for a generic representative form.

Secondly, internalism emphasises co-operation between management and staff. In its strongest form this presupposed an identity of interests between them so that disagreements are purely the result of poor communications or morale. Originally the associations did not see their role as being bargaining agents but more as a consultative link between staff and management, and the problems of dependence were considered irrelevant. Indeed many associations had been set up and maintained by the banks and it was only in the 1960's that they began to pursue greater financial independence when developing a stronger bargaining role and were influenced by new legislative requirements from 'independent' unions. It was this that led to the hostility between the associaitons and the national union (BIFU) because the latter also argued that internalists were the instrument of a management strategy designed to obstruct 'true' trade union representation.

Collective bargaining was not a method favoured by the associations until after the war and it is only recently that they have changed their constitutions to allow strike action. Even now the strike clauses of the staff unions (as the associations have become) are highly restrictive. This reluctance to adopt the more militant methods of trade unions reflects the internalist view that conflicts of interests between employers and staff in banking are non-existent. Problems and differences may certainly occur, but they can be resolved by reasoned negotiation because of the perceived common ground between the parties rather than by the explicit use of bargaining power through industrial action. If for any reason a negotiated settlement was unachievable, the associations (like BIFU) favoured arbitration by a third party.

The third point to make about internalism is that being grounded in practice it is not a fixed doctrine. In discussing the character of the associations it is therefore necessary to stress their adaptability. Indeed their strength has derived from the way they have evolved from adjuncts of managment into effective and financially independent representative bodies.

By doing this the associations appear to have countered the longstanding criticism of their rival BIFU that they were 'a spurious form of representation'.[2] In bargaining they have demonstrated a concern to defend and improve the conditions of their members, like orthodox unions, yet at the same time to combine this with a distinctive approach which is consistent with their tradition of co-operation. It can also be argued that staff unions have sustained their membership by appealing to a professional ethic which continues to exist in banking employment. Thus they seem more akin to the occupational associations which cater for the other professions, such as the British Medical Association, than to TUC unions.[3]

These factors help to explain why the staff unions have sustained a higher membership in each of the three clearing banks where they are established. Individually though the trends show some variation, with the Barclays Group Staff Union performing most strongly, at BIFU's expense, whilst in Lloyds the national union has recently outperformed its rival. It may well be that these differences are explicable largely in terms of organising resources and structures, and to some extent by management recognition policies. CBU's traditionally lower subscription rates and attractive discount services also appear to contribute to membership growth at BIFU's expense. Greater attention to recruitment and to grievance processing tends to demonstrate more visible action on behalf of members than the more professional negotiating expertise and research back-up facilities provided by BIFU.

By contrast, in Scotland BIFU was able to grow by achieving mergers with the associations which were always much smaller and thus unable to develop the resources to survive. Managerial policies were possibly also more active in promoting mergers at the company level. The question of divided representation has thus been resolved, with the exception of the Clydesdale Bank where, ASTMS (Association of scientific, Technical and

Managerial Staff) another TUC union holds a minority and declining membership.

3. ASTMS

A third union operates in the clearing banks, but with more limited rights. ASTMS gained a foothold in the banks when the Midland Bank Staff Association and the Clydesdale Association (Clydesdale Bank is owned by the Midland) elected to transfer their engagements in the early 1970's. In each case, however, ASTMS only has domestic rights to negotiation – it does not participate in pay bargaining at national level. Probably because of this its membership has steadily fallen to around 4000 in the Midland, although it is disproportionately strong among some powerful groups such as the data processing staff. Whether ASTMS can revitalise its position here and in the finance sector as a whole is debatable. Certainly its previously more militant image prompted some employers to recognise BIFU in preference or else to encourage staff associations, as in the Building Soceities. In the Bank of England, ASTMS (and BIFU) membership diminished with the development of the Bank of England Staff Organisation, (BESO) into an independent union with recognised negotiating rights for all staff. Falling membership in other areas of private industry may prompt ASTMS to turn once again to the finance sector, where it was once pre-eminent outside the banks, and particularly to compete to bring more staff associations under its wing.

National and Domestic Bargaining Machinery

National bargaining machinery was introduced in england in 1968 and in Scotland in 1970, for clerical staff. Non-clerical national negotiations were also instituted in 1970 and 1971 respectively. In each case the main conditions of employment, outlined above, were covered in these negotiations, but it proved necessary for each bank to establish a domestic procedure as well. These covered a variety of subjects not negotiated nationally, as well as conditions of employment for managerial and specialist staff such as engineers and data processors who have become more numerous in recent years. The domestic agreements mirrored the procedures established in the national machinery and joint staff sides operated except in the Midland where inter-union rivalry was particularly intense.

Although the fixing of actual rates of pay at national level did neutralize the competition for staff among the banks, as mentioned above, it entailed certain problems. Insufficient discretion was available to each bank to reward exceptional performers or use the pay system as a means of motivation. This was partly resolved in the early 1970's in a national job evaluation exercise which introduced a component of domestic pay bargaining whilst retaining a four grade national agreement. The desire for greater domestic discretion over pay has re-emerged in recent years, however, and may prompt further changes to the national machinery.

Procedurally, the banks adopted a somewhat unusual device in both their national and domestic constitutions. This was to incorporate the facility of binding arbitration which could be called upon by either side in the event of a deadlock. This has been thought desirable for several reasons. First, without having to recourse to the use of sanctions, the option of inviting a third party to determine the outcome of an issue was meant to guarantee responsible bargaining. Second, it was assumed that the majority of bank staff would prefer arbitration to the possible need to take industrial action, whether they were members of BIFU or a staff association. Similarly, the banks placed a high priority on the avoidance of disputes not only because of the effects on business but also to preserve the high-trust relationship with their staff. They wished to avoid the problems faced by some parts of manufacturing industry.

The effects of arbitration were mixed. As a device for resolving disputes without recourse to sanctions it proved successful. Moreover it did not mean, as some feared, that the inclination to bargain would be undermined with each issue only being resolved by recourse to third party. Between 1968 and 1978 there were only nine references made at the national level. There was a price for this however, as arbitrators tended to 'split the difference' between the two sides as much as possible, maximising the sense of equity rather than assessing what a free bargaining outcome would have been, given the strengths of the parties, and this caused some disquiet to the banks. After the ending of co-operation between the unions and the emergence of separate bargaining further problems developed. Each union attempted to use the option of arbitration as a means of overturning agreements reached between the banks and its rival, and neither would agree to abide by any arbitrated decision called for by the other. By 1982 the banks were finding this situation intolerable and opted to widthdraw from the compulsory arbitration arrangements.

Trade Union facilities

Despite the problems with competitive unionism, the banks have encouraged unionism without discrimination against either side. Indeed earlier criticisms of partiality towards the associations have prompted explicitly neutral policies. Facilities offered to both unions typically include the use of internal mailing systems, notice boards and access for recruitment purposes. Seconded officials were appointed by each of the banks during the 1970's; these were bank staff who spent a period of duty working as lay union officials on grievances and local problems. Some banks have extended the use of lay officials with 'jointly accredited representative' schemes. These create a system of office representatives who are empowered to deal with problems at a local level, and may have paid time off from work for this purpose. The existence of these lay representatives helps the unions overcome the problem of communicating with a widely dispersed membership. As they strengthen the local organisation of the unions they may also have helped them to extend membership relatively cheaply, a factor that has particularly assisted BIFU which was organisationally weak at local level. There are advantages for employers in these developments as well though. Given the large size of the clearers and their centralized management structures, they arguably help the orderly processing of industrial relations problems, in a manner which Professor Kessler referred to as a pluralistic approach to managing staff in the last chapter.

Bargaining Changes in the 1980s

Underlying the bargaining system in the clearing banks remains the competition between the national union, BIFU, and the staff unions in the CBU. Their rivalry led to the collapse of the joint staff sides at national and domestic levels in 1977, and the re-establishment of bargaining with separate but identical arrangements for each union only in 1983, following a period when the formal procedures were in abeyance nationally. Attempting to resolve the division the parties called in a neutral outsider, Dr Tom Johnston, in 1978, and although significant headway was made his initiative collapsed in 1980. While the failure remains of concern to the parties because of the costs in duplicating resources and the division of power at the bargaining table, their longstanding ideological differences continue to pre-empt co-operation. Although from the banks point of view there may be advantages in facing a divided staff side, they remain concerned as this competitiveness could spill over into bargaining with each union trying to outdo the other. Furthermore, the instability of separate negotiations has coincided with attempts by the banks to establish stricter controls on labour costs by pursuing firm negotiating strategies.

So confronting the banks both nationally, through the Federation of London Clearing Banks Employers, and domestically, has been the question of how to balance the risks of provoking conflict with the aim of constraining costs. One outcome has been the change in procedures at national and domestic levels with the termination of the compulsory arbitration facilities. Although this means the banks are no longer tied by the decisions of outsiders who may have little knowledge of the banking industry, it effectively compels the staff unions to resort to bargaining sanctions like an orthodox union. The first examples of this change were seen when the Barclays Group Staff Union (BGSU) executive proposed strike action over the re-introduction of Saturday opening in 1983. It should be noted though that provisions for conciliation and arbitration do remain in the new constitutions, but only if both sides agree to this beforehand, and the employers have shown reluctance to allow issues to be resolved by an outsider's decision.

Second, the range of substantive issues is also under review. Partly this reflects the loosening of the labour market, partly the banks desire to constrain labour costs and partly the growing diversification between them. This has lead to proposals to buy out or modify certain premium payments such as the Large Town Allowances and local holidays as well as adjusting the national grading structure. A firm line on Christmas opening has also been taken in response to the strong competitive threat from other financial institutions. Whilst not undermining trade union development, the competitive pressures upon the banks appear to be leading to changes in the existing arrangements which the representative bodies are very concerned about. The decision of Barclays and National Westminster to open branches on Saturday mornings, for instance, was taken without consultation with the unions and led to arguments that it contravened the previous agreements to negotiate any changes to hours of working and payments for overtime working. In response, the banks have pointed out that the branches are staffed by volunteers so that the arrangements do not contravene existing procedures. Management strategies appear now to be moving towards a position which, while accepting unionism as legitimate, sees the need to sustain clear limits to joint decision-making in order to respond to the related issues of technological change and an increasingly competitive market place.

Banking Developments and Implications for Trade Unions

Taking technological change, for example, the growth of automated payment systems (such as CHAPS), cash distribution systems (ATMS) and 'supermarket' or home banking may all have profound industrial relations effects on employment levels and career structures. If the traditional career opportunities in banking are reduced it might be argued that a source of the stability which has prevailed in banking will be removed and more conflict-orientated relationships develop. At present though there are conflicting views on the likely impact of technology on jobs.

One development which seems likely to encourage the trend towards greater diversification between the banks – already apparent in their more competitive approach to deposits – is the modification of the branch structures. Although we should not overstate the trend towards 'satellite' banking, changes in the traditional idea of the branch as a microcosm of the bank, providing a complete range of services whatever the actual demand, are likely to have an effect on the content of jobs. The existing grade structure will increasingly be rendered obsolete. It may be predicted that the national grade structure, covering all of the banks, and establishing actual pay rates, is replaced and greater discretion given to each bank. In future, while minimum rates and conditions are negotiated nationally the banks, like other industries with two tier negotiations, will supplement pay at company level to reward performance more specifically. The desire to raise productivity to internationally competitive levels may also lead each bank to tailor its reward systems more towards this goal. In short, it may be argued that the period of industry wide co-operation is past its peak.

This also has implications for the unions. With the prospect of such profound changes for bank staff, an amalgamation of resources and a unified, coherent strategy to confront the important issues facing them would appear to be strong arguments in favour of a merger, although at present such a move seems unlikely. Each remains convinced that its particular approach to representation is more appropriate. In the past, discussions on mergers have only developed when one or both parties is experiencing some sort of organisational crisis – be it financial or representational. While each is experiencing membership growth and not threatened by a loss of recognition for instance, no such crisis exists to push them together.

Changes in Union Structures

Yet each party is struggling with its identity. BIFU, in responding to its increasingly diverse areas of membership, has arguably become organisationally over-complex. It has responded to its diversified membership by creating sections which have considerable autonomy in policy making. Yet these disparate sections may see little in common with each other. Furthermore, decentralising its power into sections has weakened the industry-wide approach the union always favoured; ironically BIFU may be said to be closer to the enterprise-level approach of its rivals, the staff unions, than ever before and this might facilitate an amalgamation. The wider finance-sector ambitions of BIFU cannot easily be reconciled with the philosophy of internalism however. Nor do the staff unions find BIFU's involvement with the wider trade union movement through the TUC easy to tolerate.

Recent changes in the operational structures of the clearing banks have adversely affected BIFU. Williams and Glyn's integration with its Scottish partner, the Royal Bank of Scotland has led to the former's withdrawal from the English Federation. As BIFU had sole membership rights in Williams and Glyn's (following merger with the staff associations of the constituent banks in 1970) this means a loss of members from the English National Bargaining Council (and thus influence) which the CBU has not experienced. It also makes the CBU more representative as an industry-wide body having large numbers of members in three of the four remaining banks.

The other recent change has been in Barclays Bank with the amalgamation of the international and domestic divisions. Previously these were managed separately and the international division was not part of the Federation. Moreover BIFU had exclusive rights in the international bank and a relatively high density of membership which will now come under attack from the BGSU. (Barclays Bank Group Staff Union). If the membership performance of the two unions in the domestic bank is anything to go by, BIFU may well lose considerable numbers to its rival.

Problems of strategy and organisation face the staff unions as well. Firstly, although grouped in the CBU, their policies emphasise the old company level relationship. Whether there is sufficient to keep them together as divisions of a larger union contributing resources and power to the central body, rather than simply meeting jointly as a negotiating team as and when necessary seems doubtful. Yet on their own they may be too small to maintain the resources necessary to operate as effective, independent representative bodies. Secondly, can the staff unions reconcile the firmer bargaining strategies and the prospective changes to career opportunities with their internalist ethos? Adaptation has been their strength in the past, but at what point do they lose their distinctively co-operative approach? Already industrial action has been threatened over Saturday opening and Christmas leave and without the recourse to arbitration the staff unions may actually have to demonstrate their bargaining effectiveness, so as not to risk appearing powerless. Finally, mention should be made of ASTMS, the third clearing bank union. It has been fashionable to discount this union, but falling membership could well prompt an attempt to re-establish its position. ASTMS still has finance sector pretensions and is a sufficiently flexible organisation to offer arrangements to staff associations that establish a link by sub-contracting various services, without requiring a full merger. It is this sort of flexibility that allowed it to grow so rapidly in the past, (3) and in due course it may represent a means of re-entry into domestic as well as international banks.

International Banks

The development of the City of London as a centre of international banking and the establishment of London-based representation of nearly 400 banking groups from all over the world, in addition to the Head and branch offices of British overseas banks, has meant a steady increase in the proportion of employees in banking (and hence in potential union membership). Numbers of staff employed by foreign banks and overseas security houses rose from 9,000 in 1968 to 29,000 in 1978 and 38,000 by 1983.

Advantage of this opportunity was taken by BIFU early in the 1970s, utilising legislation (1971 Industrial Relations Act, repealed in 1974) to secure legal recognition agreements with employers, some of whom might otherwise have been reluctant to agree. A few of these have remained largely a formality. The most actively developed BIFU membership and negotiating and consultation arrangements have probably been those at Standard and Chartered Bank, but BIFU also has collective bargaining recognition agreements among a wide range of foreign banks, such as those from Australasia (in some of which ASTMS is recognised instead), the Indian Sub-continent, and many European countries, including France, Italy, Germany, Spain and Greece. Pay negotiations often follow similar lines to those of the English clearing banks with which they have links, but these have been improved upon in the Indian banks. Among the Japanese banks, only in the Bank of Tokyo is BIFU recognised, with the others preferring internal representative or consultative systems more akin to the house unions of the banks of Japan, where membership is high. The American banks represent the strongest resistance to union recognition, relying on a combination of generous employee benefits and good communications and human relations policies as well as a known policy of active discouragement of membership, (in Britain, U.S.A. and many other countries), unless this conflicts with national legislation. BIFU complained, in one instance of redundancy handling, that ILO and OECD 'Guidelines' for multi-national enterprises and labour relations, were being violated. Similar complaints of violation of agreements were made by BIFU concerning their negotiations with the Soviet-owned Moscow Narodny Bank, most of whose employees are union members.

To some extent, therefore, employer and employee traditions and policies of the parent country are reflected in the U.K. practice of respective banks, although there is often preference for an internal staff associaiton and an initial reluctance to go beyond granting unions more than representational or consultation rights, even for example in French or Italian 'nationalised' banks, accustomed to negotiating fully in their own countries. Some of the most militant union members have been those of the Indian and Pakistan banks (some of them also State owned) displaying tactics developed in their countries of origin, and with their expatriate staff retaining membership of, for example, the All India Confederation of Bank Officers.

Industrial Relations in Banking Outside the UK

Attitudes to trade union membership and collective bargaining among bank staffs in other countries tend to reflect not only different national traditions of industrial relations but, in particular, national attitudes to white collar and managerial unionism.

In Ireland, the largest group of workers outside the Irish Congress of Trade Unions (affiliated to the British TUC) is the Irish Bank Officials' Association, which organises over 90% of bank employees and is not a party to the national wages agreement. After a highly militant period in 1970s, with several strikes including one lasting for six months, industrial relations now appear to be more stable, despite lower wage settlements. This may be attributable both to the economic recession and fears of job loss, in rapid moves towards automation.

Elsewhere in Western Europe, in the Scandinavian countries and in Germany and the Netherlands, there are well developed banking unions within strong white collar federations; stable systems of wage bargaining; and rights (both statutory and bargained) to information and consultation over a wide range of working practices and conditions; as well as rights to representation on Boards and/or works councils. Similar legal rights pertain in France, although membership levels vary as between the nationalised and private banks, and union-employer relationships tend to be less stable and more volatile; although less so than in Italy, where industrial action is not uncommon.

In India, Pakistan and Sri Lanka, trade union membership is high, active and often politicised. Some of the banking unions are affiliated to different trade union federations according to their political leaning, some are regional unions, and others are very big 'internal' house unions, as in the State Bank of India and Bank of Baroda. Employers claim considerable difficulty in changing working practices, reducing inefficient overmanning or introducing new technology because of union resistance. One recent example of industrial action over a wage claim at one bank took the form of staff turning up to work normally, but with counter clerks explaining at great length and in great detail to each customer, why they were unable to fulfil their transaction for them. disputes over bonus payments and over service rules tend to proliferate.

In Hong Kong, white collar union membership is generally low in the private service sector, and in banking there are no union recognition agreements. Formal 'Staff Relations' consultative committees are, however, in operation in most of the main banks, where there are annual salary discussions and regular meetings to talk about other issues. The main terms and conditions are however largely unilaterally determined by management, taking into account informal 'soundings'. There are usually formal procedures for individual, rather than collective, handling of grievances.

In Singapore, where all trade union membership and activity is subject to considerable legal regulation, two of the biggest banks are trade union owned; but trade union leadership is also integrated into the political system.

In Malaysia, too, where lower grades of clerical staff, up to supevisor level are generally likely to be members of a registered union, some of the banks are 'Cooperative Banks' and this can appear to pose ethical problems for employees (who are also members of cooperatives) going on strike. Industrial action is usually infrequent and short-lived after some street demonstrations.

In many developing countries, (as in the industrialised world) banking industrial relations are relatively stable since employees are anxious to keep their relatively well paid and good status 'desirable' jobs, while the banks are concerned to attract and retain customers in an increasingly competitive market and to preserve a 'good employer' image. On the other hand, clerical staffs tend to be an urban, better educated, more numerate and articulate section of the population and their union activists may tend to become political activists in unstable political environments. Conversely, the scope for union membership/action may be limited by the extent of government control through state regulation of wages (in fixing minima, establishing guidelines for increases or regulating bonuses) of hours and holidays; of laws governing hire and fire procedures; of union recognition criteria; or of compulsory arbitration of disputes.

In Nigeria, British-based traditions of manual unions extended to various white collar sectors, although legislation restricts managerial representation through the same union as the employees they supervise. The majority of lower grade employees belong to the National Union of Banks, Insurance and Financial Institutions Employees which has had negotiating rights for all categories except senior staff since 1978. Industrial action is not frequent, usually consisting of short-lived, 'wild-cat' demonstrations over a particular grievance. For various reasons, employees prefer not to risk a lengthy period of absence from their jobs. Nor is membership loyalty to the union likely to be very strong in a situation in which only about a third of employees' take home pay comes from the basic wage negotiated by the union.

In Zimbabwe and in South Africa there are long established active trade unions among both white and black employees. New unions are now developing rapidly, aimed at recruiting lower grades of clerical, usually black, staff. Some of these are 'industry' based, aiming to recruit all 'finance' sector staff; some are wider, more 'general', clerical/sales workers' unions. Some are open only to blacks (and in Zimbabwe provided many political activists in the struggle for independence) while others have a more open multi-racial aim. Difficulties are therefore increasing for employers who wish to take a more pro-active stance to recognition and avoid the multi-unionism and conflict they see in British industrial relations, whether outside or inside the banking sector. New legislation is giving employees greater statutory rights to representation.

British banks overseas tend to adopt a combination of British practices and those of the host country – preferring some form of 'informal' representation where possible, providing it conforms with national legislation. Where they become independent national banks, they have often moved towards a more fully developed representational system, as for example where Barclays Bank International has now become the Republic Bank of Trinidad and Tobago.

FIET

The International Federation of Commercial, Clerical, Professional and Technical Employees (FIET) is an international trade union secretariat, with a head office in Geneva, and it claims to represent banking (as well as other white collar) staffs world wide. Its second World Conference of Bank Employees is planned to be held in Denmark in September 1985, to discuss matters of common interest. While it is also very active at EEC level (as EUROFIET) it more commonly attempts to act in support of national organisations – for example, in helping to organise the campaign for the reduction of working hours from 40 hours to 35 hours a week in Germany in 1984; to assist the Commonwealth Bank Officers Association express its concern over the likely opening of foreign bank branches in Australia; to support CONTEC in Brazil.

FIET also publishes reports on multinational banks, such as Citibank in the hope of coordinating common membership and recognition campaigns internationally, as well as on subjects of general concern to bank staffs, such as equality for women, or ATM networks and other aspects of new technology. AFRO-FIET holds seminars for banking unions in various English, French or Arab speaking nations in Africa.

Conclusions

This chapter has traced the development of a two-tiered system of bargaining at national and company level in the clearing banks and suggested that there were several advantages for the banks in combining together to fix common rates of pay and conditions. In establishing bargaining arrangements with the banking unions the unique form of competition for predominance between the national union, BIFU, and the staff association – now staff unions grouped in the CBU – has presented a special source of instability.

Changes facing the banks in their industrial relations system were seen to stem from product market conditions and technological innovations. It was suggested that more intense competition will lead to diversification between the banks, facilitated by new technologies and that the traditionaly industry-wide co-operation will probably give way to greater company level bargaining. This has profound implications for the staff bodies, but their different approaches remain, and in the absence of some sort of organisational crisis the prospects of a merger seem slim.

Industrial relations in the London offices of international banks, as in British banks overseas was shown to reflect a mixture of host country and parent country traditions, the precise balance being dependent on the strength of union activism or an employer policy. Outline examples were given of varieties of systems of industrial relations in banking in different parts of the world, and the influence of different legislative frameworks. Nevertheless, as in Britain, descriptions of the formal system need to be supplemented by an appreciation of national culture and traditions, and of informal agreements and relationships in a particular bank, in order to understand a particular pattern of industrial relations and the appropriate ways of approaching any problems experienced.

References

1. See Bain, G. S. (ed), *Industrial Relations in Britain*, 1983, (Blackwell), chapter 1, 'Union Growth: Dimensions, Determinants and Density', Table 1.5.
2. This phrase was used in a motion passed at NUBE's Annual Delegate Meeting in 1952 criticising the associations.
3. See Palmer, G., *British Industrial Relations*, 1983, (George Allen & Unwin), chapter 6 for further discussion on these types of representative body.
4. See Undy, R. et al., *Change in Trade Unions*, 1981, Hutchinson.

CHAPTER 18

Financial Reward Systems And Salary Administration

John Waine

Assistant Director, Federation of London Clearing Bank Employers

Financial reward systems comprise various methods of calculating how much a person should be paid to undertake a particular job. The amount cannot be calculated with total accuracy. The best that can be achieved is to relate the pay of an individual to that of others working for the same employer, and the pay rates of that particular employer to those of other employers in the country as a whole.

The method used to achieve this relationship varies from company to company. The very small company can negotiate individually with each employee and in each case reach agreement on a level of pay which both consider to be acceptable.

In larger companies individual negotiation is not possible and systems have to be devised which achieve the same overall level of fairness. Essentially these systems consist of two components. First, a structure whereby jobs within an organisation are related to each other and second, a method wherby the actual payment to employees in those jobs is ascertained.

Job Evaluation

The process of relating jobs to each other is usually called job evaluation. There are many methods of job evaluation but they all fall under four main headings, two quantitative, two non-quantitative. Quantitative job evaluation systems are those where the various elements of a job are allocated points or values which are then combined to produce a total. The higher the total the higher the job. Non-quantitative systems are those where jobs, or parts of them, are compared and placed in order without reference to numerical values.

1. NON-QUANTITIVE – JOB RANKING

The simplest form of non-quantitative job evaluation is job ranking. This involves comparing every complete job with every other complete job and placing them in rank order. Normally this is done by preparing job descriptions and then comparing them but in smaller companies of departments it is possible to rely on management knowledge. Whichever option is applied, the jobs should be compared systematically using suitably prepared comparison sheets.

Figure 1 is a simple comparison sheet on which a cross is placed whenever a job in the left hand column is considered more demanding than a job in the heading. Figure 1 clearly shows a loans officer at the top and a machinist at the bottom of the job ranking. Job ranking is rarely as simple as this and many jobs will be found to be of identical size. Figure 2 shows a more sophisticated job ranking table using the values of zero, one and two to signify jobs of less, equal or more value. These figures can be totalled to assist in job ranking but the totals are no more than an indication of relative size.

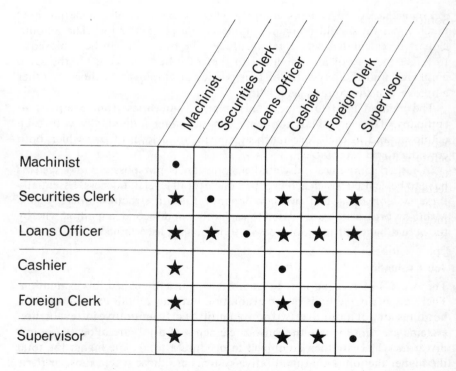

Figure 1 Job Ranking : Comparison Sheet.

	Securities Clerk	Supervisor	Manager's Clerk	Loans Officer	Senior Cashier	Cashier	
Securities Clerk	•	2	0	0	2	2	6
Supervisor	0	•	0	0	1	2	3
Manager's Clerk	2	2	•	1	2	2	9
Loans Officer	2	2	1	•	2	2	9
Senior Cashier	0	1	0	0	•	2	3
Cashier	0	0	0	0	0	•	0

Figure 2 Job Ranking : Comparison Sheet.

To ensure that the job ranking is correct it must be undertaken by several people independently and disagreements between the evaluators resolved before a final ranking is allocated to each job. Once the ranking has been agreed the jobs can, if required, be grouped into grades for the purposes of deciding salary.

Job ranking works well where jobs are readily comparable and well understood but becomes more difficult in more diverse companies or departments. In such cases the choice is either to implement a series of separate job ranking schemes, which then may have to be cross-linked, or to use a more sophisticated alternative.

2. NON-QUANTITATIVE – GRADE DESCRIPTION

A job ranking scheme places the jobs in order and then usually puts them into grades. A grade description scheme *starts* with a series of grades each of which is assigned one or more grade descriptions. These descriptions have to be general enough to cover various duties but precise enough to preclude ambiguity. There may be within any one grade a series of descriptions for different types of work. For example the following descriptions might cover grade 1:

> Typing: Undertakes simple copy typing under constant supervision. Minimum speed 40 w.p.m.
>
> Clerical: Undertakes simple routine clerical tasks under constant supervision. Duties may include filing, sorting mail and operating duplicating machines.

Other descriptions might cover staff in specialist departments such as foreign exchange or data processing.

Once grade descriptions have been completed every job must be considered in the light of these descriptions and given its appropriate grade. This can be done using management knowledge or some kind of assessment committee, but in any case it is best to complete a job description for each job which can be objectively compared with the grade descriptions and an appropriate grade assigned to the job.

3.   QUANTITATIVE – POINTS RATING

The trouble with non-quantitative systems is that decisions are entirely subjective. The aim of quantitative systems is to make decisions as objective as possible. The use of numbers can, however, be misleading because the components of a points rating system are still not defined sufficiently clearly to achieve scientific accuracy.

Points rating systems use a series of factors and sub-factors as the basis for comparison of each job. Each factor is allocated a maximum number of points and within each factor the sub-factors receive varying numbers of points up to the maximum. An example is the London Clearing Banks' scheme for clerical grades 1 to 4 in which the factors are as follows:-

Factors	*Maximum Points*
Experience	20
Complexity	25
Discretion and Initiative	15
Supervision of staff	15
Responsibility for avoiding loss	15
Personal Contact	10
	100

For example, the Factor 'Responsiblity for avoiding loss' has the following sub-factors and corresponding point scores:

(a) Errors cause delay in work – responsibility limited by regular checking provided by system 3

(b) Errors create delay and difficulty to customer or other branch or department – responsibility limited by delayed checking provided by system..6

(c) Errors could cause monetary loss. Moderate responsibility as checking provided by system does not thereby recover loss.... 10

(d) Responsible for work which is unchecked and which could cause serious monetary loss if incorrect 15

The other factors are similarly divided.

When a points rating scheme is set up, ranges are allocated to particular grades. For example a bank might select the following ranges:

Grade	Points range
1	0–20
2	21–40
3	41–60
4	61–75

Subsequently, jobs can be evaluated using the system and a points total obtained. The total will decide the grade. Under such a system new and revised jobs can be evaluated and re-evaluated easily and the system may therefore remain valid for many years.

4. QUANTITATIVE – FACTOR COMPARISON

Factor comparison is a technique which embodies the principles of points rating with the principles of ranking. It is analytical in that jobs are broken down into factors. Fewer factors are usually used than in a points system proper, for speed and simplicity, but the method can become complicated in its application, arising from the need to reconcile two independent sets of ratings. The first set of ratings consists of the rank order of jobs under various factor headings. The second set consists of monetary values ascribed to each constituent factor of a job so that the money value of any factor is in alignment with its predetermined rank order. Although this may sound relatively straightforward, it can in practice give rise to major headaches.

Factor comparison was originally applied to manual workers – and used five generic compensable factors: mental requirements, skill requirements, physical requirements, responsibility, working conditions. If the scheme is applied to clerical workers, a different factor complex might be desirable –

e.g. maybe substituting 'supervision' for 'physical requirements'. The whole idea is to identify just a few, broad, relevant factors.

The original concept of factor comparison was based on giving monetary values to each factor so that, when all the factors were combined, an actual rate for the job was produced. Even if one ignores the problems of inflation one can see that ever changing external values could make control of such a scheme difficult. Indeed, factor comparison is the most complex of all basic job evaluation systems. Moreover, the true spirit of job evaluation is not to determine absolute pay values, but simply to determine the relative worth of one job to another.

5. CONSULTANCY SCHEMES

A variety of schemes have been developed by specialist consultancy firms. Some management consultants are content to introduce a scheme to a company and then leave the company to manage it. The result is that the scheme, after a period of time, becomes specific to the company. Other management consultants, including Hay/MSL insist that control of the scheme remains with them. This enables the universality of the scheme to be maintained.

The Hay/MSL scheme is widely used throughout industry, and in three of the five London Clearing Banks where it is used for management and appointed staff job evaluation. Its particular distinction is that it attempts to combine job evaluation with external comparison of market rates as a unified package. Applicable mainly to managerial, administrative and executive jobs, it compares the relative importance of salaried jobs to each other and to total organisational objectives. It is a modification of the factor comparison method, focusing on three main job components: know-how, problem-solving and accountability.

6. 'BENCHMARK' JOBS

'Benchmark' jobs can be used with any form of job evaluation. They are jobs of agreed value which are used to help in the positioning of other jobs. Normally there will be several such jobs for each grade. The London Clearing Banks are unusual in that they have only the one 'benchmark' job for each grade as follows:

Grade	Benchmark Job Title
1	Machinist
2	Cashier
3	Junior/Trainee Securities
4	Sole or No. 1 Security Clerk in a small or medium size branch.

Some banks have taken 'benchmarks' a step further by the introduction of standard jobs. These standard jobs include all the most common jobs in each bank. The fact that these jobs are recognised as standard and have agreed points, both for each factor and in total, means that they can be used as comparators in the evaluation of new jobs in the same way as 'benchmarks'.

7. JOB ANALYSIS AND JOB DESCRIPTION

Before a job can be evaluated its contents must be clearly understood by those who are to evaluate it. It has been shown that in some cases management is sufficiently knowledgeable to evaluate jobs without special assistance but this is not practical in larger companies or departments. It is therefore necessary for the content of jobs to be known to the panel or assessment committee which is to undertake the evaluation. This is achieved by job analysis. It is possible for employees to undertake their own job analysis or for the work to be undertaken by line management but in both cases the results are unlikely to be wholly satisfactory on all occasions. The more normal approach is to use trained job analysts who are able to highlight the relevant elements in a job and set them out in a consistent manner in a job description. This job description, after it has been read and accepted by the job holder and usually by the job holder's immediate superior, is used by the panel to evaluate the job.

If the work of evaluation has been undertaken systematically and objectively the result should be that every job is placed in its correct position in the structure. There remains however in any system the risk of error or misunderstanding and it is normal for appeals against a particular evaluation to be heard by a separate appeal panel. This panel will check that a job has been correctly evaluated using the information previously provided together with any new evidence submitted by the appellant. The panel may also interview the job holder if it believes this will help to obtain the right decision.

Pay Structures

Job evaluation places a particular job in a specific grade (or at a particular point on a scale or ladder for companies which do not operate grades). Job evaluation does not set rates of pay. It is necessary therefore to apply pay rates to grades or scales.

Pay determintion, like job evaluation, is not an exact science. At its most precise it is the systematic balancing of a large number of variables of which costs on one side and the need to recruit, retain and motivate staff on the other are important.

These variables may be highlighted by a union eager for more pay or a management keen to save money, but decisions on the structure must be objective.

There are many surveys of pay and conditions which employers and employees can turn to for advice on the rate for any job. Some of these surveys are national, others are regional, some cover a specific industry whilst others relate to a particular town. Some are reliable, others are of doubtful value but when they are considered together as part of an overall picture they are a useful indication of pay for a national organisation such as a clearing bank so long as it is accepted that no two companies are precisely the same.

Job Evaluation in the banks has produced a pay and grade structure through which staff are promoted at a speed dependent upon the philosophy of the bank and whether it is expanding, remaining static or in decline. Some companies outside banking tend to keep the majority of their staff in the same grade for most of their working life. Such companies have structures which allow the full adult pay rate to be reached very quickly but it then remains static apart from possible productivity bonuses and rises resulting from structural changes or the annually negotiated pay settlement. Other businesses, like the banks, expect staff to move upwards through certain grades. These businesses tend to pay the lower grades relatively less and the higher grades relatively more than the standard rate paid to staff without career progression. It is difficult therefore to compare accurately different rates of pay without comparing different structures and different philosophies at the same time.

Salaries within a graded structure fall into four distinct groups:

1. FLAT RATE

A flat rate is a single rate for each grade. It is sometimes called the rate-for-the-job. It is sometimes achieved after a short period at a starting rate but it can be assumed that all trained employees of a particular grade are on a common rate. Flat rates are used in the London Clearing Banks for engineering staff although these staff do receive additional long service awards.

2. OVERLAPPING GRADES

Overlapping grades, possibly with a series of barriers or bars one of which may be considered as the rate for the job, allow staff to increase their remuneration over a period of years. This is the system used in the London Clearing Banks for the clerical and managerial grades. Each grade has a minimum, a standard maximum which acts as a bar and which is reached by all staff (unless they are shown to be unsatisfactory or are promoted at an earlier date) and an ultimate maximum for the outstanding person. The

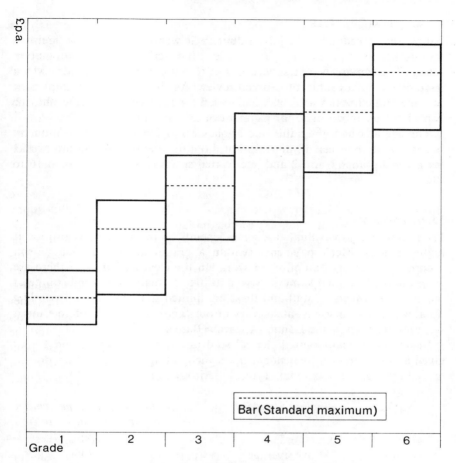

£ p.a.

Grade 1 2 3 4 5 6

Bar(Standard maximum)

Figure 3 Pay Structures : Overlapping Grades.

structure in a typical bank is set out in Figure 3 and shows that it is possible to earn more in a lower grade with long service than in a higher grade with short service.

3. NON-OVERLAPPING GRADES

Non-overlapping grades differ from overlapping ones in that the maximum of one grade is equal to or less than the minimum for the grade above. Normally the pay range for non-overlapping grades is less than the range for overlapping grades. This system allows payment for service but ensures that a higher graded member of staff always receives more pay than one in a lower grade.

4.   AGE-RELATED SCALES

Before the introduction of job evaluation it was normal for considerable importance to be placed upon age and length of service when deciding upon salary. The importance of service is still recognised in those grades which have salary ranges subject to annual review. Age has become less important but age-related scales are still widely used for staff who are below the age considered as appropriate for payment of an adult rate.

The age at which the adult rate applies varies from industry to industry but is usually between 18 and 21. The London Clearing Banks use age 21 for clerical grades 1 and 2 and age-related scales exist for staff aged 16 to 21.

Merit Payments

Promotion in a job evaluated scheme depends on the availability of jobs at higher grades. Merit payments (within a grade) are made to a person according to ability and effort at work. In the clearing banks, if there are no promotions available merit payments are the main additional source of income to members of staff and these are limited to a maximum depending upon whether a person is satisfactory or outstanding. Several different merit schemes are used in the London Clearing Banks.

In one bank unappointed clerical staff are rated between A and E and given a merit payment dependent upon their rating so long as they do not exceed their grade maximum. Typical merit ratings are:-

Rating	Implied Standard	Increase as a percentage of 'average' increase
A	Outstanding	200%
B	Above average	130%
C	Average (satisfactory)	100%
D	Below average	70%
E	Unsatisfactory	0%

Therefore, if the standard rise for an average performer in a particular grade is £200 an outstanding performer can recieve £400. Usually the highest rating requires not only a managerial recommendation but also qualifications such as certain passes in a professional examination or evidence of acceptable typing and shorthand speeds.

In other banks, merit increases of varying size are paid so that in theory the same time is taken to reach the ultimate or the standard maximum depending upon whether the recipient is outstanding or satisfactory. In one bank, some data processing staff only receive merit payments if they are better than satisfactory.

Productivity Bonuses and Profit Sharing

Productivity payments can be related to company, work group or individual achievement. They are of value in encouraging effort when other incentives, such as merit payments or promotions, are unavailable and when the results of particular effort can be clearly defined. They are of less value when the individual or group cannot influence the results that will be achieved or cannot calculate what has been achieved by extra effort. Some banks introduced productivity payments during pay restraint prior to 1980 but such payments are not normally a part of bank remuneration outside certain industrial and data processing areas.

Profit sharing is similar to the productivity bonus in that payment should increase as a result of additional useful effort. In practice, larger businesses, including the banks, have so many income and expenditure variables outside the control of the staff, that any correlation between effort and result is impossible. Profit sharing in large businesses is therefore simply a way of allowing staff to participate in the overall success of that business. It has the advantage to management that, unlike salary, it is only paid when profits are made. Profit sharing can be an incentive in small businesses, particularly those which can analyse profits on a personal basis, including some banks, but these banks are not typical of the industry as a whole.

Overall Pay

Overall, a pay structure must take account of total pay each week, each month and each year but the different components of pay must also be recognised. The pay of a typical bank clerk in a clearing bank in central London is likely to consist of salary, annual bonus, profit sharing, a special payment for working in London (usually known as a London or territorial allowance) and overtime. There is also the value of a non-contributory pension.

The most important single element of pay is salary. Not only because it is the largest single item but because it is the payment over which employees consider themselves to have most control. They believe that merit and promotion are the result of their achievements and that their salary reflects this. They also believe that failure to get promotion is reflected in their salary and this can cause resentment when promotions are, in their eyes, unreasonably withheld.

Territorial allowances can also be important in terms of size particularly for more junior staff, but the average employee feels relatively less personal involvement with them because they are usually flat rate payments. Therefore they are less likely to cause resentment so long as they are not seen to be patently 'unfair'. The same lack of involvement is true of the annual bonus and profit sharing even though both relate to salary.

Pensions fall into a rather different category. In the London and Scottish Clearing Banks all pensions are effectively non-contributory as staff receive additional pay in those banks where there are contributory schemes. The effect of non-contributory schemes is to increase real salaries of staff by at least 5% and possibly by over 10% when compared with the salaries of staff in contributory ones.

Unfortunately few people ever compare like with like, i.e. compare the grand total of all emoluments and benefits as an overall remuneration package. Usually they compare salary with salary. A bank clerk in central London with a published salary of £6000 p.a. is likely to have real earnings in excess of £8000 p.a. before taking account of pension benefits and overtime. In addition to pay there are benefits which can be considered to be substitutes for financial rewards although not provided in cash terms. These include sports and canteen facilities, loans at special rates and, for more senior staff private medical insurance and the provision of a car. Finally, there are sometimes other benefits such as above average working conditions and relative job security. All these make comparison based solely on salary unrealistic.

Salary Differentials

The previous sections, whilst emphasising the need to consider total pay, have highlighted the importance of salary in any financial reward system based upon grading and differentials. The problem is setting and maintaining the correct level of salary for each grade. It has been shown that, whilst outside information can be helpful, it is at best only an indication of possible levels. Fortunately, most companies do not introduce new job evaluation schemes and new structrues in a vacuum or into an existing structure which is so wrong that it cannot be used for reference purposes. Existing internal differentials can therefore be used as a basis for a scheme and developed as necessary. A possible way of doing this is to produce a chart of existing salary scales divided according to the new job evaluated grades as in Figure 4. It is then possible to superimpose tentative ranges for each grade as in Figure 5. This initial match might have to be adjusted if certain differentials are obviously too wide or too narrow, or if it is clear that external salaries are materially different from those indicated on the chart. For example, it would seem realistic in the example given to increase the salary bands in grade 3 to provide a better overall progression.

A check on this possible structure can be made by superimposing equivalent salary ranges from other companies on the proposed new grades. This has been done in Figure 6. It shows that whilst it was right on grounds of progression, to increase grade 3 relative to the other grades, the resultant proposals are marginally on the high side compared with the rates paid by

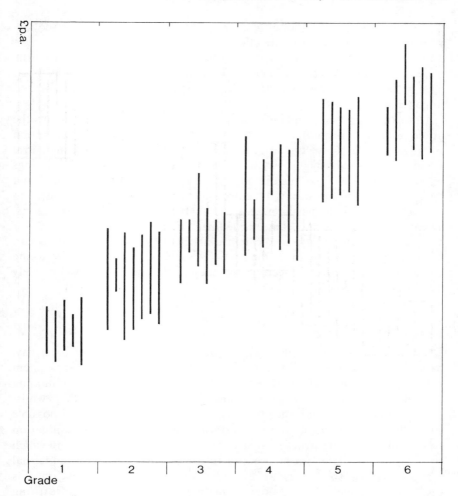

Figure 4 Salary Differentials : Existing salary ranges charted on the basis of new job evaluated grades.

other employers. There may be a good reason for this, but, if not, it may be necessary to adjust the ranges yet again.

A further check on the structure can be undertaken by calculating the expected path through the structure of various levels of staff on a time basis, as is shown in Figure 7. This chart shows that expected promotions will provide a smooth, progressive salary or 'maturity' curve. This is good so long as it is correct. It is necessary to check that the progression pattern is realistic for the foreseeable future. If it is not, then other realistic alternatives

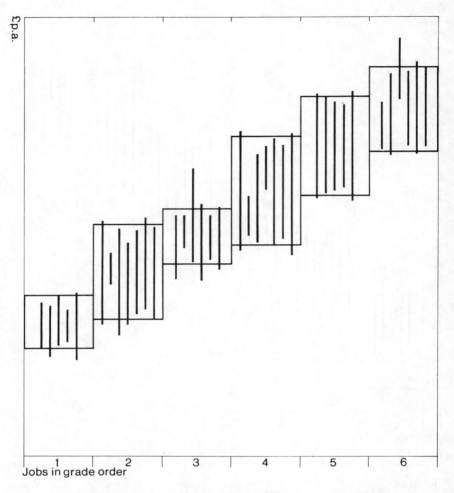

£p.a.

Jobs in grade order

1   2   3   4   5   6

Figure 5 Salary Differentials : Possible salary ranges for each grade superimposed upon existing salaries.

must be plotted and considered. Once these alternatives have been considered it may be necessary to adjust the original grade proposals.

A salary structure will finally emerge. It will be correct at a particular point in time and will survive for a period but ultimately it will have to be reviewed.

Updating a Salary Structure

If salaries are to remain constant in actual and relative terms they must be updated periodically. This can be done in a variety of ways after considering

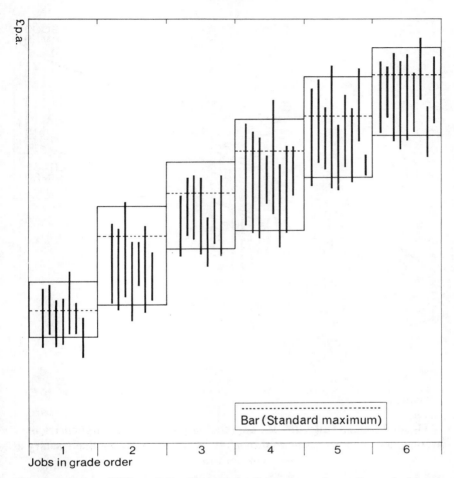

£p.a.

Bar (Standard maximum)

| 1 | 2 | 3 | 4 | 5 | 6 |

Jobs in grade order

Figure 6 Salary Differentials : Proposed salary ranges for each grade (shown as boxes) compared to salary ranges for comparable grades in other companies (Shown as vertical lines).

various statistics of which the most widely accepted are those produced by the Department of Employment. The two most commonly cited are the Retail Price Index and the Average Earnings Index. Although not perfect, these indices do reflect trends and therefore it is essential that they be considered, even if subsequently they are rejected as not relevant to the company. If a change in the RPI is not followed, real salaries will not be the same as before. Equally, if the Average Earnings Index is not followed, the relative position of company salaries to external movements in pay will be varied. Adjustments may well be necessary when it is found that company

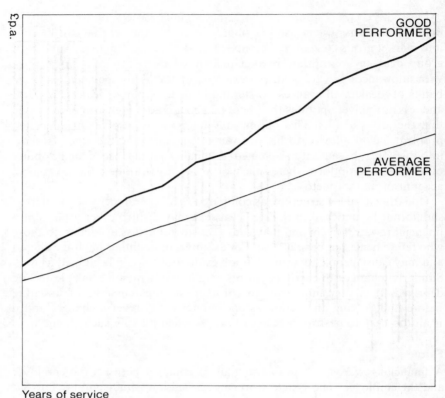

Figure 7 Salary Differentials : expected progress of 'maturity' curves of average and good performance through the structure, showing likely salary at current rates.

salaries are out of line with external ones but, in general, salary trends in one company must relate realistically to those in comparable companies, relevant industries and the country as a whole, otherwise a company will either find itself unable to recruit and retain staff or, at the other extreme, find itself paying needlessly high salaries.

A further kind of updating is that necessitated by changes in internal differentials. These changes may be between grades or between different groups of workers using the same job evaluation system. In theory, a good job evaluation system will be sufficiently flexible to cope with these changes and there are schemes which have been essentially unchanged for many years. However, in practice, the majority of schemes do need occasional amendment and some may need total replacement.

Flexibility for updating can be achieved in a variety of ways. First a financial rewards system using a single job evaluation scheme can be split into market groups (e.g. Accountants, Data Processing, Engineers) and each group paid an appropriate market related salary. Secondly a single scale with allowances can be paid. An example of this is the payment in some banks of 'dealers allowances' to sterling/foreign exchange dealers. A third, and less attractive, option is the use of personal grades higher than the grade that the job warrants. This option may temporarily resolve an immediate problem but, if allowed to happen too often, can bring the whole scheme into disrepute, because it has created 'anomalies'. It also lacks the flexibility of the first two options where salary or allowances can be adjusted to take account of market factors.

Updating a salary structure, as compared to a general increase in salaries, should not be undertaken lightly because it may disturb other aspects of a financial reward system and may cause considerable dissatisfaction to those who fail to benefit or benefit least. For example, differentials might be altered and may cause people to argue that job evaluation should be altered as well. Similarly, changes in merit payments might result in some poeple feeling deprived. It is very important to consider the repercussions of updating before undertaking any action as one cannot easily reverse changes and it is all too easy to destroy perceived fairness when making such changes.

Fairness

A financial rewards system is essentially a compact between the employer and the employee. The system works not because it is indisputably fair but because the parties consider it to be fair. A financial rewards system is likely to be considered fair when it is:

1. Systematically calculated as far as is reasonably possible.
2. Clearly explained to those involved.
3. Applied honestly and without reservation to all staff within the relevant areas.

In addition, the Job Evaluation aspects of the system should be:

1. Operated in a way that can be understood and accepted by employees.
2. Designed to allow individual appeals against proposed or outdated gradings.
3. Open to review when there is reasonable evidence that they are not working properly.

In a large company a union or some other body may represent the interests of staff, and should be able to reassure them as to the fairness or otherwise of the system.

Trade Union Involvement

A trade union has many roles of which the most obvious are the periodic claims and negotiations involving increases in pay, holidays, overtime rates and other items. It also undertakes other important but usually less obvious duties for its members of which one may be to represent the employees on job evaluation schemes.

The attitude of the banking union BIFU (formerly NUBE) to this responsibility can be seen in its publication 'Job Evaluation in the English Clearing Banks' (1971). This is probably the best single description of the London Clearing Banks scheme. It concludes with the following paragraph:

> 'Given that job evaluation is a sound economic theory, NUBE has obtained safe-guards to ensure the implementation of the fairest possible scheme. It has, furthermore, secured added protections for its members in the form of the appeals procedure, which consists of representatives from the staff side as well as management. Nothing has been overlooked by NUBE in its efforts to make certain that bank staffs are treated fairly and justly throughout the whole restructuring exercise.'

The attitude of the bank unions can also be seen in the continued participation by both BIFU and CBU in Job Evaluation procedures despite the breakdown in 1978 of joint national negotiations and the end to most other aspects of co-operation both nationally and within individual banks.

Occasionally a union might use the excuse of necessary changes to a job evaluation scheme in an attempt to improve salaries. Although possibly acceptable in certain circumstances, it contravenes the basic principle of job evaluation which is to differentiate between jobs, not to set salary levels. Salary levels should be set separately in the normal course of negotiations. For example, it is agreed policy to negotiate minimum rates for certain grades. When a new or substantially revised scheme is introduced, it is the duty of all parties to ensure that the correct salary is applied to each grade, and in some cases to each scale step or incremental point.

Straight percentage increases for particular groups of employees are often acceptable to both unions and employers because they reflect the belief of both parties that the existing job evaluated scheme accurately reflects the differentials necessary to satisfy everybody. Flat rate increases reduce differentials.

Salary Costing and Budgeting

Some businesses have so few employees that they do not need to be overly concerned about staff costs. They are the minority and most businesses, including the High Street banks, are aware that staff costs are a major part of running costs. The proportion for the London Clearing Banks is approximately two-thirds of total costs and therefore any increase in staff costs is significant. At the same time the banks know they must pay staff sufficient to achieve the following essential conditions:

1. A regular flow of suitable qualified applicants with the right attributes for the job. (Recruitment).
2. A low wastage rate in those areas or grades where there is a wish to retain staff. (Retention).
3. An attitude to work which is considered positive and attractive to both customers and management. (Motivation).

Sensible companies may attempt to limit costs by not increasing salaries when they consider the correct salary level does not require an increase. However, they will not refuse an increase if in so doing they will damage their ability to achieve the three conditions set out above as to do so could jeopardise their future commercial well being. Instead, they will look for savings elsewhere by, for instance, the use of new systems requiring less staff.

Budgeting for staff costs is therefore not simple. Account has to be taken of many variables often well outside the responsibility of personnel staff. It is not uncommon in many industries for salary administrators to apply specialist tehniques of 'grade control' such as 'compa-ratios' to facilitate monitoring global salary costs.

Deviations within the System

Very few job evaluated systems cover all staff within a large company because there are always certain people who will be paid special rates for particular purposes. In the banks the most obvious are staff on management development or accelerated career programmes. These may be paid a non-evaluated salary until such time as they reach their target grade. This is because a large amount of their time is taken up with training and gaining experience and relatively little with work which can be evaluated. They are, in effect, being paid for their future potential rather than their current work. The actual methods of payment vary. For example, some banks have totally separate development scales and others use graded salaries on a personal basis rather than on a job-evaluated one. Ultimately, these staff can expect to join the job-evaluated systems for clerical or managerial staff. The same may go for some other special groups of staff but there will be others who will always remain outside any job-evaluated scheme. This may be because employers genuinely believe a group should not be evaluated. For example, at least one bank has decided that blind telephonists should be employed on an age-related scale throughout their careers.

The various groups may all belong to one financial reward system in which all the salaries are related to each other despite the different methods of evaluation or estimation. Alternatively, a series of distinct or partially distinct financial reward systems may be used. The following example of the organisation of one bank with 50,000 staff shows the kind of structure which can exist in one large business:-

	Staff Numbers
Unappointed (Job Evaluated)	34,000
Appointed/Managerial (Job Evaluated)	14,000
Management trainees (special scale)	400
Blind telephonist (Age related scale)	200
Clerical/Managerial financial reward system	47,600*
Engineering Staff (Job Evaluated)	270*
Messenger Staff	680*
Industrial Staff (Job Evaluated)	340*
Catering Staff (Job Evaluated)	110*
Data Processing staff (Job Evaluated)	1,000*
Whole bank structure	50,000

This analysis shows six financial reward systems (marked with asterisks) of which one is dominant (in terms of employees covered) and consists of four separate sub-divisions two of which are job evaluated. The six systems are different in respect of their salary scales but identical in respect of holidays, overtime, fringe benefits and certain terms and conditions, including some allowances. Therefore there is both diversity and integration. Although 95% of the staff are in one financial reward system there are five systems for the remaining 5% of the staff. It can be seen that there are six different job evaluation schemes and three groups of workers outside any scheme. This helps to show why salary administration can be so complex.

Salary Administration

The organisation of all the foregoing and the payment of the resultant salaries is termed 'salary administration'. All companies require competent salary administration, the heart of which may be a financial rewards system of the kind that has been described. The system must be accepted as fair and must be sufficiently flexible to change as the company changes without causing undue stress on either the company or the employee. It must be the property of both employer and employee and as such must be able to stand up to the criticisms of both management and staff. Finally, it must be capable of keeping pace with the changes in salary levels and overall remuneration brought about by time and by negotiation. The effect of negotiations on a financial rewards system can be substantial and, therefore, it is important for companies to ensure that salary administration and their postures and strategies in collective bargaining spring from a common policy.

A well organised salary administration, using a properly designed financial rewards system, will go a long way towards enabling a company to operate successfully.

Further Reading

There are a number of personnel management books with chapters on Salary Administration, Financial Reward Systems and Job Evaluation. These include:-

Thomason, G., *A Textbook of Personnel Management*, (I.P.M. 1981).

Torrington, D. & Chapman, J., *Personnel Management*, (Prentice Hall International 1983).

The following books are more specialised:-

Armstrong, M. & Murliss, H., *Handbook of Salary Administration* (Kogan Page 1980).

Livy, B., *Job Evaluation, A critical review*, (Allen and Unwin 1975).

McBeath, G. & Rands, D. N., *Salary Administration*, (Business Books 1976).

Otis, J. L. & Leukart, R. H., *Job Evaluation*, (Prentice Hall 1954).

CHAPTER 19

Women in Banking

Margery Poval

Research Fellow,
Centre for Personnel Research and Enterprise Development,
City University Business School

Women now form the majority of employees in banking. They account for six out of ten of all people employed in banks, but their roles have been very different from those of men, and they still are. In the past there were good reasons for these differences. Boys entered banking assuming they would have a family to keep, and that they would work there for at least forty years. Many of them did. Most young women worked for only a few years until marriage, which was commensurate with expectations. But things have changed. Recently it was estimated that, on average, young women will have only about seven years out of the labour force while they bring up children.[1] They will be in paid work only a few years less than men. But in banks women are still mainly in the same jobs as thirty years ago – the clerical and secretarial jobs. Only just over one per cent of managers in banks, and less than 15% of appointed officers, are women. This compares with 23% of all managers who are women.

To understand why more than 90% of women in banks are in secretarial or clerical jobs, compared with just over half the men, it is necessary to look at the past as well as the current position, and at research findings on factors influencing the positions of women and men in organisations. Finally we will consider factors likely to influence the future of women in banking.

The Beginnings

Office machinery and world wars were the key to early employment in banks. Small numbers of women were employed between the 1880's and 1915 for specific jobs. They were typists, telephone operators, and later, accounting machine operators. In the First and Second World Wars (1914–1918 and 1939–1945) women moved into clerical jobs, and a small number were allowed on the counter as cashiers despite resistance from some male staff and customers. At the end of each war the women returned either to their back office machine operating jobs, or to their homes. But meanwhile, The Institute of Bankers, after much discussion, had opened their examinations to women in 1917, and admitted women to full membership from 1919.[2] In 1918 a quarter of the entrants were women.

The number of women in banking dropped once more after the Second World War, but with the expansion of banking in the 1950s it increased again, so that women later outnumbered men (Table 1). Accounting machines were now to be found in most branches, operated by women or girls. Women also staffed the clearing departments – the so-called 'factory' jobs – and increasingly worked on the counter as cashiers. Women were no longer forced to leave the bank on marriage, but usually went on to temporary conditions of employment; but some banks would still not recruit women who were already married.

In the 1960s the numbers of women in paid work continued to increase, and so did the numbers employed in banks, but women still formed a smaller proportion of banks workers than they did of clerical workers in general (Table 1). A few women in banks moved into positions of greater responsibility, usually in personnel/welfare jobs with responsibility for female staff, and one or two women in some banks became branch managers. The turnover of women was much higher than that of men, and women were still seen very much as temporary workers. G. V. Bramley said in 1969[3]: '... experience has shown that it is possible to maintain an even flow of male recruits while controlling fluctuations in numerical requirements by varying the rate of female recruitment ... If initial recruitment has been sufficiently selective, possibly 75% of [male] entrants should become managers'.

The differences in expectations for women and men were reflected in different conditions of employment and personnel policies. In the District Bank[4], for instance, up to 1967 there were different contracts of employment for men and women which said that men were 'expected to study and sit, without undue delay ... examinations of the Institute of Bankers', but women were only given 'encouragement' to study (our emphases). It was common for personnel policies in banks to lay down that boys could only be recruited if they had the minimum education levels to study for the Institute's examinations, whereas girls did not necessarily have to meet this standard. Women's and men's potential might also be assessed at different stages, using different standards, for instance women could only be assessed after the age of 25, and men at 22. Women were not, on the whole, asked to move house by the bank, whereas men, recruited on the understanding of a career, were expected to move as required. Women were not eligible for housing loans, and might be charged higher rates than men for other loans; part timers not being eligible at all. Rates of pay, too, differed. Boys and girls might have equal pay as they started work, but older women's rates were in some cases only two-thirds those of men. Because pay was age-related to 31 years of age, it was said that a young girl cashier might be working alongside an older man and doing the same job, but receive as little as a quarter of his pay.

Changes in the 1970s

In the 1970s, three Acts were passed which aimed to improve the position of women at work. These were the Equal Pay Act, Sex Discrimination Act, and the Employment Protection Act, part of which dealt with maternity provisions. They were the result of international and national pressures on employers to take account of changes in the social, economic and political environment; changes which, it was felt, also needed to be reflected in women's employment. In 1970, women were still earning on average only 63% of men's earnings, despite the major changes that had come about in women's working patterns in the preceding 20 years (see Table 2). Married women, and mothers of young children, increasingly had a paid job. Hakim[5] said: 'Over a period of about twenty to thirty years, the profile of the typical working woman has completely changed. Before the Second World War she was typically single and young. By 1971 she was typically married and of a mature age.'

Women were taking less and less time out of the labour force to bring up children. By 1971 two out of five mothers with dependent children were in a paid job (Table 3). There had been changes, too, in education and in family structure. Girls were no longer less well educated than boys, and were leaving school with qualifications as good as boys, and with rising expectations. The numbers of single parent households were growing steadily, and most of these were headed by women. Increasingly, for a variety of reasons, women were becoming the sole or major breadwinner. But women were still found, in the majority, in the low pay, low opportunity jobs, done mainly or only by women.

In banks women now formed the majority of workers (53% in 1971 – Table 1), but few more were in managerial jobs (Table 4). In 1974 Egan[6] found that more than 9 out of 10 women in many banks were in clerical or secretarial jobs (compared with fewer than six out of ten men). The numbers of women managers were small. At most, 1% of all managers were women, and these were mainly in personnel and other support functions.[7] Few were in jobs involving lending, especially commercial lending. In the big four clearers it seems unlikely that there were ever more than around two or three women branch managers for every thousand men. These women managed only small branches or sub branches which had a large private customer base.

In the 1970s the formal position of women in the industry was to change quite dramatically. First, equal pay was introduced in banking in 1972, three years before it was required to come into force by the Equal Pay Act of 1970. Equal pay came with the introduction of job evaluation for clerical jobs, and is seen by some as the most important change yet made in the position of women in banks. With job evaluation there was, for the first time, formal grading and therefore a career structure in clerical grades. Until then everyone was a clerk until their first appointment, and paid according to age and sex. One banker said: 'It meant that for the first time people were paid the same for doing a job. We changed to looking for the best person for the job. Life really began for girls at that stage'.

The passing of the Sex Discrimination and the Employment Protection Acts in 1975 did not initially result in many noticeable changes. As a result of the latter, women became entitled to maternity leave (paid and unpaid), and to the right of reinstatement to the same or a 'suitable alternative' job if they returned to work up to 29 weeks after the birth of their child. Few women in banks used their right of reinstatement initially. Daniel[8] found in 1979 that two out of five mothers of eight month old babies who had been in a paid job before had returned to paid work or were actively seeking jobs. But few returned to their old job as the maternity provisions did not allow full-time workers to return as part-timers, which is what most of the mothers wanted (Table 3).

Banks were little different from other organisations in their initial response to the Sex Discrimination Act. In 1977 a research team found[9] that 'changes due to the Sex Discrimination Act were few and on the whole superficial'. In large banks, reviews of personnel policies, procedures and statistics were carried out, and some small changes took place, the most significant probably being the revision of the terms of staff loans. This was because the Act had also made it illegal to discriminate on grounds of marriage, so loans had to be made available to married women. The legislation also resulted in a discrimination case which ended in the European Court of Justice. Lloyds Bank had paid young men more than young women in order to cover the men's compulsory pension contributions, and the legality of this was disputed, successfully, by BIFU with assistance from the Equal Opportunities Commission.

By the end of the 1970s, women formed nearly a half of the membership of both BIFU (Table 1) and the CBU, but this was still below their representation in the industry overall. Unions have therefore had two areas of concern for women in banks, how to increase female membership of unions, and women's active participation in the union, as well as safeguarding the jobs of women in banks and trying to improve their position.

To start dealing with these issues, BIFU formed an 'equality working party' in 1975 which, from 1980, operated as an Equal Opportunities Committee. They also established Equality Committees in all the large banks. Within CBU a Women's Committee was established by Barclays Group Staff Union.

Research Studies

An international study of equal opportunity in banks in the late 1970s[7] found that legislation had resulted in the disappearance of directly discriminatory personnel policies in banks except for pensions and retirement conditions which were not covered by legislation. But this and other studies[6,9] at this time showed that some personnel practices were either still discriminatory or acted in such a way that women did not in reality have equal opportunities.

For instance, all three studies pointed to continuing discriminatory recruitment practices. The women recruited were on average less well qualified and younger than men recruited.[10] That this was common in banks in other countries as well was shown in the international study. 'Analysis of applications and interviews with managers show that the emphasis on higher-qualified men and low-qualified women is not a result of chance. In the British and in the Dutch banks, some managers will not interview boys unless they have the minimum requirement for study for The Institute of Bankers examinations ... They assume that the (unqualified) boy will remain with them until retirement and will become a married man with obligations, but no future ... One reason why in each bank a lower percentage of women than of men have progressed is thus the deliberate recruitment of greater numbers of lower-qualified women and of higher-qualified men ... the managers concerned, even if aware of the (sex discrimination) legislation, feel their decisions to be quite valid ... managers feel no need to discontinue practices which they see as sensible and even essential'.[7]

More women were studying for professional qualifications, but numbers of qualified women were still low (Table 5). In 1978, fewer than 3% of Associates of The Institute of Bankers were women. The low numbers could be explained in part by managers attitudes and assumptions. The studies found that, in the past, women had been actively discouraged from becoming qualified ' ... young women may be less career-oriented than their male colleagues. It is therefore likely that girls would require additional encouragement and evidence of available opportunities. In practice, they received less'[10]

The studies pointed to another factor influencing women's ability to realise career ambitions. This was the fact that careers in banks were built slowly over a lifetime in an organisation. 'The bank operated a closed, inflexible system of career development in domestic banking. The system required continuous full-time employment from the time the employee left school until the mid/late 30s age-range before a management post was attained. Prior to the provision of maternity leave, this requirement could only be met by single or married childless women, who form a small minority of the total female population'[10] The international study showed that where, as in France and Belgium maternity and parental leave, childcare facilities, and reduced or flexible working hours were available, more women had been able to combine motherhood and a career, and there were therefore more women managers. Of banks studied in four European countries and the United States, those in Britain and the Netherlands had the lowest percentage of women in management jobs. This was partly because many young women left the banks, but even those that stayed did not progress at the same rate as men.

The studies showed the importance of attitudes, both of the managers and of the women themselves, to women working, and how they can affect personnel practices. 'Assumptions regarding women's employment patterns and stereotyped views of women's abilities and aspirations are widespread. These were reflected in, and reinforced by, past discriminatory practices, for example discouragement for women from taking the examinations, the use of proficiency grades for women, job channelling of young men and women in the clerical grades . . . Some of these practices linger on, as do the associated attitudes.[10] The stereotypes which exist 'could lead to assumptions and decision being made in individual cases, which could be premature and incorrect'.[10] The Ashridge team felt that, in the bank they studied, 'career development for women was based on a number of outdated attitudes and assumptions regarding the work patterns of women', and that 'without more positive remedial action, the bank would continue to recruit the vast majority of its managers from amongst the minority of its staff'.[10]

An American, Professor Rosabeth Kanter, has shown how some of the differences in the attitudes and behaviour of women and men in organisations can be related to the situation within the organisation in which people find themselves.[11] In an EEC seminar for bankers on equal opportunity[12] she demonstrated how 'some jobs provide more chance to develop and advance than others'. This tends to result in two kinds of people, the 'moving' and the 'stuck'. The 'moving' raise their aspirations, highly value their own skills, are strongly engaged with work, form political alliances with upward orientation, use active forms of protest, whilst the 'stuck' lower their aspirations, down-value their own skills, are disengaged from work, form protective peer groups, resist passively. These characteristics are the very ones often attributed to men and to women respectively. Professor Kanter showed how, in organisations, men tend to have more power (the capacity to get results) than do women. She also showed what effect the presence of someone who is a member of a minority group, and is different, will have on both themselves and the group with whom they work. In organisations women who have reached positions of responsibility are usually in a minority, and may therefore be treated, probably unconsciously, quite differently from their male colleagues. This in turn can limit their effectiveness at work, and thus their ability to progress. She showed that the elements of Opportunity, Power and Numbers are key in helping or hindering women's progress in organisations.

Egan,[6] in his study of the position of women in banks and in BIFU, pointed to the attitudinal barriers as well as the personnel practices which either directly or indirectly inhibit women's career development. The existence of a large area of 'female' work, that of the secretarial jobs which are quite separate in all banks from the clerical career stream, means many women are cut off from possibilities of any but the most limited career development. In looking at women's position in unions he found that ' . . . despite equality (or even a female majority) in membership, and despite in some cases a reasonable level of attendance by women, men predominate to a very considerable extent in all 'official' positions.'

The 1980s

From the late 1970s onwards, two different aspects of women's employment in banking were receiving attention. Whilst unions were expressing fears about the future of women workers in the industry because of technological and structural change, in some banks efforts were being made to reduce career barriers for women. The author[13] found there were nine main reasons why banks in various countries introduced what have become known as positive action programmes. These were:

The existence of laws and, in some countries, of their enforcement;

Growing union interest in the subject of equal opportunity;

Women employees or external women's groups questioning women's lack of progress;

Awareness of the economic and social consequences of the failure to utilise the experience and training of women;

Possible commercial advantages in encouraging women to develop their potential, e.g. the provision of better quality staff, and the positive publicity which could attract more women customers or high quality women recruits;

Shortages of traditional quality male staff;

Research findings including research in their own organisations;

Media publicity about the small number of women managers in a particular organisation or sector, and

Contact with women in North America who were competently doing jobs either considered unsuitable for women in Europe or of which it had been thought women were not capable.

In some banks the numbers of women in appointed officer and senior clerical jobs were increasing slowly. For instance in Midland Bank the proportion of women Appointed Officers rose from 10% to 12% between 1978 and 1982. This was not unexpected because the number of well qualified women and girls available for employment was also increasing. By 1983, 41% of undergraduates in universities were women, as were 46% of those securing GCE 'A' level passes.

Banks began to realise at this time that there were actions they could take to change the under-representation of women in higher level jobs. In Britain, Barclays Bank International was the first, in 1974, to appoint an internal consultant for five years to advise, amongst other things, on the career development of women. As a result of her research they introduced 'Personal Effectiveness' training for clerical staff, which was later extended to management level. In addition, after reappraisal of the situation, a small number of able women who had got 'stuck' were promoted. Ten years later, in 1984, Barclays Bank Group appointed a Manager, Equal Opportunities. Her main aim is to ensure that the bank's policy of treating all employees and applicants equally regardless of sex, race, or marital status is put into practice. She will do this by communicating policies to all staff, training personnel managers in all aspects of sex and race discrimination, and monitoring statistics to ensure that the policy is effective.[14]

At the end of 1984, 19% of the staff on the Management Development Programme in Barclays Bank UK were women (69 people). Women accounted for only 5% of those put on the programme through internal transfer, but 23% of the graduate intake to the programme.

In 1978, Midland Bank appointed a Manager to advise on the legal aspects of equal opportunity, and on company policy. After an initial audit, a programme was started including one day seminars, and later one week courses for career women. A working party was set up, with a consultant to advise it, workshops for senior personnel and line managers were run, and a monitoring system was established requiring information to be sent to and from personnel managers.

Instructions to managers on the setting up of a Management Development Programme in 1983 included equal opportunity aspects. 21% of the staff accepted as management trainees were women, and in 1984 the figure rose slightly to 22%, a total of 832 women.[14]

In 1985, a retainer scheme will be launched which will allow management trainees, appointed officers and managers with young children, to be reinstated at the same level as that at which they left, after up to five years for pre-school child care. During this period they will maintain links by working at least two weeks each year.

National Westminster Bank also reviewed the position of women in the 1970s, and a Women's Workshop was held in which 15 career women analysed the position of women in the bank and made recommendations. These, along with others based on independent research, resulted in the development of various actions. A Career Planning Adviser was appointed in 1980 with special responsibilties for women's careers. A policy statement on equal opportunities was issued by senior management. The inventory of 'women with good management potential' was completely revised, new guidelines were drawn up, and control maintained at Group level with regular audits being carried out. Career Workshops for women (and a Management Development Course for women run for staff both from the bank and outside) have been held. In 1981, a re-entry/reservist scheme was set up which allowed women (and men) to take a break up to a maximum of five years after the birth of their child. In January 1985 there were 50 women on this scheme. The number of women rated as having executive potential, or potential to reach appointed status comparatively early, has increased from 127 (4% of the total) at the beginning of 1979 to 304 (9%) at the end of 1984, the increase being at both clerical and appointed officer levels, the clerical rate rising from 10% to 17%, and appointed officers from 1% to 4%.[14]

Lloyds Bank[14], too, has taken a number of steps to move more women further up the management ladder. These include changing the practice of requiring confirmation of mobility from young women candidates for the management development programme. Now they are presumed to be mobile and are dropped from the programme only if they decline a reasonable request to move for further training and experience. The number of women on the management development programme increased, between the end of 1980 and 1983, from 107 to 240 (8.4% to 15.3%). Clear instructions have been given to all involved with recruitment and selection to abandon any attempt to procure predetermined ratios of men to women at any level. In 1982, an arrangement was introduced for extended absences of up to five years for women leaving the bank to have children. The scheme permits their return to posts in the same grade with appropriate retraining.

Other banks, too, have taken action. For instance, the Royal Bank of Canada has run courses specially for women.

The re-entry arrangements various banks have made are vital if women are to have careers.[16] In the absence of extended maternity leave, and with inadequate child care facilities, only a minority of women will return to full time work at the end of the statutory maternity leave. One in five women were returning to some banks at the end of maternity leave in 1983, but the number seems no longer to be increasing.

Graduates have traditionally formed only a small part of banks' intake, but increasingly they form a sizeable proportion of the large banks' management development programmes. In some, but not all banks, the proportion of women graduates recruited now approximates to the proportion of women undergraduates in university (two out of five). For Instance, Barclays Bank recruited 17% women graudates in 1984; Lloyds Bank 38% in 1983, and National Westminster 39% in 1984.

Some banks now have a woman on their board, such as Midland and Lloyds, and Barclays on their UK board. Women themselves are actively co-operating more. In the world of finance there are two women's groups, the City Women's Network set up in 1978 to bring together women in senior positions in the City of London to share common interests and solve mutual problems, and Women in Banking, formed in 1980 to encourage and promote the role of women in the banking industry.

Unions have been promoting the interests of women. BIFU has negotiated the inclusion of the TUC equality clause into most of its procedural agreeements. It has issued proposals for positive action with recommendations both on negotiating with employers and on equality within the union. It provides training for women members. Other publications for members deal with sexual harassment, the implications of micro technology, part-timers and workplace nurseries. The CBU has issued a discussion document on new technology. Lloyds Bank Group Staff Union has issued a guide to maternity rights, set up a Typing and Secretarial Advisory Committee, and is issuing a charter for part-time staff. Barclays Group Staff Union, too, have issued a booklet on part-time workers.[18]

These activities point to the current issues which seem likely to affect the future of women in banking.

Issues for the future of Women in Banking

1. THE EXTENT TO WHICH BANKING EMPLOYMENT MIGHT CONTINUE TO GROW

The gloomy predictions of a decline in banking employment of a few years ago have not been fulfilled. What has happened is that the *growth* in employment has continued to slow down. Rajan[17] found that the annual growth had slowed from 4% to 3% and that the deceleration is expected to continue in the period 1983 to 1987, with an annual rate of increase in staff numbers likely to be between one and two per cent. Between 1972 and 1983, the proportion of women in banking had increased from 54% to 59%.[18] If the rate of growth falls still further, or if growth stops altogether, it is likely that the proportion of full-time women employees will drop because of the higher turnover of women than of men in banks.

2. THE GROWTH OF PART-TIME EMPLOYMENT

Banks traditionally employed few part-timers, but this is changing. In 1975 part-timers comprised only 6% of employees (11% of female employees). By 1983 the proportion were 8% and 14% respectively.[19] Rajan[17] found that this trend was likely to continue, one quarter of the growth in staff numbers from 1983 to 1987 being forecast to be in part-time employment. As almost all part-timers are women, there will be an overall increase in female employment.

Many women want part-time work when their children are young, and the growth in part-time jobs enables some women bank employees to keep their toe in the world of paid work, thus facilitating a later return to full-time work and career. There are, however, two aspects of part-time work which concern those in unions and elsewhere who are promoting equality for both women and men.

These are:

(a) the extent to which part-time jobs are found only at the lowest levels. It would seem in the banks' interest to convert some higher level jobs to make them suitable for part-timers, or job sharers, i.e. two people between them doing one full-time job, but there is resistance to this;

(b) the terms and conditions of part-timers in some banks which are, in various ways, not comparable with those of full-timers. This is a matter of considerable concern to unions.

3. THE EFFECT ON JOBS OF TECHNOLOGICAL AND STRUCTURAL DEVELOPMENTS

Rajan[17] points to the changing nature of clerical jobs in financial institutions. Some jobs are being enlarged with, for instance, a growing emphasis on social skills, but others are becoming more specialised, such as keyboard operators in central data processing departments. 'There is little doubt that job enlargement and enrichment are occurring alongside the loss of job-specific skills in the financial sector'. Women, who form the bulk of clerical workers, stand both to lose and to gain from changes. Rajan points to a shift to non-clerical and professional jobs as well as what he calls 'non career' and part-time jobs. If these result in a squeeze in promotion opportunities at the top of the clerical ladder, and bottom of the appointed officer ladder, women may well suffer. Increasing numbers of women are in these positions seeking promotion. But with current attitudes towards men as breadwinners and women as secondary earners, they may well find promotion increasingly difficult if opportunities are limited. A second factor could be a growth in more *de facto* dead-end jobs, in small service branches and operations centres. These provide limited breadth of experience, and if they are staffed, as would seem likely, with 'non career' staff, these could be predominantly women.

4. THE ROLE, PAY AND CAREERS OF SECRETARIES

Currently, about one in ten women in banks are secretaries and typists. Most of their jobs are not evaluated, their career progression depends largely on that of their manager, and few have been able to transfer to other work. Their situation and the effect on their jobs of technical change have become a cause for union concern.

5. THE EXTENT TO WHICH WOMEN ARE IN MANAGEMENT TRAINING PROGRAMMES

Two and even three tier recruitment, which has existed informally in banks for years, is being formalised. Women were traditionally over-represented in the 'non career stream', and under-represented in management training programmes. Their representation in management training programmes is increasing as we have shown, but still does not approximate the proportion of 'A' level and graduate job seekers who are women. With the formalisation of 'career' and 'non career' streams, it could become increasingly difficult for anyone, man or woman, who has been labelled as a 'non careerist' to take a late career decision. The assumption is still that one must start young if one is to have sufficient years in which to develop a career. If study leave is limited to 'career' staff, another barrier will be placed in the way of the late developer. Because women tend more than men to take late career decisions, they could be adversely affected.

6. THE FUTURE OF THE POSITIVE ACTION PROGRAMME STARTED BY BANKS AND UNIONS

The extent to which these programmes continue and develop, and take account of women's greater domestic responsibilities, will be key to the future. Measures such as improved maternity leave, the introduction of parental leave, the extension of flexitime, and the development of retraining and re-entry schemes, will affect women's career opportunities as will adaptations of other personnel policies such as mobility requirements.

7. THE LABOUR MARKET AND LEGISLATIVE DEVELOPMENTS

Finally, the banks do not of course exist in a vacuum. Their personnel policies must be influence by labour market conditions, although they are large enough employers to influence developments themselves, as they take a considerable proportion of the 'O' and 'A' level school-leaving population.

Employment forecasts to 1991 include a continuing increase in the numbers of women employed, particularly in the 25–54 age groups, and a decline in male employment. It could be argued that banks can benefit by taking steps to retain their experienced female staff by means of re-entry schemes and part-time work, but if it is to be done at the expense of giving an unemployed young person a job it may not happen. The drop between 1981 and 1991 of over a quarter in the number of school leavers with 'O' and 'A' levels will, however, restrict the numbers of traditional recruits available to the banks. An obvious alternative source of staff is women ex-employees who have left to raise a family.

Developments in British law in 1984 and possible future changes because of EEC activity could bring about far reaching alterations in the situation of women at work. The Equal Pay Act has been changed at EEC insistence to allow for claims of equal pay for work of equal value, even where a job evaluation system does not exist. This change raises questions in banks as to the value of such jobs as secretary (mainly female) and messenger (mainly male) in relation to clerical jobs.

Another development is the bringing of successful cases under the Sex Discrimination Act, which has resulted in women with responsibility for bringing up children being allowed to work part-time, or to have flexible working hours. Such cases could affect employment practices in many sectors including banking.

The EEC has been active in other areas particularly relevant to women in employment. Changes may be forced (or pressure put) on employers in relation to the terms and conditions of part-timers, the granting of parental leave, the equalisation of retirement provisions and benefits, and the desirability of their taking positive action to improve the position of women employees.

The future of women in banking, as so much else in banking, is in the melting pot. Whether out of the pot there will emerge a large number of highly effective corporate leaders, or only a number of part-time machine minders and clerks, remains to be seen.

Table 1: Proportion of women in labour force, as clerks: in banking: members of BIFU, 1911–1981

	Women as % of labour force*	Women as % of clerks*	Women as % of bank employees	Women as % of BIFU members***
1911	30	21	1****	–
1911	30	45	20****	9 (1922)
1931	30	46	15****	8
1951	31	60	23****	25
1961	33	65	48**	35
1971	37	73	53**	47
1981	39	67	57**	48

Sources: * Hakim[15] and UK Census
    ** Annual census of employment
   *** BIFU records
  **** National Westminster Bank records

Table 2: Composition of female labour force by marital status, 1931–1981

Percentage of working women who are:

	Single	Married	Divorced/ Widowed	Total
1931	77	16	7	100
1951	52	40	8	100
1961	40	52	8	100
1971	28	64	8	100
1981	27	65	8	100

Source: Hakim[5] and General Household Survey

Table 3: Proportion of mothers of dependent children in paid work

%	Full time	Part time	Total working
1971	15	26	41
1980	17	36	54
1982	15	35	50

Sources: Hakim[5] and general Household Survey

Table 4: Proportion of managers in the four major clearing banks who are women, 1973–1984

	1973–1975		1978–1979		1983–1984	
	No. of women	% of total	No. of women	% of total	No. of women	% of total
Barclays*	96	2.1	84	1.9	175	2.8
Lloyds	19	0.7	31	1.1	43	1.4
	31.12.73		31.12.78		31.12.83	
Midland			29	0.9	26	0.8
			1.1.79		1.1.84	
National Westminster	44	1.0	53	1.2	84	1.6
	1.1.75		1.1.79		31.12.84	

*Board appointed staff in the UK

Source: Individual banks

Table 5: Proportion of IOB members who are women

		Grade of Membership Nos. of women		
Membership as at 1 January	Fellows	Ordinary Members	Associates	% of Associates that are women
1973	6	4,148	380	1.3%
1978	8	12,283	973	2.7%
1984	11	14,412	2,094	5.1%

Source: Institute of Bankers

References
1. Joshi and Owen, *Demographic Predictors of Women's Work Participation in Post-War Britain*. Centre for Population Studies Working Paper 81–3, August 1981.
2. Green, E., *Debtors to their profession: A History of the Institute of Bankers*, The Institute of Bankers, 1979.
3. Bramley, G. V., Paper given at The Institute of Bankers Cambridge Seminar, The Institute of Bankers, 1969.
4. Bank records.

5. Hakim, C., *Occupational segregation*, Research paper no. 9., Department of Employment, London, 1979.
6. Egan, A., *Women in Banking: a study in inequality*, Industrial Relations Journal vol. 13 no. 3. Autumn, 1982.
7. Povall, M., DeJong, A., Chalude, M. et al, *Banking on Women Managers*, Management Today. February, 1982.
8. Daniel, W. W., *Maternity rights*, PSI Reports nos. 588 (June 1980) and 596 (August 1981). Policy Studies Institute, London.
9. Snell, M. W., Glucklich, P. & Povall, M., *Equal Pay and Opportunities*, Research paper no. 20. Department of Employment, London, 1981.
10. Ashridge Management College, *Employment Potential: Issues in the development of women*, IPM. London, 1980.
11. Kanter, R. M., *Men and Women of the Coporation*, Basic Books, New York, 1977.
12. Seear, B. N. & Povall, M., *Equal Opportunities in Banking*, Report of the EEC Seminar held at Knokke, Belgium, 1982. EEC V/981/82–EN, Brussels.
13. Povall, M., *Overcoming barriers to women's advancement in European organisations*, Personnel Review, vol. 13, no. 1. 1984.
14. Communications from individual banks.
15. Povall, M. & Hastings, J. (Ed.) *Managing or removing the career break*, A report of a workshop held in 1981, Manpower Services Commission, Sheffield, 1983.
16. Povall, M. & Hastings, J., *A re-entry and retainer scheme for women: guidelines for employers*, Manpower Services Commission, Sheffield, 1983.
17. Rajan, A., *New technology and employment in insurance, banking and building societies*, IMS, Gower, 1984.
18. Information from unions.
19. Committee of London Clearing Bankers.

CHAPTER 20

Legal Aspects of Employment

Jane Welch

Senior Research Fellow in Company and Commercial Law, The Institute of Advanced Legal Studies, University of London

The legal relationship between employer and employee has shifted dramatically in favour of the latter in the last fifteen years. Legislation, both domestic and EEC, has played a dual role: on the one hand it reflects changing attitudes in society and on the other it acts as a catalyst by forcing change on those who will not adjust of their own accord. The full effects and implications of legislation take time to percolate through the sytem. Attitudes, which have developed and been reinforced over the decades, adjust with difficulty to seemingly arbitrary changes imposed overnight. Employers tend to resent the intrusion of legislation into the way they handle their workforce. They frequently advance the argument 'but we've always done it this way' as sufficient justification for refusing to change. Employers complain too, and with some reason, about the management costs of employment legislation, both in terms of monitoring developments and of ensuring compliance. Against this it may be argued that the costs of non-compliance may be even greater, not simply as a result of legal sanctions but because of employee disaffection. In any event, employment legislation is here to stay; trade union legislation may continue to be a political football but it seems inconceivable that a future government would seek to reverse the basic trend towards improved individual employment rights. That being so, a knowledge of employment law has become as essential a part of every bank manager's training as a knowledge of the credit clearing.

The ever-increasing flood of employment legislation has been matched by a sharp increase in the number of reported cases on employment law. The creation of industrial tribunals gave employees the means to pursue employment grievances informally and cheaply. The result has, predictably, been a much greater willingness to resort to law, which in turn has placed a severe burden on managerial resources, since time and money must be spent on defending every claim, however hopeless. The inconsistent and sometimes conflicting interpretations of employment legislation handed down by industrial tribunals have often confused, rather than enlightened, the manager seeking guidance.

There is now a growing awareness of the EEC dimension – a realisation that domestic statutes and regulations can be challenged on the grounds that they contravene EEC law. The Court of Justice of the European Communities is increasingly being used as a kind of supranational court of appeal, and the Government has been forced to amend the 1970 Equal Pay Act as a result of its decisions.

Apart from statute and case law, the employer also has to be aware of the underlying role of the common law in employment relations. The basic principles of contract law will determine, for example, if and how an employer can change an employee's contract of employment. Common law actions continue to exist alongside their statutory counterparts so that, for instance, an employee may well be able to bring a common law action for wrongful dismissal where a statutory action for unfair dismissal would not be possible.

Contracts of employment

Under section 1 of the Employment Protection (Consolidation) Act 1978, employees have the right to obtain a written statement from their employer setting out the terms of their employment. The statement must identify the employer and employee, state when the employment began and when the period of 'continuous employment' began, stating in addition whether any previous employment counts as part of the employee's continuous employment. This is important as regards entitlement to various employment rights, such as maternity and redundancy rights and the right not to be unfairly dismissed. Where two banks merge, for example, it would be normal for the period of employment with each of the merging banks to count as continuous employment with the new bank. If the merger is an 'assets merger' as opposed to a share merger, continuity of the employment relationship is a legal requirement by virtue of the EEC Acquired Rights Directive implemented in the UK by the Transfer of Undertakings (Protection of Employment) Regulations 1982.

The written statement must contain details of the scale of remuneration, holiday entitlement, hours of work, sickness provisions, pension arrangements, periods of notice, and the employee's job title. In addition the employee is entitled to be told about any disciplinary rules and grievance procedures that apply. This does not include health and safety matters which must be covered in a separate written statement of policy which every employer is required to bring to the attention of his employees under section 2(3) of the Health and Safety at Work Act of 1974

Not all 'employees' are covered by these requirements. Casual workers will normally be excluded since the obligations only extend to employees who work 16 hours or more a week and who have been employed for at least 13 weeks, and to those with five years' service who work at least 8 hours a week.

The written statement is not conclusive evidence of the terms of employment. There may be other implied terms, such as the duties of cooperation, care and loyalty expected from employees. Conversely there is a growing body of case law which appears to establish an implied term that every employer must treat his employers fairly and reasonably – though what is reasonable will depend on the individual circumstances. Matters governed by collective agreements may be incorporated in individual contracts of employment even though they are not expressly mentioned in the written statement. Office rule books may also become part of the implied or express terms of the contract, depending on how they are brought to the attention of the employee.

The fact that a particular term is expressly incorporated in the written statement and accepted by the employee does not necessarily mean that the employer will be able to enforce it. Any terms which purport to exclude or limit rights guaranteed by the Employment Protection (Consolidation) Act 1978 are void.

The contract of employment, like any other contract, may only be varied with the consent of both parties – the employer and employee. A unilateral variation by the employer amounts to a repudiation of the contract. For example, if a manager dismisses an employee for refusing to carry out duties other than those which he was engaged to perform, he risks a claim for unfair dismissal. This could have been avoided either by including in the contract an obligation to perform such other duties as may be assigned from time to time or, alternatively, in the case of a major and essential reorganisation, by terminating the existing contract and offering the employee a new one. If the new contract is reasonable, the refusal of the employee to accept it will be substantial reason justifying dismissal.

Disciplinary Procedures

The law has intervened too in the area of disciplinary procedures. In the past, many employers tended to deal with questions of discipline on an *ad hoc* basis. Now they have to comply with a Code of Practice on Disciplinary Practice and Procedures drawn up by the Advisory, Conciliation and Arbitration Service (ACAS). Although this Code does not have the force of law, failure to observe its provisions will count against an employer in any proceedings before an industrial tribunal. Employers therefore ignore it at their peril.

According to the Code of Practice, an employee should know in advance what conduct will lead to disciplinary action, the persons entitled to take that action, and what his rights of appeal are. In addition, the Code recommends that an employee who faces disciplinary action be allowed to ask his union or staff association to put his case for him.

Inevitably, the result is that disciplinary procedures have become much more formal than would otherwise be necessary or desirable. Employers may have to record minor instances of misconduct to protect themselves, since behaviour which might not warrant dismissal if it were an isolated instance, may do so if it marks the culmination of a series of breaches of discipline. On the other hand, disciplinary action cannot come as a surprise to the employee since he will be reprimanded for each breach of discipline as and when it occurs and he will be told the consequences of any repetition. In particular he will be left in no doubt as to the type of conduct which will lead to dismissal. The range of sanctions which can be imposed is limited to those set out in the contract of employment and any attempt to enforce different sanctions may be treated by the employee as constructive dismissal.

Grievance Procedures

Grievance procedures are now similarly regulated by a combination of statute law and a Code of Practice. Again they must be set out in the contract of employment, so that an employee knows how and to whom to make a complaint. He should also be allowed to ask his union to handle his complaint. The Code of Practice recommends the inclusion of a right of appeal and that provision be made for independent conciliation and arbitration.

Sex Discrimination

Apart from imposing an obligation to inform employees of their rights, the law has also changed substantially the content of those rights. Nowhere has this been more evident than in the area of sex discrimination.

It is now illegal for an employer to discriminate against a woman as regards access to employment, training, promotion, remuneration and working conditions. A woman is entitled to receive the same remuneration as a man for doing the same work and, more importantly, for doing work 'of equal value'. The latter right has only recently become fully available under English law, which did not comply with EEC law on this point until brought into line by the Equal Pay (Amendment) Regulations of 1983.

Previously a woman could only claim equal pay with a man doing a different job if a job evaluation study had been carried out. Now if she can establish that her job requires the same or greater skills than a more highly paid man in a different job, she can bring an equal pay claim. The difficulties of proof may be considerable but this did not deter one woman employed as a cook from successfully claiming the same pay as painters and joiners in a shipyard.

The concept of 'pay' is far wider than might be assumed. Even if men and woman receive the same net salary, difference in gross salary may lead to reduced entitlement to fringe benefits such as low interest loans, mortgage benefits etc. which will be based on gross income. In the case of *Worringham* v. *Lloyds Bank* the European Court of Justice had to examine the bank's non-contributory pension scheme for employees under the age of 25. Female clerical officers were not required to contribute, whereas male clerical officers were required to do so, but received by way of compensation an additional 5% in salary. The bank argued that provisions made in 'connection with death or retirement' were outside the scope of the Equal Pay Act, but the European Court held that a contribution to a pension scheme which was paid by means of an addition to the gross salary was 'pay' within the meaning of Article 119 of the EEC Treaty which took precedence over any provision of the Equal Pay Act. The women were therefore entitled to be paid a sum of money equal in amount to the refund of pension contributions which they would have received had they been male employees employed in similar work. This case is a salutary reminder that compliance with English law may not be enough; regard must be had to European Community law and in particular to the growing case law of the European Court of Justice on this point.

The maintenance of different retiring ages for men and women is still legal under EEC law, but the principle of equal treatment applies to the conditions of access to voluntary redundancy schemes. Similarly, where an employer provides special benefits for male employees after retirement, this constitutes discrimination against female employees who do not receive the same facilities.

Discrimination on grounds of pay is usually easier to detect than other forms of discrimination. The employer should beware, in particular, of classifying jobs as 'male' and 'female'. We can no longer automatically expect secretaries to be female and messengers to be male. This means that recruitment policies, advertising, training programmes and selection for promotion must be non-discriminatory, except where training programmes are organised to redress an imbalance in the number of women or men employed doing a particular job.

Over-protective attitudes may also involve employers in claims of discrimination. Being a man or a woman may in some circumstances be a 'genuine occupational qualification' in the words of the Act, justifying discrimination, but the exception is strictly limited. The fact that a job requires physical strength or stamina will not justify it being restricted to men. Nor will exposure to risk of personal injury justify the exclusion of female employees from a particular job.

Racial Discrimination

Very much the same penalties apply to racial discrimination as to sex discrimination. The 1976 Race Relations Act makes it illegal to discriminate on grounds of colour, race, ethnic or national origins. Indirect discrimination is also illegal, particularly in cases where a condition or requirement discriminates against a certain racial group and is unjustifiable. Thus a requirement that all employees have a good command of English may contravene the Act if it is not an essential requirement for a manual job, for example. As with sex discrimination, positive discrimination in favour of minority groups is allowed, so that an employer will not be acting illegally if he were to organise English lessons and special training courses for immigrant staff.

Before the Act came into force, many employers deliberately sought to achieve a 'racial balance' in their staff. This is now illegal and an employer will face damages and a possible injunction if he refuses to recruit from certain racial groups on the grounds that it will upset the balance of his staff. If a company is found guilty of general discrimination, it can be served with a non-discrimination notice and if it persists, with a court order or injunction.

Maternity Rights

Banks invest considerable resources in training their staff, both male and female. It makes sense therefore to encourage female employees to return to work after childbirth if they wish to do so. The law has provided women with two guarantees – first the right to return to work 29 weeks after the birth of the child, and secondly the right to receive nine-tenths of her normal weekly salary (less the standard social security maternity allowance) for the first six weeks' absence. These guarantees are extended only to those employees who have been continously employed for a period of not less than two years at the beginning of the eleventh week before the expected week of confinement.

The employer is entitled to three weeks' written notice of the employee's intention to stop work, which she is entitled to do from eleven weeks before the expected week of confinement. In order to secure the right to return to work, she must state her intention of returning in the written notice.

Seven weeks after the birth, the employer may ask her for written confirmation of her intention to return to work. This must be given within two weeks or as soon as reasonably practicable. The employee is entitled to a further 29 weeks maternity leave after the birth and can postpone the date of return for a further four weeks if she produces a medical certificate stating that she is unfit for work. The employer may also ask her to postpone her return for up to four weeks.

The right to return to work can obviously cause problems for employers through these are likely to be fewer in large organisations like banks where the opportunities for alternative employment are greater. The length of time away from work will not always amount to 40 weeks; it may be greater where the birth was later than expected or less where the birth was earlier, since the 29 week period runs from the actual date of birth rather than the expected date.

Unfair Dismissal

Gone are the days where an employer could dismiss an employee for no reason at all. The concept of unfair dismissal was first introduced by the Industrial Relations Act of 1971 and is now found in the Employment Protection (Consolidation) Act of 1978. It is no exaggeration to say that it has fundamentally altered the nature of the employer/employee relationship. An employer now has to be in a position where he can establish that a dismissal was 'fair', within the meaning of the Act. To do this, he has to produce valid reasons justifying the dismissal; these must relate to competence, conduct, redundancy or a statutory prohibition. On top of this, the employer must demonstrate that he acted reasonably in regarding the reason as a *sufficient* reason for dismissing the employee. The Act sets out various grounds for dismissal which are automatically unfair. These are dismissals for so-called 'inadmissible reasons' relating to trade union membership or activity, or refusal to join a trade union on grounds of conscientious belief or in certain closed shop situations; redundancy for an inadmissible reason or in contravention of agreed procedures; and pregnancy.

Claims for unfair dismissal do not only arise where an employee has been formally dismissed by an employer. The employee may resign with or without notice, because 'he can't stand it any longer', a situation regarded as 'constructive dismissal'. The fairness or otherwise of the dismissal will then be determined in the usual way.

Apart from circumstances justifying instant or summary dismissal (which are few), the importance of adhering to strict procedural rules cannot be too highly stressed. It has been recognised by the House of Lords that a procedural omission may render a dismissal unfair. The ACAS Code of Practice on Disciplinary Practice and Procedure in Employment has laid down guidelines which have been recognised by the courts. These include oral and written warnings where necessary, the right to be heard and the right of appeal. However, there will be occasions where the employee's conduct warrants summary dismissal and the requirement of fair procedure will not apply. It has to be borne in mind that conduct which might once have justified summary dismissal will not necessarily do so today. A passage from one case, *Wilson* v. *Roche*, illustrates the change in social conditions:

> 'What would today be regarded as almost an attitute of Czar-serf, which is to be found in some of the older cases where a dismissed employee failed to recover damages would, I venture to think, be decided differently today. We have by now come to realise that a contract of service imposes upon the parties a duty of mutual respect.'

Nevertheless theft, dishonesty, or a serious breach of security would be likely to justify summary dismissal from employment in a bank but, as always, the misconduct has to be examined in all the surrounding circumstances.

An employee who has been continuously employed for more than 26 weeks is now entitled to a written statement of the reasons for his dismissal. This statement is admissible in any proceedings before a court or tribunal. Whether a dismissal was fair or unfair can only be determined on the basis of the facts which were available at the time of the dismissal. Evidence of misconduct which arises subsequently cannot be used to provide an alternative reason for dismissal. Thus in *Devis v. Atkins*, evidence of gross misconduct which came to light subsequently, was not admitted to justify the dismissal for which other reasons had originally been put forward. The evidence was, however, admissible when it came to assessing the amount of compensation which should be paid.

Redundancy

Redundancy may be grounds for dismissal, entitling the employee to a redundancy payment but the dismissal will not necessarily be fair. Under Part VI of the Employment Protection (Consolidation) Act 1978, an employee who is made redundant is entitled to receive a redundancy payment from his employer, who can then be reimbursed out of the Government's Redundancy Fund. The amount of redundancy payment is determined by the age of the employee, the length of time in qualifying employment and his normal rate of pay. The statutory limit imposed by the Act does not prevent an employer paying more redundancy compensation if he so wishes but he will not be reimbursed by the Redundancy Fund for the excess payment.

The redundancy payment is designed to compensate the employee for the loss of his job and he will accordingly be entitled to the payment even if he succeeds in finding alternative employment immediately. To qualify, the employee must normally have at least two years' continuous employment, and he will be presumed redundant unless the employer can prove that he was dismissed for another reason. Redundancy will arise in three situations: (a) where the business closes down; (b) where the employer moves his business; and (c) where fewer employers are required. Where the redundant employee is offered suitable alternative work (and the suitability of the offer will depend on the employee's personal circumstances) which is refused, the employee will lose the right to redundancy payment.

It is illegal to select individual employees for redundancy on the basis of union membership, sex, race or colour and any redundancies which are in breach of agreed procedures may give rise to unfair dismissal claims against the employer, unless there are special reasons justifying a departure from the rules.

Where the employer recognises an independent trade union, he must consult union representatives about any proposed redundancy affecting union members. He must also notify the Secretary of State if he is proposing to make more than 10 employees redundant over a period of 30 days or less. A sliding scale of notice applies depending on the number of redundancies involved and the date on which they take effect.

In consulting the unions involved, the employer has to disclose the reasons for the redundancies, the numbers and occupations of employees involved, the total number of employees in each occupational group at the establishment in question, the proposed method of selecting the employees to be made redundant and the redundancy procedures to be followed including proposed timing.

The trade union has in turn the right to make representations to the employer, which he must consider. If the employer decides to reject them, he must state the reasons but he has the final right of decision.

It will in some cases be impracticable for the employer to consult the unions, e.g. where a receiver is appointed unexpectedly. In these circumstances the employer's duty is to take all the steps which are reasonably practicable. Where the employer fails to consult for no good reason, the trade union may complain to an industrial tribunal and, if successful, may obtain a protective award of salary for up to 90 days for the redundant employees. Failure to notify the Secretary of State may reduce any redundancy rebate to which the employer is entitled under the Employment Protection (Consolidation) Act by up to one-tenth, subject to a right of appeal to an industrial tribunal.

Health and Safety at Work

The 1974 Health and Safety at Work Act is arguably the most important safety statute ever introduced. Its basic aim is to maintain and improve the standards of health, safety and welfare of employees. It tries to achieve this through a combination of legislation and Codes of Practice, enforced by a Health and Safety Commission and Executive. Most employees will have been made aware of the Act by virtue of the provision requiring employers to provide staff with a written statement on health and safety policy.

Trade unions have been given a greater role in that the Act requires employers to consult employee representatives on health and safety matters. There are also provisions dealing with the disclosure of safety information to union representatives.

To comply with the Act, employers must give their staff adequate information about possible hazards to health and guidance on how to avoid them. Staff should be trained in the use of first aid and fire-fighting equipment and all manual operations should be thoroughly examined to assess the possible dangers to health. Any processes or equipment which involve increased safety risks should be identified and staff given special training to enable them to cope with them.

There are other obvious safety checklists to be carried out – fire certificates, fire drills, the safety of all entrances and exits, electrical appliances, ventilation, lighting, protective clothing and the use of dangerous machinery etc.

Enforcement of safety measures is the job of the Health and Safety Executive and local authorities who can appoint inspectors to go round and check up on companies. The inspectors have power to serve improvement or prohibition notices on anyone breaking the law – a power which is crucial to the effective implementation of the Act. In the first month after the provisions came into force, 77 such notices were served, which indicates that the inspectors mean business. The sanctions which can be invoked are fairly severe: company officers and managers are liable to unlimited fines on indictment or imprisonment of up to two years if found guilty of an offence under the Act.

Membership of Trade Unions

One of the most politically sensitive and legally complex areas of employment law concerns the rights of trade unions and their members. Despite recent legislative attempts to curtail the privileges and immunities enjoyed by trade unions, employers tend to feel that they are in a 'no win' situation. On the one hand, they cannot risk infringing legislation protecting trade union members, e.g. by dismissing an employee because he wants to join an independent trade union, but on the other hand, employers can rarely avail themselves of the protection offered by legislation against e.g. unlawful picketing or secondary strike action simply because to do so may exacerbate an already bitter industrial dispute. In the British system of industrial relations, legal rights are often irrelevant from the employer's point of view.

Compliance with the obligations imposed by union legislation is another matter. Employers cannot prevent or deter an employee from joining an independent trade union or from taking part in its activities at 'any appropriate time'. An 'appropriate time' means either outside working hours or within working hours with the employer's consent. As mentioned above, dismissal of an employee for belonging to an independent trade union is automatically unfair. Employees who are union officials must be given reasonable paid leave for union duties and training, in accordance with the ACAS Code of Practice on time off for union duties and activities. The Code also recommends that employers make facilites available to enable union officials to perform their duties efficiently and to communicate effectively with members and fellow officers. These facilities may 'include accommodation for meetings, access to a telephone, notice boards and, where the volume of the official's work justifies it, the use of office facilities.'

In return, union officials should bear in mind management's responsibility for maintaining services to customers and should seek to ensure that their activities cause the minimum disruption possible. On the delicate question of whether union officials are entitled to paid leave to organise industrial action against their employer, the Code of Practice recommends only making a distinction between those cases where an official is engaged in industrial action along with his members and those where it is not. The 'normal' arrangements for time off with pay should apply in the latter case but 'there is no obligation on employers to permit time off for union activities which themselves consist of industrial action.'

Although employers may not discriminate against independent union members in their employment, they remain free to refuse to engage a person because he is a member of a trade union. The Employment Act 1980 intervened to protect individuals who lost their job or were refused jobs because of expulsion or exclusion from a trade union. Section 4 of the 1980 Act provides that any person who is, or is seeking to be in employment with an employer who operates a closed shop, has the right not to have an application for membership of the union unreasonably refused and the right not to be unreasonaly expelled from that union. Where a closed shop exists, it will be unfair to dismiss an employee who refuses to join the union if (a) the employee genuinely objects on grounds of conscience or other deeply held personal conviction to being a member of any trade union whatsoever or of a particular trade union or (b) the employee belonged to the class of employee covered by the closed shop agreement before it took effect and has not been a member of the union specified in the agreement since, or (c) the closed shop agreement came into effect for the first time on or after August 15, 1980 and had been approved in a secret ballot by at least 80% of those entitled to vote.

Disclosure of information to Trade Unions

Unions that are recognised by the employer have a legal right to obtain information from the employer for the purposes of collective bargaining. The information requested must be in the employer's possession or in the possession of an associated employer and must relate to the employer's undertaking. The test is whether a union representative would be 'impeded to a material extent' in bargaining, and whether it would be in 'accordance with good industrial relations practice' to disclose the information for the purpose of collective bargaining. In determining the latter, the provisions of the ACAS Code of Disclosure of Information to Trade Unions for Collective Bargaining Purposes are to be taken into account. The Central Arbitration Committee in an early decision held that 'materially impeded' meant that the information should be both relevant and important. The law does allow employers to refuse to disclose information if *inter alia* it would cause 'substantial injury to the employer's business for reasons other than its effect on collective bargaining', or if the information was obtained in confidence.

Conclusion

Employment law is a complex subject fraught with potential hazards for the unwary employer. But the legislation becomes much less threatening once the basic philosphy behind it is grasped. Employees have certain guaranteed rights; they must be informed of these rights and employment procedures must be applied fairly and without discrimination. If employers are in sympathy with the spirit of the law, they are much less likely to infringe the letter of the law.

Legislation
Disabled Persons (Employment) Acts 1944, 1958.
Employment Act 1980
Employment Act 1982
Employment Protection Act 1975
Employment Protection (Consolidation) Act 1978
Equal Pay Act 1970
Equal Pay Regulations 1983
Health and Safety at Work Act 1974
Payment of Wages Act 1960
Race Relations Act 1976

Rehabilitation of Offenders Act 1974
Sex Discrimination Act 1975
Trade Union and Labour Relations Act 1974
Trade Union Act 1984
Transfer of Undertakings (Protection of Employment) Regulations
Unfair Contract Terms Act 1977

EEC Law
EEC Treaty 1957
 Article 7
 Article 48
 Article 119
Council Regulation 1612/68 on free movement of workers
Council Directive 75/117 on equal pay
Council Directive 75/129 on mass dismissals
Council Directive 76/207 on equal treatment for men and women
Council Directive 77/187 on acquired rights for employees in the event of transfers of undertakings

Codes of Practice
Industrial Relations Code of Practice (H.M.S.O.)
Closed Shop Agreements and Arrangements (H.M.S.O.)
Disciplinary Practice and Procedure in Employment (H.M.S.O.)
Disclosure of Information to Trade Unions for Collective Bargaining Purposes (H.M.S.O.)
Elimination of Racial Discrimination and the Promotion of Equality of Opportunity in Employment (H.M.S.O.)
Health and Safety Representatives and Safety Committees
Picketing (H.M.S.O.)
Time off for Trade Union Duties and Activities (H.M.S.O.)
Time off for the Training of Safety Representatives (H.M.S.O.)

Further reading
Encyclopedia of Labour Relations Law by B. A. Hepple and Paul O'Higgins, London: Sweet and Maxwell
Law of Employment by Norman M. Selwyn, London: Butterworths 1982
Labour Relations Statutes and Materials edited by B. A. Hepple, P. O'Higgins and Lord Wedderburn, London: Sweet and Maxwell, 1983

Notes

Notes

Notes

Notes

Notes

Notes

Notes

Notes

Notes

Notes

Notes